contemporary

native

american

artists

contemporary

native american artists

Dawn E. Reno

Alliance Publishing, Inc.

Cover and Interior Design by Cynthia Dunne
Produced by Publisher's Studio, Albany, New York

Alliance Books are available
at special discounts for bulk purchase
for sales promotions, premiums, fund
raising, or educational use
For details, contact:

Alliance Publishing, Inc.
P.O. Box 080377
Brooklyn, New York 11208-0002

Distributed to the trade by National Book Network, Inc.

10 8 6 4 2 1 3 5 6 7 9

Dedicated to the artists,
those who recreate the beauty.

Beauty before me

With it I wander.

Beauty behind me,

With it I wander.

Beauty below me,

With it I wander.

Beauty all around me,

With it I wander.

In old age traveling,

With it I wander.

On the beautiful trail I am,

With it I wander.

FROM NAVAJO NIGHT CHANT

acknowledgments

My deepest gratitude for helping with the birth of this book goes out to many people. First, to my editor, Dottie Harris, who agreed that it was time for a listing of contemporary Native American artists. My thanks for her faith in me and for giving me the opportunity to learn more about the ancient and contemporary cultures of this country's *original* owners.

Second, to my friends, the artists who create objects filled with their spirits. A special thank-you goes to those I know personally—Jamie Tawodi Reason, Andy and Roberta Abeita, Gib Nez, Jake Livingston, Joe Jojola and Allan Wallace. An additional thank-you goes to the dealers and auctioneers I've met through the years—especially Al Anthony, Will Channing, Ken Canfield, and Colonel Doug Allard—who all fostered my love of Native American arts. Also, much appreciation goes to the staff of the United States Department of the Interior, who helped make my research easier with their brochures listing the artists and galleries and various museums across the country. Thanks also goes to the Iroquois Museum in New York, which supplied me with books, pamphlets, and names of artists to contact, and to the many galleries and artists (listed as contributors) who kindly sent photos and biographies.

Third, and probably most important, my gratitude goes to the librarians at Daytona Beach Community College's West Campus—Pat and Beverly—who gave me the "seat of honor" so that I could pore through their on-line book search systems for hours. They also loaned me their personal books when they thought it might help. Their tireless support made what I was trying to do much easier.

I also feel a great debt of gratitude to R. Carlos Nakai, a Native American (Navajo/Ute') flutist, whose music relaxed me and pulled me into the art created by the people listed in this volume. There were many days when I thought this task was insurmountable, but if I put on my headphones and listened to Nakai, all of my stress magically disappeared.

And last in this list, but first in my heart, my husband, Bobby, who continues to stand beside me—sometimes *behind* me—offering his wholehearted support. To him, as well as to the rest of my family, my deepest thanks for believing in me.

vii

introduction

This book was written with the intention of including as many contemporary Native American artists as possible. I contacted everyone who was within mailing distance; spread the word among galleries and dealers; received pieces of information from friends, students, and editors; examined hundreds of books and articles; and tried to leave no stone unturned in my research. The plan was, from the very beginning, to make this book the most complete listing of Native American painters, sculptors, potters, jewelers, weavers, basketmakers, and carvers to date.

My editor and I wanted to offer not only the nuts-and-bolts information about the artists (such as their birthdates, birthplaces, tribal affiliations, and the type of art they create), but also a little more, perhaps tidbits about what the artists create, or how they feel about their work. Though this guide can be used as a formal piece of research, we also wanted it to be readable. However, we could not give you everything known about each artist because the book would have become unwieldy. We came to the conclusion that the more artists we could include, the better; thus the information about each artist may be brief.

The more research I did, however, the more I realized that there are far more Native American artists working in this country than this book could possibly contain. Though I diligently sent mailings to artists I wanted to include, I know some were simply too busy or too skeptical to respond. I hope that when I do the next edition of this book, I will be able to write about the artists who were left out of this edition. All artists deserve recognition and I would like to present the most comprehensive directory possible.

As the author, I did not take it upon myself to check each contributor's Native American heritage. Though I received several letters from possible contributors stating that they could not participate because they were not "enrolled in a tribe," I did not consider enrollment a prerequisite for being listed in this volume. Therefore, when I listed artists, I listed the tribes to which they were born. If the artists' parents were from different tribes, I listed both tribes. In addition, I listed the artists in the tribe appendix under every tribe to which they might lay claim via heritage or birthright. Anyone with no Native American blood was informed by mail that they would not be included. In future volumes, we might be able to include those artists who work in "Native American disciplines" regardless of heritage, but for now, I have decided to stick with my original vision, which was to find as many Native American artists as possible and list them in a single volume. As I stated before, this undertaking has just skimmed the surface of artists, and I hope to add to these first thousand when we go into another edition.

If you, the reader, discover a new piece of information about one of the artists listed here and can add it to what I already know, I urge you to forward it to my publisher. And if you discover a discrepancy, I accept full responsibility and would appreciate being informed so that I may offer the correct information in the next edition of this book.

I hope you enjoy learning about the artists as much as I did and that you will be able to add some pieces of their work to your collections. These artists are keeping important pieces of American history alive and deserve all of your support.

the artists

JEANNINE AARON

Iroquois (1956 –)
Beadworker

EDUCATION: Self-taught.

ABOUT THE ARTIST: Aaron shows her work at pow-wows, schools, and other places. Her whole family practices beadwork, and Aaron has been experimenting with new techniques.

ANDY AND ROBERTA ABEITA

Andy–Isleta Pueblo (N/A)
Roberta–Navajo (N/A
Sculptors, jewelers

AWARDS: The Abeitas have won many awards at the shows and festivals they attend around the country.

REPRESENTATION: Silver Sun Traders, Santa Fe, New Mexico

ABOUT THE ARTISTS: This husband-and-wife team creates carved fetishes, both large and small. Their signature is a heart-line and their fetishes are decorated with inlaid, semiprecious stones and feathers. The couple travel all over the country educating others about their craft, their heritage, and their history.

JIMMY ABEITA

Navajo (1948 –) Arizona
Painter

AWARDS: Abeita's many awards include the Grand Prize at the Gallup Inter-Tribal Ceremonials (New Mexico) and Tanner's All-Indian Invitational (Scottsdale).

REPRESENTATION: SunWest Silver, Albuquerque, New Mexico.

ABOUT THE ARTIST: In 1976, a book called *The American Indians of Abeita: "His People"* was published about this artist. The author, Joseph Stacey, called Abeita a "genius" and stated that Abeita's work was "executed to the superlative degree of Indian, Navajo, Western, and American art standards."

Jimmy Abeita's oil-on-canvas painting of Plains warrior, courtesy of SunWest Silver, Albuquerque, New Mexico.

KAREN ABEITA

Hopi (1961 –)
Potter

EDUCATION: Studied in Albuquerque, New Mexico in the late 1970s to early 1980s to become an optical technician. Learned pottery-making skills from contemporaries such as Fawn Garcia and Mark Tahbo.

Jimmy Abeita's oil-on-canvas painting of young Native American woman sitting on a table next to pottery with modern newspaper stored inside, 7Up® can, and white kitten to her left, courtesy of SunWest Silver, Albuquerque, New Mexico.

4

REPRESENTATION: Robert F. Nichols Gallery, Santa Fe, New Mexico.

ABOUT THE ARTIST: Abeita comes from a long line of potters. Her grandmother's first cousins, Sadie Adams, Joy Navasie, and Beth Sakeva, are well known in the business. Abeita's pottery is traditional. It is made from native materials she and her husband gather and is often decorated in the prehistoric Sikyatki style.

TAMRA L. ABEITA
> *Acoma (N/A) Acoma Pueblo, New Mexico*
> *Potter*

ABOUT THE ARTIST: Abeita is a young and up-and-coming artist.

MARY ABEL
> *Okanagan (N/A) Okanagan Lake, Canada*
> *Leatherworker*

ABOUT THE ARTIST: Abel soaks, tans, and prepares all of her own deer hides. She taught her daughter, Hilda Belanger, the trade.

ELIZABETH ABEYTA
> *Navajo (N/A)*
> *Potter, clayworker, sculptor*

ABOUT THE ARTIST: Abeyta makes ethereal, free-flowing clay figurines that are airbrushed to look like sandstone.

NARCISSO PLATERO ABEYTA
(a.k.a. Ha So De, Narciso Abeyta, "Ascending")
> *Navajo (1918 –   ) Canoncito, New Mexico*
> *Artist—various media*

EDUCATION: Studied with Dorothy Dunn at the Santa Fe Indian School (1939), attended Somerset Academy School (1940) and received a Bachelor of Fine Arts degree from the University of New Mexico (1953).

AWARDS: Abeyta has won fourteen awards, including the Inter-Tribal Indian Ceremonial Grand Award.

ABOUT THE ARTIST: Abeyta's work has been published by Clara Lee Tanner (1957) and others in publications such as *Art in America*. His works have been exhibited in shows such as the San Francisco World's Fair (1939–1940) and pieces are held at the University of Oklahoma, the Museum of New Mexico, and the Arizona State Museum. Though he follows the conventions set forth by the Santa Fe Indian School, Abeyta is considered an innovative painter.

PAULINE ABEYTA
> *Acoma (N/A) Acoma Pueblo, New Mexico*
> *Potter*

ABOUT THE ARTIST: Pauline is an up-and-coming artist whose work is becoming collectible.

TONY ABEYTA

Navajo (1965 –   ) Gallup, New Mexico
Painter, printmaker

EDUCATION: Institute of American Indian Arts, Santa Fe; Maryland Institute College of Art; Lacoste, Ecole Des Beaux Arts (France) S.A.C.I. (Florence, Italy); Chicago Art Institute.

AWARDS: Abeyta has won various awards, including first and third places in Mixed Media at the Indian Market, first place in Two-Dimensional Painting, second place in lithographs, and many others.

REPRESENTATION: Glen Green Galleries, Santa Fe, New Mexico; John Cacciola Galleries, New York; Turquoise Tortoise, Sedona, Arizona; Adobe Gallery, Albuquerque, New Mexico.

ABOUT THE ARTIST: Abeyta has experimented with sand and uses it in his paintings, working in a three-dimensional style. His style covers a wide range, from working with black and white to using primary colors. He painted the cover of 1992 *Indian Market* magazine.

ELIZA ABRAHAM

Haida (N/A) Masset, British Columbia, Canada
Basketmaker

ABOUT THE ARTIST: Abraham gathers roots and bark for her baskets in the summer (usually in August).

D. MONROE ABRAMS

(a.k.a. Ten Nooshagh, "Sugar Bear")
Seneca (1948 –   ) Steamburg, New York
Beadworker, leatherworker, featherworker, quillworker, carver, dollmaker

EDUCATION; Learned many of his skills from his parents; attended Ithaca College, Ithaca, New York.

ABOUT THE ARTIST: This multitalented artist makes beadwork medallions, necklaces, earrings, wristbands, watchbands, belts, headbands, chokers, and necklaces. He also decorates leather vests, purses, and costumes with beadwork; makes porcupine-quill chokers and earrings; carves wooden statuettes, pipes, hatchets, and baskethandles; makes rattles from turtle, horn, and hickory; and makes cornhusk dolls. In addition, Abrams is a dancer and takes his work with him when he travels to dancing ceremonies.

MARY ADAMS

Mohawk (1917 –   ) St. Regis, Quebec, Canada
Basketmaker, splintworker, quilter

EDUCATION: Learned how to weave baskets by watching her mother.

AWARDS: Adams won the New York State Iroquois Conference award (1975); first prizes at the New York State Fair; and many others.

ABOUT THE ARTIST: Adams creates many types of baskets using black-ash splints, sweet grass, natural or plastic twine, and cloth. She has taught others, demonstrated, and exhibited her basketry throughout the Northwest, as well as at Brigham Young University.

SALLY ANNE ADAMS

Mohawk (1943 –   )
Basketmaker, quilter

EDUCATION: Learned her trades from her mother, Agnes Sunday.

ABOUT THE ARTIST: Adams uses black-ash splints and sweet grass for her baskets and cloth for her quilts. She prefers smaller baskets, gathering sweet grass herself, and using natural dyes. She has taught basketry to grade-school children.

NADEMA AGARD

Sioux/Cherokee/Powatan (N/A)
Artist

EDUCATION: Bachelor of Science in art education from New York University; Master in Art and Education from Columbia University, concentrations in painting and drawing.

ABOUT THE ARTIST: Agard has taught art through the New York Board of Education as well as in the American Indian community. She is multitalented, having illustrated a children's book, lectured and counseled in addition to teaching. Because she is also multilingual, Agard travels around the world participating in various summer study programs and exhibiting her work.

FLORENCE AGUILAR

Santo Domingo (N/A) Santo Domingo Pueblo,
New Mexico
Jeweler—mosaic

ABOUT THE ARTIST: Aguilar works in a mosaic technique.

JOSÉ VICENTE AGUILAR

San Ildefonso (1924 –) San Ildefonso Pueblo,
New Mexico
Artist—watercolor

EDUCATION: Otis Institute, California; University of New Mexico; Los Angeles Trade Technical Junior College; Los Angeles County Art Institute (1954); Los Angeles Art Center School (1958–1959).

ABOUT THE ARTIST: At first, Aguilar followed the traditional Native American style of painting, but he has experimented with different abstract techniques in his career. He has painted Koshares, the clowns of ceremonial activities, and other subjects.

MARIE AGUILAR

Santo Domingo (1924 –   )
Jeweler

EDUCATION: Learned some of her craft from family members.

AWARDS: During the twenty years Aguilar has entered the Indian Market, She has won many prizes for her necklaces.

ABOUT THE ARTIST: Aguilar works almost exclusively with coral, but sometimes adds Navajo tooled beads to her necklaces.

TONY AGUILAR

Santo Domingo (1919 –   )
Jeweler

EDUCATION: Worked at Skip Maisel's Indian Jewelry and Craft, Inc., in Albuquerque as a silver polisher, then took a course from Wilfred Jones, a Navajo silversmith, at the Santa Fe Indian School.

REPRESENTATION: Elaine Horwitch Gallery, Santa Fe, New Mexico.

ABOUT THE ARTIST: Aguilar creates classic *heishi* pieces with unique touches, such as metal, turquoise, coral, and jet.

GEORGE A. AHGUPUK

Eskimo (1911 –   ) Shishmaref, Seward Peninsula,
Alaska
Artist—pen and ink on reindeer skin

EDUCATION: Self-taught.

REPRESENTATION: University of Alaska Museum Shop, Fairbanks, Alaska; Alaska State Museum Show, Juneau, Alaska.

ABOUT THE ARTIST: Though Ahgupuk had no formal training, he was one of the first Eskimos to achieve notoriety as a fine-art artist. Under the guidance of illustrator Rockwell Kent, Ahgupuk joined the American Artist group and exhibited with them (1937). He became so popular that, often, his work was copied outright. Ahgupuk refers to his work as "Bering Sea pictures."

PEGIE AHVAKANA

Suquamish (N/A) Washington
Ceramist, painter

EDUCATION: Institute of American Indian Arts, Santa Fe, New Mexico; Ray Vogue School of Chicago; Chicago Circle University.

REPRESENTATION: Via Gambaro Gallery, Washington, D.C.

ABOUT THE ARTIST: Ahvakana has worked as a ceramics instructor and commercial artist. Her ceramics incorporate her vision of the meaning of her Native American roots. Her works are held by numerous private and public collections and she has exhibited all over the United States.

DANNY AKEE
Navajo (N/A) Tuba City, Arizona
Sandpainter

ABOUT THE ARTIST: Akee's work is experimental both in color and in design. He has produced a technique called "split paintings" where one half of the painting is, for instance, a still life and the other half is an abstract of a spirit. He has combined traditional and nontraditional subjects in this way.

NORMAN AKERS
Osage/Pawnee (1958 –)
Painter

EDUCATION: Master of Fine Art, University of Illinois (1991); Certificate of Museum Training, Institute of American Indian Arts (1983); Bachelor of Fine Art, Kansas City Art Institute (1982).

AWARDS: First Place, 1987 Scottsdale Indian Arts and Crafts Exhibition; Third Place, 1988 S.W.A.I.A. (Southwestern Association on Indian Affairs) Indian Market; Graduate Fellowship Award, 1988-89, University of Illinois.

REPRESENTATION: Jan Cicero Gallery, Chicago, Illinois.

ABOUT THE ARTIST: Akers has exhibited his abstract, surreal paintings all over the country and has quite a few shows and exhibits to his credit.

Akers's oil-on-paper painting entitled "The Big Step," 30 x 22 inches, 1989, courtesy of the artist and Jan Cicero Gallery, Chicago, Illinois.

GAIL ALBANY
(a.k.a. Picking Leaves)
Mohawk (1949 –) Caughnawaga, Quebec
Painter

EDUCATION: Mostly self-taught; took a pottery course at Manitou Community College.

ABOUT THE ARTIST: Albany paints on leather and her themes are usually Native American in nature. She also writes poetry.

AGNES ALFRED
Kwakiutl, Mamalelekala tribe (N/A) Village Island, British Columbia
Basketmaker

ABOUT THE ARTIST: Alfred is the only person who makes cedar-root and cedar-bark handled baskets. She states "(W)e used to make big ones for clams, fish, and berries" (*Artists at Work* by Ulli Steltzer).

ALVAREZ
Comanche (N/A)
Jeweler, silversmith

EDUCATION: Taught by his father, White Buffalo.

ABOUT THE ARTIST: A fourth-generation silversmith, Alvarez often shows with his father.

ALVIN ELI AMASON

Aleut (1948 –   ) Arkansas
Artist—mixed media

EDUCATION: Formally educated with three degrees.

ABOUT THE ARTIST: Amason's work is abstract, dramatic, and vivid. He is a highly respected teacher whose experience as an Indian is reflected in the way he passes on his education to others.

ARTHUR D. AMIOTTE

Ogala Sioux (1942 –   ) Pine Ridge, South
Dakota
Leatherwork, petroglyphs, miscellaneous media

EDUCATION: University of Montana Master of Interdisciplinary Studies: Anthropology, Religion, and Art (1983); University of South Dakota (1969); Pennsylvania State University (summers 1967, 1968, and 1971); University of Oklahoma (1966); Northern State College (1964), Bachelor of Science Education (double major: Art Education and Commercial Art).

AWARDS: Amiotte's awards, appointments, publications, films, and lectures number in the hundreds and include an award for "Outstanding Contribution to South Dakota History" given by the Dakota History Conference and Center for Western Studies at Augustana College (May 1992) and an Honorary Doctorate of Lakota Studies given by the Ogala Lakota College in Kyle, South Dakota (1988).

REPRESENTATION: The Heritage Center, Inc., Pine Ridge, South Dakota.

ABOUT THE ARTIST: Amiotte's work has been exhibited extensively throughout the United States in the last thirty years. His commissions and published art have become book covers, Governor's Awards (South Dakota) posters for Okala Lakota College, and limited editions. He lectures all over the country about Plains art and traditional and contemporary Indian artists. He also teaches and writes extensively about the Native American experience and the arts.

Amiotte's petroglyphs on paper, courtesy of The Heritage Center, Inc., Pine Ridge, South Dakota.

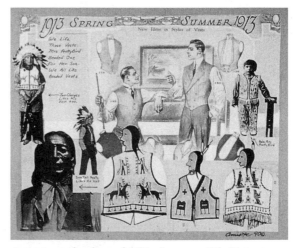

Amiotte's mixed media entitled "Vests," courtesy of The Heritage Center, Inc., Pine Ridge, South Dakota.

ABRAHAM APAKARK ANGHIK

(a.k.a. Abe Ruben)
Eskimo (1951 –   ) Paulatuk, Northwest
Territory, Canada
Sculptor, silversmith, carver, printmaker

EDUCATION: University of Alaska.

ABOUT THE ARTIST: Anghik's work is both Eskimo and Inuit. He uses his educational background, as well as what he learned from an Inuit teacher, Ronald Sengungetuk.

JOSEPHINE ANGUS

(a.k.a. Ka En Ten Ha Wi)
Mohawk (1920 –) St. Regis, Quebec, Canada
Basketmaker, splintworker, quilter

EDUCATION: Taught by her grandmother.

REPRESENTATION: Mohawk Craft Fund.

ABOUT THE ARTIST: Angus makes a number of different types of baskets, including cone-shaped, doll bassinets, comb holders, and strawberry. She usually uses natural splints. A founding member and president of Akwesasne Homemakers and Cultural Committee, Angus often shares her skills with others in the community.

EULA ANTONE

Oneida (1917 –) Southwold, Ontario, Canada
Beadworker, leatherworker, quilter, rugweaver

EDUCATION: Mostly self-taught; took beadwork classes in 1965.

AWARDS: Various prizes for her beadwork and pipes from the Oneida Fall Fair and the Homemakers' Convention.

ABOUT THE ARTIST: Antone has taught beadwork and exhibited her work extensively. She especially likes to use turtles, eagles, and wolves on her medallions and bolo ties. During the winter, Antone's husband, Russell, helps her with loomwork; both of their children also bead. Antone is deeply involved with Oneida affairs.

NORMA ANTONE

Tohono O'odham (N/A)
Basketmaker

ABOUT THE ARTIST: Antone makes miniature horsehair baskets in the Papago style.

BLANCHE ANTONIO

Acoma (1927 –) New Mexico
Potter

EDUCATION: Learned how to pot from her mother, Juana Pasqual, and her grandmother, Juana Concho.

ABOUT THE ARTIST: Other members of Antonio's family who also create pottery include Antonio's clan grandmother, Marie Z. Chino; her sister, Mary Lukee; her sister-in-law, Romolda Pasqual; and her nieces, Bonnie Leno and Kimberly Pasqual. Antonio creates bowls, jars, wedding vases, figurines, and Storytellers in the traditional colors and designs of the Acoma Pueblo potters. She made her first Storyteller in the late 1970s.

HILDA ANTONIO

Acoma (1938 –) New Mexico
Potter–Storyteller figures

EDUCATION: Learned how to pot from mother, Eva B. Histia.

AWARDS: Since the mid 1970s, has regularly won prizes at the Indian Market for her Storytellers and Storyteller owls.

ABOUT THE ARTIST: Antonio comes from a line of well-known potters, including her aunts, Lucy Lewis and Elizabeth Woncada; her grandmother, Helice Valdo; her daughter, Mary A. Garcia; and her sister, Rose Torivio. Hilda created her first Storyteller in the late 1950s, one of the first to do so.

JOHNSON ANTONIO

Navajo (1932 –) New Mexico
Carver

ABOUT THE ARTIST: Antonio carves wooden dolls which are folk art in design that are now becoming collector's items. The dolls capture the Navajo spirit through authentic clothing and costumes. His work has been shown at the Wheelwright Museum of the American Indian in a one-person show and at other museums and galleries.

ARNOLD D. ARAGON

(a.k.a. "Buck" Aragon)
> *Crow/Laguna (1953 –   ) Crow Agency, Montana*
> *Sculptor—stone*

EDUCATION: Associate of Art, three-dimensional arts, Institute of American Indian Arts; three years in Economics and Art at University of Nevada, Reno.

AWARDS: Aragon's awards include First place/ sculpture, Fort Hall Art Show, Fort Hall, Indiana (1994); First place, Nevada Day Art Show (1989); First place/Best of Show, California Indian Market (1988); First and Second places, California Indian Market/Nevada Museum of Art, "Native Visions Show" (1987).

REPRESENTATION: Riata Gallery, Virginia City, Nevada; Vigil's Native American Gallery, Nevada

Aragon's stone sculpture entitled "Woman with Baby," courtesy of the artist.

City, California; Out West, Walker, California; Three Flags, Walker, California.

ABOUT THE ARTIST: Aragon's stone sculptures are owned by collectors such as Randy Travis and held in private collections in the United States, Canada, and France. His sculptures and art reflect the culture and heritage of both Plains and Pueblo peoples. He carves warrior figures, bear fetishes, and other stone pieces.

CLARICE ARAGON

> *Acoma (N/A) Acoma Pueblo, New Mexico*
> *Potter*

EDUCATION: Learned some of her art from her mother, Wanda Aragon.

ABOUT THE ARTIST: An active, contemporary potter, Aragon has experimented with her pottery by creating pottery hot-air balloons decorated with traditional Acoma designs and has even designed human figures to ride in the gondola.

Portrait of Arnold Aragon, sculptor, at work, courtesy of the artist.

DELORES ARAGON

Acoma (1969 –) New Mexico
Potter

EDUCATION: Learned potting skills from her mother, Marie Juanico; her mother-in-law, Wanda Aragon; and her husband, Marvia Aragon, Jr.

REPRESENTATION: Robert Nichols Gallery, Santa Fe, New Mexico.

ABOUT THE ARTIST: Aragon began creating small clay animals at age five. She is now teaching her son, Marvis III, how to make pottery. She works in miniature, does fine-line work, and has combined modern elements with ancient ones in decorating her pots.

JOHN ARAGON

Acoma (N/A) Acoma Pueblo, New Mexico
Potter

EDUCATION: Encouraged by his mother and his grandmother, Lupe Aragon, Aragon began potting at a young age.

ABOUT THE ARTIST: Because the pottery he creates is in demand, Aragon now pots year-round rather than only during the summer months, as his grandmother did. He uses the parrot design only on water jars and uses other designs for other pots, depending on the pot's shape and style.

WANDA ARAGON

Acoma (1948 –) New Mexico
Potter

EDUCATION: Learned how to pot from her mother, Frances Torivio Pino.

ABOUT THE ARTIST: Aragon, Delores Aragon's mother-in-law, has taught other members of her family the time-honored traditional techniques by which she works. Other members of Aragon's family who are potters include Aragon's sister, Lillian Salvador; her mother-in-law, Daisy Aragon; her sister-in-law, Rose Torivio; and her aunts. In addition to creating traditional pots in the Acoma style, Aragon also creates miniature pots. Among the first things Aragon created were pottery owls during the 1960s. Aragon made her first Storyteller in the early 1970s. She also makes nativities and bird and animal figurines, all painted in the Acoma style with traditional pottery designs.

CLARA ARCHILTA

Kiowa/Apache/Tonkawa (1912 –) Tonkawa, Oklahoma
Artist

EDUCATION: Self-taught.

AWARDS: Two First Awards, Indian Art Exhibition, Anadarko, Oklahoma, and many others.

ABOUT THE ARTIST: Archilta began painting in 1957 and has exhibited in many group showings in the Southwest.

ESTHER ARCHULETA

Santa Clara (N/A) New Mexico
Potter

EDUCATION: Learned the pottery-making tradition from her famous mother, Margaret Tafoya.

MARY E. ARCHULETA

Santa Clara/San Juan (N/A) New Mexico
Potter

ABOUT THE ARTIST: Archuleta creates both the Santa Clara style pottery (she was raised there) and the San Juan style (she married into the tribe). Sometimes she blends the two styles to create a new and distinct style.

JOSEPHINE ARQUERO

Cochiti (1928 –) New Mexico
Potter–Storyteller

EDUCATION: Learned the art of pottery making from mother, Damacia Cordero.

AWARDS: Won an award in 1971 for a Storyteller and has won many more awards since that time.

ABOUT THE ARTIST: Arquero comes from a long line of potters, including her sisters, Martha and Gloria Arquero; and Marie Lewake. She made her first Storyteller in 1969 and has also created human and animal figures.

MARTHA ARQUERO

Cochiti (1945 —   ) New Mexico
Potter—Storyteller figures

EDUCATION: Learned the art of potting from her mother, Damacia Cordero.

AWARDS: Arquero's frog and human Storytellers have won awards at such places as the Indian Market and the New Mexico State Fair.

ABOUT THE ARTIST: Arquero created her first Storyteller in 1975. Her whole family has been involved in pottery making; most make Storytellers like the ones created Arquero's mother, Damacia Cordero. Arquero has created human and animal figures, as well as a kangaroo Storyteller with a baby in its pouch (1982). She gathers her clay and paints from hills near her home, makes her black paint from wild plants, then fires the pieces with a hot fire consisting of cow chips and plenty of wood.

CHRISTIE ARQUETTE

(a.k.a. Kia Wenh Toe)
Mohawk (1924 —   ) Hogansburg, New York
Basketmaker, splintworker

EDUCATION: Learned from her mother.

REPRESENTATION: Mohawk Craft Fund; Margaret David (Arquette's mother).

ABOUT THE ARTIST: Arquette uses black-ash splints and sweet grass in her baskets. She makes strawberry baskets that are pink, red, or natural in color.

JAKE ARQUETTE

(a.k.a. Zock)
Mohawk (1905 —   )
Basketmaker

EDUCATION: Learned his skills from his father.

REPRESENTATION: Mohawk Craft Fund; Arquette himself.

ABOUT THE ARTIST: Arquette makes lunch baskets, market, laundry, pack, and fancy baskets. He uses black-ash splints, sweet grass, and hickory. Though Arquette taught his children how to make baskets, they have not continued the art form.

MARGARET ARQUETTE

Mohawk (1915 —   ) Hogansburg, New York
Basketmaker, quilter

EDUCATION: Arquette learned from her sister; and her mother, Anne Thompson, and her three sisters, who are also basketmakers.

AWARDS: Has won first prizes at the New York State Fair for both her baskets and her quilts.

REPRESENTATION: Mohawk Craft Fund.

ABOUT THE ARTIST: Arquette uses black-ash splints and sweet grass to make sewing, fancy, strawberry, wastepaper, and button baskets; flowerpots; filing trays; purses; and matchbook holders. She often dyes the splints different colors and is very skillful at combining the splints to make attractive baskets. Arquette demonstrates or exhibits her work.

PITSEOLAK ASHOONA

Inuit (1900 —   ) Near Cape Dorset, Canada
Artist—mixed media

EDUCATION: Self-taught.

ABOUT THE ARTIST: Ashoona began to draw in midlife. She has recreated the world that today's Inuits have nearly forgotten by telling of the shamans, the tribal legends, and the stories her father told her of the old days.

ALICE ASMAR

Artist—all media, colored ink specialty

EDUCATION: Bachelor of Art, Lewis and Clark College, Portland, Oregon; Master of Fine Art, University of Washington.

ABOUT THE ARTIST: Asmar paints Indians because she sees them "as America's real ecologists." Solo shows of her work have been held at Gallerie de Fondation des Etas-Unis, Paris; New York; Italy; the Minnesota Museum of Art; and the Western Association of Art Museums.

GILBERT ATENCIO

(a.k.a. Wah Peen, "Mountain of the Sacred Wind")
San Ildefonso/Spanish/Navajo (1930 –   )
Greeley, Colorado
Artist—various media

EDUCATION: Santa Fe Indian School (1947).

AWARDS: Two years after graduating from Santa Fe Indian School, Atencio had already won seventeen competitions. He continued to win many awards after that time.

ABOUT THE ARTIST: Atencio comes from an artistic family (his aunt was Maria Martinez) and uses traditional Pueblo ceremonial figures in his work. In the 1950s his work was realistic, but in the 1960s, he became interested in abstract representations of dance figures, pottery, and other symbols of Pueblo life.

JAMES AUCHIAH

(a.k.a. Tse-koy-ate, "Big Bow")
Kiowa (1906–1975) Meers, Oklahoma
Artist—opaque watercolor

EDUCATION: Special training in art, University of Oklahoma, Norman, Oklahoma (1947).

AWARDS: Certificate of Appreciation, Indian Arts and Crafts Board/United States Department of Interior, 1966.

ABOUT THE ARTIST: Auchiah was associated with the original "Five Kiowa Artists." He did murals for the St. Patrick's Mission School, the United States Department of the Interior, and the Oklahoma Historical Society from the 1920s to the 1930s; and painted in the Oklahoma style.

MARY AVERY

Navajo (N/A) New Mexico
Jeweler

ABOUT THE ARTIST: Avery's jewelry is reminiscent of the old style, but she gives each piece her own stamp by incorporating something new.

SONJA K. AYRES

AWARDS: Best of Division (graphics) at the 1994 Five Civilized Tribes Competitive Show at Muskogee, Oklahoma.

CHARLA BACH

Seneca (1946 –   ) Salamanca, New York
Beadworker, dollmaker

EDUCATION: Self-taught; has also taken classes in working with cornhusks at the Allegany Indian Arts & Crafts Coop.

REPRESENTATION: Allegany Indian Arts & Crafts Coop.

ABOUT THE ARTIST: After being hospitalized in the late 1970s, Bach became interested in beadwork and now sells her craftwork. She also makes cornhusk dolls and takes her work to fairs and festivals. Bach, like many other Indian artists, encourages young people to carry on Iroquois crafts.

RUTH BAIRD

Oneida (1905 –   )
Beadworker, quilter

EDUCATION: Self-taught.

ABOUT THE ARTIST: Baird watched members of her family make baskets, but did not become interested

13

in creating her own items until the 1970s when she learned how to do beadwork. She receives orders for both her freehand and loomed jewelry and medallions. She often uses green and orange (Green Bay Packer colors). An active member of the Oneida community, Baird has headed the Oneida Indian Singers and often teaches the Oneida language.

BESSIE BARBER

Navajo (1955 –   ) Aneth, Utah
Rugweaver

EDUCATION: Learned how to weave in her late teens from her mother, Anna Mae Barber.

REPRESENTATION: Toh Atin Gallery, Durango, Colorado.

ABOUT THE ARTIST: Barber and several of the women in the Barber/Begay family developed a distinctive style by using only native, handspun sheep wool and small accents of bright dyes. This changed the Two Grey Hills style just enough to make it the family's own and it is now called the Burnham style. The family of weavers includes Anna Mae Barber; Alice, Helen, and Sandy Begay (her sisters), Laverne, Lorene, and Bessie (her daughters); Teresa and Julia (her young nieces); as well as a sister of a brother-in-law.

MARJORIE BARNES

Mohawk (1957 –   ) Hogansburg, New York
Painter, photographer, ceramist

EDUCATION: Took art classes at the Salmon River Central School; Fine Arts major at City College of New York (1975–1977); St. Lawrence University (1977–1979).

ABOUT THE ARTIST: Barnes uses Iroquois symbols in her work and gets some of her inspiration from traditional Iroquois stories. She paints in an abstract style, with clean lines and blocks of color. She teaches art, has done illustrations, and is known as a photographer and sculptor as well.

RICK E. BARTOW

Yurok (1946 –   ) So. Beach, Oregon
Artist; sculptor–mixed media

EDUCATION: Bachelor of Art, Western Oregon State College, Monmouth (1969).

AWARDS: Many awards and commissions include being part of Washington State Arts Commission, "Who We Are: Autobiographies in Art" (1991); the Brandywine Visiting Artist Fellowship, Philadelphia, Pennsylvania, and the Oregon Arts Commission Fellowship in Visual Arts.

Portrait of Bartow, artist (mixed media). Photograph by Rebekah Johnson, courtesy of Jamison Thomas Gallery, Portland, Oregon.

Bartow's "Drifting VI," pastel and graphite on paper, 26 x 40 inches, 1994, courtesy of Jamison Thomas Gallery, Portland, Oregon.

14

REPRESENTATION: Jamison Thomas Gallery, Portland, Oregon.

ABOUT THE ARTIST: Influenced by Northwest Coast masks and carvings, Bartow's contemporary sculptures are often mistaken for the traditional ones carved many years ago. His paintings and drawings have been part of many solo and group exhibits, including some held at the Jamison/Thomas Gallery and at galleries in Japan, Germany, and the United States. Collections of Bartow's work are held by the Portland Art Museum, the Heard Museum, and the Metropolitan Arts Commission in Portland, Oregon, to name a few.

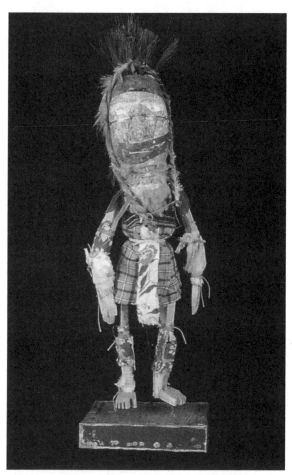

Bartow's "Doll Figure I," wood, copper, rope, and cloth, 26 x 7¼ x 5¾ inches, 1994, courtesy of Jamison Thomas Gallery, Portland, Oregon.

EMMA BEANS
> *Kwakiutl (N/A) Alert Bay, British Columbia, Canada*
> *Blanketmaker*

ABOUT THE ARTIST: Beans designs blankets with buttons, abalone and sequins designs. She uses the animal motifs of the Northwest Coast (i.e., Eagle design).

JOSEPH BEAUVAIS
(a.k.a. Kanawarenton)
> *Mohawk (1922 – mid 1970s)*
> *Painter, framer*

EDUCATION: Self-taught.

ABOUT THE ARTIST: After an accident that left him paralyzed, Beauvais recovered and eventually set up a studio so that he could paint. He taught himself the art by reading and listening to art critics.

FRED BEAVER
(a.k.a. Eka Le Ne, "Brown Head")
> *Creek/Seminole (1911 – 1980) Eufala, Oklahoma*
> *Artist—watercolor*

EDUCATION: Bacone Junior College, Oklahoma; Haskell Indian Institute, Kansas.

ABOUT THE ARTIST: Beaver spent his life speaking for his people and showing their history through his art. His paintings show the Seminole and Creek peoples before the Great Seminole War and the Trail of Tears. In 1970 Beaver said, "I wanted to change the non-Indian's image of my people." Beaver's trademark was his use of monochromatic color.

VIRGINIA (HILL) BEAVER
> *Mohawk (1930 –)*
> *Beadworker, weaver, leatherworker, cornhusk worker, basketmaker, quillworker*

EDUCATION: Learned beadwork from her grandmother; fingerweaving from Audrey Spencer; basketry from Mary Adams and Margaret Torrence; and has taught herself other crafts.

AWARDS: Has won several grants for different types of research and work.

ABOUT THE ARTIST: A prolific craftsperson, Beaver has done beadwork since she was a child and has passed on what she knows by teaching classes. She has done quite a bit of research about the traditional crafts, discovering that the beadwork used on antique Native American clothing was subtle in color. She has also educated herself and others about the Indians who lived in the Grand River area before the Six Nations settled there.

CLIFFORD BECK
Navajo (N/A)
Artist

ABOUT THE ARTIST: Beck often does pastel portraits. He sometimes uses the old Anasazi symbols in his paintings.

LARRY BECK
Yup'ik (1938 —   ) Seattle, Washington
Sculptor—mixed media, painter

EDUCATION: Bachelor of Fine Art, Sculpture, and Master of Fine Art, Painting, University of Washington, Seattle.

ABOUT THE ARTIST: As with many other Native artists, Beck's inspiration comes from the stories he knows of his ancestors. He is especially influenced by Yup'ik masks. His materials are often recycled or "found" objects.

VICTOR BECK
Navajo (1941 —   ) New Mexico
Jeweler

EDUCATION: One of the first young artists to participate in an art internship at the Museum of Northern Arizona Art Institute in 1975.

AWARDS: Awarded the Heard Museum's Ted Charveze Memorial Award (1991); commissioned by Pope Paul VI (1978).

REPRESENTATION: Gallery 10, Inc., Scottsdale and Carefree, Arizona, and Santa Fe, New Mexico; The Squash Blossom, Aspen, Vail, and Denver, Colorado; Merrill B. Dumas American Indian Art, New Orleans, Louisiana; Four Winds Gallery, Pittsburgh, Pennsylvania.

ABOUT THE ARTIST: Beck creates contemporarily styled jewelry, using the same stone (turquoise) as his ancestors and some other semiprecious stones. He was strongly influenced by the work of Charles Loloma and Kenneth Begay and is especially known for his side inlay rings in silver and gold, as well as for his unusual bolo-tie designs.

MARY (THOMPSON) BECKMAN
(a.k.a. Jostwi)

Onondaga (N/A) Nedrow, New York
Painter, beadworker, jeweler, clothing designer

EDUCATION: Took painting classes at Roosevelt School in Syracuse and at the Cayuga Museum.

ABOUT THE ARTIST: Beckman's work has been exhibited throughout New York State. She also teaches, writes, and is musical. Her paintings are landscapes, still lifes, wildlife, and, sometimes, portraits.

ABRAHAM BEGAY
Navajo (N/A)
Jeweler, silversmith

REPRESENTATION: Long Ago and Far Away, Manchester, Vermont.

ABOUT THE ARTIST: Begay, a master silversmith, is known for his innovative designs. His jewelry is striking and original, often large and chunky.

ALICE N. BEGAY

Navajo (1940 —) Pinon, Arizona
Weaver

EDUCATION: Learned from her grandmother in the early 1960s how to make the cross-shaped wall hangings; learned how to make standard rectangular rugs from her mother.

AWARDS: Begay's unusually shaped rugs have won many prizes.

ABOUT THE ARTIST: A Mormon, Begay often makes rugs shaped like Latin crosses, but denies that they have any symbolic Christian meanings. Most of Begay's designs are based on Ganado Red patterns, though she also weaves in the Two Grey Hills style. Her weavings are from her imagination and she intentionally stays away from photographs and others' weaving techniques.

ALVIN BEGAY

Navajo (N/A)
Jeweler

ABOUT THE ARTIST: In addition to being a well-known jeweler, Alvin is also a champion bull rider.

AMY BEGAY

Navajo (1965 —) Chinle, Arizona
Weaver, basketmaker

EDUCATION: Learned how to make tufted rugs from her mother, Elsie Nez; degree in early childhood education and special education from Northern Arizona University.

AWARDS: Regularly wins prizes in the Novelty Weave category of the Museum of Northern Arizona's annual Navajo Show.

ABOUT THE ARTIST: Begay uses fleece from large goats to create her tufted rugs which are normally single- or double-saddle blanket size (36 inches square or 30 x 60 inches). The mohair is washed and used for tufts; the sheep wool is carded and spun, then used for the wefts and warps.

GLORIA BEGAY

Navajo (1970 —) Ganado, Arizona
Weaver

EDUCATION: Learned how to weave from her mother, Mary Lee Begay; Associate in Art in computer science at Scottsdale Community College.

AWARDS: Miss Indian Scottsdale Community College (1991).

ABOUT THE ARTIST: Begay's whole family weaves, but Begay is considering a career that may take up most of her time and leave her little time for weaving. It takes Begay approximately six months to finish a rug, and she uses the same designs her mother and grandmother have.

HARRISON BEGAY

(a.k.a. Warrior Who Walked Up to His Enemy/Haskay Yah Ne Yah)
Navajo (1917 —) White Cone, Arizona
Artist—painter, illustrator, printmaker, muralist

EDUCATION: The Santa Fe Indian School (1939) under Dorothy Dunn (The Studio); architecture Black Mountain (1940-41); attended Phoenix Junior College (1941).

AWARDS: Begay's work has won many awards and has been exhibited in shows such as the First Annual American Indian Art Exhibition at Wayne State University (1964), the Museum of Modern Art in New York, and the Philbrook Art Center.

REPRESENTATION: Amerind Foundation Museum Shop, Dragoon, Arizona.

ABOUT THE ARTIST: Begay likes to paint scenes from the traditional Navajo past, as well as today's events. Internationally known, Begay's work has greatly influenced other Navajo artists. Begay is the best known Navajo artist of the Southwest movement. His works have been published by Frederick Dockstader (Director of the Museum of the American Indian—1961) and in a number of publications.

17

HARRY A. BEGAY

Navajo (N/A) Sheep Springs, New Mexico
Sandpainter

ABOUT THE ARTIST: Begay's late 1970s sandpaintings were created with the tourist in mind. His Holy People are generalized figures, created without the specificity that they would have had had they been done by a medicine man using the sandpainting in its original intent—as a healing tool that could be blown away when finished.

HARVEY BEGAY

Navajo (1938 –   ) New Mexico
Jeweler

EDUCATION: Learned most of his jeweler's skills from his father, Kenneth Begay; apprenticed with Pierre Touraine; earned a Bachelor of Science degree from Arizona State University.

REPRESENTATION: Lovena Ohl Gallery, Scottsdale, Arizona; Gallery of the American West, Sacramento, California; Galeria Capistrano, San Juan Capistrano, California; The Indian Craft Shop, Washington, D.C.; Beckwith Gallery, Wellesley, Massachusetts; Adobe East Gallery, Millburn, New Jersey; La Fonda Indian Shop and Gallery, Santa Fe, New Mexico; Red Rock Trading Company, Alexandria, Virginia.

ABOUT THE ARTIST: Begay incorporates traditional styles with modern techniques, often using the textile patterns he learned from his mother, Eleanor Begay, a weaver. In the 1970s, Begay opened a shop called the Navajo Craftsman in Steamboat Springs, Colorado, where he sold work created by Native American artists. Eventually, Begay's jewelry began to take over, and he soon began to earn his living from what he created. He is adept at all types of casting, works in silver and gold, and uses precut and polished stones in his pieces. Also a metalcraft artist, Begay creates flatware, plates, and goblets.

JOE BEGAY

Navajo (N/A) Sheep Springs, New Mexico
Sandpainter

ABOUT THE ARTIST: Begay has done some full sandpainting reproductions that are easily named and identified, though changes are made to them so that they do not offend religious people. Some of Begay's work was adapted from Newcomb and Reichard's books of sandpaintings.

KEITH BEGAY

Navajo (N/A) Shiprock, New Mexico
Sandpainter

AWARDS: Begay's work has won awards that include first prize at the New Mexico State Fair (1978).

KENNETH BEGAY

Navajo (1914 – 1977) New Mexico
Jeweler

EDUCATION: Taught by Fred Peshlakai at the Fort Wingate Boarding School for Native Americans during the 1930s.

AWARDS: Begay won many awards for the work he did with John C. Bonnell and built a national reputation for his work.

ABOUT THE ARTIST: Begay was responsible for creating a style of Navajo jewelry that was simple and designed with bold lines around a single stone. He worked with John C. Bonnell at the White Hogan in Arizona from 1946–1950. They collaborated to created metalwork of all kinds, each with its own distinct design. After leaving the White Hogan, Begay taught silversmithing at the Navajo Community College where he influenced the new generation of jewelers. He is called the Father of Modern Navajo Jewelry.

KYLE BEGAY

Navajo (N/A)
Jeweler

18

EDUCATION: Taught the family jewelry tradition by his father, Harvey Begay.

ABOUT THE ARTIST: Like the other Begays, Kyle creates award-winning pieces of jewelry.

MAMIE P. BEGAY

Navajo (1949 –   ) Sweetwater, Teec Nos Pas, Arizona
Weaver

EDUCATION: Learned how to weave from her grandmother at age twelve.

ABOUT THE ARTIST: Begay's serrated-outline rugs are large and in the Teec Nos Pas/Red Mesa style. She sells her rugs at the Crownpoint Rug Auction in New Mexico and tries to have a new rug ready every six weeks.

MARY LEE BEGAY

Navajo (1941 –   ) Ganado, Arizona
Weaver

EDUCATION: Learned how to weave from her mother, Grace Henderson Nez.

REPRESENTATION: Hubbell Trading Post, Ganado, Arizona.

ABOUT THE ARTIST: Begay started weaving rugs for the Hubbell Trading Post in 1971 and is often commissioned to design patterns for customers such as the Denver Art Museum. She makes Burntwater, Two Grey Hills, Storm, Wide Ruins, revival patterns, and other designs. She demonstrates weaving at the Hubbell Trading Post and her work is often shown in urban art galleries.

NATHAN BEGAY

Navajo/Hopi (N/A)
Potter

ABOUT THE ARTIST: Begay creates a variety of styles and is influenced by both modern and traditional designs.

VERA BEGAY

Navajo (1922 –   ) New Mexico
Weaver

EDUCATION: Learned from her mother and other weavers; began making her own weavings at age fifteen.

ABOUT THE ARTIST: Begay's first weaving, a saddle blanket, is still in her possession and she refuses to sell it. She creates what the traders tell her people want and supports herself selling her weavings.

DENNIS BELINDO

(a.k.a. Aun-So-Te, "Foot")
Kiowa/Navajo (1938 –   ) Phoenix, Arizona
Artist

EDUCATION: Studied art at Bacone College, Northeastern State College, and the University of Oklahoma.

AWARDS: Has won many awards throughout the Southwest.

ABOUT THE ARTIST: Belindo, a law student who turned to art, eventually became a professor of art at the University of California at Berkley. He has exhibited in group and one-person shows throughout the United States.

GLADYS BEN

Navajo (N/A) Shiprock, New Mexico
Sandpainter

AWARDS: Ben has won several awards for her sandpaintings, including third prize at the Gallup Ceremonial (1978).

JOE BEN, JR.

Navajo (N/A)
Sandpainter.

EDUCATION: University of New Mexico.

19

ABOUT THE ARTIST: Ben uses original ceremonial designs but changes the colors because it is considered sacrilegious to use the original colors. He creates sandpaintings because people have been cured by them and because "(t)his is my way of life."

WILSON BENALLY
Navajo (N/A) New Mexico
Sandpainter

ABOUT THE ARTIST: Benally has created some sandpaintings in which the four Cloud People have been moved from their original positions. Because sandpainting is considered a medicine man's art that has gone commercial, it is theorized that the reason sandpainters make errors in their paintings is so that they become more secular and less religious.

MIKE BERO
Mohawk (1921 –   ) St. Regis, Quebec, Canada
Painter; sculptor—acrylics, oil, pencil, charcoal,
pastels, clay

EDUCATION: Self-taught.

ABOUT THE ARTIST: Bero paints scenes of traditional Iroquois life. He likes to work with oils best and has a realistic style. Some of his work is on permanent display at the Akwesasne Cultural Center. He exhibits his work and also accepts commissions.

HELEN BIA
Navajo (1945 –   ) Three Turkey Ruins, Arizona
Weaver

EDUCATION: Bia's mother, Mary Bia, taught her the Three Turkey Ruins style which is now shared by Bia; her sisters, Ruth Ann Tracey, Lucy Begay, and Alice B. Begay; her daughter, Gloria; and her niece, Irene.

AWARDS: Best of Show, Heard Museum's Indian arts and crafts exhibition (1974).

ABOUT THE ARTIST: Bia's Three Turkey Ruin rugs are different from Burntwaters as they have fewer colors and incorporate more symmetrical design components. Bia creates both small and large rugs, often shopping around for the best price for her work or taking commissions. Bia and her daughter, Gloria, often set their looms up side by side to work on their rugs.

WOODY BIG BOW
(a.k.a. Tse-Koy-Ate, "Big Bow")
Kiowa (1914 –   ) Carnegie, Oklahoma
Artist

EDUCATION: University of Oklahoma, Oklahoma.

ABOUT THE ARTIST: Big Bow has shown his work throughout the United States and has painted murals for the RCA Building in New York, as well as others.

CHARLIE BIRD
Laguna/Santo Domingo (1943 –   ) New Mexico
Jeweler

EDUCATION: Comes from a family of artists, but did not develop his own style of jewelry until the 1970s; taught himself mosaic work.

REPRESENTATION: Dewey Galleries, Ltd., Santa Fe, New Mexico; Packard's Indian Trading Co., Inc., Santa Fe, New Mexico.

ABOUT THE ARTIST: Bird is inspired by nature. Some of his jewelry reflect the designs he sees in places like the Chaco Canyon and the cliffs at Jemez Pueblo.

GAIL BIRD AND YAZZIE JOHNSON
Gail—Santo Domingo/Laguna (1949 –   )
California
Yazzie—Navajo (1946 –   ) Arizona
Jewelers

EDUCATION: Self-taught.

20

AWARDS: Fellowship from the Southwestern Association on Indian Affairs (1980); Best of Show award, Santa Fe Indian Market (1981); work held by Museum of Man, San Diego; the Wheelwright Museum; the Millicent Rogers Museum; Albuquerque International Airport.

REPRESENTATION: Joanne Lyon Treasures, Aspen, Colorado; Dewey Galleries, Ltd., Santa Fe, New Mexico.

ABOUT THE ARTISTS: Bird designs the jewelry and Johnson fabricates the pieces. The two have worked in brass, silver, copper, and gold and have used precious and semiprecious beads and stones from all over the world. Bird keeps a notebook of her designs, as well as clippings of ideas for future pieces.

MIKE BIRD

San Juan Pueblo (1946 –) New Mexico
Jeweler

EDUCATION: Basically self-taught, Bird was inspired to create jewelry after watching Julian Lovato.

AWARDS: Has won awards at the Santa Fe Indian Market for his petroglyph figural pins.

REPRESENTATION: Gallery 10, Inc., Scottsdale and Carefree, Arizona, and Santa Fe, New Mexico; Federico on Montana, Santa Monica, California; Galeria Primitivo, Santa Monica, California; Merrill B. Domas American Indian Art, New Orleans, Louisiana; Dewey Galleries, Ltd., Santa Fe, New Mexico; Four Winds Gallery, Pittsburgh, Pennsylvania.

ABOUT THE ARTIST: Bird did not take up jewelry as a career until in his mid thirties. He and his wife, Allison, research Navajo and Pueblo traditional styles, then Bird uses their designs to create his own jewelry. He has even copied some petroglyph designs and recreated them, giving them new life as pieces of jewelry. His work is held in the Millicent Rogers Museum.

DOROTHY M. BISCUP

(a.k.a. Gain Ee)
Seneca (1911 –) Steamburg, New York
Beadworker

EDUCATION: Taught by her aunt, Kathryn Jamerson; also taught herself some skills.

ABOUT THE ARTIST: Biscup was a president of the Iroquois Senior Citizens and also taught Seneca at the Haley Community Building. She was a member of the Allegany Indian Arts & Crafts Coop from its inception. She finds making beadwork chokers, daisy chains, and ladder-stitch necklaces to be quite relaxing, and she prefers to use brightly colored glass beads in her work.

AGNES BLACK

Navajo (N/A)
Basketmaker

ABOUT THE ARTIST: Black uses deer, butterflies, and human forms to decorate her traditionally coiled trays.

LORRAINE BLACK

Navajo (N/A)
Basketmaker

ABOUT THE ARTIST: Like Agnes, Lorraine decorates her traditionally coiled trays with deer, butterflies, and human forms.

MARY BLACK

Navajo/Ute (N/A)
Basketmaker

ABOUT THE ARTIST: Black often creates baskets reminiscent of Pima designs.

ARCHIE BLACKOWL

(a.k.a. Mis Ta Moo To Va, "Flying Hawk")
Cheyenne (1912 –) Weatherford, Oklahoma
Artist—various media; illustrator; muralist

21

EDUCATION: The Seger Indian School; the Chilocco Indian School; studied under muralist Olaf Nordmark at the Indian Art Center in Fort Sill, Oklahoma; studied water color at University of Kansas; studied art at the Art Institute of Chicago, the Rockefeller Art Center, and the Washington, D.C. School of Fine Arts.

AWARDS: Numerous.

ABOUT THE ARTIST: Blackowl painted murals for quite a few institutions, painted portraits of public officials, and created illustrations for the Georgia Agricultural Extension Service. He was also author/illustrator of "Charts for Visual Instruction." Various publications have printed his work. Blackowl has held exhibits at galleries and museums throughout the United States, at places such as the Agra Gallery in Washington, D.C.; the Oklahoma Art Center; and various colleges and universities. His work is held in collections throughout the United States. Made a chief of the Cheyenne Sun Dance Clan in 1945, Blackowl resigned from his duties for financial reasons. After that time, he continued to paint the Cheyenne rituals and traditions.

WINONA ESTHER BLUEYE

(a.k.a. Ko Woo Wiitha')
> Seneca (1903 –) Basom, New York
> Beadworker, leatherworker

EDUCATION: Self-taught; took some classes.

AWARDS: Among Blueye's honors is the recognition she received from the New York Iroquois Conference in 1975 when they named her one of the Ten Prominent Women of the Year in New York State.

ABOUT THE ARTIST: Blueye has exhibited her work at powwows and art exhibits. She prefers to do beadwork medallions, but also works with leather. She teaches the Seneca language at several area schools.

DEMPSEY BOB

> Tahltan-Tlingit (1948 –) Telegraph Creek,
> British Columbia, Canada
> Carver

EDUCATION: Self-taught; uses the ancient art of carving and the old designs and drawings.

ABOUT THE ARTIST: Bob works with wood because he likes its feel. He uses alder for masks, bowls, and spoons (because it has no taste); red cedar for canoes, houses and large totem poles; and birch for rattles. He carves human figure bowls and all other types of wooden objects using the old designs that were once incorporated into blankets, rattles, drums, and masks. He is considered the artistic spokesperson for his people.

CHRISTINE BOBB

> Northwest Coast (1890 –)Boothroyd Reserve,
> British Columbia, Canada
> Basketmaker

ABOUT THE ARTIST: Bobb gathers her own materials to make her decorated baskets.

CAROLYN BOBELU

> Zuni (N/A) Arizona
> Jeweler

ABOUT THE ARTIST: Bobelu often uses intricate inlay designs in her work.

ALEX BOMBERRY

> Lower Cayuga (1953 –) Caledona, Ontario,
> Canada
> Artist—acrylics, pen and ink, pencil, watercolors

EDUCATION: Took some art classes in high school and summer classes with the Manitou Art Foundation.

ABOUT THE ARTIST: Bomberry's paintings are stylized, photolike portraits of Native Americans. He gives all of his paintings titles and has exhibited his work in Canadian exhibits. Bomberry is also interested in photography and filmmaking.

22

GRACE BONSPILLE

(a.k.a. Takahawakwen)
Mohawk (1930 –   ) Oka, Quebec, Canada
Beadworker, leatherworker

EDUCATION: Took classes in beadwork, leather-work, and leather tooling.

BOUT THE ARTIST: Bonspille has made beaded belts, necklaces, watchbands, and headbands; leather moccasins, jackets, vests, and purses; and has decorated leather changepurses, key holders, and wallets. Her whole family is involved in the arts, especially her mother, Margaret Etienne, a basketmaker.

PERRY BONSPILLE

Mohawk (1960 –   )
Beadworker, leatherworker

EDUCATION: Took classes in beadwork and leather-work.

ABOUT THE ARTIST: Like his mother, Grace, Bonspille has been doing craftswork since a young age. He likes to use stars and geometric patterns in his beadwork designs and continues to experiment with different media.

F. BLACKBEAR BOSIN

(a.k.a. Tsate Kongia, Sate-Kon-Gia, "Blackbear")
Kiowa/Comanche (1921 – 1980) near
Anadarko, Oklahoma
Artist—watercolor, gouache on illustration board

EDUCATION: Self-taught.

AWARDS: Fellow, International Institute of Arts and Letters, Kreuzlingen, Switzerland (1956); Certificate of Appreciation, Indian Arts and Crafts Board, United States Department of Interior, 1966; Waite Phillips Trophy for Outstanding Contributions to American Indian Art, Philbrook Art Center, Tulsa (1967); many others.

ABOUT THE ARTIST: Bosin's art reflected his feelings about what this country would have been like if Columbus had not discovered it in 1492. Bosin painted the spiritual history, tribal history, and myths of Native American life. He was the first generation after his tribe had been "conquered" and put on reservations, and thus felt a moral obligation to paint his people in the same manner the storytellers of the tribe used to tell their history. Former owner and operator of the Great Plains Studio and Gallery in Wichita, Kansas, Bosin exhibited his work in group and one-person shows throughout the United States and abroad.

ARKENE BOVA

(a.k.a. Gah Na Sah Gnaha)
Seneca (1961 –   ) Salamanca, New York
Beadworker

EDUCATION: Learned from her mother, Ella Bowen.

ABOUT THE ARTIST: Bova has been doing beadwork since she was nine. She prefers loom beadwork because it allows her to work with many different colors and designs. She tries to never use the same design twice with the same colors. Bova took a number of art courses at Salamanca Central School, and she also dances with the Seneca Dancers.

DARLENE BOVA

(a.k.a. Gay Yeh Na)
Seneca (1960 –   ) Salamanca, New York
Beadworker, quillworker

EDUCATION: Learned her skills from her mother, Ella Bowen, and her aunt, Delores Oldshield.

ABOUT THE ARTIST: Bova has been working with beads since she was nine. She especially likes to make porcupine-quill and bead earrings in the peyote stitches.

PARKER BOYIDDLE, JR.

Wichita/Delaware/Chickasaw/Kiowa (1948 –   )
Oklahoma
Artist—oil; sculptor

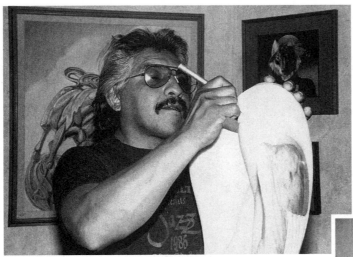

Portrait of Boyiddle at work on a sculpture. Photograph by Mary Goodman, courtesy of SunWest Silver, Albuquerque, New Mexico.

EDUCATION: Classen High School, Oklahoma City (1965); art scholarship to the Oklahoma Science and Art Foundation.

REPRESENTATION: SunWest Silver, Inc., Santa Fe, New Mexico.

ABOUT THE ARTIST: Boyiddle's work has been exhibited at Riverside Museum in New York.

Boyiddle's painted 48 inch round shield. Slide by Sanford Maldin, courtesy of SunWest Silver, Albuquerque, New Mexico.

Limited edition bronze sculpture by Boyiddle entitled "New Life," 18 inches high. Slide by Sanford Maldin, courtesy of SunWest Silver, Albuquerque, New Mexico.

LYNDA (HAYFIELD) BRANT
Mohawk (1954 –   ) Kingston, Ontario, Canada
Artist—oils, watercolors, pastels, pencil, pen and ink

EDUCATION: Art major at the Ontario College of Arts.

ABOUT THE ARTIST: Continuously learning, Brant has added photography, beadwork, and pottery to her list of arts. She often sketches from life, then later paints the scene. She has exhibited her work at the Mohawk Fall Fair.

MABEL BROWN
Acoma (N/A) Acoma Pueblo, New Mexico
Potter

ABOUT THE ARTIST: Though she creates traditional Acoma pottery, this innovative potter has also created some nontraditional pieces, such as cream pitchers in the form of a cow.

MAMIE BROWN
(a.k.a. Gan Nah Jah Leet)
Oneida (1921 –   ) Afton, New York
Beadworker, quillworker, dollmaker, featherworker

EDUCATION: Learned from her mother.

ABOUT THE ARTIST: Brown's mother was an active craftsperson at Onondaga. Her father carved wood basket handles and axe handles. Mamie has made baskets, but she now does mostly quillwork and beadwork, as well as makes cornhusk dolls. She dresses her dolls in traditional clothing and often makes male-female pairs. One such doll went into Rose Kennedy's collection. Brown exhibits at the New York State Fair and travels to shows all over the country.

MARY BROWN
Navajo (1950 –   ) Phoenix, Arizona
Weaver

EDUCATION: Learned how to weave from her mother, but gave it up for quite a while until challenged by a friend to make a seat cover for his pickup.

ABOUT THE ARTIST: The rug Brown made for her friend's pickup is a "Stacked Boxes" design, which is one of the patterns used for saddle blankets and throw rugs. It is an optical illusion design, often used by Navajo weavers because of its figure/ground ambiguity. After weaving the rug, Brown kept on weaving, creating at least four more rugs in the year following.

CLIFFORD BRYCELEA
Navajo (N/A)
Painter

EDUCATION: Fort Lewis College, Durango, Colorado.

ABOUT THE ARTIST: If Brycelea paints a sacred ceremonial scene or object, he "say[s] a prayer and sprinkle[s] corn pollen."

LES BUCKTOOTH
Onondaga (1957 –   ) Nedrow, New York
Illustrator—pen and ink, pencil, chalk, acrylics

EDUCATION: Self-taught.

AWARDS: Among Bucktooth's awards are ribbons from the New York State Fair, a Gold Key Award, and many others.

ABOUT THE ARTIST: Bucktooth likes to do traditional drawings as well as modern ones. He is especially drawn to nature and animals. He can also string lacrosse sticks and works with beads, leather, and wood.

BENJAMIN FRANKLIN BUFFALO
(a.k..a. Bennie Franklin Buffalo, "Going South")
Cheyenne (1948 –   ) Clinton, Oklahoma
Artist—acrylic

EDUCATION: Studied painting at the San Francisco Art Institute, California.

ABOUT THE ARTIST: Buffalo's style has gotten away from the traditional and is now focused on an almost photographic realism, portraying his people as they are today.

WHITE BUFFALO
Comanche (N/A)
Jeweler

EDUCATION: Learned some of his technique from a master silversmith in Europe.

ABOUT THE ARTIST: White Buffalo is known for his flatware, vases, trays, jewelry, and coffee and tea sets.

HELEN BURBANK
Navajo (N/A) near Ganado, Arizona
Weaver

EDUCATION: Learned to weave from her aunt and grandmother.

ABOUT THE ARTIST: Burbank sold her first weaving at age eight. She does Yeibichai rugs and is starting to incorporate features into her rugs which go beyond the traditional regional style.

HELEN BURNING
Onondaga (1918 –   ) Oshweken, Ontario, Canada
Beadworker, clothing designer, leatherworker

EDUCATION: Learned from Huron Miller.

AWARDS: Best in show (beadwork), Six Nations Fall Fair (1977).

ABOUT THE ARTIST: Burning makes beaded jewelry, barrettes, and hair and bolo ties. She also does beadwork decoration on native clothing and moccasins. Burning travels extensively to fairs, festivals, and powwows to sell the work that she and her daughters, Shirley and Ruth, have created. Helen shades and blends her beads, striving for an original design and style. She experiments with beadwork and also holds classes in the art.

DIANE M. BURNS
Anishinabe/Chemehuevi (1953 –   )
Painter

EDUCATION: Institute of American Indian Arts, Santa Fe (1974); Barnard College, Columbia University, New York.

AWARDS: Received the Manuel J. Lujan Congressional Medal of Merit for academic and artistic excellence while at the Institute of American Indian Arts.

ABOUT THE ARTIST: Burns has exhibited her paintings all over the United States, including the 1974 Minnesota Governor's Invitational, the 1979 American Indian Community House Gallery Invitational, and the 1980 National American Indian Women's Art Show.

JEROME GILBERT BUSHYHEAD
(a.k.a. "Coyote Walks By")
Cheyenne (1929 –   ) Calumet, Oklahoma
Artist—tempera on illustration board and other media

EDUCATION: Studied art at Centenary College, Shreveport, Louisiana.

ABOUT THE ARTIST: Bushyhead paints in the traditional Indian style, often depicting his people as they were in the past.

NORMAN BUSHYHEAD
Cheyenne (N/A)
Textiles

AWARDS: Best of Division, Cultural items/textiles, at the Red Earth Awards Ceremony, Oklahoma, 1994.

MARY CAIN
Santa Clara (N/A) New Mexico
Potter

EDUCATION: Learned the Tafoya pottery tradition from her mother, Christina Naranjo.

ABOUT THE ARTIST: Cain worked with her mother during the 1970s. The pieces they made together are signed by both of them. Cain's daughter, Linda, and many other members of this famous pottery-making family are in the business. Cain makes black polished pots.

"CA WIN" JIMMY CALABAZA
Santo Domingo (1949 –   ) New Mexico
Jeweler, silversmith

EDUCATION: Self-taught silversmith.

ABOUT THE ARTIST: Calabaza makes jewelry in the Santo Domingo Pueblo craft tradition. He is well-known for his polished turquoise necklaces. He also started using silver in his necklaces at the end of the 1980s and his signature piece became a silver side box.

CECIL CALNIMPTEWA

Hopi (1950 –) Moenkopi, Arizona
Carver–Kachina dolls

EDUCATION: Learned carving from father.

AWARDS: Calnimptewa's awards are numerous, including many won at the Santa Fe Indian Market for his lifelike Kachinas.

REPRESENTATION: Adobe Gallery, Albuquerque, New Mexico.

ABOUT THE ARTIST: Calnimptewa is well known for his true one-piece carved Kachinas, as well as for his understanding of draping materials. He has passed on his knowledge to his students, such as Dennis Tewa, winner of Kachina carving category of the 1983 Gallup Inter-Tribal Ceremonial. The artist's innovations have given new nuances of artistic rendering to his Kachina carvings.

DALE CAMPBELL

Tahltan (N/A) Telegraph Creek, British Columbia,
Canada
Carver

ABOUT THE ARTIST: Campbell carves such items as Eagle frontlets. Sometimes she decorates them with abalone inlay.

TOM WAYNE CANNON

(a.k.a. T.C. Cannon, Pai Doung U Day, "One Who Stands in the Sun")
Caddo/Kiowa (1946 – 1978) Lawton,
Oklahoma
Artist–oil on canvas, acrylic on canvas

EDUCATION: Studied at the American Indian Art in Santa Fe under Fritz Scholder (1964–1966); studied painting at the San Francisco Art Institute (1966); studied at the College of Santa Fe, New Mexico (1969–1970) and at Central State University, Edmond, Oklahoma (1970).

AWARDS: Governor's Trophy at Scottsdale National Indian Art Exhibition (1966); many other awards.

REPRESENTATION: Broschofsky Galleries, Ketchum, Idaho; 21st Century Fox Fine Art, Santa Fe, New Mexico; Wheelwright Museum of the American Indian/Case Trading Post, Arizona.

ABOUT THE ARTIST: Cannon used abstract expressionism and pop art to depict the two levels on which the modern Native American lives—one set in the white world and the second in the native Indian world. Cannon worked as a mainstream modern artist and was often compared to Fritz Scholder.

JOE AND ROSEY CATÉ

Joe—Santo Domingo (1944 –) New Mexico
Rose—Santo Domingo (1948 –) New Mexico
Jewelers

EDUCATION: This husband-and-wife team learned some of its techniques from family members; Rosey also studied at the Institute of American Indian Art in Santa Fe.

REPRESENTATION: Dewey Galleries, Ltd., Santa Fe, New Mexico; Packard's Indian Trading Co., Inc., Santa Fe, New Mexico; Wheelwright Museum of the American Indian/Case Trading Post, Santa Fe, New Mexico.

ABOUT THE ARTISTS: The Catés' trademark is the addition of a *jacla* (means "ear string" in Navajo) to their *heishi* necklaces. The jacla can be worn as earrings or left attached to each side of the necklace.

CONNIE CERNO

Acoma (N/A) Acoma Pueblo, New Mexico
Potter

ABOUT THE ARTIST: Cerno likes her pots to be nicely shaped and prettily presented. Her well-shaped forms rise gracefully from the bases of her pots.

JOE AND BARBARA CERNO

Acoma (N/A) Acoma Pueblo, New Mexico
Potters

ABOUT THE ARTISTS: This talented couple make kiln-fired polychrome pottery. Their seed jars are often decorated with Mimbres motifs and very large pottery vessels they create influenced by Acoma, Mimbres, and Zuni designs.

POP CHALEE

(a.k.a. Marena Lujan, Marina Lujan Hopkins, "Blue Flower")
Taos/East Indian (1908 –) Castle Dale, Utah
Artist

EDUCATION: Tutored by Dorothy Dunn, Santa Fe Indian School (1930s).

ABOUT THE ARTIST: Chalee's style, a light, surrealistic fantasy world, shows the influence of both cultures in which she was raised (her mother was

Chapman's watercolor entitled "Mrs. Hunter," 30 x 22 inches, 1990. Slide courtesy of the artist and Jan Cicero Gallery, Chicago, Illinois.

from India). Her work is filled usually with forest creatures who are stylized and delicate (what has since been called the "Bambi" style of painting). She has exhibited all over the world.

JEFFREY CHAPMAN

Chippewa (early 1960s –)
Painter, carver, sculptor

EDUCATION: Bachelor of Fine Art, Minneapolis College of Art and Design (1984); Minneapolis Community College (1977–1978).

AWARDS: Many awards, including first and second places for both watercolor painting and graphics at the Annual Minnesota Ojibway Art Expo.

REPRESENTATION: Jan Cicero Gallery, Chicago, Illinois.

ABOUT THE ARTIST: Chapman has exhibited his work in both solo and group shows throughout the Midwest, has been commissioned to create works for the Science Museum of Minnesota, and is active in his community. He is also known as a flute carver and has held many demonstrations of that talent.

CHARGING THUNDER FAMILY

Lakota

This contemporary-artist family includes working artists Earl Charging Thunder, Alma Charging Thunder, Faye Charging Thunder, Agnes Charging Thunder, Kathy Charging Thunder, Pauline Charging Thunder, and Nora Brings Him Back.

ABOUT THE ARTISTS: The Charging Thunder Family's genealogy extends into other artistic families. One of the reasons this family is grouped as artists in this book, and at exhibits held at The Heritage Center, Inc., is because the family members learn from each other, work together and depend on each other in their daily and artistic lives. For further information on each artist, contact The Heritage Center, Inc., in South Dakota (see the gallery contributors list in the back of this book).

KAREN KAHE CHARLEY
Hopi (N/A) Arizona
Potter

EDUCATION: Taught to pot by her mother, Marcella Kahe.

ABOUT THE ARTIST: Charley did not begin creating pottery pieces until 1983. She uses the orange-red color Charley's family has kept secret and which other Hopi potters have not yet imitated. She has shown her work at the Tulsa Indian Arts Festival, the Santa Fe Indian Market, and the Pueblo Grande in Phoenix.

CARRIE CHINO CHARLIE
Acoma (N/A) Acoma Pueblo, New Mexico
Potter

EDUCATION: Inspired by the large seed jars her aunt, Grace Chino, created.

ABOUT THE ARTIST: Charlie produces traditional ceramics made with native clay and painted with natural pigments; however, she fires her work in an electric kiln. She considers her work to be a blend of traditional and modern styles.

DENNIS AND MARGE CHARLIE
Cowichan (N/A) Penelakut Reserve, British Columbia, Canada
Knitters

EDUCATION: Some of Marge's designs (such as the Bird and Sea Monster patterns) were passed down to her by her mother who had received them from her mother. The designs have been used by many generations.

ABOUT THE ARTISTS: This husband-and-wife team work together to shear the sheep and make the wool with which they create.

ELSIE CHARLIE
Northwest Coast (N/A) Yale, British Columbia, Canada
Basketmaker

EDUCATION: Charlie's mother taught her how to weave baskets, telling her to speak to the tree and make sure it realizes she would not waste any of it. Charlie still uses her mother's tools.

ABOUT THE ARTIST: Charlie makes all kinds of baskets, including decorated baby baskets. She uses deerbone awls as tools (just as her ancestors did) and makes baskets out of cedar roots, white straw, and wild cherry bark.

RIC CHARLIE
Navajo (1959 –   ) New Mexico
Jeweler

REPRESENTATION: Sherwoods, Beverly Hills, California.

ABOUT THE ARTIST: Charlie creates one-of-a-kind gold pieces, using tufa casting and setting them with semiprecious stones. He carves his design on the tufa with dental tools and often applies patinas to his metals. Charlie often creates *yeibeichai* designs on his jewelry.

SIMON CHARLIE
Coast Salish/Malahat (N/A) Canada
Carver

ABOUT THE ARTIST: Charlie listened to his family tell him of hiring men to carve potlatch figures. The figure would have two open hands, welcoming the friends who were coming to the potlatch. By listening to his uncle's description, Charlie has been able to reproduce the figures. In 1974, Charlie made a replica of a decaying house board which was used at the University of British Columbia.

TED CHARVEZE
Isleta (N/A) Isleta Pueblo, New Mexico
Jeweler

EDUCATION: Studied with Pierre Touraine, a French jeweler.

ABOUT THE ARTIST: Charveze's jewelry is owned by royalty, including the Queen of Denmark and the Princess of Luxembourg. He has designed for Cartier in Paris and Imperial Enterprises in Japan.

ELIZABETH CHARVEZE-CAPLINGER

Isleta (N/A) Isleta Pueblo, New Mexico
Jeweler—gold, diamonds, precious/semiprecious stones

EDUCATION: Ted Charveze, Elizabeth's father, taught her.

ABOUT THE ARTIST: At age fourteen, Elizabeth started making jewelry. She has continued to improve and is already considered important enough to be included in major art books. Charveze-Caplinger shows in major galleries.

FLORENCE NUPOK CHAUNCEY

(a.k.a. Malewotkuk)
Eskimo (1906 – 1971) Village of Gambell,
St. Lawrence Island, Alaska
Artist—pen and ink on seal skin

EDUCATION: Self-taught.

ABOUT THE ARTIST: Chauncey drew scenes of her people, the walrus, and other animals around her, and earned the title "Grandma Moses of the Bering Sea."

STELLA CHAVARRIA

Santa Clara (N/A) New Mexico
Potter

EDUCATION: Learned her skills from the many illustrious potters in her family, the Tafoyas and Naranjos.

ABOUT THE ARTIST: Daughter of Teresita Naranjo, Stella has learned the trade from some of the best potters in the business, her family, and is expected to become as well known as they are. She pencils in her decoration before carving

it into the leather-hard clay with an old kitchen paring knife.

RICHARD CHAVEZ

San Felipe (1949 –   ) New Mexico
Jeweler

EDUCATION: Studied architecture at University of New Mexico; learned how to make jewelry from his grandfather.

AWARDS: Grand Prize at the Eight Northern Indian Pueblo Artist and Craftsman Show (1975); Fellowship from Southwestern Association on Indian Affairs (1981); many subsequent awards and honors.

REPRESENTATION: The Squash Blossom, Aspen, Vail, and Denver, Colorado; Merrill B. Domas American Indian Art, New Orleans, Louisiana; Beckwith Gallery, Wellesley, Massachusetts; La Fonda Indian Shop and Gallery, Santa Fe, New Mexico; October Art Ltd., New York; Four Winds Gallery, Pittsburgh, Pennsylvania; Texas Art Gallery, Dallas, Texas.

ABOUT THE ARTIST: Chavez began making *heishi* and turquoise necklaces, but switched to silver because the price of silver was low. He taught himself how to smith and has been influenced by the simplistic manner of Scandinavian jewelry. He only uses three colors at a time and often perfects the sculpture of his jewelry by working outward before filling the pieces with color.

NOTAH H. CHEE

Navajo (N/A) Newcomb, New Mexico
Sandpainter

ABOUT THE ARTIST: Chee is one of the sandpainters who will create a sacred sandpainting template but change something about it. For example, in a painting done in 1975, Chee eliminated the number of outlines which surround the sun's face and changed the number of feathers in each quadrant of the painting.

ROBERT CHEE

Navajo (1938 – 1971) Billemont, Arizona
Artist—watercolor and pencil

EDUCATION: Attended school in Billemont, Arizona.

ABOUT THE ARTIST: Chee's works have been published by such magazines as *New Mexico Magazine* and the *Inter-Tribal Indian Ceremonial Annual Magazine.* Some exhibits of his work include the Museum of New Mexico and the Philbrook Art Center. Public collections of his work are held by the Museum of New Mexico, the Philbrook Art Center, the Bureau of Indian Affairs, and many others.

EVELYN CHEROMIAH

Laguna (N/A) Laguna Pueblo, New Mexico
Potter

ABOUT THE ARTIST: When creating new pottery, Cheromiah asks her ancestors (deceased potters) for help. In her many years as a potter, Cheromiah has seen the change in the way Laguna pottery was created—changes made during the advent of the tourist season and the invasion of the railroad and all it carried into the once-quiet reservations. Evelyn was responsible for reviving the art of making large ollas at the Laguna Pueblo.

LEE ANN CHEROMIAH

Laguna (NA) Laguna Pueblo, New Mexico
Potter

EDUCATION: Learned most of her craft from her mother, Evelyn.

ABOUT THE ARTIST: Cheromiah believes that the spirit of the clay works with the potter's spirit; if the clay and spirit agree, then the design works. If they do not, the pot will not come out right. Cheromiah makes older styles of pottery.

GERTRUDE CHEW

Onondaga (1903 –   ) Lewiston, New York
Beadworker

EDUCATION: Taught by her grandmother.

AWARDS: Received prizes at the New York State Fair for her beaded cushions.

ABOUT THE ARTIST: Chew exhibited and sold her beaded velvet cushions, picture frames, jewelry holders, birds, and other items at Niagara Falls Park. She often instructed curious tourists and family members in beading techniques.

GILBERT CHINO

Acoma (N/A) Acoma Pueblo, New Mexico
Potter

ABOUT THE ARTIST: Chino believes that some of today's potters are wage earners—some even manufacture their pottery which makes the pots lose much of their value. Other potters, he says, put their spirit into pottery making, keeping it an art.

GRACE CHINO

Acoma (N/A) Acoma Pueblo, New Mexico
Potter

EDUCATION: Her mother, Marie Chino, taught her much of what she knows about pottery.

ABOUT THE ARTIST: Chino knows that some pottery is made specifically for the deceased (buried with the body). Chino is responsible for teaching many Chino family members, including her niece, Carrie Chino Charlie. Chino lets each pot "decide" which design she will use and does not believe in a "design trademark" as do other potters of her generation.

KEITH CHINO

Acoma (N/A) Acoma Pueblo, New Mexico
Potter

ABOUT THE ARTIST: Chino creates commercial pottery in red clay that is painted in blue-and-yellow underglaze and decorated in sgraffito.

RANDALL CHITTO

Choctaw (N/A)
Sculptor

EDUCATION: Institute of American Indian Arts, Santa Fe, New Mexico.

AWARDS: Chitto's clay turtles have won numerous awards and wide recognition.

REPRESENTATION: Long Ago and Far Away, Manchester, Vermont.

ABOUT THE ARTIST: Chitto's turtles represent Storytellers, warriors, dancers, and musicians. His creations echo his Choctaw heritage; the Choctaw believe that the turtle is the keeper of their history.

JOHN CHRISTIANSEN

(a.k.a. Keokuk)
> *Sac and Fox (Sauk-Fox) (N/A) Michigan*
> *Jeweler*

ABOUT THE ARTIST: Christiansen creates fine necklaces of turquoise and other semiprecious stones. He also creates miniature (stone) beads that are hand-rolled and hand-polished.

DENNIS R. CHRISTY

> *Saginaw Chippewa (1955 –) Mt. Pleasant,*
> *Michigan*
> *Sculptor—stone, wood, bronze*

EDUCATION: Institute of American Indian Arts, Santa Fe, Associate of Fine Arts, Three-Dimensional Design and Sculptor (1976).

AWARDS: Christy's many awards include first, second, and third places; honorable mentions; special merit awards; and best of class recognition from such places as the Annual Indian Market in Dayton, Ohio; the Michigan Indian Arts Show in Mt. Pleasant, Michigan; and the Eiteljorg Museum in Indianapolis.

REPRESENTATION: SunWest Silver, Albuquerque, New Mexico.

ABOUT THE ARTIST: A member of the Black River Swan Creek tribe of the Saginaw Chippewa, Christy began carving wood as a young boy. He often worked alongside his grandmother, a basket-maker. Now Christy's work has been shown in both solo and group shows throughout the country and is owned by museums such as the Heard, the Wheelwright, and the Institute of American Indian Arts, and by private collectors.

Black-and-white portrait of Christy with owl sculpture, courtesy of SunWest Silver, Albuquerque, New Mexico.

Christy's owl sculpture done in alabaster, courtesy of SunWest Silver, Albuquerque, New Mexico.

CARL AND IRENE CLARK

Carl–Navajo (1952 –) Arizona
Irene–Navajo (1950 –) Arizona
Jewelers

EDUCATION: Carl learned how to make jewelry by observing silversmiths when he managed a jewelry production shop in Winslow, Arizona.

AWARDS: The Clarks have exhibited all over the world and have won awards at the Gallup Inter-Tribal Ceremonial and the Museum of Northern Arizona and Heard Museum competitions.

REPRESENTATION: Gallery 10, Inc., Scottsdale and Carefree, Arizona, and Santa Fe, New Mexico; Many Hands, Sedona, Arizona; Southwest Trading Company, Saint Charles, Illinois.

ABOUT THE ARTISTS: This couple researches historical jewelry styles, then incorporates Navajo themes into their designs. They often create Yei figures in their jewelry with thousands of microscopic stones so that the figures look like sandpaintings.

DORIAL CLARK

Tuscarora/Cayuga (1940 –)
Beadworker, wireworker, headdress worker

EDUCATION: Murial Hewitt, Clark's cousin, taught her.

ABOUT THE ARTIST: In addition to making her own patterns, Clark uses a variety of beading techniques to fill her orders and uses as many as 200 colors. She has been especially influenced by the beadwork made in Manitoulin Island.

IRENE CLARK

Navajo (1934 –) Crystal, New Mexico
Weaver

EDUCATION: Clark began to weave after her children were grown, and she was in her late forties. She worked with her mother, Glenabah Hardy, to design a distinctive version of the Crystal style.

AWARDS: Best of Textiles and Best of Show at the 1990 Museum of Northern Arizona Navajo show; other awards.

ABOUT THE ARTIST: Clark's rugs are owned by private collectors as well as museums such as the Denver Art Museum, Denver, Colorado. She is often commissioned by collectors to create a specific kind of rug. One such rug, titled "Rainbow," was made in 1990 for Gloria F. Ross Tapestries and features ten stripes of different colors. Clark states that "(E)very strand of naturally dyed yarn interwoven is my family's clanship and the belonging to one another. All the colors of the rug symbolize the array of colors depicted in the rainbow." Clark has guided her daughter, Teresa, daughters-in-law, Evelyna and Julie, and sister-in-law, Marjorie Hardy, in weaving techniques.

KAREN CLARK

Seneca (1948 –) Steamburg, New York
Beadworker, also creates rattles

EDUCATION: Though mostly self-taught, Clark learned the daisy chain stitch from her mother, Martha Bucktooth, and learned other skills by watching others.

ABOUT THE ARTIST: An experienced beadworker, Clark uses porcupine quills with her beadwork medallions, necklaces, and earrings. She almost never uses the same pattern and enjoys working with whatever pattern her customer suggests or designs. She has decorated costumes with beadwork and has also beaded leather purses. In addition, she makes turtle rattles and passes on what she has learned to others.

LESLIE CLAUS

Mohawk (1909 -) Tyendinaga Reserve, Ontario,
Canada
Painter, sculptor, photographer

EDUCATION: During his career, Claus has worked with many well-known artists in Canada.

AWARDS: Claus has participated in juried shows since 1968.

ABOUT THE ARTIST: An active schoolteacher, Leslie always worked to perfect his skills. Much of his early work is pencil, pen and ink, or oil, but he began working in watercolors during the late 1970s and has also taken pottery and leatherworking classes. Claus has been active in Native American art and cultural programs and was a member of the Board of Governors of the Woodland Indian Cultural Education Centre. He retired from teaching in 1974.

DARELYN CLAUSE
Mohawk/Algonquin (1957 –   ) Sanborn, New York
Beadworker

EDUCATION: Took beading classes from Doris Hudson.

ABOUT THE ARTIST: Since the early 1970s, Clause has been exhibiting her work at the New York State Fair, the Erie County Fair and Exhibition, and other fairs. Her beadwork includes barrettes, medallions, hair ties, jewelry, lighter covers, and key chains. She also decorates pipe stems with beadwork.

FARRELL COCKRUM
Blackfoot (N/A) Northern Montana
Painter, sculptor, miscellaneous media

EDUCATION: Institute of American Indian Arts, Santa Fe, New Mexico.

REPRESENTATION: SunWest Silver, Albuquerque, New Mexico.

ABOUT THE ARTIST: Cockrum attempts to introduce the world to his people via his contemporary art. He works in several different media and is inspired by his dreams and beliefs in the Creator.

Cockrum's acrylic-on-canvas painting of Indian facing left, 36 x 36 inches. Slide courtesy of the artist and SunWest Silver, Albuquerque, New Mexico.

Cockrum's acrylic-on-canvas painting of Indian Day Parade/Three Indians on Horseback, 54 x 54 inches. Slide courtesy of the artist and SunWest Silver, Albuquerque, New Mexico.

KARITA COFFEY
Comanche (1947 –   ) Oklahoma
Potter, ceramist

EDUCATION: Institute of American Indian Arts, Santa Fe (1965); Bachelor of Fine Art, University of Oklahoma (1971); teacher's certification in art and Master in Education, University of Oklahoma.

AWARDS: Coffey's many awards include being included in *Who's Who in American Indian Art* and the *Dictionary of International Biographies*, and she was appointed to the Native American Council of Regents of the Institute of American Indian Art.

ABOUT THE ARTISTS: Coffey makes ceramic forms that interpret the Plains Indian culture, from the traditional forms to the contemporary. She creates different types of pots, such as sculpted tall moccasins made of clay. She has shown her work in national competitions all over the United States. Some of her works were also selected for a traveling exhibit called "Arts of Indian America" which showed in Germany, Scotland, England, and Turkey.

ANN COHO
Ramah Navajo (N/A) Arizona
Beadworker

ABOUT THE ARTIST: Coho creates beaded ornaments.

GREY COHOE
Navajo (1944 –   ) New Mexico
Artist—oil and acrylic

ABOUT THE ARTIST: Cohoe's work often addresses the gap between the white world and the Indian with biting sarcasm and portents of evil.

CAROLYN CONCHO
Acoma (N/A) Acoma Pueblo, New Mexico
Potter

ABOUT THE ARTIST: Concho creates commercial Acoma ware that is slip-cast ceramic. She has made figurines (i.e., statues of the Virgin Mary) as well as traditional pottery.

SHEILA CONCHO
Acoma (N/A) Acoma Pueblo, New Mexico
Potter

ABOUT THE ARTIST: Sheila has created commercial Acoma pottery that uses post-fired pigments. One seed jar she made in 1991 had shades of purple and green, as well as the traditional white and black.

DON CONKLIN
Seneca (1957 –   ) Irving, New York
Painter—acrylics, pen and ink; Block printmaker

EDUCATION: Art major, State University at New York at Fredonia.

AWARDS: Conklin has garnered several honors for his work.

ABOUT THE ARTIST: Conklin works mostly with acrylics and pen and ink. He enjoys drawing landscapes and wildlife. He has also done some sculpture and silversmithing.

RUTH CONKLIN
Seneca (1936 –   ) Irving, New York
Beadworker, dollmaker

EDUCATION: Learned some beadwork skills from Virginia Snow; taught herself additional beadwork designs and how to make cornhusk dolls.

ABOUT THE ARTIST: Conklin has been creating beadwork since the early 1970s, preferring the older beaded designs done on velvet. She uses raised beading in her medallions. She also makes cornhusk dolls and is passing on her skills to her son.

VICTOR COOCHWYTEWA
Hopi (N/A)
Jeweler, silversmith

AWARDS: Designated one of Arizona's Indian Living Treasures in 1994.

ABOUT THE ARTIST: Coochwytewa uses gold, diamonds, and Hopi symbolism, an unusual combination.

CARL COOK

Mohawk (1942 –   ) Hogansburg, New York
Beadworker

EDUCATION: Self-taught; also learned some basic techniques in school.

ABOUT THE ARTIST: Cook designs his own patterns to create beadwork on belts, wristbands, and watchbands. His designs often portray the Mohawk longhouse or clan animals. Cook also takes special orders.

FLORENCE COOK

(a.k.a. Ana)
Mohawk (1930 –   ) Hogansburg, New York
Basketmaker, quilter

EDUCATION: Her mother taught her basketmaking; however, she learned how to quilt in grammar school.

AWARDS: She has won first prizes for her quilts at the New York State Fair.

REPRESENTATION: Mohawk Craft Fund; Akwesasne Notes; Christina Jock.

ABOUT THE ARTIST: One of the unusual shapes Cook creates is a square handkerchief basket. However, she makes a wide variety of shapes and sizes and uses black-ash splints, sweet grass, and dyes. She often uses green, brown, orange, and red dyes, but will make a basket out of very white splints if she has enough. Her quilts have been recognized nationally and have even been exhibited at the New York Metropolitan Museum of Art Gift Shop. They are brightly colored appliqué or in star, fan, or crazy quilt designs.

JULIUS COOK

(a.k.a. Jo Jo)
Mohawk (1955 –   ) Hogansburg, New York
Basketmaker

EDUCATION: Learned by watching his mother, Florence Cook, and his grandmother, Josephine Lazore; Norwich University, Vermont (Business Administration).

REPRESENTATION: Mohawk Craft Fund.

ABOUT THE ARTIST: Julius prepares the splints, pounds the logs, and carves the handles for the baskets he creates. He does not use a mold and makes all types of baskets in various sizes.

TONI COOKE

(a.k.a. Gus Ah Doong Gwas)
Oneida (1961 –   ) Onondaga Nation, Nedrow, New York
Beadworker, quillworker, clothing designer, painter; potter, weaver

EDUCATION: Took pottery classes at Lafayette Central School (1975–1979); art major at Cazenovia College, New York.

AWARDS: Many awards, including the Gold Key Award and Mony Scholastics Award.

ABOUT THE ARTIST: A multitalented artist, Cooke has been selling her beadwork since age fourteen. She experiments with different forms and traditions, as well as arts. She incorporates what she learns into the clothing, beadwork, quillwork, weaving, pottery, and painting she creates.

DARREN COOPER

(N/A)

AWARDS: Best of Division/Miniatures at the 1994 Five Civilized Tribes Competitive Show in Muskogee, Oklahoma.

RITA JOE CORDALIS

Navajo (1954 –   ) New Mexico
Jeweler

EDUCATION: Grew up in a family of silversmiths.

REPRESENTATION: Dewey Galleries, Ltd., Santa Fe, New Mexico; October Art Ltd., New York.

ABOUT THE ARTIST: Cordalis has chosen to create jewelry that she hopes will be "multicultural," more contemporary than traditional, and made out of wood, ivory, malachite, and other nontraditional materials.

BUFFY CORDERO

*Cochiti (1969 –   ) Cochiti Pueblo, New Mexico
Potter—Storyteller figures*

EDUCATION: Learned the trade from her grandmother, Helen Cordero, as well as from a teacher at school.

REPRESENTATION: Adobe Gallery, Albuquerque, New Mexico.

ABOUT THE ARTIST: Cordero began making Storytellers around 1980 and has learned much about the art from the members of her family, most of whom are potters.

DAMACIA CORDERO

*Cochiti (1905 –   ) Cochiti Pueblo, New Mexico
Potter—Storyteller figures*

EDUCATION: Learned from her mother, Lucinda Suina.

REPRESENTATION: Adobe Gallery, Albuquerque, New Mexico.

ABOUT THE ARTIST: Cordero has kept pottery making in her family, passing on what she learned from her mother to her daughters, Josephine Arquero, Martha Arquero, Gloria Arquero, and Marie Lewake. Cordero began creating pottery in the 1920s. Her early Storytellers, made in the mid to late 1950s and into the 1960s, are held by the Museum of New Mexico. These early pieces depict "singing" Storytellers—figures of mothers singing to their children. One of the first shows to exhibit Cordero's work was held in 1973 by the Museum of International Folk Art in Santa Fe and was called "What is Folk Art?"

GEORGE CORDERO

*Cochiti (1944 –   ) Cochiti Pueblo, New Mexico
Potter—Storyteller figures*

EDUCATION: Learned the trade from his mother, master Storyteller creator Helen Cordero.

REPRESENTATION: Adobe Gallery, Albuquerque, New Mexico.

ABOUT THE ARTIST: Cordero began making Storytellers in 1982 and has shared what he has learned with his daughter, Buffy; his nephews, Tim Cordero and Kevin Peshlakai; and his sister, Antonita Suina.

HELEN CORDERO

*Cochiti (1915 –   ) Cochiti Pueblo, New Mexico
Potter—Storyteller figures*

EDUCATION: Learned how to make pottery from her cousin-in-law, Juanita Arquero.

AWARDS: Many awards throughout the years, including recognition in *National Geographic*. Cordero's first Storytellers won first, second, and third prizes at the 1964 New Mexico State Fair, and first prize at the 1965 SWAIA's Santa Fe Indian Market.

REPRESENTATION: Adobe Gallery, Albuquerque, New Mexico.

ABOUT THE ARTIST: Cordero is the premier Storyteller creator in the Southwest and has passed on her skill and technique to family members such as her son, George; her daughter, Tony (Antonita Suina); grandchildren, Tim Cordero, Buffy Cordero; and great-nephew, Kevin Peshalakai. She created her first Storytellers as a tribute to her grandfather, Santiago Quintana. Cordero's work has been internationally exhibited.

TIM CORDERO

*Cochiti (1963 –   ) Cochiti Pueblo, New Mexico
Potter—Storyteller figures*

EDUCATION: Taught the traditional storytelling pottery art by his grandmother, Helen Cordero.

REPRESENTATION: Adobe Gallery, Albuquerque, New Mexico.

ABOUT THE ARTIST: Cordero comes from a long line of famous potters. He made his first Storyteller in 1980 while living in Cochiti with his grandmother. Like his grandmother's figures, most of Cordero's adult Storytellers' eyes are closed and the mouths are open. Because as a Cochiti he is traditionally not allowed to make clown and Kachina figures, Cordero incorporates them into his Storyteller figures.

BLUE CORN

San Ildefonso (N/A) New Mexico
Potter

EDUCATION: Began making pottery at age three at her grandmother's knee.

ABOUT THE ARTIST: Blue Corn originally made only black pottery, but then decided to do polychrome. She makes her pots in the traditional way. Like other potters, Blue Corn believes her mood influences the pot, and vice versa. Her pots are white-white, a hard-to-polish slip that is the base for her polychrome.

RAY P. CORNELIUS

Oneida (1955 –   ) Southwold, Ontario, Canada
Artist—drawings, soapstone carvings

EDUCATION: Largely self-taught, though he has taken classes at Laurier Secondary School in London.

AWARDS: Cornelius's awards include several first prizes for drawings at the Oneida Fall Fair.

ABOUT THE ARTIST: Cornelius's media of choice is pencil or pen and ink. Though most of his subjects are Native American, he sometimes draws cartoons or comic book characters. He also works in soapstone, carving figures and faces.

LARRY D. B. (BUTCH) COTTRELL

Oneida (1959 –   ) Oneida, Wisconsin
Painter

EDUCATION: Attended art classes in school.

ABOUT THE ARTIST: Cottrell has been sketching and illustrating for many years. He does cartoons, portraits, scenery, and some Native American subjects.

DOUG CRANMER

Haida (N/A) Canada
Carver

EDUCATION: Worked with Bill Reid.

ABOUT THE ARTIST: One of the totem poles Cranmer worked on was resurrected by Bill Reid in Anthony Island. Cranmer assisted Reid in recarving and painting the pole, which was finished in 1959. He also worked with Reid on several other totem poles which were part of the collection held by the University of Columbia Museum of Anthropology. Cranmer was also responsible for carving a memorial pole for his father, Dan Cranmer.

CIPPY CRAZY HORSE

(a.k.a. Cipriano Quintana)
Cochiti (1946 –   ) New Mexico
Jeweler, silversmith

EDUCATION: Observed his father, Joe H. Quintana, a silversmith who worked in Santa Fe's production shops in the 1930s. Also taught himself silversmithing techniques and how to make all of his own tools.

AWARDS: Crazy Horse has won top honors for all of his work—jewelry, canteens, and buckles—at the Santa Fe Indian Market, and has acted as curator for an exhibit at the Museum of Indian Art and Culture in Santa Fe.

REPRESENTATION: The Indian Craft Shop, Washington, D.C.; Dewey Galleries, Ltd., Santa Fe,

New Mexico; Packard's Indian Trading Co., Inc., Santa Fe, New Mexico; Indian Post, Allentown, Pennsylvania; Texas Art Gallery, Dallas, Texas.

ABOUT THE ARTIST: Crazy Horse did not start making jewelry until 1974 when he was left partially disabled after an accident at work. He uses early Navajo and Pueblo patterns for his work and likes the First-Phase jewelry style. His designs are drawn from items he sees every day.

CECILIA CREE

Mohawk (1920 –)
Basketmaker, quilter

EDUCATION: Anna and Richard Sunday, Cree's parents, taught her.

REPRESENTATION: Mohawk Craft Fund.

ABOUT THE ARTIST: Cree makes lighter baskets, instead of the large ones with wood handles. She prefers to work with naturally colored and brown-dyed splints. Cree occasionally demonstrates her craft and teaches children at a local grammar school.

GORDON CROSS

Haida (N/A) Skidegate, British Columbia, Canada
Jeweler, carver

ABOUT THE ARTIST: After an accident in 1965, Cross gave up his fishing business and began carving silver. He carves the Haida animal symbols into his pennants, bracelets, pins, and rings.

NELSON CROSS

Haida (N/A) Skidegate, British Columbia, Canada
Jeweler, carver

ABOUT THE ARTIST: Cross creates silver jewelry. He believes the piece must speak to him, that he must feel the urge to create, and that what he does is not just a job.

BERNICE CROUSE

Seneca (1902 –) Salamanca, New York
Beadworker

EDUCATION: Learned how to do beadwork through summer crafts classes.

ABOUT THE ARTIST: Crouse is noted for her daisy chain necklaces which are delicate combinations of reds, blues, and white.

BILL CROUSE

(a.k.a. Gahatageyat)

Seneca (1963 –) Salamanca, New York
Painter, carver—acrylics, oils, watercolors, pencil, pen
and ink, charcoal, pastels, wood

EDUCATION: Mostly self-taught, although he has taken some classes in woodcarving.

ABOUT THE ARTIST: Crouse sketches portraits, Iroquois games and dances, and also does some woodcarving. In addition to his art, Crouse writes poetry and has been dancing and singing all of his life. He is an avid believer in Longhouse customs.

WOODROW WILSON CRUMBO

(a.k.a. Woody Crumbo)

Creek/Potawatomi (1912 – 1989) Lexington,
Oklahoma
Artist—oil, watercolor, drawing, murals

EDUCATION: Studied under Susie Peters, muralist Olaf Nordmark, watercolorist Clayton Henri Staples, and artist O.B. Jacobson; attended Chilocoo Indian School, American Indian Institute in Wichita, Wichita University (1933–1936); University of Oklahoma; and Wichita State University; director of Art for Bacone College in Muskogee, Oklahoma.

AWARDS: Many honors, including the Julius Rosenwald Fellowship; inducted into the Oklahoma Hall of Fame in 1978.

REPRESENTATION: Philbrook Museum, Tulsa, Oklahoma; Eagles Roost Gallery, Colorado Springs, Colorado.

ABOUT THE ARTIST: Crumbo's first painting, "Deer and Birds," was given to the Philbrook Art Center in 1939. In 1944, Crumbo convinced the Philbrook to sponsor the first national Indian art show. Crumbo, the artist-in-residence at the Gilcrease Museum, assembled an American Indian and Western art collection in 1945 and also served as the assistant director of the El Paso Museum of Art (1962–1968). Exhibitions of his work have been held nationally and internationally. Collections are held by the Philbrook Art Center, the Gilcrease Institute, the Southeast Museum of the North American Indian, and many others. Crumbo is considered a major influence on Native American painting, especially in the Southwest.

SADIE CURTIS and ALICE BELONE
Navajo (1930 –   ) Kinlichee, Arizona
Weavers

EDUCATION: Curtis learned how to weave from her mother, Elsie Jim Wilson, and often collaborates with her aunt, Alice Belone.

AWARDS: Her American flag rug appeared on an *Arizona Highways* magazine cover in July 1976.

ABOUT THE ARTISTS: Considered a masterful weaver, Curtis once worked for the Hubbell Trading Post but is now retired. She likes to create chief blankets and revivals of early designs. She prefers to make small rugs because the large ones take up so much time. Her sisters, Elsie Wilson and Mae Jim, her daughter, two daughters-in-law, and her granddaughter are all weavers. Curtis's son, Earl, is a silversmith and leatherworker. When Curtis and Belone work, together they have used dye artists from one area and weavers from another.

DAWN'A D
Navajo (N/A)
Potter

AWARDS: First Prize in the Fine Arts Contemporary Ceramics category (for the "Anasazi Pot"), Museum of Northern Arizona Annual Navajo Artists Exhibition (1987).

ABOUT THE ARTIST: Dawn'a often creates pottery with a new variation on a traditional theme. One of her pottery pieces had the appearance of leather ("The Anasazi Pot").

POPOVI DA
(a.k.a. Red Fox)
San Ildefonso (1923 – 1971) San Ildefonso Pueblo, New Mexico
Potter, silversmith

EDUCATION: Taught by his mother and father, Maria and Julian Martinez, as well as by instructors at the Santa Fe Indian School.

ABOUT THE ARTIST: The eldest son of the famous Maria and Julian, Martinez decorated his mother's pottery from 1953–1971. In 1948, he opened his own studio in San Ildefonso. He also accumulated a collection of his mother's work which was on display at the Popovi Da Studio of Indian Art at San Ildefonso. In addition to being a potter, Martinez also made silver jewelry and was regarded by the Santa Fe art patrons as a talented, innovative artist.

TONY DA
San Ildefonso (1940 –   ) San Ildefonso, New Mexico
Potter, artist

EDUCATION: Learned his traditional style from his grandmother, Maria Martinez, as well as from other members of his well-known family.

ABOUT THE ARTIST: Da was one of the foremost male traditional potters before his automobile accident. He no longer pots, though he does paint. Considered by many to be a great innovator, Da's work is still copied by today's up-and-coming potters. Da is also an artist who has had no formal training. He uses traditional abstract designs in his work and usually chooses earth and water tones, the same colors used in Pueblo pottery.

SUSIE SHIRLEY DALE

Navajo (1931 –   ) Kinlichee, Arizona
Weaver

EDUCATION: Dale learned basic and herringbone twill weaves by watching her mother, then taught herself two-faced rugs after watching her aunt, Edith James.

REPRESENTATION: Hubbell Trading Post, Ganado, Arizona; J. B. Tanner's, Ya-Ta-Hey, Arizona.

ABOUT THE ARTIST: Dale's rugs are pastoral scenes of Navajo life the way it used to be. She uses geometric designs in her rugs and likes to create the medium-sized pictorials because they usually bring in a little more money. She makes *yei* pictorials as well. Three of Dale's four sisters weave, but only a few members of the younger generation have learned the art.

TONY DALLAS

Hopi (1956 –   ) Arizona
Potter—Storyteller figures

EDUCATION: Learned his trade from mother-in-law, Lucy Suina, who introduced him to pottery in 1982.

REPRESENTATION: Adobe Gallery, Albuquerque, New Mexico.

ABOUT THE ARTIST: After being taught by his mother-in-law, Dallas started creating mudhead Storytellers, which usually hold a bowl and have little mudheads crawling all over the larger Storyteller. Because it is tradition that only Cochitis are allowed to make and sell Storytellers, Dallas is unique to the craft.

FELICITY DAN

Mount Currie (N/A) Mount Currie, British
Columbia, Canada
Basketmaker

ABOUT THE ARTIST: This basketweaver collects all of her own materials and weaves all types of baskets from them.

RICHARD GLAZER DANAY

(a.k.a. Ric Danay)
Mohawk (1942 –   ) Coney Island, New York
Artist—various media

EDUCATION: Bachelor of Art, California State University, Northridge; Master of Fine Art, University of California, Davis.

ABOUT THE ARTIST: Danay's three-dimensional works are sexy, dry, ironic, humorous, sarcastic, and biting. One can safely say each of the works would have a different interpretation depending upon who was doing the interpreting. Danay often creates art in response to a historical event or theme.

KATHLEEN D'ARCY

Seneca (1935 –   )
Beadworker, quillworker

EDUCATION: Learned her skills while attending Thomas Indian School, Cattaraugus.

AWARDS: Several honors, including first prize for a barrette at the Indian Fall Festival.

ABOUT THE ARTIST: D'Arcy experiments with new designs and forms in her beadwork, using both traditional and modern styles. She creates jewelry and barrettes with her beadwork and has made porcupine-quill chokers and earrings. Turquoise, black, and white are in her favorite color combinations. She sells from her home and does not attend fairs.

FLORENCE DAVID

Mohawk (1934 –   ) Hogansburg, New York
Basketmaker, splintworker, quilter, leatherworker,
beadworker

EDUCATION: Eva Point, David's mother, taught her.

REPRESENTATION: Mohawk Craft Fund.

ABOUT THE ARTIST: David produces a wide variety of basketry items, usually featuring plain splints, but sometimes using colors in her work. She also is a skilled sewer, knitter, crocheter, beadworker,

41

and leatherworker, and is passing her skills down to her children.

JOE DAVID

> *Haida (N/A) Canada*
> *Carver, artist*

ABOUT THE ARTIST: David recalls certain Northwest Coast legends in his paintings. He has done some totem-pole carving, notably assisting Art Thompson in carving a pole for the University of British Columbia's Museum of Anthropology.

NEIL DAVID, SR.

> *Hopi (1944 –) First Mesa, Arizona*
> *Painter, carver—various media*

EDUCATION: David is a third-generation artist.

ABOUT THE ARTIST: David belongs to the Artist Hopid, a group of Hopi artists, and may have been the first to convert the painted Kachina into a three-dimensional being. He is prolific and versatile and brings a feeling of reality to his Kachina figures which makes them truly appear alive. His paintings are geometric and often use both traditional and modern designs.

CLAUDE DAVIDSON

> *Haida (N/A) Canada*
> *Carver*

ABOUT THE ARTIST: Davidson sells few of his pieces because he hates to sell them after putting his time and soul into them. The piece of paper means less to him than what he has created.

FLORENCE DAVIDSON

> *Haida (N/A) Masset, British Columbia, Canada*
> *Basketmaker*

ABOUT THE ARTIST: Davidson personally collects the cedar bark and spruce roots for her baskets, then hangs the materials to dry on clothesline strung in

42

her backyard. She works her baskets and hats the way the Raven taught her people in the beginning.

REG DAVIDSON

> *Haida (N/A) Masset, British Columbia, Canada*
> *Carver*

EDUCATION: Learned the finer carving skills from Robert Davidson, his role model.

ABOUT THE ARTIST: Davidson works mostly with wood.

ROBERT DAVIDSON

(a.k.a. Guud San Glans, Jaa-daa Guulx)
> *Haida (1946 –) Hydaburg, Alaska*
> *Carver, artist, printmaker*

EDUCATION: Davidson's father urged him to begin carving at a young age in order to continue a family tradition. Bringing his work one step further, Davidson visited museums to learn about the carved items his ancestors had made and was guided by Bill Reid and Bill Holm.

AWARDS: In 1993, Davidson became the second Northwest Coast artist to have a one-person exhibit at a major gallery.

ABOUT THE ARTIST: Called a great innovator by his contemporaries, Davidson carves large totem poles, masks, bowls and other items. He paints the items and often uses alder wood with an abalone inlay. He also carves on silver to make jewelry, spoons, boxes, and other items. Davidson continues to learn about his culture and often lectures on the subject; he passes on his education to the new generation of Haida carvers.

FRED DAVIS

> *Haida (N/A) Masset, British Columbia, Canada*
> *Carver*

ABOUT THE ARTIST: Davis creates wooden and argilite carvings that are often mythical.

DAVID DAWANGYUMPTEWA
Hopi (N/A)
Painter

ABOUT THE ARTIST: Dawangyumptewa paints in the abstract style and uses a lot of symbolism in his work. He frequently uses water as a staple in his painting as a reflection of his membership in the Water Clan.

FRANK DAY
Maidu (1902 – 1976) Berry Creek, California
Artist—oil on canvas

EDUCATION: Self-taught.

ABOUT THE ARTIST: Day's father taught him the old ways of his people. Day felt obligated to pass on his knowledge in his art to the younger generation. He was part of a revitalization movement among California, Native American artists in the 1960s.

VIRGINIA DEAL
Navajo (1929 –   ) Toadlena, New Mexico
Weaver

EDUCATION: Learned how to weave by helping her mother, as did her sisters, Elizabeth Mute and Marie Lapahie.

ABOUT THE ARTIST: Deal sold her first rug at age thirteen and is now passing her skills on to her daughter, Caralena.

AGNES DECAIRE
Mohawk (1951 –   ) Caughnawaga, Quebec, Canada
Quillworker, beadworker

EDUCATION: Learned beadwork from Nora Deering.

ABOUT THE ARTIST: A founding member of the Kanawake Handicraft Workshop, Decaire makes a wide variety of items, including porcupine-quill chokers and earrings; beaded chokers, earrings, medallions, and barrettes; and bone chokers. She works closely with her mother, Isabell Myiow, when selling her work.

JON DeCELLES
Gros Ventre / Assiniboin Sioux (1958 –   )
Tillamook, Oregon
Sculptor—stone

EDUCATION: Associate in Fine Art, Three Dimensional Design, Institute of American Indian Art, Santa Fe (1984); Portland State University, Portland, Oregon (1977).

AWARDS: DeCelles's many awards include Best of Show at the 1992 New Mexico State Fair and first prize for sculpture at the 1984 Big Lake Trading Post and Museum Indian Market, Page, Arizona.

REPRESENTATION: SunWest Silver, Albuquerque, New Mexico.

ABOUT THE ARTIST: DeCelles became interested in art as a child, but it was not until he studied at the Institute of American Indian Art that he found his real love in stone sculpture. He has studied both classical and modern sculpture, believing that "the fusion of these two styles allows me optimal expression." DeCelles exhibits in solo and group shows throughout the Southwest. His work is held in private collections and by the Institute of American Indian Art.

ANDY DEER
Onondaga (1951 –   ) Nedrow, New York
Painter

EDUCATION: Self-taught.

ABOUT THE ARTIST: Deer comes from an artistic family (his mother, Mary Beckman, and his brother, John). He experiments with color and paints in an abstract style.

JOHN DEER
Onondaga (1950 –   ) Nedrow, New York
Sketcher, carver, leatherworker, jeweler

EDUCATION: Self-taught.

ABOUT THE ARTIST: Deer sketches in a realistic fashion, drawing animals, landscapes, people, and

43

whatever else interests him. He has also done some beadwork, carves animals out of wood, and is trying to pass on what he knows to others.

KRISTEN DEER

Mohawk (1963 –   ) Caughnawaga, Quebec, Canada
Beadworker

EDUCATION: Learned her beadworking skills at the Caughnawaga Boys & Girls Club.

ABOUT THE ARTIST: Deer does most of her work on a loom, though she can also do freehand items. She likes blue and white beads and though some of her designs are geometric, she has been known to make moose or eagle patterns. She also likes to make ribbon shirts.

NORA DEERING

Mohawk (1911 – 1976)
Beadworker, dollmaker, basketmaker, knitter,
clothing maker

EDUCATION: Self-taught.

ABOUT THE ARTIST: This well-respected craftswoman attended quite a few fairs, taught her craft to anyone who wanted to learn, worked to keep the Mohawk language alive, and accepted any creative challenge given her. She experimented with new techniques and often gave some materials to others to make their works. Her most important contribution to Iroquois culture was a dictionary of the Mohawk language and a grammar book which she co-authored.

CHARLOTTE DELORMIER

(a.k.a. Warisarot Kenetahawi)
Mohawk (1910 –   ) Cornwall Island, Ontario,
Canada
Basketmaker, splintworker, quilter

EDUCATION: Self-taught.

ABOUT THE ARTIST: Delormier makes sewing, strawberry, button, bingo chip, and thimble baskets

using black-ash splints, sweet grass, and rope. She collects her sweet grass in the summer, then works on making baskets throughout the winter. Her mother, Josephine Thompson, and her sisters, Minnie Delormier and Mary Leaf, are also basketmakers. Charlotte has taught others and has held demonstrations of basketmaking.

MINNIE DELORMIER

Mohawk (1921 –   ) Cornwall Island, Ontario,
Canada
Basketmaker, splintworker

EDUCATION: Josephine Thompson, Delormier's mother, taught her.

ABOUT THE ARTIST: Delormier has been making baskets since her adolescent years and still uses her mother's distinctively styled molds. Minnie uses many colors in her work and creates many different types of baskets. She now passes her skills on to her own daughters.

DIANE DEMARCO

Tuscarora (1937 –   )
Beadworker, dollmaker, painter, carver

EDUCATION: Learned from her grandmother, Harriet Pembleton.

ABOUT THE ARTIST: Since the early 1970s, Demarco has made beaded items in both the raised and flat style and has exhibited her work at the Tuscarora Indian Culture Night and Earl Bridges Art Park. Her work includes beaded light covers, barrettes, medallions, jewelry, velvet cushions; cornhusk dolls, and other items. She also paints and does stonecarving.

ELIZABETH (BETTY) DENNISON

Oneida (N/A) Oneida, Wisconsin
Beadworker, quillworker, leatherworker, quilter

EDUCATION: Diane Funmaker taught Dennison how to bead. She learned the other crafts on her own or from friends.

ABOUT THE ARTIST: Dennison creates beaded head-bands, chokers, wristbands and watchbands, jewelry, hair ties, and barrettes. In addition, she makes porcupine-quill-decorated chokers and earrings, moccasins, and quilts.

LUELLA DERRICK

Onondaga (1925 –   ) Nedrow, New York
Beadworker–textiles

EDUCATION: Learned some of her skills from her grandmother, Minni Shanadore.

AWARDS: Derrick has won many sewing awards at the New York State Fair.

ABOUT THE ARTIST: An active creator, Derrick attends fairs and exhibits with her items. She makes beaded jewelry, headbands, keychains, belts, and wristbands, as well as ribbon shirts and other types of clothing.

RAYMOND LEE DESCHENE

Dineh (1971 –   ) Winslow, Arizona
Pottery

EDUCATION: Studied commercial arts.

REPRESENTATION: Native Reflections, Salt Lake City, Utah.

Deschene painting on pottery, courtesy of the artist and Native Reflections, Salt Lake City, Utah.

ABOUT THE ARTIST: Deschene uses an etching-and-airbrush technique to decorate his pottery with wildlife. Married with two children, this artist is also a singer/drummer with "Indian Creek," a powwow drum group with a recording on the market.

Deschene's painted eagle on pottery plate, courtesy of the artist and Native Reflections, Salt Lake City, Utah.

DESIDER

San Ildefonso (N/A) New Mexico
Potter

EDUCATION: Learned how to pot with other members of her family, including Maria Martinez, her sister.

ABOUT THE ARTIST: As did her famous sister, Desider potted and created valuable works which are in prized collections today.

PATRICK DesJARLAIT

(a.k.a. Magawbo, "Boy of the Woods")
Chippewa (1921 – 1973) Red Lakes Reservation,
Minnesota
Artist–watercolor

EDUCATION: Pipestone Indian Training School, Pipestone, Minnesota; Phoenix Junior College, Arizona.

ABOUT THE ARTIST: Though discouraged from speaking in his native language or learning anything about the history, traditions, or culture of his people, DesJarlait rebelled and began to learn about his heritage anyway—he used all he learned about the culture and traditions of the Chippewa people in his stylized paintings. His work was often reflective of Mexican muralists' work and had touches of cubism.

ALICE DIABO

Mohawk (1906 —   ) Caughnawaga, Quebec, Canada
Beadworker, leatherworker, dollmaker, headdress worker

EDUCATION: Learned from her mother.

ABOUT THE ARTIST: Diabo created many of her items with the traditional raised-beadwork-on-velvet-style. Though she often substituted leather for the traditional turn-of-the-century velvet, she preserved the old designs. Like others, Diabo has taught the young so that the Iroquois traditions will not be lost.

CHARLOTTE DIABO

(a.k.a. Warisaro Wasontanoron)
Mohawk (1921 —   ) Caughnawaga, Quebec, Canada
Basketmaker

EDUCATION: Learned from her mother.

REPRESENTATION: Akwesasne Notes.

ABOUT THE ARTIST: Diabo's whole family were basketmakers from the St. Regis Reservation. She learned a lot from them and has returned the favor by passing on her skill to her granddaughter. Diabo makes colorful baskets using all the colors of the rainbow and often attaches flowers and leaves made from sweet grass and splints.

MARJORIE DIABO

Mohawk (1937 —   ) Caughnawaga, Quebec, Canada
Beadworker, dollmaker, quillworker

EDUCATION: Diabo's mother taught her some skills and she also took beadwork classes from Nora Deering.

ABOUT THE ARTIST: Diabo makes beaded chokers, key chains, barrettes, and watchbands both freehand and on the loom. She also works with leather, quilts, crochets, knits, and hooks rugs. A founding member of the Kanawake Handicrafts Workshop, Diabo also wants children to learn the art of beadwork.

VICTOR K. DIABO

Mohawk (1956 —   ) Caughnawaga, Quebec, Canada
Beaded leatherworker, painter, carver, sculptor, silversmith

EDUCATION: Mostly self-taught, Diabo learned some of his skills from his grandmother, Alice Diabo, and learned about soapstone sculpture from Olga Korper.

ABOUT THE ARTIST: Diabo has traveled to many places to demonstrate his crafts and to teach others. Some of his work is held in private collections in Switzerland, Australia, Scotland, and Canada. He is noted for his original designs and never uses the same design twice. He gets ideas for his paintings from the people, animal, and land around him and his soapstone carvings are delicately carved.

CECIL DICK

(a.k.a. Dagadahga, "Standing Alone")
Cherokee (1915 —   ) Rose, Oklahoma
Artist—watercolor, tempera

EDUCATION: Educated in government boarding schools; studied painting at Santa Fe Indian School (The Studio) under Dorothy Dunn and at Bacone Junior College under Woody Crumbo.

ABOUT THE ARTIST: Dick is an authority on Cherokee myth and language. He paints highly active, competitive scenes of Cherokee life and legend, frequently including horses in his work. He uses brightly colored paints in his work. The Studio strongly influenced his work and gave it a monumental quality.

46

GRACIE DICK

Navajo (N/A) Two Grey Hills, New Mexico
Sandpainter

ABOUT THE ARTIST: Dick often incorporates Zuni fetishes into her sandpaintings. Her interpretations often resemble pottery.

JIMMY DICK

Kwakiutl (N/A) Kingcome Inlet, Canada
Carver

ABOUT THE ARTIST: Dick carves masks, poles, and other pieces of art from wood. He often colors and paints them.

FREDA DIESING

Haida (N/A) Prince Rupert, Canada
Carver, artist

EDUCATION: Studied at the Gitanmaax School of Northwest Coast Indian Art in 'Ksan.

ABOUT THE ARTIST: Diesing often decorates totem poles carved by others in the Northwest Coast tradition (i.e. Freda and Josiah Tait) . She also carves decorated masks, bowls, and other items. Diesing is one of the few women carvers in the Northwest Coast to carve totem poles.

BILL DIXON

Navajo (1950 –   ) Winslow, Arizona
Rock art and rock painter

EDUCATION: Self-taught.

REPRESENTATION: SunWest Silver, Albuquerque, New Mexico.

ABOUT THE ARTIST: Dixon does work similar to the ancient petroglyphs. He has sold paintings as well as stone art and says he is currently "working on my own style."

Dixon's petroglyph ("rock") art, paint on paper, courtesy of SunWest Silver, Albuquerque, New Mexico.

47

Dixon's acrylic on canvas of pots and petroglyphs, 24 x 48 inches, courtesy of the artist and SunWest Silver, Albuquerque, New Mexico.

PAT DIXON

Haida (N/A) Skidegate, British Columbia, Canada
Carver; jeweler—stone, wood, other materials

ABOUT THE ARTIST: Dixon's carvings imitate the totems common to the Northwest and are done in minute detail.

MAVIS DOERING

Cherokee (N/A)
Basketmaker

ABOUT THE ARTIST: Doering uses wicker in unusual colors, such as pink and purple (natural dyes), and adds feathers for decoration.

TOM "TWO ARROWS" DORSEY

(a.k.a. Ga Hes Ka, "Two Arrows")
Onondaga (1920 –   ) Onondage Reservation, New York
Artist—watercolor; potter; jeweler; weaver

EDUCATION: Self-taught.

ABOUT THE ARTIST: Dorsey is a member of the Falseface Society and Onondaga Wolf Clan. He is known worldwide as an expert on Native American design and legend and often uses Woodlands symbols in his work.

TOMAS DOUGI, JR.

Navajo (N/A)
Sculptor; painter—variety of stones

ABOUT THE ARTIST: Dougi, who works with alabaster and other stones, will not create any sculptures or paintings that would offend his people.

ALTA DOXTADOR

Cayuga (1909 –   ) Caledonia, Ontario, Canada
Painter—oils

EDUCATION: Mostly self-taught.

ABOUT THE ARTIST: Doxtador's paintings were of nature scenes or birds. She was the granddaughter of Jim Beaver, the earliest acknowledged Iroquois painter.

BETTY DOXTATOR

Mohawk (1960 –   ) Oshweken, Ontario, Canada
Beadworker, breastplatemaker, gauntletmaker,
headband and beltmaker, clothing designer

EDUCATION: Self-taught.

ABOUT THE ARTIST: Doxtator started becoming more prolific with beadwork when she began beading her own dress costumes. She makes native clothing for men, women, and children in both the Iroquois and Western styles.

LAURA DOXTATOR

Oneida (1935 –   ) Southwold, Ontario, Canada
Beadworker, leatherworker, knitter, crocheter, quilter

EDUCATION: Doxtator has taken various classes, including beadwork. Her mother taught her how to sew and Doxtator taught herself how to work with leather.

AWARDS: Doxtator has won various prizes for her work at the Oneida Fall Fair.

ABOUT THE ARTIST: Some of the items Doxtator makes include medallions, necklaces, neckties, guitar straps, belts, wallets, key chains, belts, and purses. She creates new patterns and is always experimenting with the decorating she does on leather. In addition to creating her own work, Doxtator teaches craft classes and the Oneida language.

DEBORAH DROUIN

Mohawk (1953 –   )
Beadworker, leatherworker, dollmaker

EDUCATION: Learned how to create beadwork from Nora Deering and Elaine Lahache.

ABOUT THE ARTIST: A founding member of the Kanawake Handicrafts Workshop, Drouin started working with leather at age fifteen when a neighbor gave her a pattern for a vest. She does both raised and flat beadwork and is teaching her children the art.

NANCY DIABO DROUIN

Mohawk (1926 –   ) Caughnawaga, Quebec, Canada
Beadworker, leatherworker, dollmaker

EDUCATION: Self-taught.

48

ABOUT THE ARTIST: Drouin is a founding member of the Kanawake Handicrafts Workshop and did not begin making Indian crafts until that shop opened in 1976. She works with silver, bone, quality beads, and material to make necklaces and chokers. She also makes fringed and decorated leather vests.

JUANITA DuBRAY

Taos (N/A) Taos Pueblo, New Mexico
Potter

EDUCATION: Learned from people in the pueblo.

ABOUT THE ARTIST: DuBray began making micaceous pottery during the 1980s. At first, her designs were plain, but they gradually became adorned with unique corn motifs, the symbol "of the gift of life," DuBray says.

SARAH DUBUC

(a.k.a. Yeh Sah Gehs)
Tuscarora (1916 –   ) Sanborn, New York
Wireworker, beadworker, dollmaker

EDUCATION: Learned from her mother and her sister.

ABOUT THE ARTIST: Dubuc has often sent her work to the New York State Fair. She has made beaded wirework (miniature) chairs, cups and saucers, turtles and baskets, cornhusk dolls, beaded velvet picture frames, cushions, boots and boxes, and beaded medallions and necklaces.

VIRGINIA DURAN

Picuris (N/A) New Mexico
Potter

EDUCATION: Some of the methods Duran uses were shared by Taos potter Virginia Romero, a friendly rival.

ABOUT THE ARTIST: Duran creates pottery that is purely utilitarian (i.e., bean pots) used for cooking. Most New Mexicans agree that beans taste best in Picuris bean pots.

ANTHONY DURAND

Picuris (N/A) New Mexico
Potter

EDUCATION: Learned his pottery skills from his grandmother, Cora.

ABOUT THE ARTIST: Durand is one of Picuris's most active potters. He gets his clay from the Picuris Mountain foothills and creates utilitarian pots that he hopes buyers will use for cooking over campfires or woodstoves.

CORA DURAND

Picuris (N/A) New Mexico
Potter

ABOUT THE ARTIST: Durand has passed on some of her secrets to her grandson, Anthony. She also holds a small class to teach the younger women.

BLACK EAGLE

Shoshone/Yokut (N/A) Elko, Nevada
Traditional artist—leatherworker, beadworker, drawer, printmaker, textile worker, painter, jeweler

Black Eagle: weaver, jeweler, painter, drawer. Photograph by Bob Western, courtesy of the artist.

EDUCATION: Self-taught; derives inspiration from experience, research, and heritage such as memories of his grandmother and other ancestors.

AWARDS: Black Eagle won Best of Division at the Red Earth awards ceremony of 1994 (for drawing/printmaking), Best of Class/Best of Division at the 1994 Heard Museum Indian Fair and Market, and Best of Class for Textiles and Attire at the 1994 Eitejorg Museum Indian Market in Indianapolis, as well as many other awards.

ABOUT THE ARTIST: Black Eagle is unique in that he began his professional art career in 1991 and began winning awards for his creations immediately. He "takes great pride in using genuine materials in his art . . . real bison and deer sinews, rawhides, and

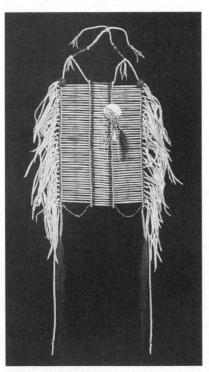

Black Eagle's "Breastplate with Russian Blue Beads." Created true to the spirit of original breastplates, this piece includes authentic decorations and Russian Blue hand-faceted trade beads, hawkbells, horsehair, abalone, red wool trade cloth, and other traditionally used materials. Won "Best of Division, Cultural Items," at the 1993 Heard Museum Indian Fair and Market. Transparency by Bob Western, courtesy of the artist.

ground pigments from Mother Earth . . . Shoshone brain-tanned smoked deerskin and pre-1900 antique beads . . . ."

VIRGINIA EBELACKER
Santa Clara (N/A) New Mexico
Potter

EDUCATION: Taught by her mother, the well-known potter Margaret Tafoya.

ABOUT THE ARTIST: Virginia's work has become collectible and will be more so with the passage of time.

TENNYSON ECKIWAUDAH
(a.k.a. Yutsuwuna, "Able to Stand Up Again")
Comanche (1912 –   ) Anadarko, Oklahoma
Artist—oil on canvas

EDUCATION: Largely self-taught, Eckiwaudah also studied illustration through a correspondence course.

AWARDS: Eckiwaudah's many awards include those won at the Indian Art Exhibition in Anadarko, Oklahoma (1961–62) and the All American Indian Days, Sheridan, Wyoming (1966).

ABOUT THE ARTIST: Eckiwaudah was commissioned to design paintings for several Native American tribal groups and is widely known for his spiritual paintings. He is often inspired by the rites of the Native American Church.

DENNIS AND NANCY EDAAKIE
Dennis—Zuni (1931 –   ) Arizona
Nancy—Zuni (N/A) Arizona
Jewelers, silversmiths—silver, turquoise, jet, coral,
mother-of-pearl, other inlays

AWARDS: First place, Gallup Inter-Tribal Ceremonial (1972); many others.

REPRESENTATION: McGee's Indian Art, Keams Canyon, Arizona; Gallery of the American West,

Sacramento, California; The Indian Craft Shop, Washington, D.C.; Tanner Chaney Gallery, Albuquerque, New Mexico; Joe Milo's Trading Company, Vanderwagen, New Mexico.

ABOUT THE ARTISTS: The Edaakies create silverwork and inlaid belt buckles and jewelry in their studio in Zuni, New Mexico. Dennis does all the figurative work while Nancy inlays the borders. Dennis has experimented with new designs, such as cardinals and blue jays, and in 1985 made his first Koshare figure. Dennis, who led the way in refining the Zuni inlay technique, is Jake Livingston's uncle.

FRANCES EDGAR

Northwest Coast (N/A) Nitinat, British Columbia, Canada
Basketweaver

ABOUT THE ARTIST: Edgar collects her own swamp grass, cedar bark, and three-corner grass for the baskets she creates. She began making baskets at age eight and then used cedar baskets for gathering berries, kindling, and seafood.

KEN EDWARDS

(a.k.a. Ken Rainbow Cougar)
Colville Confederated Tribes (1956 –)
Greenville, South Carolina
Painter—pen and ink, watercolor

EDUCATION: Institute of American Indian Arts, Santa Fe (high school and college); Haskell Indian Jr. College, Lawrence, Kansas.

AWARDS: First place, Painting, Hunter Mountain Eagle Indian Festival, Hunter, New York (1994); Third place, Painting, Aspen Celebration for the American Indian, Aspen, Colorado (1994); Second place, Painting, Milwaukee Indian Summer Festival, Milwaukee, Wisconsin (1994); many others.

REPRESENTATION: Micah Gallery, Calgary, Alberta, Canada; EarthStar, Klamath Falls, Oregon; Black

Edward's lithograph of painting entitled "Nature's Daughters," courtesy of the artist.

Wolf Art Gallery, Lake Worth, Florida; The Mill Gallery, Seneca, South Carolina.

ABOUT THE ARTIST: Edwards not only paints, he travels around the country lecturing about Native American topics, bringing his storytelling talents to schools, fairs, festivals, and markets. His paintings have been sold all over the United States and Canada and one of his creations was used on a T-shirt sold at the Santa Fe Powwow.

SHANNON ELIJAH

(a.k.a. Guna Da How)
Oneida (1952 –) Southwold, Ontario, Canada
Beadworker

EDUCATION: Mostly self-taught, Elijah has also taken some beadwork classes.

AWARDS: Received a grant from the Young Canada Works program (1975); has won many prizes at fairs and festivals; work illustrated in *Redbook* magazine.

ABOUT THE ARTIST: An innovative artist, Elijah creates her own patterns for the freehand and loom beadwork she makes. Her beaded wallets, changepurses, and cuffs are unusual. Though she uses flower or feather designs, Elijah also incorporates traditional Iroquois designs into her clothing. She exhibits widely and does shows in the Northeast.

ELK WOMAN

(a.k.a. Kathy Whitman)
Mandan/Hidatsa, Arikara/Norwegian (1952 –   )
Bismarck, North Dakota
Sculptor; painter; jeweler—alabaster, soapstone, marble

AWARDS: Many honors, including Best of Show at the 1991 Pasadena Western Relic and Native American Show and first place at the 1990 Eight Northern Pueblos Arts and Show.

REPRESENTATION: Silver Sun/Hardin Estate, Santa Fe, New Mexico; Attic-Hogan Gallery, Prescott, Arizona; Crazy Horse, Frandor, Illinois; Fred Harvey Enterprises, Grand Canyon, Arizona; Heard Museum Gift Shop, Phoenix, Arizona; Lovena Ohl Gallery, Scottsdale, Arizona; Moodancer Gallery, Redondo Beach, California; Morefields Gallery, Ruidoso, New Mexico; O B Enterprises, Denver, Colorado; Phoenix Gallery, Coeur d'Alene, Indiana; Santa Fe Connection, San Antonio, Texas; Sun Silver West Gallery, Sedona, Arizona; Tanner Chaney Gallery, Albuquerque, New Mexico; Tribal Expressions Gallery, Arlington Heights, Illinois; Turquoise Tortoise, Tubac, Arizona; Vision Quest, Dallas, Texas; White Pelican, Dana Point, California; Wrights Gallery, Albuquerque, New Mexico, Yahta-hey Gallery, New London, Connecticut.

ABOUT THE ARTIST: Elk Woman creates works that are symbols of nature. Her strong belief in spiritual aspects of the world inspire her work and help her to "find" the subject and spirit of the art within. Whitman received her Indian name, Elk Woman, in a 1977 Sun Dance ceremony held in South Dakota.

GAIL ELLIS

Oneida (1953 –   ) Oneida, Wisconsin
Beadworker, quillworker, weaver

EDUCATION: Institute of American Indian Arts (1969–1972); University of New Mexico (1975–76); University of Wisconsin, Green Bay (1979).

AWARDS: Received Vincent Price Award for her poetry.

ABOUT THE ARTIST: When she returned home from college, Ellis studied under Josephine Wapp, learning traditional weaving techniques and the history of other Native American crafts. Her preference is beadwork, and she constantly studies the old designs. Her work recalls the wampum beltwork done in the early days. She specializes in making leather pouches and teaches not only the crafts of the Oneida but the language as well to children in grammar schools.

MARSHALL ELLIS

Oneida (1959 –   ) Oneida, Wisconsin
Painter, silversmith, potter

EDUCATION: Institute of American Indian Arts (1975–1977); College of Art Design, New Mexico (1978).

AWARDS: Ellis has received many awards, including the Award of Merit for Outstanding Achievement, Exhibition Techniques and Curatorial Functions, Institute of American Indian Arts (1977).

ABOUT THE ARTIST: Ellis paints nature and what it means to him, though he occasionally will paint Indian scenes, too. In addition to painting, Marshall works with and knows how to repair silver. He has also done some pottery work.

JANE ELM

Oneida (1917 –   )
Beadworker

EDUCATION: Taught by her daughters.

ABOUT THE ARTIST: Elm likes to do loom-beaded and freehand items with floral or geometric designs in shiny beads.

MARGARET EMERY

Salish (N/A) Yale, British Columbia, Canada
Weaver

ABOUT THE ARTIST: Emery often finishes two rugs a year. She does everything from start to finish herself.

SAM ENGLISH

Chippewa (N/A)
Painter—watercolor

AWARDS: Best of Division, Painting, at the Red Earth Awards Ceremony of 1994.

REPRESENTATION: Long Ago and Far Away Gallery, Manchester Center, Vermont.

ABOUT THE ARTIST: English's bold watercolors of contemporary Native Americans have brought him much deserved attention. One such painting, entitled "Them Two, the First Americans," depicts an Indian man and his wife wrapped in one American flag. The figures are elongated, their faces raised to the sky. English's paintings are often made into prints.

ADELINE ETIENNE

(a.k.a. Nikawonna A)
Mohawk (1950 —) West Oka, Quebec, Canada
Beadworker, leatherworker, weaver

EDUCATION: Etienne took beading classes.

REPRESENTATION: Kanesatake Indian Arts & Crafts.

ABOUT THE ARTIST: A multitalented woman, Adeline prefers beadwork, though she has made many other items. She uses floral and geometric designs when decorating her leather tooled pieces and floral designs in her loomwork. She also weaves rugs and ponchos.

KAREN ETIENNE

(a.k.a. Whentenhawi)
Mohawk (N/A)
Beadworker, leatherworker

EDUCATION: Largely self-taught; also took some classes in leatherwork and tooling.

ABOUT THE ARTIST: Etienne's whole family is working in the arts. Karen's talents lie in creating beaded and porcupine-quill earrings, feathered hair ties, embroidered duffle garments, and leatherwork decorated with tooled designs.

MARGARET ETIENNE

(a.k.a. Konwakeri Kahentoretha)
Mohawk (1907 —)
Artist, basketweaver, beadworker, leatherworker

EDUCATION: Self-taught; took beadwork classes.

ABOUT THE ARTIST: Etienne has had her work exhibited all over the world. She does local scenery, animals, and portraits. When she makes baskets, her specialty is white baskets with potato-stamped flower designs.

CHRISTINA EUSTACE

Zuni/Cochiti (1954 —) Albuquerque, New Mexico
Jeweler

EDUCATION: Learned her trade by helping her parents, both of whom were jewelers. Eustace also studied fine arts at the University of New Mexico and took some stained-glass classes in New York in 1976.

REPRESENTATION: Gallery 10, Inc., Scottsdale and Carefree, Arizona and Santa Fe, New Mexico; American Indian Contemporary Arts, San Francisco, California; Galeria Primitivo, Santa Monica, California; Dewey Galleries, Ltd., Santa Fe, New Mexico; Wadle Galleries, Ltd., Santa Fe, New Mexico; October Art Ltd., New York, New York.

ABOUT THE ARTIST: Eustace uses petroglyphs to design some of her jewelry. She uses a variety of stones and does all her own lapidary work. Her stained-glass background has influenced her jewelry designs. She has made masks as pins and concha belts.

JOHN FADDEN

(a.k.a. Kahionhes)
> *Mohawk (1938 –   ) Onchiota, New York*
> *Painter, wood and stone carver*

EDUCATION: Bachelor of Fine Art, Rochester Institute of Technology.

AWARDS: Fadden's many awards include the United Teachers Journalism Award, many awards for his illustrations, and Best Original Cartoon from New York State's *NY Teacher*.

ABOUT THE ARTIST: Fadden has illustrated many books, articles, and films. His work was first published when he was thirteen and one of his sketches was used for a poster for the Six Nations Indian Museum. At first Fadden wanted to be a commercial illustrator, but when he began taking education courses, he realized he liked teaching.

MITCH FARMER

> *Onondaga (1957 – 1979)*
> *Painter, carver, silkscreener*

EDUCATION: Self-taught.

ABOUT THE ARTIST: Farmer worked as layout and graphic artist for *Akwesasne Notes* from 1977–1978. He designed a special silkscreen T-shirt to commemorate the Longest Walk, did deerskin wall hangings, and made pipes and water drums.

JOE FEDDERSON

> *Colville Confederated Tribes (early 1960s –   )*
> *Painter, printmaker, graphic artist, photographer*

EDUCATION: Master of Fine Art, University of Wisconsin (1989); Bachelor of Fine Art, University of Wisconsin (1983); Wenatchee Valley College (1979).

Fedderson's monotype entitled "Black Star," 38½ x 27 inches, 1990. Slide courtesy of the artist and Jan Cicero Gallery, Chicago, Illinois.

REPRESENTATION: Jan Cicero Gallery, Chicago, Illinois.

ABOUT THE ARTIST: Fedderson has exhibited his work in solo and group shows throughout the country. He is a versatile artist who is adept at computer graphics as well as traditional art.

ANITA FIELDS

> *Osage/Creek (1951 –   ) Hominy, Oklahoma*
> *Sculptor—clay; ribbonworker; clothing*
> *designer/decorator*

EDUCATION: Bachelor of Fine Art, Oklahoma State University (1991); Northeastern Oklahoma State University (1980).

AWARDS: Best of Division/Diversified Art Forms, 1994 Red Earth Festival; other awards for sculpture and pottery.

REPRESENTATION: Artables Gallery, Houston, Texas.

ABOUT THE ARTIST: Fields considers her art "an expression of my spirit. It is about transforming

Fields's "Women with Mask," made of earthenware clay and terra sigillath slip, 10 x 3 x ½ inches, 1994, courtesy of the artist.

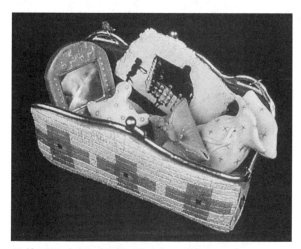

Fields's "Turtle Women's Purse," made of earthenware clay, 4½ x 6 x 2 inches, 1994, courtesy of the artist.

my dreams, thoughts, and inspirations into clay objects and forms." She has participated in group shows and museum exhibits throughout the Southwest. In addition to her art, Fields has taught elementary students how to create Osage ribbonwork, clay, pottery, and sculpture.

PHYLLIS FIFE
> Creek (1948 –   ) Alabama
> Artist–acrylic

EDUCATION: Fife comes from a long line of artists and educators.

ABOUT THE ARTISIT: Fife's work is a reflection of her subconscious. She blurs the images in her work so that one is not sure whether one is looking at a traditional Indian scene or at something that relays how Fife feels about how the world of her Indian heritage affects her and those around her.

GRACE MEDICINE FLOWER
(a.k.a. Wopovi, "Medicine Flower")
> Santa Clara (1938 –   ) Santa Clara Pueblo,
>   New Mexico
> Potter

EDUCATION: Learned the trade from her mother and from her famous father, Camilio Tafoya, one of the first male potters in the pueblo.

ABOUT THE ARTIST: Medicine Flower uses an incised style of decoration on her miniature pottery, often embellishing it with feathers, flowers, and butterflies. Her brother, Joseph Lonewolf, also uses this style. She works in both black and red and is one branch of the family who popularized the sgraffito style. Her tools were made by her father and she bakes the clay the traditional way.

JODY FOLWELL
> Santa Clara (N/A) Santa Clara, New Mexico
> Potter

REPRESENTATION: Gallery 10 (Lee Cohen), New York.

Four pieces of pottery representative of Folwell's style (two black decorated pieces, one tan piece, and one brown), courtesy of the artist and Gallery 10, Inc., Scottsdale, Arizona.

ABOUT THE ARTIST: Folwell feels that her pottery pieces are spiritual creations, as if they molded themselves. She also believes that the people who pick up pieces of pottery feel the spiritual power. Folwell has taken many traditional Santa Clara styles and made them abstract. She often gets inspiration from ancient ruins like those at Chaco Canyon, New Mexico.

HARRY FONSECA
Maidu/Portuguese/Hawaiian (1946 –   )
Sacramento, California
Artist—mixed media

EDUCATION: Influenced by the University of California at Davis art community.

REPRESENTATION: Suzanne Brown Galleries, Scottsdale, Arizona; Jerome Evans Gallery, Lake Tahoe, Nevada; Rena Haveson Gallery, Pittsburgh, Pennsylvania.

ABOUT THE ARTIST: Fonseca paints Maidu dances and legends, but is best known for his Coyote series of paintings. Each Coyote is painted from a different perspective, depicting contemporary ways to follow the Native American into the twentieth century. In *Shared Visions*, Fonseca was quoted as saying, "I believe my Coyote paintings to be the most contemporary statements I have painted in regard to traditional beliefs and contemporary reality."

CLIFF FRAGUA
Jemez (N/A)
Sculptor

ABOUT THE ARTIST: Fragua uses Utah alabaster and other stones in his abstract, symbolic sculptures.

JUANITA FRAGUA
Jemez (N/A) New Mexico
Potter

EDUCATION: Fragua often studies the old pots to get design ideas, but credits Al Momaday (N. Scott Momaday's father) for teaching her how to draw.

ABOUT THE ARTIST: A member of the Corn Clan, Fragua often uses corn designs on her pottery. Her pieces are painted with soft grey-blues, tans, and chalky whites. She introduced melon bowls to the Jemez pueblo and is best known for those pieces.

DELFINA FRANCISCO
(N/A)
Basketmaker

AWARDS: Francisco was designated one of Arizona's Indian Living Treasures in 1994.

W. B. FRANKLIN
Navajo (N/A)
Painter—acrylic on linen and other media

ABOUT THE ARTIST: Franklin works spiritual figures and symbols into paintings that resemble everyday items (i.e. Navajo rug with abstract images). His paintings are abstract and use complex symbolism.

JAMES (JIM) FRED

Hopi (1945 –) Bacavi, Arizona
Carver–Kachinas

REPRESENTATION: Adobe Gallery, Albuquerque, New Mexico.

ABOUT THE ARTIST: Fred creates realistic all-wood Kachinas, even carving the feathers which adorn his creations. He began carving full-time after spending some time working for the Hopi Center for Human Services teaching the mentally handicapped. Fred tries to carve the dolls the way they move during the traditional dances, capturing certain motions. He does not attempt to carve unless he is "in the mood to carve a particular type of doll."

JOHN FREDERICKS

Hopi (N/A)
Carver

ABOUT THE ARTIST: Fredericks carves stylistic rather than realistic Kachinas.

IDA GABRIEL

(a.k.a. Kwatsitsaienni)
Mohawk (1938 –) Oka, Quebec, Canada
Beadworker, leatherworker

EDUCATION: Gabriel's sister, Violet, taught her.

ABOUT THE ARTIST: Gabriel beads men's ties, necklaces, headbands, daisy chains, and rosettes, and also beads leather hair ties and vests. She does most of her work during the winter and passes on that piece of Iroquois culture to others.

MARY MITCHELL GABRIEL

Passamaquoddy (1909 –) Passamaquoddy
Indian Reservation, Maine
Basketmaker

EDUCATION: Gabriel's grandmother taught her the art of basketweaving.

AWARDS: Gabriel is the first Maine Indian basketmaker to win the National Heritage Fellowship of the National Endowment of the Arts.

ABOUT THE ARTIST: Gabriel creates sweet-grass and ash round baskets; some are covered with sweet-grass patterns and their lids topped with "frog" handles. She is keeping the basketmaking tradition alive by teaching some of her seven children the art of weaving.

SYLVIA GABRIEL

Passamaquoddy (1930 –) Maine
Basketmaker

EDUCATION: Gabriel's mother, Mary Mitchell Gabriel, taught her how to weave a basket.

ABOUT THE ARTIST: Gabriel creates sweet-grass baskets, which are usually round and topped with lids. Her styles often imitate those her mother taught her.

CANDELARIA GACHUPIN

Zia (N/A) New Mexico
Potter

EDUCATION: Learned her skills from her family.

ABOUT THE ARTIST: Gachupin passed her pottery-making knowledge on to her daughter, Dora Tse Pe Pena. Gachupin often told her children that if a pot is ruined in the process of creation, then it just was not meant to be.

RETHA WALDEN GAMBARO

Creek (1917 –) Lenna, Oklahoma
Sculptor–bronze, wood, stone

EDUCATION: Corcoran School of Arts, Washington, D.C.; apprenticeship with Berthold Schmutzhart, Washington, D.C.; daily observation of spirituality in art forms since childhood.

AWARDS: Gambaro's main awards include Best in Sculpture (1985); Mystic Harbor Invitational, Mystic, Connecticut; and Best in Show (1989), Whirlwind Gallery, Florida.

REPRESENTATION: Amerind Gallery, Daleville, Virginia; Buffalo Gallery, Alexandria, Virginia; Four Winds Gallery, Naples, Florida; Kline's Gallery, Boonesboro, Maryland; Western Heritage Art Gallery, Taos, New Mexico; Yah-Ta-Hey Gallery, New London, Connecticut.

ABOUT THE ARTIST: A member of the Muscogee Indian Nation, Gambara started sculpting at age fifty-two and since that time has taught; held one-person shows all over the country; exhibited at many museums, festivals, and shows; and has been commissioned to produce her sculptures by such associations as the International Franchise Foundation, Hawaii, and Howard University. She states that "(A)ccomplishing a special communication among sculptor, sculpture, and viewer is my aim and my reward."

DELORES LEWIS GARCIA
Acoma (N/A) Acoma Pueblo, New Mexico
Potter

ABOUT THE ARTIST: Garcia is a traditional potter who says that the deer design, which has a spiritual and symbolic connection to the Acoma tribe, is an important symbol to their pottery. She also believes that pottery cannot be copied because it is never the same.

DOLORES GARCIA
Acoma (N/A) New Mexico
Potter

ABOUT THE ARTIST: After mixing the clay with her hands, Garcia wedges it with her feet.

DORINA AND RUBY GARCIA
Tohono O'odham (N/A)
Basketmakers

ABOUT THE ARTISTS: This pair weave miniature baskets.

58

Portrait of artist Gambaro with "Grandfather," a cold cast copper bust. Photograph by Stephen A. Gambaro, courtesy of the artist.

Gambaro's "Medicine Flower" (c), bronze, 12 x 12 x 26 inches high, courtesy of the artist.

GOLDENROD GARCIA
Santa Clara (N/A) New Mexico
Potter

EDUCATION: Learned the trade from her mother, Petra Gutierrez, as well as other members of her family.

ABOUT THE ARTIST: Garcia comes from a large family of potters—her mother and all of her sisters are potters. Garcia creates sgrafitto pots.

JOANNE CHINO GARCIA
Acoma (N/A) Acoma Pueblo, New Mexico
Potter

EDUCATION: The granddaughter of the late Marie Z. Chino and daughter of Carrie Chino Charlie, Joanne learned how to pot from the experts in her family.

ABOUT THE ARTIST: Garcia considers seed jars created by Grace Chino, her aunt, some of the most beautiful.

RAYMOND AND BARBARA GARCIA
Santo Domingo (N/A) New Mexico
Jewelers

AWARDS: Three blue ribbons at Indian Market (1990).

ABOUT THE ARTISTS: Raymond cuts and grinds the shells for the couple's twenty to forty strand necklaces. Barbara then drills the shells and strings the beads on wire. The necklaces are finished with a "squaw wrap" (the couple intertwine the ends of their strands, then wrap them tightly in cotton) rather than with commercially made clasps. The Garcias sell most of their work directly to collectors.

TAMMY GARCIA
Santa Clara (N/A) Santa Clara Pueblo
Potter

EDUCATION: Taught by her mother and grandmother.

AWARDS: Garcia's awards include 1987 and 1988 First Prize Awards at Gallup's Inter-Tribal Indian Ceremonial; 1990 & 1992 Best of Category Ribbons at Casa Grande's O'odham Tash; and many others.

REPRESENTATION: Gallery 10, Inc., Scottsdale, Arizona.

ABOUT THE ARTIST: Garcia works from old photographs of Santa Clara pottery and incorporates her new style into it. She particularly enjoys Margaret Tafoya's large water and storage jars and remarks that, for her, "a large jar would stand about sixteen inches tall." Garcia's family includes Sarafina Tafoya, Margaret Tafoya, Mary Esther Archuleta, Shirley Tafoya, Nancy Youngblood, Camilio Sunflower Tafoya, Joseph Lone Wolf, Grace Medicine Flower, and many other famous potters.

Three pieces of Garcia's pottery (from left to right): black jar, 10½ x 6 inches diameter, red jar, 4½ x 6½ inches, red jar, 8½ x 9 inches), courtesy of the artist and Gallery 10, Inc., Scottsdale, Arizona.

WILFRED AND SANDRA GARCIA
Acoma (N/A)
Potters

ABOUT THE ARTISTS: The Garcias create elegant, single-color pieces with innovative accents.

MILDRED GARLOW
Seneca (1889 —   )
Beadworker, dollmaker, basketmaker

EDUCATION: Learned how to bead from her mother-in-law; learned how to make cornhusk dolls from her mother.

ABOUT THE ARTIST: Garlow made unique items, such as beaded pincushions, velvet dolls, cornhusk dolls, and other items which she sold at Prospect Point, Niagara Falls, for more than sixty years. She had a distinct beadwork style, elaborating on the raised beadwork styles. Her red-velvet dolls were made from cloth Queen Victoria gave to Garlow's mother, Deerfoot.

RUTH GARLOW
(a.k.a. Yah Wenh Gwas)
Seneca (1914 —   ) Lewiston, New York
Beadworker, dollmaker, leatherworker

EDUCATION: Learned how to bead from her grandmother and mother; learned how to make beaded velvet birds from her cousin; learned how to create cornhusk dolls from her grandmother.

AWARDS: Garlow has received numerous prizes at the New York State Fair for her beaded birds.

ABOUT THE ARTIST: Garlow's specialty are her velvet and satin beaded birds, which she tries to make look as realistic as possible. Because of the great demand for her work, Garlow has been able to devote her time solely to creating items to sell to her customers.

TED GARNER
Sioux (N/A)
Sculptor

AWARDS: Garner has won numerous awards and honors, including the Sith Martin and Doris Rosen Award from Appalachian State University, North Carolina (1992) and the First Award of Excellence in the "New Horizons in Art—22nd Exhibit of Illinois Artists" (1992).

REPRESENTATION: Jan Cicero Gallery, Chicago, Illinois.

ABOUT THE ARTIST: Garner's work has been installed in dozens of major exhibits across the United States and has been included in four major touring exhibits (all of which were printed in catalogs). He has also constructed major projects for internationally known artists and institutions. In addition, Garner was invited to give the 1993 inaugural lecture at the National Museum of Natural History in Washington, D.C.

AGNES GARROW
Mohawk (1900 —   ) St. Regis, Quebec
Basketmaker, splintworker

EDUCATION: Learned from her mother.

REPRESENTATION: Mohawk Craft Fund.

ABOUT THE ARTIST: Garrow makes a variety of baskets using black ash splints, sweet grass, ribbon, and rope. She has a reputation for fine craftsmanship and usually creates sewing baskets made with undyed splints (sometimes she uses a brown dye).

SARAH GARROW
Mohawk (1954 —   ) Bombay, New York
Beadworker, quillworker

EDUCATION: Learned beadwork from her sister, Martha Cook; learned loom beadwork at Salmon River Central School in late 1970s.

ABOUT THE ARTIST: Garrow uses beads, sequins, pearls, and porcupine quills to create both loom and freehand beadwork. Some of the items Garrow makes include beaded key chains, earrings, barrettes, medallions, hair ties, watchbands, and barrettes. She also does porcupine-quill-designed earrings and chokers. Garrow believes it is important for Iroquois children to know the old ways and crafts; thus she teaches the culture at the Salmon River School and at the Twin Rivers School in Massena.

GASTON GASPÉ

Mohawk (1933 –   ) Oka, Quebec, Canada
Graphic artist, photographer, painter

EDUCATION: Attended Montreal College (1947–1953); received Bachelor of Fine Art in design from the Fine Arts School of Montreal (1959–1963); earned a Pedagogie Artistique degree (1963–1966).

ABOUT THE ARTIST: Gaspé has taught school, exhibited his work, and also does some photography. He has spent most of his time passing on his knowledge to his children.

GEORGE GEIONETY

(a.k.a. Bei-Koi-Gei, "Water Bag to Travel")
Kiowa (1913 –   ) Lawton, Oklahoma
Artist—watercolor on illustration board

EDUCATION: Learned from his grandfather Haungooah (Silverhorn), a well-known Kiowa artist during the turn of the century.

AWARDS: Has exhibited in group and one-person shows.

ABOUT THE ARTIST: Geionety paints in the traditional manner, depicting his ancestors and the way they lived.

JACK TÓ BAAHE GENE

Navajo (1953 –   ) Winslow, Arizona
Painting, sandpainting

EDUCATION: Mostly self-taught, Gene has received grants from the French/Navajo Intercultural Art Exchange; the Southwestern Association on Indian Affairs; and the Arizona Commission on the Arts, which assisted in his study of art.

AWARDS: Among Gene's many awards are Best of Division/Fine Arts from the Southwest Museum (1993), Best of Show from the Heard Museum Indian Fair (1993), and First and Second Place/Pastel Paintings from the Santa Fe Indian Market (1992).

REPRESENTATION: TóBaahe Fine Art, Winslow, Arizona

ABOUT THE ARTIST: Gene states that he is "a traditional Navajo cultural painter depicting my experiences of the rawness of the natural being as contained within contemporary society." Gene uses sand and pastel paints in his paintings, trying to "go beyond the two-dimensional surface to express the soul of the image."

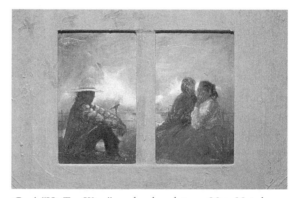

Gene's "His Two Wives," pastel and sand, image 19 x 11 inches, courtesy of the artist.

Gene's "The Enduring Night Way," pastel, 40 x 30 inches, 1992. Slide by Jerry Jacka Photography, courtesy of the artist.

AGNES GEORGE

*Carrier (N/A) Nautley Reserve, British Columbia,
Canada*
Basketmaker

ABOUT THE ARTIST: George creates birch-bark
baskets, some of which are shaped like bowls.

BESSIE GEORGE

Navajo (1932 –   ) Wide Ruins, Arizona
Weaver

EDUCATION: Learned how to weave from her
mother; one of her sisters also weaves.

ABOUT THE ARTIST: George has fifteen children,
but only one weaves. George supports her family
with her efforts.

FIDELIA GEORGE

Seneca (1955 –   )
Beadworker

EDUCATION: Learned by watching her mother.

ABOUT THE ARTIST: George creates beaded jewelry
as well as bolo ties, wristbands, barrettes, hair ties,
belt buckles, and cigarette cases. She has exhibited
her work and is always trying something new. In
addition, George dances, sings, and spreads the Iroquois traditions whenever she gets the chance.

MILDRED GEORGE

Seneca (1916 –   )
Beadworker

EDUCATION: Learned how to bead by watching
others.

ABOUT THE ARTIST: George creates beaded jewelry,
preferring to make clan medallions in patterns she
has created.

ROS GEORGE

Hopi (N/A)
Carver

ABOUT THE ARTIST: George carves one-piece Kachinas.

JOHN GEORGE-MATHEWS

Ojibway/Chippewa (1963 –   ) Sarnia, Canada
Painter, muralist

EDUCATION: Self-taught, independent freelance
artist.

ABOUT THE ARTIST: George-Mathews does fine art
on commission or contract, whether it be a mural
for an office building or a T-shirt design. George-
Mathews states that, "As an artist I strive to induce
shock, surprise, joy, fear, starkness, and shivers
down the viewers' spine."

*Portrait of George-Mathews holding his portrait of a Native
American man, courtesy of the artist.*

JOHN GIBSON

Mohawk (1962 –   ) Hagersville, Ontario, Canada
Painter

EDUCATION: Gibson took some art classes in high
school, but is mostly self-taught.

ABOUT THE ARTIST: Gibson was the youngest student allowed to attend art courses at the Art
Gallery of Brant. His style is romantic realism,
though he has experimented with various modern
techniques.

RICK GLAZER-DANAY

Mohawk/White (1942 –   ) Coney Island, New York
Painter

EDUCATION: Bachelor of Art in Fine Arts, California State University, Northridge; Master of Art in Fine Arts, California State; Master of Fine Art, University of California at Davis.

AWARDS: Glazer-Danay has many honors from exhibiting all over the United States. His work is held in many permanent and private collections, including the Philbrook Museum and the United States Department of the Interior.

ABOUT THE ARTIST: On his fiftieth birthday in August 1992, Glazer-Danay stated that he would "sell my creations no more forever." A controversial artist whose work was once called "soft porn," Glazer-Danay has created pop-culture, satire, and political-commentary paintings. He has also taught American Indian history at the University of California at Riverside, taught at the University of Wisconsin-Green Bay from 1980–1985 and taught art at the California State University at Long Beach from 1985–1991.

JACK GLOVER

Cherokee (N/A) Texas
Sculptor–bronze

EDUCATION: Largely self-taught.

REPRESENTATION: Glover's Old West Museum and Trading Post, Bowie, Texas.

ABOUT THE ARTIST: As author of fourteen books on the Indian culture, collector of Indian artifacts, and owner of an old West museum and trading post in Bowie, Texas; Glover sculpts investment-quality bronzes.

HENRY GOBIN

Skohomish (1941 –   ) Washington
Artist–watercolor

EDUCATION: Gobin has experimented with many of the "schools of Indian painting." He studied at the pre-Institute Santa Fe Boarding School, then studied the Northwest Coast cultures.

ABOUT THE ARTIST: Gobin's style could be called surrealistic, though it does incorporate some of the Northwest Coast symbols and stylized masks.

PAT COURTNEY GOLD

Tlingit/Wasco (1939 –   ) Warm Springs, Oregon
Basketmaker

EDUCATION: Learned basketry from local basket weavers in Oregon and Washington (1991 and 1992); Bachelor of Art in Mathematics-Physics, Whitman College.

AWARDS: Invited to participate in Governor Barbara Roberts and Oregon Arts Commission show (June–August 1991); special invitation to the Ancient Images of the Columbia River Gorge show at the Maryhill Museum (March–July 1992); received the Timberline Purchase Award at the Tribal Member Art Show at the Museum of Warm Springs, Oregon (September 1993–January 1994).

Portrait of Gold, courtesy of the artist.

Gold's contemporary Wasco basket, "Urban Indian Couple,"
9 diameter x 13 inches high, courtesy of the artist.

REPRESENTATION: Snow Goose Associates, Inc., Seattle, Washington; Ancestral Spirits Gallery, Port Townsend, Washington; Perry House Galleries, Alexandria, Virginia; Indian Way Gallery, Olympia, Washington; Lelooska Gallery, Ariel, Washington.

ABOUT THE ARTIST: When Gold had had enough of the business world, she and her sister, Bernyce, started a business—reviving the art of Wasco basketweaving. The business, called "The Sally Sisters," means to preserve the art for future generations. Gold has exhibited and sold her work and has taught the art of basketry throughout the western United States.

LARRY GOLSH
Pala Mission / Cherokee (1942 –) Phoenix, Arizona
Jeweler, painter, sculptor

EDUCATION: Golsh worked with Pierre Touraine from 1972–1983 and was the first Native American to study at the Gemological Institute of America. He also observed Charles Loloma at work and learned from him how to set diamonds. Golsh majored in fine arts at Arizona State University where he studied with Ben Goo, a renowned sculptor. Manfred Susunkewa, a Hopi

silversmith and Kachina carver, taught Golsh how to work with silver.

AWARDS: National Endowment for the Arts grant; Arizona Commission on Arts and Humanities grant; numerous awards for jewelry creations; judges jewelers at the Heard Museum, Scottsdale National Indian Art Show, and Santa Fe Indian Market; featured in a television special (PBS, 1984) entitled "Larry Golsh—American Indian Artist."

REPRESENTATION: Lovena Ohl Gallery, Scottsdale, Arizona; Galeria Capistrano, San Juan Capistrano, California; The Squash Blossom, Vail, Aspen, and Denver, Colorado; Glen Green Galleries, Santa Fe, New Mexico.

ABOUT THE ARTIST: Golsh works with numerous sketches to create his jewelry and often makes facsimiles of the final product in wood, silver, or plaster before the work is finished. He uses exotic and unusual stones, is innovative, and uses all of his art training when creating jewelry.

CORDI AND GLEN GOMEZ
Pojoaque (N/A) Pojoaque Pueblo, New Mexico
Potters

EDUCATION: Cordi, Glen's mother, learned how to pot from her mother, Glen's grandmother. Cordi has passed on her skills to her son.

ABOUT THE ARTISTS: This mother-son team produces small- to medium-sized micaceous pots. Glen's innovative designs include subtle diagonal textures on the exterior of his pots. Cordi makes Indian bread and molding pots.

STEPHEN GONYEA
Onondaga (1946 –) Alexandria, Virginia
Artist—acrylics, pen and ink, pencil

EDUCATION: Gonyea did post-graduate work at the Institute of American Indian Arts (1964–1966) and received a Bachelor of Fine Art with Honors (illustration major) from the Art Center College of Design, Los Angeles.

ABOUT THE ARTIST: Gonyea's work has been exhibited extensively. He has also acted as a freelance illustrator; his work has appeared in magazines such as *American Artist*.

BARBARA GONZALES

San Ildefonso (N/A) New Mexico
Potter

EDUCATION: Learned how to pot with other members of her family, including Maria Martinez, her great-grandmother.

ABOUT THE ARTIST: Gonzales learned her trade from her illustrious family and has created works that are valued by collectors all over the world. In the 1950s and 1960s, Gonzales revived the painted polychrome designs that Popovi Da, Maria's son, had used.

ROSE GONZALES

San Ildefonso (N/A) New Mexico
Potter

EDUCATION: Learned how to make pottery from her mother-in-law.

ABOUT THE ARTIST: An innovator in the pottery art, Gonzales came from San Juan when she married a man from the San Ildefonso in 1920. Her pottery has a distinctive rounded edge. She made the first carved and modern pottery at the pueblo. Gonzales has taught her son, Tse-Pe, and his wife, Dora, the art.

DAVID A. GORDON

Seneca (1948 –   ) Irving, New York
Painter, sculptor, ceramist, potter

EDUCATION: Gordon's parents and art teachers influenced him. He also took silversmithing classes at the United South Eastern Tribes Indian Center.

ABOUT THE ARTIST: Gordon's work has been exhibited throughout the Southwest by the Institute of American Indian Art. He continues to learn new skills while working to improve his painting.

HARLEY GORDON

(a.k.a. Gah-En-Teh)
Seneca (1922 –   ) Tonawanda Reservation,
Basom, New York
Artist—sketches; carver

EDUCATION: Self-taught.

ABOUT THE ARTIST: Harley's sketches are usually of people he knows, animals, or local activities. He also carves spoons, ladles, and paddles.

R.C. GORMAN

Navajo (1932 –   ) Chinle, Arizona
Artist—oil, pastels, other media; sculptor—bronze

EDUCATION: Gorman's father, painter Carl Nelson Gorman, inspired Gorman to paint. Gorman attended Mexico City College to study art and was Carlos Merida's pupil. In addition, he attended Guam Territorial College, Marianas Islands; California State University, San Francisco; and Arizona State College, Tempe.

REPRESENTATION: Joan Cawley Gallery, Scottsdale, Arizona; Allard's Gallery, Fresno, California; Georgetown Gallery of Art, Washington, D.C.; Fields and Rosen Fine Arts, Inc., Jupiter, Florida; Santa Fe Trails Gallery of Southwestern Art, Sarasota, Florida; Donna Rose Galleries/Art Brokerage, Inc., Ketchum, Indiana; Freeport Art Museum and Cultural Center, Freeport, Illinois; R. Michelson Galleries, Amherst, Massachusetts; J. Todd Galleries, Wellesley, Massachusetts; Saper Galleries, East Lansing, Michigan; John A. Boler, Indian and Western Art, Minneapolis, Minnesota; Gomes Gallery Inc., St. Louis, Missouri; The New Riverside Gallery, Red Bank, New Jersey; Roswell Museum and Art Center, Roswell, New Mexico; 21st Century Fox Fine Art, Santa Fe, New Mexico; Wheelwright Museum of the American Indian/Case Trading Post, Santa Fe, New Mexico; Grycner Studio/ Gallery Taos, Taos, New Mexico; Navajo Gallery, Taos, New Mexico; C & L Fine Arts, Inc., Bohemia, New York; Studio 53, New York; Fields and Rosen Fine Arts, Inc., Southampton, New York; Landing Gallery of Woodbury, Inc., Woodbury, New York; Argus Fine

Arts, Eugene, Oregon; JRS Fine Art, Providence, Rhode Island; El Taller Gallery, Austin, Texas; Gallery Mack NW , Seattle, Washington; Santa Fe Gallery, Madison, Wisconsin.

ABOUT THE ARTIST: One of the best-known contemporary Native American artists, Gorman's sensuous style and large canvases are well known and have given him commercial success which reaches far beyond the circle of those who collect strictly Native American art. Posters and lithographs of Gorman's Navajo women are sold almost everywhere. Gorman has also written books such as *R. C. Gorman: The Radiance of My People* (1992).

CRAIG GOSEYUN
(N/A)
Sculptor

AWARDS: Best of Division at the Red Earth awards ceremony, (1994).

SHAL GOSHORN
(a.k.a. Noon da Da Lon a ga el, "Yellow Moon")
Cherokee (1957 –   ) Baltimore, Maryland
Jeweler, photographer, painter

EDUCATION: Majored in silversmithing at the Cleveland Institute of Art, Cleveland; changed her major to photography in her third year; then transferred to the Atlanta College of Art in Atlanta, Georgia; and graduated with a Bachelor of Fine Art, double major in painting and photography (1980).

AWARDS: Goshorn's work has been commissioned by many public and private institutions and has been awarded many prizes.

ABOUT THE ARTIST: Goshorn has done cover art and photographic illustrations for many publications. Her work is held in many collections such as the Indian Arts and Crafts Board and Prudential Insurance. Her photographs are currently being assembled for a book that will document contemporary Native-American life.

ROLLIE A. GRANDBOIS
Chippewa/Cree/French (1955 –   ) Belcourt, North Dakota
Sculptor–stone

EDUCATION: Institute of American Indian Art, Santa Fe, New Mexico.

AWARDS: First Place Sculpture, Santa Fe Indian Market (1992); Best of Show, Inter-Tribal Arts Expo (1991); Sculptor of the Year, Grand National Art Show American Endangered Species Foundation (1990); and many others.

REPRESENTATION: SunWest Silver, Albuquerque, New Mexico.

ABOUT THE ARTIST: Grandbois works with life- and heroic-size stone sculptures. One piece, "Ancient Guardian," is a nine-foot sculpture made of marble, neon, and steel. Grandbois believes "(T)he light represents the spirit, the marble is antiquity, and the steel is strength."

GERTRUDE GRAY
Mohawk (1942 –   ) Hogansburg, New York
Basketmaker, quilter, clothing designer

EDUCATION: Gray learned by helping her mother, Mary Adams.

AWARDS: Gray has won prizes at the New York State Fair for her work and has a small bassinet on exhibit at the United Nations building in New York.

ABOUT THE ARTIST: Gray's first basket was an Easter basket, but today she makes a wide variety of sewing baskets (often made with velvet linings and pincushions on top), as well as flower baskets decorated with ribbons and large hampers decorated with sweet grass.

LEONA GRAY
Mohawk (1959 –   ) Hogansburg, New York
Beadworker, quillworker, carver

EDUCATION: Learned some of her skills from a friend and developed her other skills personally.

ABOUT THE ARTIST: Gray taught herself how to bead as a child of seven, then learned other stitches at the Longhouse. She does freehand and loom work and uses geometric and floral designs. In addition, Gray carves cradleboards from red pen. She also teaches crafts in the Native American Program in Rochester and has worked with that city's language program.

TOM GRAY
(a.k.a. Kaion Ha Te Ni Or)
Mohawk (1895 –) Hogansburg, New York
Basketmaker

EDUCATION: Self-taught.

AWARDS: The New York State Fair has awarded Gray's baskets many times.

ABOUT THE ARTIST: Gray uses black-ash splints to make large pack baskets. His nephew helps him pound the logs, but Gray still carves his own handles.

HERBERT GREEN
Gitksan (N/A) British Columbia, Canada
Carver

ABOUT THE ARTIST: Green carves Talking Sticks out of yellow cedar and other wooden objects.

IRENE GREENE
Oneida (1925 –) Nedrow, New York
Beadworker, clothing designer, leatherworker

EDUCATION: Self-taught.

AWARDS: Greene has won prizes for her work at the New York State Fair.

ABOUT THE ARTIST: Greene creates beaded jewelry, children's native clothing, beaded leather wristbands, and other items. She has been working at her craft since she was a youngster and has also taught her own children how to bead. She rarely exhibits her work.

JUDITH GREENE
Seneca (1940 –) Buffalo, New York
Sculptor–mixed media

EDUCATION: Bachelor of Fine Art, State University of New York College of Ceramics, Alfred University, 1984; Master of Fine Art, University of Massachusetts, Dartmouth, 1990.

ABOUT THE ARTIST: Greene, a member of the Deer Clan, works in mixed media and is formally trained. She does shows throughout her area and represents her own work.

STAN GREENE
Coast Salish (N/A) Canada
Carver

ABOUT THE ARTIST: Because the Coast Salish did not have totem poles that displayed crests, Greene's carvings are often simple posts which may have acted as support beams for dance houses in the Northwest. He replicated one such pole in 1986 for the Vancouver Expo.

LOIS GUTIERREZ-DE LA CRUZ
Santa Clara (N/A) New Mexico
Potter

ABOUT THE ARTIST: Gutierrez-de la Cruz' husband, Derek de la Cruz, helps her gather clay. When she began potting, they were partners; now Gutierrez-de la Cruz signs the pottery herself. She uses smoothing stones passed down through her family and uses a symbol of the four sacred Tewa mountains on the rim of her pots. Her pottery is polychrome, a distinct buff color, and she often decorates her pieces with lizards, hummingbirds, and humpbacked flute players.

MARGARET AND LUTHER GUTIERREZ
Santa Clara (N/A) New Mexico
Potters

EDUCATION: Learned from Lela and Van Gutierrez, responsible for modifying a polychrome method that is distinctly their own.

ABOUT THE ARTISTS: Margaret and Luther are carrying on their parents' work. Using a red base and a tan background, they paint their designs in pastels. Their clay sources are secret.

PETRA GUTIERREZ
Santa Clara (N/A) New Mexico
Potter

ABOUT THE ARTIST: Gutierrez' whole family is involved with pottery—daughters Minnie Vigil, Goldenrod Garcia, Thelma Talachy, and Lois Gutierrez; and daughter-in-law Virginia Gutierrez. Gutierrez' daughters are half Santa Clara and half Pojoaque.

STEPHANIE GUTIERREZ
Santa Clara (N/A) New Mexico
Potter

EDUCATION: Learned the distinctive Gutierrez style from her grandfather, Luther Gutierrez.

ABOUT THE ARTIST: Gutierrez is the fourth generation of her potting family. She carries on the tradition of polishing her pots with a rag instead of a stone, giving the pottery a silky feel.

VAL AND PULA GUTIERREZ
Santa Clara (N/A) New Mexico
Potters

ABOUT THE ARTISTS: This couple create blackware animals that are hand-shaped and polished. One animal often requires a full day's worth of polishing.

VIRGINIA GUTIERREZ
Nambé/Pojoaque (N/A) Arizona
Potter

EDUCATION: Gutierrez' aunt, the last working Nambé potter, taught her how to work the clay.

ABOUT THE ARTIST: Gutierrez married into the Santa Clara pueblo and her design is distinctive: part Nambé (where she learned) and part her own. Her artwork is complex, created on clays from Nambé and Pojoaque, sand from Nambé, and paints from northern New Mexico. She does not polish her pottery and frequently creates seed jars.

MARY HALFTOWN
(a.k.a. Jo Yan Non)
Seneca (1903 –)
Beadworker

EDUCATION: Learned beadwork from a friend.

ABOUT THE ARTIST: Halftown has sold her beadwork at a number of fairs. She creates medallions, bolo ties, and necklaces, and decorates leather purses and vests with beadwork. She has also made baskets and cornhusk dolls. Halftown's daughters also make baskets and do beadwork.

RON HAMILTON
Northwest Coast (N/A) Port Alberni, British Columbia, Canada
Carver—slate, wood

ABOUT THE ARTIST: Hamilton carves some pieces on slate from the Campbell River, stating that it is harder than the pieces the Haida people use in their carvings. He also states that his style of carving and design is more realistic than the tribes farther north. He regularly uses the Sea Serpent in his work.

ENOCH KELLY HANEY
Seminole/Creek (1940 –) Seminole, Oklahoma
Artist—acrylic, watercolor, monotype, lithographs, tempera

EDUCATION: Associate in Art from Bacone College; Bachelor of Art in Fine Arts from a Rockefeller Foundation Scholarship for art.

Haney's limited edition print "Crazy Horse," 16 x 21 inches, courtesy of Haney, Inc.

Haney's limited edition print "American Eagle," 16 x 21 inches, courtesy of Haney, Inc.

AWARDS: Master Artist of the Five Civilized Tribes (1975); Governor's Art Award/ Oklahoma; Oklahoma City University Distinguished Alumni Award; honorary Doctor of Law degree from Oklahoma City University (1994); inducted into the Bacone Junior College Hall of Fame.

REPRESENTATION: Kelly Haney Art Gallery, Shawnee, Oklahoma.

ABOUT THE ARTIST: Haney's work is faithful to his heritage. Every detail is painstakingly painted and accurate. In addition to being a versatile artist,

Haney has served three terms in the Oklahoma House of Representatives and is currently serving in the Oklahoma State Senate (1994).

MONICA HANSEN
(N/A)
Carver, sculptor

AWARDS: In 1994, Hansen won both the Grand Heritage Award and Best of Division (sculpture/wood carving) at the Five Civilized Tribes Competitive Show.

ROY HANUSE
Kwakiutl/Owikeeno (N/A) Rivers Inlet, British Columbia, Canada
Carver, painter

ABOUT THE ARTIST: Hanuse started by painting in the traditional Northwest Coast manner. Later, he began carving and has been able to incorporate his painting style into the design of the carving.

ROBERT HAOZOUS
Chiricahua Apache/Navajo/English/Spanish (1943 –   ) Los Angeles, California
Sculptor—stone, metals

EDUCATION: Utah State University, Logan; California College of Arts and Crafts, Oakland.

REPRESENTATION: David Rettig Fine Arts, Inc., Santa Fe, New Mexico; Wheelwright Museum of the American Indian/Case Trading Post, Santa Fe, New Mexico; Philbrook Museum of Art, Tulsa, Oklahoma.

ABOUT THE ARTIST: Haozous humorously (bordering on the sarcastic) depicts the way the white man's civilization poses a threat to traditional Indian life. He often uses steel, stainless steel, mahogany, and stone.

LIZ HAPPYNOOK

Northwest Coast (N/A) Bamfield, British Columbia,
Canada
Basketmaker

EDUCATION: Taught how to weave baskets by
her aunt.

ABOUT THE ARTIST: Happynook's baskets are often
in the shape of bottles, created with designs she
learned from family members.

HELEN HARDIN

(a.k.a. Tsa-sah-wee-eh, "Little Standing Spruce")
Santa Clara (1943 – 1984) Santa Clara Pueblo,
New Mexico
Artist—oil

EDUCATION: At the University of New Mexico,
Hardin studied art history and anthropology, later
winning a painting scholarship to a special school
for Indians at the University of Arizona.

AWARDS: Hardin won her first art contest at age
six. After showing her work in South America, she
won major awards in the United States and was one
of the Southwest's leading artists.

REPRESENTATION: Silver Sun/Hardin Estate,
Santa Fe, New Mexico; Inee Yang Slaughter
Gallery, Santa Fe, New Mexico.

ABOUT THE ARTIST: Hardin was Pablita Velarde's
daughter. Influenced by Joe Herrera, Hardin's style
was more modern and abstract than traditional
Indian painting and often integrated the designs of
the potters of Acoma and Mimbres. Her first art
show in Bogota, Colombia, was almost a sell-out.
Her work, by her own admission, was definitely not
traditional nor classic. During the 1970s, Hardin
developed a series of Kachina paintings, then went
on to her "Women" series.

MARGUERITE LEE HARING

Seneca (1944 –   ) Irving, New York
Painter, graphic artist, ceramist

EDUCATION: Associate in Art, Bacone College,
Oklahoma (1963–1965); Bachelor of Science in
Art Education, Rosary Hill College (1967–1970);
Master in Art Education, State University of New
York College at Buffalo.

AWARDS: Haring has won many honors during her
career, including being part of an exhibit at the
Museum of the American Indian.

ABOUT THE ARTIST: Haring was influenced by
Richard West while at Bacone. She does abstract,
modern work but also does pieces that deal with
Indian culture. She has exhibited at art shows, but
most of her work is for herself and her family.

MARCELLE SHARRON AHTONE HARJO

(Sain-Tah-Oodie, "Killed with a Blunted Arrow")
Kiowa (N/A) Oklahoma
Artist—acrylic on canvas

EDUCATION: Bacone College, Muskogee,
Oklahoma (1963–1965); Northeastern State
College, Tahlequah, Oklahoma (1965); Colorado
Women's College, Denver (1965).

AWARDS: Miss Indian America XII (1966); exhibited in group and one-person shows in Oklahoma.

ABOUT THE ARTIST: Harjo works in an abstract
style, painting scenes of Indian life in an almost
geometric fashion.

ARIEL HARRIS

(a.k.a. Ga Wen He Henz, "Holding Flower")
Onondaga (1929 –   ) Ohsweken, Ontario, Canada
Wireworker, clothing designer, beadworker, crocheter

EDUCATION: Learned wireworking from a woman
at Tuscarora; learned some of her other skills on
her own or from her mother.

ABOUT THE ARTIST: Harris displays her many craft
items at fairs and powwows. She has made a living
with her work since age fourteen. Her wirework
items include chairs, bracelets, rings, baskets, tur-

tle earrings and Indian-head earrings. She does beadwork jewelry, crocheted items, and novelty items as well.

RICHARD HARRIS
Gitksan (N/A) Canada
Carver

EDUCATION: Harris learned some of his carving skills from his father, Walter Harris. This practice is unusual because carvers traditionally train their *nephews*.

ABOUT THE ARTIST: Harris worked with his father on a totem pole that was commissioned by Sunrise Films of Toronto. The film showed the traditional skills of making a totem pole and the raising of the pole on August 24, 1980.

SADIE HARRIS
Kispiox (N/A) British Columbia, Canada
Blanketmaker

ABOUT THE ARTIST: Harris handsews blankets for the 'Ksan ceremonial functions or dances. Blankets for her own family may be decorated with the Double Killer Whale design, her husband Walter's family crest.

WALTER HARRIS
Gitskan (N/A) British Columbia, Canada
Carver

ABOUT THE ARTIST: Harris is married to blanket-maker Sadie Harris. He often provides the designs for the blankets she creates in addition to the designs for the carvings he produces. He has carved doors for the Royal Centre in Vancouver; masks, some with abalone inlay and moveable parts; and totem poles. He and his son, Richard, were part of a film made by Sunrise Films of Toronto in 1980. The documentary followed the making of a totem pole for the University of British Columbia's outdoor exhibit. Harris also guided the 'Ksan carvers

who made the carved folding doors at the Museum of Anthropology's entrance.

HAZEL HARRISON
Seneca (1933 –) Jamestown, New York
Beadworker

EDUCATION: Harrison learned some techniques from a friend and others through a class at the Allegany Indian Arts & Crafts Coop.

ABOUT THE ARTIST: Though a full-time emergency medical technician (EMT) for the Seneca Nation, Harrison fills her free time with beadwork. She has passed on her skills to her sons and daughters. She usually makes clan medallions, medallions, daisy chain, and other types of necklaces.

JAMES HART
Haida (N/A) Canada
Artist, carver

ABOUT THE ARTIST: Hart has carved totem poles for the Museum of Anthropology of the University of British Columbia. Hart resurrected one that was originally a house pole carved before the turn of the century. It took him almost a year to complete the carving. The pole was officially raised in 1982.

TIMOTHY HARVEY
Navajo (N/A) Lukachukai, Arizona
Sandpainter

ABOUT THE ARTIST: In the late 1970s, Harvey was one of the sandpainters who created nontraditional works such as his "Father Peyote" (1977), a sandpainting depicting that personage. Harvey has attempted to bring his work to a higher level by using more details and employing all his skill so that his work will be called "fine art." He has also been one of the only sandpainters to create action shots and one of the few who signs and dates his work.

JAMES HAVARD

Choctaw/Chippewa (1937 –   ) Mississippi
Artist—oil and acrylic

REPRESENTATION: Robert Kidd Gallery, Birmingham, Michigan; Channing, Santa Fe, New Mexico; Allene LaPides Gallery, Santa Fe, New Mexico; Naravisa Press, Santa Fe, New Mexico.

ABOUT THE ARTIST: Havard's style is abstract and often difficult to interpret. His work is totally nontraditional and often reminiscent of *trompe l'oleil.*

HACHIVI EDGAR HEAP OF BIRDS

Cheyenne/Arapaho (1954 –   ) Wichita, Kansas
Artist

EDUCATION: California College of Arts and Crafts, Oakland, California (1975); Bachelor of Fine Art, University of Kansas (1976); Master of Fine Art, Tyler School of Art, Temple University (1979); graduate work in painting at the Royal College of Art, London (1977).

AWARDS: Heap of Birds has received numerous awards and commissions for his work, including "Building Minnesota," a work installed at the Walker Art Center, Minneapolis, from March 10–August 20, 1990. He also received the National Art Award from the Tiffany Foundation in 1989.

Heap of Birds's "Neuf Series," 56 x 72 inches, courtesy of the artist and Jan Cicero Gallery, Chicago, Illinois.

REPRESENTATION: Jan Cicero Gallery, Chicago, Illinois; Cleveland Institute of Art Reinberger Galleries, Cleveland, Ohio; University of North Texas University Art Gallery/Cora Stafford Gallery, Denton, Texas.

ABOUT THE ARTIST: Heap of Birds lectures on art throughout North America and Europe, curates exhibits of art, teaches at the University of Oklahoma, and exhibits his own work in group and solo shows. He has painted commuter buses, park and freeway signs, and the normal canvas. He believes that it is important to unify language and image in his pieces.

BILL HENDERSON

Kwakiutl (N/A) Canada
Carver

EDUCATION: Henderson learned some of his skills from his father, Sam Henderson.

ABOUT THE ARTIST: Henderson is known for helping his father carve some house posts, such as the one at one end of the traditional plank house erected in Campbell River's Foreshore Park (British Columbia).

ERNIE HENDERSON

Kwakiutl (N/A) Canada
Carver

EDUCATION: Henderson learned some of his carving skills from his father, Sam Henderson.

ABOUT THE ARTIST: Henderson and his brother, Bill, assisted their father in carving two house posts and crosspieces for a traditional plank house erected in Campbell River's Foreshore Park (British Columbia).

MARK HENDERSON

Kwakiutl (N/A) Canada
Carver, artist

EDUCATION: Henderson learned some of his carving skills from his father, Sam Henderson.

ABOUT THE ARTIST: Henderson and his brothers have carried on the carving tradition their father began. In fact, Mark was responsible for repainting one of his father's poles.

SAM HENDERSON

Kwakiutl (1905 – 1982) Canada
Carver, dancer, composer, singer, speaker

EDUCATION: Henderson learned his carving skills from members of his family.

ABOUT THE ARTIST: Considered one of the most renowned of the Northwest Coast carvers, Henderson passed on the traditions he had learned to other members of his family, as well as to many others. He carved totem poles that now stand along the Campbell River.

HILDA HENRY

Cowichan (N/A) Khenipsen Reserve, British Columbia, Canada
Knitter

ABOUT THE ARTIST: Henry uses the old method of loosening and cleaning the wool by hand, cards it, then spins it on a device made from a treadle sewing machine.

JAMES PEPPER HENRY

Kanza (Kaw)/Creek (1966 –   ) Portland, Oregon
Sculptor—bronze, terra-cotta

EDUCATION: Bachelor of Art in Fine Arts, University of Oregon.

REPRESENTATION: Littman Gallery, Portland, Oregon.

ABOUT THE ARTIST: As guest curator for special exhibits at the Portland Art Museum, gallery coordinator of the Firehouse Cultural Center (in Port-

land), and a mask carver who also exhibits, Henry is a busy artist who is constantly spreading his knowledge and love of Native American art. Henry, a descendant of the Chiricahua Apache leader, Geronimo, learned about Northwest Coast art when his family moved to British Columbia. He uses what he has learned through his family and the courses he took in school to produce his own style of sculpture. He has sold to private collectors and does shows throughout the Northwest.

LOUISE HENRY

Tuscarora (N/A)
Beadworker, clothing designer

EDUCATION: Henry's sister, Doris Hudson, gave Henry classes on how to bead.

ABOUT THE ARTIST: Henry has decorated velvet, cloth, and leather with her beadwork and has also passed on what she knows by teaching beading classes at conferences, colleges, and churches. She has exhibited at the New York State Fair with her beaded medallions, bolo ties, barrettes, beaded velvet picture frames and cushions, Iroquois clothing, and beaded leather purses and moccasins.

MARGIE HENRY

(a.k.a. Kawinetá)

Cayuga (N/A) Ohsweken, Ontario, Canada
Beadworker, weaver, cornhusk dollmaker, silverworker

EDUCATION: Mostly self-taught; has taken classes in silversmithing and fingerweaving; was taught how to work with cornhusk by her mother.

ABOUT THE ARTIST: Henry's work is held in collections at the Woodland Indian Cultural Educational Centre and the North American Traveling Indian College. She is very active in her community, teaches all kinds of classes, and instructs students in the Cayuga language. Her work is traditional; she makes beadwork jewelry, fingerwoven sashes, felt and cornhusk dolls, and silver jewelry.

MARY HERNE

Mohawk (1928 –   )
Basketmaker, quilter

EDUCATION: Learned from her mother, Josephine Lazore, and shared experiences with her sisters, Florence Cook and Sarah Lazore.

REPRESENTATION: Mohawk Craft Fund, New York.

ABOUT THE ARTIST: Herne's baskets are usually made of black-ash splints and sweet grass. She makes sewing and wastepaper baskets in natural colors. Her quilts are made in a variety of patterns.

SUE ELLEN HERNE

(a.k.a. Kwa Ne Ra Ta Ieni)
Mohawk (1960 –   ) Hogansburg, New York
Painter—oils, oil pastels, charcoal

EDUCATION: Trained at the Institute of American Indian Art (1977–1978); majored in painting at the Rhode Island School of Design.

AWARDS: First prize, Painting, New York State Fair (1976).

ABOUT THE ARTIST: Herne's work is nonrepresentational, somewhat abstract and not necessarily concerned with Iroquois tradition or style. She has exhibited at the New York State Fair and other fairs/exhibitions.

JOE H. HERRERA

(a.k.a. See Ru, "Blue Bird")
Cochiti (1923 –   ) Cochiti Pueblo, New Mexico
Artist—watercolor, casein

EDUCATION: Studied the basics with his mother, Tonita Peña, one of the first Rio Grande painters; later studied with Dorothy Dunn (Santa Fe Studio); received a Bachelor of Art in Art (1953) and a Master of Art in Art Education (1963) from the University of New Mexico. At the university, Raymond Jonson taught Herrera about cubist techniques.

ABOUT THE ARTIST: Herrera is one of the first Native American artists to win acclaim for his abstract imagery. He has acted as mentor to other artists who want to create art that is considered mainstream. He had exhibited his work all over the country, but stopped painting in 1958.

MARIAN HERRERA

Navajo (N/A) Torreon, New Mexico
Sandpainter

ABOUT THE ARTIST: In the late 1970s, Herrera painted Pollen Boy in different colors and added the four sacred plants to her painting, as well as four rainbow bars, in order to make her work different enough from the original sacred sandpainting that the Holy People would be pacified.

VELINO SHIJE HERRERA

(a.k.a. Velino Shije, Ma Pe Wi, or Oriole)
Zia (1902 – 1973) Zia Pueblo, New Mexico
Artist, illustrator

EDUCATION: Studied in Santa Fe with E. Hewett.

ABOUT THE ARTIST: Herrera was commissioned to do murals for the Albuquerque Indian School and others; illustrated books during the 1940s; had his work published in magazines such as *School Arts*, *American Magazine of Art*, and *Arizona Highways*; and in books such as *Compton's Picture Encyclopedia*. He was also commissioned to do work for the Amon Carter Museum, American Museum of Natural History, the Corcoran Gallery, the Denver Art Museum, and the Museum of New Mexico. Exhibits of his work were held at the Heard Museum in Phoenix, various tribal ceremonials, the Museum of New Mexico, and at the Southwest Museum. His works are included in private and public collections. Herrera's art career ended when he was injured for life in a car accident in the 1950s.

VALJEAN McCARTY HESSING

Choctaw (1934 –   ) Tulsa, Oklahoma
Artist—watercolor

EDUCATION: Summer program at Philbrook Museum (on scholarship at eleven years old); studied art in college at Mary Hardin-Baylor College, Texas, and Tulsa University, Oklahoma.

ABOUT THE ARTIST: Hessing is known as a master painter of horses and she also weaves narratives or stories through her paintings. Her art reflects the confusion and disillusionment through which her people suffered when on the Trail of Tears. A painting with that subject was part of an exhibit sponsored by the Cherokee Historical Center in Tahlequah, Oklahoma.

ALVA MARTIN HILL

Mohawk (1930 –   ) Hagersville, Ontario, Canada
Painter—oils

EDUCATION: Hill has taken painting classes in Cleveland, Miami, and Fort Erie.

AWARDS: First and second prizes at the Six Nations Fall Fair; many others.

ABOUT THE ARTIST: Most of Hill's paintings are still lifes or nature scenes. She mixes colors with a good sense of how they work together. Hill gives away most of her paintings.

BOBBY HILL

(a.k.a. Pau-Tain-Dae, "Whitebuffalo")
Kiowa (1933 –   ) Lawton, Oklahoma
Artist—watercolor

EDUCATION: Self-taught.

AWARDS: Grand Award, Indian Art Exhibition, Anadarko, Oklahoma (1968); many others.

ABOUT THE ARTIST: Hill began painting in 1953, then worked at several jobs, including as a commercial artist for several Oklahoma City television stations and as a scenic artist for ABC. His realistic and highly detailed work has been shown throughout the United States.

DONALD HILL

Cayuga/Tuscarora/Mohawk (1959 –   )
Lewiston, New York
Painter; carver; ceramist—pen and ink, acrylics, steatite, clay

EDUCATION: Hill is mostly self-taught, though he has taken art courses at the State University of New York at Buffalo.

ABOUT THE ARTIST: Hill exhibits his work and experiments with different media. He explores his heritage and puts what he learns into his work.

ETHEL HILL

(a.k.a. Gah Wonh Ho Donh)
Seneca (1910 –   )
Beadworker, clothing designer

EDUCATION: Self-taught.

AWARDS: Include a first prize for a woman's native dress shown at the New York State Fair in 1977.

ABOUT THE ARTIST: Hill began beading in the mid 1950s and exhibited regularly after that time. She uses her own designs for clan medallions and often takes orders for native costumes which she designs and sews herself. She taught her daughter and grandchildren the skills she had learned.

JOAN HILL

(a.k.a. Chea-se-quah, "Redbird")
Creek/Cherokee (1930 –   ) Muskogee, Oklahoma
Artist—watercolor, tempera, other media

EDUCATION: Muskogee Junior College, Oklahoma; Bachelor of Art, Northeastern University, Oklahoma; studied with W. Richard West, Bacone Junior College, Oklahoma.

AWARDS: During her career, Hill has won more than 200 awards, including ten Grand Awards and four special trophies.

ABOUT THE ARTIST: Hill was one of the first female Native American artists to become successful. Her work bridged the gap between traditional and contemporary Native American painting. A well-known artist, Hill's paintings and drawings are in many permanent museum and college collections, including the United States Department of the Interior, Washington, D.C.; the Philbrook Art Center; the Heard Museum; and the Museum of the American Indian in New York City. Her work is also held in private collections throughout the world.

RICK HILL

Tuscarora (1950 –   ) near Buffalo, New York
Painter, writer, photographer

EDUCATION: Art Institute of Chicago (1968), studied with Walker Evans and Robert Frank; Master degree in American Studies from the State University of New York in Buffalo.

AWARDS: Hill's career has brought him many honors and awards.

ABOUT THE ARTIST: Currently acting as museum director at the Institute of American Indian Arts, Hill has held many jobs throughout his diverse career. He worked for the New York State Historical Society as a photographer of Indian artists; worked in various museums in and around Buffalo, New York; coordinated the development of the new Institute of American Indian Arts museum in Santa Fe; and will be working at the National Museum of the American Indian scheduled to open in the late 1990s. Hill also curates many shows; his own work is held in a number of public and private collections throughout the world.

RITA HILL

Seneca (N/A)
Beadworker, leatherworker, quillworker, clothes designer

EDUCATION: Self-taught.

ABOUT THE ARTIST: Hill's beadwork is done by request. She makes ribbon shirts and moccasins, as well as porcupine-quill jewelry and beaded leatherwork. Her whole family is involved in the arts.

RON HILL

Oneida (1956 –   )
Painter, sculptor, silversmith

EDUCATION: Art major, Institute of American Indian Arts (1973–1974).

ABOUT THE ARTIST: Hill has been sketching since he was a young boy, has worked with a variety of other media, and has exhibited his work at annual shows.

TOM HILL

Seneca (1943 –   ) Ohsweken, Ontario, Canada
Artist—oils, acrylics, pen and ink, plastic, wood products, murals

EDUCATION: Majored in Fine Arts, Medical Illustration, and Advertising at Ontario College of Arts (1963–1967).

AWARDS: Hill has been recognized throughout Ontario for his murals and paintings.

ABOUT THE ARTIST: As a young boy, Hill was encouraged by his uncle's, Reg Hill's, dedication to art. Hill has been using his talents as an artist to promote Native American art and has been involved with the Six Nations Arts Council. His paintings and drawings sometimes express his feelings about the political situations in his community.

JACK HOKEAH

Kiowa (1902 – 1973) Kiowa Reservation in western Oklahoma
Artist—watercolor, tempera, oil

EDUCATION: University of Oklahoma (non-credit art course); Santa Fe Indian School, New Mexico

ABOUT THE ARTIST: Though Hokeah painted during the time that the Kiowa Oklahoma style was being perfected, his portraits are not often characteristic of the full-figure Kiowa style.

DELBRIDGE HONANIE

(a.k.a. Coochsiwukioma, "Falling Snow")
Hopi (1946 –   ) Arizona
Artist–acrylic; carver; sculptor

REPRESENTATION: Lovena Ohl Gallery, Scottsdale, Arizona.

ABOUT THE ARTIST: Honanie uses traditional Hopi symbols and pottery motifs in his work to link the present with the past. His sculptures are of Hopi daily life.

WATSON HONANIE

Hopi (1953 –   ) Arizona
Jeweler–often works with gold

AWARDS: Best of Classification in all jewelry categories at Santa Fe Indian Market (1991).

REPRESENTATION: Monongye's Gallery, Old Oraibi, Arizona; McGee's Indian Art, Keams Canyon, Arizona; Many Hands, Sedona, Arizona; Tanner Chaney Gallery, Albuquerque, New Mexico; Silver and Sand Trading Company, Taos, New Mexico; October Art Ltd., New York, New York; Red Rock Trading Company, Alexandria, Virginia.

ABOUT THE ARTIST: Honanie has popularized his overlay gold style. He often carves Hopi Kachinas or scenes of Hopi life into his overlay jewelry.

SHERIAN HONHONGVA

Hopi (1960 –   ) Arizona
Jeweler

EDUCATION: Honhongva apprenticed with her uncle, Charles Loloma, and studied with her sister, Verma Nequatewa.

REPRESENTATION: Lovena Ohl Gallery, Scottsdale, Arizona.

ABOUT THE ARTIST: Honhongva and her sister began exhibiting their jewelry in 1989 under the name *Sonwai*, which in Hopi means "beautiful." They worked with Loloma for twenty-three years, perfecting a skill that is distinctive and high quality.

BRIAN HONYOUTI

Hopi (N/A) Arizona
Carver–Kachinas

ABOUT THE ARTIST: Honyouti carved a Crow Mother emerging from the kiva which is said to be one of the first wood Kachinas that was only partially painted. (Howato did the other.)

Brian Honyouti's Kachina "Sheep Herder (Laiaya)," 12¼ inches tall. Courtesy of the Adobe Gallery, Albuquerque, New Mexico.

Brian Honyouti's sculpture "Hai i Wohti," 18¼ inches tall. Courtesy of the Adobe Gallery, Albuquerque, New Mexico.

CLYDE HONYOUTI

Hopi (N/A) Arizona
Carver–Kachinas

REPRESENTATION: Adobe Gallery, Albuquerque, New Mexico.

ABOUT THE ARTIST: Honyouti is the father of Brian, Loren, Ronald, and Richard. All the boys (except Richard) are Kachina carvers of the highest regard. Richard works with oak and makes traditional Hopi furniture out of that wood.

Clyde Honyouti's Kachina "Monongya (Lizard)," 7¼ inches tall, courtesy of the Adobe Gallery, Albuquerque, New Mexico.

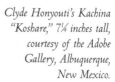

Clyde Honyouti's Kachina "Koshare," 7¼ inches tall, courtesy of the Adobe Gallery, Albuquerque, New Mexico.

LOREN HONYOUTI

Hopi (N/A) Arizona
Carver–Kachinas

AWARDS: Loren has won many awards at the Santa Fe Indian Market.

REPRESENTATION: Adobe Gallery, Albuquerque, New Mexico.

ABOUT THE ARTIST: Loren Honyouti has been a premier carver of Hopi Kachinas since learning the craft from his father, Clyde, and working with his brothers, Ronald, Brian, and Richard.

Loren Honyouti's sculpture "Tewa Maiden," 13¼ inches tall, courtesy of the Adobe Gallery, Albuquerque, New Mexico.

RONALD HONYOUTI

Hopi (N/A) Arizona
Carver–Kachinas

AWARDS: Best of Class, Gallup Inter-Tribal Ceremonial (1983).

REPRESENTATION: Adobe Gallery, Albuquerque, New Mexico.

ABOUT THE ARTIST: The brother of Brian Honyouti, Honyouti began carving after Brian. He does realistic Kachinas.

Ronald Honyouti's Kachina "Poli (Butterfly)," 10¼ inches tall, courtesy of the Adobe Gallery, Albuquerque, New Mexico.

Ronald Honyouti's Kachina "Supai Uncle," 13 inches tall, courtesy of the Adobe Gallery, Albuquerque, New Mexico.

ABOUT THE ARTIST: Hood paints Comanche scenes as they were in the past: a proud, hunting and warring people. His painting style changes as he captures images of scenes that were gone long before he was born. He began exhibiting his work in 1962 and has since shown it throughout the United States.

DAISY HOOEE
Hopi/Tewa (N/A) Arizona
Potter

EDUCATION: Hooee's grandmother, Nampeyo, taught Daisy how to paint freehand. Today, Hooee talks to young pottery artists and urges them to use the old ways instead of the commercial clay.

ABOUT THE ARTIST: Hooee still paints the same way her grandmother taught her eighty years ago.

SIDNEY HOOEE
Zuni (N/A) Arizona
Jeweler

ABOUT THE ARTIST: Hooee is a traditional Zuni craftsman.

JOHN J. HOOVER
Aleut (1919 –   ) Cordova, Arkansas
Sculptor—polychrome wood, bronze, aluminum

EDUCATION: Leon Derbyshire School of the Fine Arts, Seattle; artist-in-residence, Institute of American Indian Art, Santa Fe.

AWARDS: Hoover was asked to judge the sculpture at the Santa Fe Indian Market in 1990. He has received many awards for his sculptures, including first place at the 1978 Heard Museum show, a first award in sculpture at the 1974 Philbrook Art Center show, and many more.

REPRESENTATION: Glen Green Gallery, Santa Fe, New Mexico; Stonington Gallery, Anchorage, Alaska, and Seattle, Washington; Quintana Gallery,

RANCE HOOD
(a.k.a. Aut-Tup-Ta, "Yellow Hair")
Comanche (1941 –   ) Lawton, Oklahoma
Artist—tempera

EDUCATION: Hood's style of painting is his own, though he learned some of his technique from Blackbear Bosin's work.

AWARDS: Hood's numerous awards include First Award at the American Indian Artists Exhibition, Philbrook Art Center, Tulsa (1970) and three Grand Awards at the Indian Art Exhibits in Anadarko, Oklahoma (1968, 1969, 1971).

Portland, Oregon; Amy Burnett Gallery, Bremerton, Washington.

ABOUT THE ARTIST: Because Hoover grew up knowing little of his heritage, he soaked in the Northwest Coast's myths and legends when he became an adult. He features Indian myths, legends and shamans in his sculptured pieces. He uses traditional colors and tools in his work and experiments with his own interpretations of the ancient arts. Hoover's sculpted pieces have been exhibited all over the world.

Portrait of Hoover by Kiyoshi Yagi (c), courtesy of the artist.

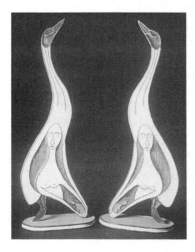

Hoover's "Loon Children," polychromed red cedar, 5 feet high x 3 feet wide, 1993, courtesy of the artist.

ALLAN C. HOUSER

(a.k.a. Haozous, "Pulling Roots")
 *Chiricahua Apache (1915–1994) Apache, Oklahoma
 Artist—painter, sculptor*

EDUCATION: Studied with the muralist Olaf Nordmark and also worked with Dorothy Dunn in Santa Fe; director of the sculpture division of the Institute of American Indian Arts (1971–1975).

AWARDS: Scholarship for sculpture and painting from John Simon Guggenheim; a Certificate of Appreciation by the IACB (Indian Arts and Crafts Board) (1967); three Grand Awards and a trophy for outstanding work in Indian art from the Santa Fe Indian School.

REPRESENTATION: American Foundation Museum, Dragoon, Arizona; Philharmonic Galleries/Philharmonic Center for the Arts, Naples, Florida; Glen Green Galleries, Santa Fe, New Mexico; Wheelwright Museum of the American Indian/Case Trading Post, Santa Fe, New Mexico.

ABOUT THE ARTIST: Houser painted murals in Indian schools such as Fort Sill, Riverside, and Jicarilla, and he sculpted the marble war memorial entitled "Comrades in Mourning" at the Haskell Institute in 1948. Exhibitions include the 1937 National Exhibition of Indian Art in New York where Houser was the only American Indian represented; the O'Hara Exhibition in Maine (1937); the New York World's Fair (1939); and one-person shows at the Chicago Art Institute, the Denver Art Museum, and others. Houser's work is held in collections such as the Fort Sill Indian School in Oklahoma, the Museum of New Mexico, the Philbrook Art Center, and the Arizona State Capitol.

WALTER HOWATO

 *Hopi (N/A) Arizona
 Carver—Kachinas*

ABOUT THE ARTIST: One of the first Kachina carvers to partially paint his figures, Howato entered his Kachina in the Santa Fe Indian Market in the early 1970s.

OSCAR HOWE

(a.k.a. Mazuha Hokshina, "Trader Boy")
*Yanktonai Sioux (1915 – 1983) Crow Creek
Reservation, South Dakota
Artist–various media*

EDUCATION: The Studio, Santa Fe Indian School, New Mexico (1935); Bachelor of Art, Dakota Wesleyan University, South Dakota; Master of Fine Art, University of Oklahoma.

REPRESENTATION: Civic Fine Arts Center, Sioux Falls, South Dakota; University of South Dakota/University Art Galleries, Vermillion, South Dakota.

ABOUT THE ARTIST: Howe's style was cubist and surreal; however, he felt that his paintings were still in the mainstream of Native American art because his need to tell the Dakota Sioux's history was stronger than any other. Howe taught that cubism and surrealism are effective ways in which to relate the mystery and power of Native American beliefs.

PENNY HUDSON

*Tuscarora (1956 –   ) Sanborn, New York
Beadworker, weaver*

EDUCATION: Learned from her mother, Doris Hudson.

AWARDS: Hudson has won numerous awards at the New York State Fair and the New York State Iroquois Conference for her beaded work.

ABOUT THE ARTIST: From a very young age, Hudson began to help her mother with beadwork and attended the New York State Fair. She uses geometric designs or clan animals to decorate. She prefers to use blacks, reds, yellows, and browns in her designs, uses both regular or cut-glass beads. Hudson does special orders.

RONDINA HUMA

*Hopi (N/A) Arizona
Potter*

ABOUT THE ARTIST: Huma believes, as do other potters, that firing problems can mean something bad will happen in the family.

JAMES HUMETEWA, JR.

(a.k.a. Saw-whu, "Morning Star")
*Hopi (1926 –   ) Arizona
Artist–watercolor*

EDUCATION: Santa Fe Indian School (1945).

ABOUT THE ARTIST: Humetewa, Jr., has painted Hopi traditions and ceremonial dances, often showing the spectators as well as the dancers. His work has been shown quite often—the first exhibit was in 1947 when the Museum of New Mexico chose his work for a one-person show.

CALVIN HUNT

*Kwakiutl (N/A) Canada
Carver*

ABOUT THE ARTIST: Hunt was responsible for carving the pole that was erected in Comox Reserve in 1989 and dedicated to Andy Frank, the past Chief of the Comox Reserve.

HENRY HUNT

*Kwakiutl (N/A) Fort Rupert, British Columbia, Canada
Carver*

EDUCATION: Learned some of his skills from his stepgrandfather-in-law, Mungo Martin. Henry passed on his own knowledge to four of his six sons.

AWARDS: His totem pole in Swartz Bay was awarded first prize in the "Route of the Totems."

ABOUT THE ARTIST: Hunt was the chief carver at the Royal British Columbia Museum in Victoria, British Columbia, for fourteen years. His totem poles of all sizes are parts of collections all over the world. He is considered one of the finest carvers in the world.

RICHARD HUNT

Kwakiutl (N/A) Fort Rupert, British Columbia,
*   Canada*
Carver

EDUCATION: Taught by his father, Henry Hunt.

ABOUT THE ARTIST: Hunt carves colorful tall and
small totem poles. He acts as head carver at the
Provincial Museum. He also makes ceremonial
potlatch masks.

TONY HUNT

Kwakiutl (1942 –   ) Alert Bay, Canada
Carver

EDUCATION: Learned from his parents and apprenticed with his uncle, Mungo Martin, master carver,
for ten years. His father, Henry Hunt, was also a
master carver.

REPRESENTATION: Orca Art Gallery, Chicago, Illinois; personal gallery in the Northwest.

ABOUT THE ARTIST: Hunt works in the Northwest
Coast style. He carves certain animals, fish, birds,
and other symbols. Hunt has passed on the skills
he has to others who have become accomplished
carvers. His work has been featured in exhibits held
around the world; he has also carved totem poles
for Mexican, European, and South American cities
and universities. Hunt has done work for the Royal
British Columbia Museum. One of his poles,
located in Sidney on Vancouver Island, is on the
"Route of the Totems."

DOUG HYDE

Nez Percé/Chippewa/Assiniboin (1946 –   )
*   North Dakota*
Sculptor–stone, wood, bronze

EDUCATION: Influenced by his mentor, Allan
Houser; Institute of American Indian Art in Santa
Fe, New Mexico.

REPRESENTATION: Hahn Gallery, Philadelphia,
Pennsylvania.

ABOUT THE ARTIST: Hyde does not have a particular idea what his subject is going to be when he
begins a project. Instead, he lets the material with
which he is working suggest a design. Like other
Native American artists, Hyde depicts the legends
and rituals of his people in his work.

JERRY INGRAM

Choctaw (1941 –   ) Oklahoma
Artist–watercolor; beadworker; lithographer; graphic
*   artist*

EDUCATION: Chilocco Indian School, Oklahoma;
Institute of American Indian Arts (1963); Bache-
lor of Art in Commercial Art, Oklahoma State
Tech (1966).

AWARDS: Ingram's first award was an Honorable
Mention in the 1966 Annual American Indian
Artists Exhibition at the Philbrook Art Center; it
was the beginning of many awards and honors.

REPRESENTATION: SunWest Silver, Albuquerque,
New Mexico.

ABOUT THE ARTIST: Ingram has been exposed to
many different Indian cultures and has relayed their

Portrait of Ingram, courtesy of the artist and SunWest Silver,
Albuquerque, New Mexico.

82

Ingram's Sioux Style Bonnet, courtesy of the artist and SunWest Silver, Albuquerque, New Mexico.

mystic religious rites and customs through his art. He paints both historical and contemporary scenes in what may be described as a romantic style. A "peyote school" painter, Ingram is one of the most experimental in Indian art. Ingram is also well known for his prizewinning beadwork. He has done shows all over the world and is included in many books on the subject of art.

GŌWÁ DJŌWA ALSEA ISAACS

(a.k.a. Gonwaka 'son)
*Cayuga (1959 –   ) Ohsweken, Ontario, Canada
Beadworker*

EDUCATION: Learned how to bead from her father.

ABOUT THE ARTIST: Isaacs' family ran a crafts shop called Iroqcrafts. She learned at a young age to do beadwork and tend the store. She chooses to work with pony beads and large beads which she strings on sinew to make chokers, earrings, yoke necklaces, and danglers. Isaacs often uses bone, brass,

and glass beads, as well as leather, shell, or beaded rosettes.

MAGGIE AND VERNON JACK

*Penelakut (N/A) Penelakut Reserve, British
Columbia, Canada
Basketmaker*

ABOUT THE ARTISTS: This husband-and-wife team collect the cedar roots for the baskets Maggie creates. Vernon prepares the bark for her and often makes canoe bailers out of leftover pieces.

JIM JACKSON

*Klamath Modoc (1963 –   ) Klamath Falls, Oregon
Sculptor–clay, bronze*

EDUCATION: Mostly self-taught; took some classes at the Institute of American Indian Arts and Portland Community College.

AWARDS: Jackson's awards are many, including first, second, and third places, honorable mention, and

Jackson's limited edition "Whispers in the Wind," bronze casting, 30 x 16 x 8 inches, courtesy of the artist.

best craftsman awards from such places as the Lawrence, Kansas, Indian Art Show; the South West American Indian Art Market, Santa Fe; the Red Earth Art Show; and many others.

ABOUT THE ARTIST: Jackson's bronze and clay sculptures are in much demand by collectors throughout the United States. His work usually represents traditional tribal members in lifelike stances.

MARY JACKSON
Sechelt (N/A) British Columbia, Canada
Basketmaker

ABOUT THE ARTIST: Jackson collects the cedar roots, wild cherry bark, and white straw to make her lidded, hamper-style baskets.

ROBERT JACKSON
Gitksan (N/A) British Columbia, Canada
Carver

ABOUT THE ARTIST: Jackson carves and decorates masks. Often the masks have carved beards which represent beaks.

ARNOLD JACOBS
(a.k.a. Nah-Gwa-Say)
Cayuga (1942 –   ) Ohsweken, Ontario, Canada
Painter—oils, acrylics

EDUCATION: Jacobs has taken special art classes at Central Technical School in Toronto.

AWARDS: Jacobs has shown his work from Canada to Cuba and won honors and recognition for it.

ABOUT THE ARTIST: Jacobs developed his artistic skill in the commercial art field. Though he has worked with all types of media, he prefers oils and acrylics. His style varies from very modern to realistic. His work usually includes the symbols of the earth and sky, the spiritual forces which are vital to him. His painting "Creation" was used by the Iroquois Museum to raise funds to publish its directory of artists.

CONNIE JACOBS
Mohawk (1936 –   ) Caughnawaga, Quebec, Canada
Beadworker

EDUCATION: Self-taught.

REPRESENTATION: Kanawake Handicrafts Workshop, Quebec, Canada.

ABOUT THE ARTIST: Jacobs began beading on velvet in 1976 and uses only floral designs. She uses her mother's patterns and lets her daughter watch her work so that she will learn how to continue the tradition.

EMILY JACOBS
Oneida (1923 –   )
Beadworker

EDUCATION: Self-taught.

ABOUT THE ARTIST: Jacobs makes beaded medallions, jewelry, neckties, belts, moccasins, and other items. She does both regular and loom beading to create her own designs and patterns. She likes using a lot of white beads in her work, but lets the customer choose the colors if they order a particular item.

MARY SCOTT JABOBS
(a.k.a. Kanekenhawi)
Mohawk (1907 –   ) Caughnawaga, Quebec, Canada
Beadworker, leatherworker, costume designer, quilter

EDUCATION: Self-taught.

ABOUT THE ARTIST: Jacobs has exhibited all over Canada and the United States and has sold her work in her own shop as well as door-to-door. She beads velvet and satin cushions and change purses, makes leather moccasins, beadwork medallions, designs Native costumes, and sews quilts which have Indian designs. She is active in the community; she was elected one of the first women counselors in 1964 and has been president of the Retarded Children Association.

ALVIN JAMES, SR.
(a.k.a. Makya)
Hopi (N/A)
Carver

ABOUT THE ARTIST: James, Sr., creates lifelike features on his Kachinas and does not cover the wood's natural qualities. He was one of the first to produce bronze castings of his work.

MARTHA JAMES
Salish (N/A) Skwaw Reserve, Chilliwack, British Columbia, Canada
Weaver

ABOUT THE ARTIST: James's rugs often have a narrative story woven into them.

JACQUELINE "MIDGE" JAMISON
Mohawk (1934 –) Irving, New York
Beadworker, dollmaker

EDUCATION: Self-taught.

ABOUT THE ARTIST: Jamison learned how to do beadwork in the 1960s, preferring variety in all she does. She does most of her beadwork in the winter, creating medallions, necklaces, Indian head rings, watchbands, wristbands, and pincushions. She also makes stand-up cornhusk dolls.

G. PETER JEMISON
Cattaraugus Seneca (1945 –) Silver Creek, New York
Artist; illustrator—acrylic, various other media

EDUCATION: Bachelor of Science in Art Education, the State University of New York in Buffalo (1967); studied Italian art and culture at University of Siena, Italy; self-imposed learning of Native culture from his own people.

ABOUT THE ARTIST: Jemison is considered one of the most active artists in the Northeast. He is dedicated to preserving Indian art and culture, has illustrated *The Iroquois and the Founding of the American Nation*, has established community programs for Native Americans, has directed the gallery of the American Indian Community House in New York City, and is a member of the New York State Iroquois Conference. Jemison's style emerged from the different types of training he has had, which show his love for Matisse's cut-paper works as well as his fascination in his own heritage. He continues to experiment with different artistic expressions.

THERESA JEMISON
(a.k.a. Teres Kanawiosta)
Mohawk (1918 –) Basom, New York
Basketmaker, beadworker

EDUCATION: Learned some of her basketmaking skills from her mother and grandmother and learned loom beadwork at the National Youth Association Training Camp.

ABOUT THE ARTIST: Jemison has lectured on the art of basketry, taught the art, and has owned her own craft shop. She has been recognized in local publications. Her baskets are made from black-ash splints. Jemison also does loom beadwork, occasionally making a piece for one of her friends. She has taught the Mohawk language and continually researches her heritage.

DOREEN JENSEN
Gitksan (N/A) British Columbia, Canada
Carver

ABOUT THE ARTIST: Jensen creates masks that are often decorated with paint, bark fringes, and human hair.

EDWARD JIM
Navajo (N/A) Shonto, Arizona
Sandpainter

ABOUT THE ARTIST: Jim paints subjects that use symbols from the Native American Church, like his portrait of a sacred deer depicted with cloud symbols, a wand, and sacred hoof prints.

MATILDA JIM

Mount Currie (1890? –   ) Mount Currie,
British Columbia, Canada
Basketmaker

EDUCATION: Jim learned her skills from fellow family members.

ABOUT THE ARTIST: Jim continued making baskets until she was well over 100 years old. Her daughter, Julianna Williams, learned the art from Jim.

THOMAS JIM

Navajo (1955 –   ) Arizona
Jeweler

REPRESENTATION: Lovena Ohl Gallery, Scottsdale, Arizona; Waddell Trading Company, Tempe, Arizona; Packard's Indian Trading Co., Inc., Santa Fe, New Mexico; Gilcrease Museum Gift Shop, Tulsa, Oklahoma.

ABOUT THE ARTIST: Jim's work is often made of silver-stamped beads which he chisels, stamps, and files with decorations.

FIDELIA JIMERSON

Seneca (1915 –   )
Beadworker, clothing designer, dollmaker, basketmaker

EDUCATION: Jimerson is mostly self-taught; however, she learned basketry from her grandmother and how to work with cornhusks from her grandmother and Dorothy Jimerson.

ABOUT THE ARTIST: Jimerson, a well-known speaker on Indian traditions, music, and dance, is also a talented craftsperson. She has made and sold baskets; began doing beadwork in the late 1940s; makes native clothing, and moccasins; and makes beaded cloth picture frames. She and her husband were very involved with Longhouse affairs and have taught the Seneca language and Iroquois culture at high schools and colleges in New York, Pennsylvania, and Massachusetts.

MARGARET JIMMIE

Salish (N/A) Squialla Reserve, British Columbia,
Canada
Weaver

ABOUT THE ARTIST: Jimmie often weaves rugs with typical Northwest Coast designs (i.e., the Eagle).

THERESA JIMMIE

Salish (N/A) Squialla Reserve, British Columbia,
Canada
Weaver

ABOUT THE ARTIST: Jimmie has taught the art of spinning, knitting, and weaving to the Salish Weavers.

CHRISTINA JOCK

(a.k.a. Ka Wennite)
Mohawk (1920 –   ) Hogansburg, New York
Basketmaker, leatherworker, beadworker, quillworker

EDUCATION: Learned her basketry skills from her mother; Malone School of Practical Nursing (1968); Associate of Art in Education, Mater Dei College (1975).

ABOUT THE ARTIST: Jock began selling Iroquois baskets in the 1960s and creating hampers and other types of baskets. She sometimes dyes her own splints and usually uses sweet grass. In addition, this multitalented artist makes pipestone and *heishi* shell necklaces, and sometimes uses glass beads. She is also dedicated to teaching the Mohawk language to others and passing on her skills to whomever wants to learn.

WILLIE JOCK

(a.k.a. Shaklunia)
Mohawk (1946 –   ) Hogansburg, New York
Painter—acrylics, watercolors, tempera, pen and
ink, hide

EDUCATION: Jock took some art courses in high school, but is mostly self-taught.

ABOUT THE ARTIST: Jock has exhibited his work at the Native American Center for Living Arts, as well as at other shows/exhibitions. His work is held in private collections and his cartoons have been published. His work usually involves painting wildlife and nature scenes on deerhide or moosehide that is stretched on barn board.

VELMA JOCKO
(a.k.a. Kahontawakon)
Mohawk (1927 –   ) Hogansburg, New York
Leatherworker; beadworker; artist—pencil, watercolor

EDUCATION: Learned the basics of leatherwork and beadwork from her father.

AWARDS: Awards include a blue ribbon for a purse exhibited at the New York State Fair in 1978.

REPRESENTATION: Kanesatake Indian Arts & Crafts, Oka, Quebec.

ABOUT THE ARTIST: Jocko makes a variety of items, often using designs inspired by nature or traditional Iroquois patterns. She uses a raised beadwork technique and decorates vests, pocketbooks, pouches, and moccasins. She is also an artist who draws or paints nature scenes. Jocko often exhibits at the New York State Fair and takes individual orders to work on at home.

EUGENE JOE
Navajo (N/A) Shiprock, Arizona
Sandpainting

ABOUT THE ARTIST: Joe has attempted to move the art of sandpainting into the realm of fine arts. His still lifes are often drawn from the crafts of the Southwest (i.e., pottery, fetishes, baskets).

EVELYN JOE
Cowichan (N/A) Comiaken Reserve, British
Columbia, Canada
Knitter

ABOUT THE ARTIST: Joe, like many women of her reserve, cards the wool personally and spins it before knitting.

GRACE JOE
Navajo (1908 –   ) Red Valley, Arizona
Weaver

EDUCATION: Learned how to weave from her aunt, Louise Chee; Grace's mother taught her the finer points.

ABOUT THE ARTIST: Joe sold her first rug when she was twenty and has supported herself and her family by weaving ever since.

JAMES JOE
Navajo (N/A) Shiprock, New Mexico
Sandpainter

REPRESENTATION: The Heard Museum, Phoenix, Arizona.

ABOUT THE ARTIST: In 1965, Joe made the first nontraditional sandpainting. He is known for creating a sandpainting of Water Creature from Beautyway, a figure most Navajos will not recreate. He also teaches others the technique of sandpainting.

MONICA JOE
Cowichan (N/A) Comiaken Reserve, British
Columbia, Canada
Knitter

EDUCATION: Joe has been knitting all of her life and has passed on her skills to other members of her family.

ABOUT THE ARTIST: Joe knits sweaters and other items.

ORELAND JOE
Ute/Navajo (N/A)
Sculptor—stone, bronze

REPRESENTATION: Pierce Fine Art, Santa Fe, New Mexico.

ABOUT THE ARTIST: Joe formed a group of fledgling artists called "Eagles in Flight" in Shiprock, Arizona.

ELAINE JOHN
Seneca (1945 –   )
Beadworker

EDUCATION: Learned from her aunt, Rose John.

ABOUT THE ARTIST: John is quite active in Seneca Nation affairs. She began to do beadwork at age nine and has learned some new techniques since then. She had also learned the rudimentary skills of making baskets and hopes to continue making them.

ESTELLA JOHN
Seneca (1924 –   ) Salamanca, New York
Beadworker, dollmaker, leatherworker

EDUCATION: Learned how to do bead and leatherwork at Thomas Indian School in Cattaragus and took cornhusk classes.

ABOUT THE ARTIST: John creates a wide variety of freehand and loom beadwork patterns, including floral, star, and clan medallions. She dresses her cornhusk dolls in traditional Iroquois costumes. She attends a number of fairs to sell her work and also takes individual orders.

ISABELL JOHN
Navajo (1933 –   ) Many Farms, Arizona
Weaver

EDUCATION: Learned how to weave when she was about eight years old.

AWARDS: Many of John's rugs have been prize winners.

ABOUT THE ARTIST: John creates pictorial rugs that often feature the *yeibeichai* ceremonials. She hopes to keep the Navajo identity and traditions alive through her rugs and to show people what the Navajo people are all about. She was the first to put people, animals, and landscapes into her rugs in the 1970s, but other weavers quickly imitated her. Sometimes John's rugs are signed, but their large size and distinctive pictorals give her little need to do so.

JIMMY JOHN
Nootka (approximately 1873 – 1987) Friendly
Cove, British Columbia, Canada
Carver

EDUCATION: Learned how to carve from family members and passed his skills on to his son, Norman John.

ABOUT THE ARTIST: John, a direct descendant of Chief Maquinna, carved for close to 100 years. He was estimated to be 114 years old when he died. His body of works include masks, headdresses, totem poles, and feastbowls.

NORMAN JOHN
Nootka (N/A) Friendly Cove, British Columbia,
Canada
Carver

EDUCATION: Learned most of his carving skills from his father, Jimmy John.

ABOUT THE ARTIST: John assisted his father in carving some of the larger totem poles, such as the one in Nanaimo on the north end of the Pearson Bridge. It is one of the poles on the "Route of the Totems."

ROSE JOHN
Seneca (1924 –   ) Salamanca, New York
Beadworker

EDUCATION: Learned how to work with beads from a bead importer.

REPRESENTATION: Bear Skin Trading Company, New York.

ABOUT THE ARTIST: Most of John's work is done with only one hand because she has been confined to her bed with rheumatoid arthritis for many years.

DAVID JOHNS
Navajo (N/A)
Painter

EDUCATION: Northern Arizona University, concentration in printmaking.

AWARDS: Lovena Ohl Foundation Award (1979), and others.

REPRESENTATION: Lovena Ohl Gallery, Scottsdale, Arizona

ABOUT THE ARTIST: Johns began painting full-time in 1980 and presented his fifth collection at the Lovena Ohl Gallery in the fall of 1984. A young, prolific painter, he is gaining a national reputation. His portraits of Navajo faces are drawn from his imagination.

GEORGE JOHNS
Navajo (N/A) Farmington, New Mexico
Sandpainter

ABOUT THE ARTIST: Johns is a master at working with sand and in 1977 was commissioned to do a portrait of Jesus Christ. The portrait was done in such detail that some of the grains of sand were laid individually to create contours on the face.

MARGARET JOHNS
Navajo (N/A) Farmington, New Mexico
Sandpainter

ABOUT THE ARTIST: Johns creates sandpaintings that often depict still lifes. She is one painter who hopes that the Navajo art will escalate in importance and artistic value.

DARLA JOHNSON
Seneca (1945 –) Salamanca, New York
Beadworker, featherworker, costume designer,
dollmaker, painter

EDUCATION: Self-taught.

ABOUT THE ARTIST: Johnson began doing loom beadwork when she was seven and wanted to learn how to work with leather when she saw her father working. As a child, Johnson did beadwork for the Indian Village in Onoville, then stopped for a while. When she became a member of the Allegany Indian Arts & Crafts Coop, Johnson began beading again. She has made beaded medallions, chokers, necklaces, earrings, belts, hatbands, headbands, watchbands and leatherwork clothing. She also creates feathered war bonnets, fancy dance costumes, bone and bead chokers, and cornhusk dolls. She also paints.

JOYCE JOHNSON
Cherokee/Mississippi Choctaw (1928 –) Tulsa,
Oklahoma
Basketmaker—buckbush, oak, honeysuckle, reed

EDUCATION: In 1978, when a person was brought in to teach couples how to make baskets, Johnson

Portrait of Johnson and her work, courtesy of the artist.

was taught basketry at Mulberry Tree in the Cherokee Nation.

REPRESENTATION: Gilcrease Museum, Tulsa, Oklahoma; Philbrook Museum, Tulsa, Oklahoma; Okmulgee Creek Museum, Okmulgee, Oklahoma; Red River Indian Museum, Bartleville, Oklahoma; Davis Museum, Claremare, Oklahoma; Seminole Museum, Wewoka, Oklahoma; Natchez Indian Museum, Natchez, Michigan.

ABOUT THE ARTIST: An experienced basketweaver, Johnson takes her knowledge to groups, schools, and museums, offering demonstrations and lectures of the art. She was taught how to gather natural dyes to color her basketry materials. All of her baskets are double weave, which makes them stronger. Johnson believes the spirit of the Creator goes into each and every basket she makes and that the spirit travels with the basket to each owner.

TRACY JOHNSON
(a.k.a. Ahosta)
> *Tuscarora (1940 —) Lewiston, New York*
> *Carver; beadworker; leatherworker;*
> *collagemaker—acrylics, deerskin, leather, bone,*
> *stone, quills, feathers, horsehair, fur, ermine tails,*
> *beads, ironwood, elk, moose horn, caribou*

EDUCATION: Johnson learned most of his skills by watching his parents, Norma and Tracy Johnson.

ABOUT THE ARTIST: Johnson draws on his heritage to make various items, such as cradleboards, collages, clan staffs, pipe bowls, knife cases, and bracelets. His family is also active in the arts. He has exhibited his work throughout the Northeast.

JOE JOJOLA
> *Isleta (1945-) Isleta Pueblo, New Mexico*
> *Jeweler, silversmith*

EDUCATION: Self-taught silversmith; Santa Monica City College; New Mexico State University (Associate Degree Undesignated); Bachelor of Science in Liberal Arts, Regents College, New York.

Portrait of Joe Jojola at work. Photograph by Ann-Marie Jojola, courtesy of the artist.

REPRESENTATION: Jojola represents himself, has been a member of the IACA (Indian Arts and Crafts Association) since 1980, and usually works on order.

ABOUT THE ARTIST: Jojola started silversmithing as a young man and continued his craft while stationed in Germany with the Army. His work has been featured by the Indian Arts and Crafts Association. He makes custom-ordered jewelry, belt buckles, rings, necklaces, and watchbands for his clients using both old and modern tools. To help his customers with decisions, Jojola provides a photo package (for a fee) and also registers the work.

TONY JOJOLA
> *Isleta (early 1960s —)*
> *Glassmaker*

EDUCATION: Apprenticed under hot-glass artist Dale Chihuly at the Pilchuk Glass School (1980–1981).

REPRESENTATION: Jan Cicero Gallery, Chicago, Illinois.

ABOUT THE ARTIST: Jojola began working with hot glass in the late 1970s and has continued to improve on what he learned in his apprenticeships with various glassmakers. He got his inspiration from his maternal grandfather, Patricio Olguin, who was a silversmith, carver and beekeeper. Jojola's work reflects his knowledge of traditional Pueblo pottery and has been exhibited throughout the country.

Tony Jojola's hot glass vase in blue. Photograph by Robert Reck, courtesy of the artist and Jan Cicero Gallery, Chicago, Illinois.

EVELYN JONATHAN

Seneca (1934 –   )
Beadworker, quillworker

EDUCATION: Jonathan took classes at the Tonawanda Indian Community House.

ABOUT THE ARTIST: Jonathan has exhibited her work quite regularly and has passed on the skills she has learned to others. She makes beaded jewelry that is often decorated with geometric and floral designs. In addition, she does appliqué beadwork on clothing and is investigating other crafts.

PETER B. JONES

Onondaga/Seneca/Iroquois Confederacy (N/A)
Potter—ceramic, stoneware, clay

ABOUT THE ARTIST: Jones creates mystical serene figures.

LOUISE JOSEPH

Okanagan/Hagwilget (N/A) near New Hazelton, British Columbia, Canada
Beadworker

ABOUT THE ARTIST: Works with beadwork designs, sometimes sewing rabbit fur or other such decoration on pieces created for special occasions.

CHARLENE JUAN

Tohono O'odham (N/A)
Basketmaker

ABOUT THE ARTIST: Juan weaves miniature baskets.

HARRISON JUAN

Dineh (N/A) Lake Valley, New Mexico
Potter; painter; sculptor; carver—etchings, airbrush work, watercolors, oils, acrylics, stone, wood, sand

EDUCATION: Associate of Art in Elementary Education/Recreation.

AWARDS: Juan's awards include first place honors in Woodburning Art and Pencil Sketch, Oil/Acrylic (Mixed) and Painting at the Indian Arts Festival in Farmington, New Mexico (1994).

REPRESENTATION: Native Reflections, Salt Lake City, Utah.

Portrait of Juan, courtesy of the artist and Native Reflections, Salt Lake City, Utah.

91

ABOUT THE ARTIST: Juan is of the Mountain Clan and the Folding Arm People. He has been commissioned to do murals at La Vida Mission in New Mexico. A versatile artist, Juan does shows in New Mexico and has sold his work to collectors all over the United States.

MARIE JUANICO

Acoma (N/A) Acoma Pueblo, New Mexico
Potter

EDUCATION: Learned from her mother, Delores Sanchez.

REPRESENTATION: Robert F. Nichols Gallery, Canyon Road, Santa Fe, New Mexico.

ABOUT THE ARTIST: Juanico began making pottery at age four. Today she incorporates both traditional and complex Mimbres designs into her work, passing on what she has learned to her daughter, Delores Aragon. Juanico digs and mixes her own clay, makes her own colors, and creates her pots by hand. She strongly believes that Acoma potters should return to original, traditional techniques and use their ancient language, Tewa.

ELLEN JUMBO

Northwest Coast (N/A) Port Alberni, British
Columbia, Canada
Basketmaker

ABOUT THE ARTIST: Jumbo creates smaller decorated baskets which often have lids.

JULIA JUMBO

Navajo (1929 –) Newcomb, New Mexico
Weaver

EDUCATION: Learned how to weave from her mother.

ABOUT THE ARTIST: Jumbo sold her first rug at age twenty and has had continued success with her weavings. She keeps her own herd of sheep, shears

them, then prepares the wool to make her textiles. She specializes in smaller, superfine weavings.

LENA JUMBO

Northwest Coast (N/A) Ahousat, British
Columbia, Canada
Basketmaker

EDUCATION: Her grandmother started to teach her how to weave when Jumbo was five.

ABOUT THE ARTIST: Jumbo often creates pocketbook-style baskets complete with zippers and decorated with eagles, whales, and other typical Northwest Coast designs.

JOSEPH KABANCE

Potawatomi (1945 –) Horton, Kansas
Artist—mixed media

EDUCATION: Studied art ceramics at the Institute of American Indian Arts, Santa Fe (1963–1964); majored in art, Fort Lewis College, Durango, Colorado (1964–1965); Bachelor of Art in Sociology, Wichita State University, Wichita, Kansas (1965–1970).

AWARDS: Kabance's awards include first place in a ceramic competition at the South Dakota State Fair (1961–1963).

ABOUT THE ARTIST: Kabance's work has been exhibited both at one-person and group shows. He has an almost abstract style that reminds one of *trompe d'oleil* and uses various types of media to create his art.

FRED KABOTIE

(a.k.a. Fred Nakavoma, "Day After Day")
Hopi (1900 – 1986) Shungopovi, Second Mesa,
Arizona
Artist; illustrator—various media; jeweler; silversmith

EDUCATION: Studied at Santa Fe Indian School and encouraged to explore art as a career by school superintendent John DeHuff; went to Santa Fe

High School (1925); studied at the Museum of New Mexico; took private lessons from Mrs. J. D. DeHuff of Santa Fe.

ABOUT THE ARTIST: Kabotie illustrated several picture books in the 1930s, worked for the Heye Foundation, and painted murals for some of the Fred Harvey Company's hotels. Kabotie painted the ceremonies and traditions of his people. He taught and/or inspired young artists to be innovative, as well as to continue the Hopi artistic traditions. He is the best-known artist of the 1920s and is thought to be responsible for bringing traditional Indian painting to the forefront and gaining the support of wealthy collectors.

MICHAEL KABOTIE
(a.k.a. Lomawywesa, "Walking in Harmony")
Hopi (1942 –) Shungopavi, Second Mesa, Arizona
Artist—mixed media

EDUCATION: Learned some of his technique from his father, painter and silversmith Fred Kabotie; studied with Southwest Indian Art Project, University of Arizona, Tucson; graduated from the Haskell Institute in Lawrence, Kansas (1961).

REPRESENTATION: Lovena Ohl Gallery, Scottsdale, Arizona; Kopavi International, Sedona, Arizona.

ABOUT THE ARTIST: Kabotie paints petroglyph images that reiterate basic Hopi beliefs and traditions. Symbols of Kabotie's Hopi ancestors, such as clan symbols, rain clouds, snow, and other signs, are often incorporated into his paintings. He was one of the founders of The Artist Hopid in 1973. Kabotie's work has been exhibited throughout the United States, both in solo and group shows.

BENNETT KAGENVEAMA
Hopi (1964 –) Arizona
Jeweler

REPRESENTATION: Waddell Trading Company, Tempe, Arizona; The Indian Craft Shop, Washington, D.C.

ABOUT THE ARTIST: Kagenveama often creates silver overlay pieces decorated with Kachinas and other Hopi motifs.

MARCELLA KAHE
Hopi (N/A) Arizona
Potter

ABOUT THE ARTIST: Kahe is the mother of Karen Kahe Charley and taught her daughter the art of potting. Kahe has shown her work at most of the Southwestern markets.

RODERICK KASKALLA AND LELA ROMERO
Roderick—Zuni (1955 –) Zuni Pueblo, New Mexico
Lela—Nambé/Cherokee (N/A)
Jewelers

EDUCATION: Kaskalla learned silversmithing by watching his aunts, Rose Hustito and Perlita Boone. His grandmother, Mabel Lonjose, introduced him to channel inlay work. He also took some modern art courses at Fort Lewis College.

AWARDS: One of Kaskalla's bracelets is on permanent exhibit at the Albuquerque International Airport.

ABOUT THE ARTISTS: Kaskalla creates abstract, clean-edged patterns for his jewelry. His work follows the Zuni roots and he uses colors to indicate the six directions of that culture (north, west, east, south, zenith, and nadir). His wife, Lela Romero, often assists him.

RENA KAVENA
Hopi (N/A) Arizona
Potter

ABOUT THE ARTIST: Kavena has days when she believes the clay knows she is not interested in working. The tendency to be in tune with the creation has been passed on to others in her family, particularly her granddaughter, Tracy.

93

TRACY KAVENA
Hopi (N/A) Arizona
Potter

EDUCATION: Learned her skills from her grandmother, Rena.

ABOUT THE ARTIST: Like potters before her, Kavena talks to the clay and believes that it has life. She feeds her pottery fire with sheep dung brought from the Navajo. When Kavena tried to use commercial paintbrushes, the Hopi paint ate through them, so she returned to using the traditional yucca brush.

ERNIE KEAHBONE
(a.k.a. To-Gem-Hote, "Blue Jay")
Kiowa (1933 –   ) Anadarko, Oklahoma
Artist—casein on illustration board

EDUCATION: Self-taught artist who began painting in 1966.

AWARDS: Keahbone's many awards include the First Award in the Amateur Division, Indian Art Exhibit, at the American Indian Exposition in 1966.

ABOUT THE ARTIST: Keahbone is a member of the Ton-Kon-Ko Black Leggings Warrior Society. His simplistic, folk-art style is reminiscent of the ledger drawings of the Plains Indians. He has exhibited his work in group and one-person shows throughout the United States.

GEORGE KEAHBONE
(a.k.a. Asaute)
Kiowa (1916 –   ) Oklahoma
Artist—watercolor

EDUCATION: Santa Fe Indian School; Taos Valley School of Art.

ABOUT THE ARTIST: Keahbone has painted the Kiowa people as they were in the past. After his marriage, he lived with his wife's people at the Taos Pueblo.

MAUDE KEGG
Ojibwa (N/A) Minnesota
Beadworker

ABOUT THE ARTIST: Kegg weaves beads into floral, leaf, and geometric patterns in the Great Lakes tradition.

JOSEPHINE KELLY
Salish (N/A) Soowahlie Reserve, British Columbia, Canada
Weaver

EDUCATION: Kelly learned the art of weaving from Oliver Wells. He researched the art and revived it by sharing what he had learned with the local women.

ABOUT THE ARTIST: Kelly works with the Salish Weavers, often cooperating with the others by sharing dyes or other tools. She makes her own dye and explains that the time of year determines what colors she will get from particular plants.

BEATRICE KENTON
Apache (N/A)
Basketmaker

ABOUT THE ARTIST: Kenton incorporates traditional animal, figural, and geometric designs into her burden baskets.

CELESTE (ROONEY) KETTLE
Seneca (1956 –   )
Beadworker, clothes designer, quillworker

EDUCATION: Learned from parents; self-taught.

ABOUT THE ARTIST: Rooney began making beadwork pieces in the tenth grade and continued to expand her repertoire after that time. She has mastered the challenge of weaving porcupine-quill designs into leather and cloth, and also draws and does some fingerweaving.

IVY KIBBE
(a.k.a. Wasontiio)
Mohawk (1949 –)
Beadworker, leatherworker

EDUCATION: Most of what Kibbe knows was learned from her mother; she has also attended classes for beadwork and leather tooling.

ABOUT THE ARTIST: Both of Kibbe's parents, as well as her siblings, have been involved in Iroquois arts. Kibbe uses Indian designs and flowers on her loomwork and leather pieces.

MICHAEL LACAPA
Apache/Hopi/Tewa (N/A)
Painter, storyteller

REPRESENTATION: Sage Brush Limited Editions, Flagstaff, Arizona.

ABOUT THE ARTIST: Lacapa's traditions are as much incorporated into his paintings as they are into the stories he tells to classrooms full of children. He has illustrated and authored children's books. Many of the prints from those books have been made into limited editions.

GREG LA FORME
Onondaga (1963 –)
Artist—oils, watercolors, acrylics, tempera, pen and ink

EDUCATION: Buffalo Academy of Visual and Performing Arts.

ABOUT THE ARTIST: LaForme is experimenting with his work to develop his individual style.

PRESLEY LA FOUNTAIN
Chippewa (1956 –) Lynwood, California
Sculptor, carver

EDUCATION: Mostly self-taught.

AWARDS: One of the first awards LaFountain won was "Most Promising Young Sculptor and Carver"

at the 65th Annual Indian Market/Wheelwright Museum Award in 1986. Since then, he has been honored many times.

REPRESENTATION: SunWest Silver, Albuquerque, New Mexico.

ABOUT THE ARTIST: LaFountain works with stone and is often amazed at how pieces come together naturally. He used black African wonderstone in his sculpture "Night Wind" and has also used Utah alabaster and other stones. He states that he "carve(s) deliberately without detail; I carve shadows, using shadows as lines. I don't want to carve just beautiful objects . . . I want to carve a whole spectrum of emotions."

La Fountain's sculpture of eagle in alabaster, courtesy of the artist and SunWest Silver, Albuquerque, New Mexico.

DOROTHY K. LAHACHE
(a.k.a. Kawannes)
Mohawk (1954 –) Caughnawaga, Quebec, Canada
Painter, beadworker, leatherworker, silversmith, carver

EDUCATION: Elaine Lahache, Dorothy's mother, taught her some of her skills. Dorothy was also an arts major at Manitou Community College.

AWARDS: Lahache's career has been recognized with awards for her painting, beadwork, and dancing.

ABOUT THE ARTIST: Lahache's work has been exhibited, but it is not for sale. She does not title any of her work.

ELGIN W. LAMARR

Wichita (1918 –   ) Anadarko, Oklahoma
Artist–oil

EDUCATION: Studied Art Education and Music at the University of Tulsa (1945–1949); graduate studies at the same school (1950).

ABOUT THE ARTIST: Lamarr has passed on his skill to younger generations by teaching at the Indian City Pottery Works in Anadarko, Oklahoma. An abstract artist, he also has worked as a commercial illustrator.

JEAN LAMARR

Pitt River / Paiute (1945 –   ) Susanville,
California
Photographer, artist–mixed media

EDUCATION: Philco-Ford Technical Institute, Santa Clara, California; San Jose City College, California; University of California, Berkeley.

REPRESENTATION: Jerome Evans Gallery, Lake Tahoe, Nevada.

ABOUT THE ARTIST: Lamarr has created art in response to anniversaries (i.e. Christopher Columbus's arrival in America) and combines his photographs with other media.

MADELINE LAMSON

Hopi (N/A)
Basketmaker

AWARDS: Won Best of Show (1986) at the Annual Museum of Northern Arizona Hopi Artist's Exhibition.

ABOUT THE ARTIST: Lamson creates traditionally coiled Hopi baskets and trays.

MARIE LAPAHIE

Navajo (1938 –   ) Toadlena, New Mexico
Weaver

EDUCATION: Learned how to weave from Daisy Taugelchee, a well-known weaver. Lapahie's sisters, Virginia Deal and Elizabeth Mute, are also weavers.

ABOUT THE ARTIST: Though she started weaving at age ten, Lapahie sold her first rug at age fifteen. She often uses a light-pink wool made from the belly of a newborn lamb.

FRANK LAPENA

Nomtipom Wintu (1937 –   ) San Francisco,
California
Artist–acrylic, various media; poet; writer

EDUCATION: Bachelor of Art, California State College, Chico (1965); Life Issue, Teaching Credential, San Francisco State University, California; Master of Art in Anthropology from California State University, Sacramento.

AWARDS: LaPena has exhibited in solo and group shows since 1960, winning numerous honors. His work is held in permanent collections of the Heard Museum; the Indian Arts and Crafts Board in Washington, D.C.; and others.

REPRESENTATION: Jerome Evans Gallery, Lake Tahoe, Nevada; Wheelwright Museum of the American Indian / Case Trading Post, Santa Fe, New Mexico.

ABOUT THE ARTIST: LaPena is a modernistic artist who paints the myths and traditions of Indian art. His work often shows how he is searching for an understanding of the universe and its power, as did his people before him. In 1992, LaPena created a work which was a response to the anniversary of Columbus's arrival in America. LaPena has acted as consultant to the Smithsonian, the California State Indian Museum, and the Ishi Project at Berkeley; has written and published poetry, as well as an arts column; is fluent in the Wintu language; and is now professor of art and ethnic studies and director of the Native American Studies Program at the California State University at Sacramento.

BRENDA LAUGHING

Mohawk (1957 –   ) Hogansburg, New York
Beadworker, leatherworker

EDUCATION: Learned from her parents, Ida and Angus Laughing.

ABOUT THE ARTIST: Laughing's whole family are active in crafts and often travel together to exhibits, including the New York State Fair. Brenda makes men's and women's leather outfits; beaded pieces, especially clothing, in both raised or flat style; and bone beads, which she works on with her brother. She is very active in the American Indian Nationalist Movement and travels extensively to promote Indian causes and arts.

JAMES LAVADOUR

Walla Walla (1951 –   ) Cayuse, Oregon
Artist—oil on linen

EDUCATION: Self-taught.

ABOUT THE ARTIST: Lavadour uses many canvases to create his illusionistic landscapes. He applies paint thinly so that the spirit images he creates can become part of the real world.

JUANITA LAY

Seneca (1905 –   ) Irving, New York
Beadworker, dollmaker

EDUCATION: Learned from her mother.

ABOUT THE ARTIST: Lay beads clan medallions, medallions, necklaces, cigarette-lighter covers, and rings. Her medallions often feature animals such as the turtle, hawk, beaver, heron, snipe, bear, deer, and wolf. Lay also uses some flower designs. Lay and her daughters often work together to create items which they sell at Indian functions.

AGNES LAZORE

(a.k.a. Ka He Ro Ton Kwas)
Mohawk (1924 –   ) St. Regis, Quebec
Basketmaker, splintworker

EDUCATION: Learned how to make baskets at Akwesasne Homemakers and Cultural Committee.

REPRESENTATION: Mohawk Craft Fund, Quebec

ABOUT THE ARTIST: Lazore often makes large stars from splints. She likes to use white- or orange-colored splints. Her basketry specialty is small sewing baskets, but she also knows how to make other types.

MARGARET R. LAZORE

(a.k.a. Kon Wa Ke Ri Saionatonti)
Mohawk (1923 –   ) St. Regis, Quebec
Basketmaker, splintworker

EDUCATION: Learned by watching her mother, Dorothy Curry.

ABOUT THE ARTIST: Lazore uses black-ash splints, sweet grass, and twine to make various types of baskets, both large and small. She likes using colored splints, but usually bends to the customer's preference. She often teaches basketry classes.

ROBBIE LAZORE

Mohawk (1961 –   )
Beadworker

EDUCATION: Self-taught.

ABOUT THE ARTIST: Robbie's grandmother, Louise Buckshot, gave him a loom and encouraged him to learn how to bead. He often creates his own designs and usually uses a black background. Though he knows how to bead freehand, Lazore prefers to work on a loom.

SARAH LAZORE

Mohawk (1918 –   ) St. Regis, Quebec
Basketmaker, splintworker, clothing designer, quilter

EDUCATION: Learned from her grandmother and mother.

REPRESENTATION: Mohawk Craft Fund, Hogansburg, New York.

ABOUT THE ARTIST: Sarah makes a wide variety of baskets, including lampshades and baskets in the shape of turtles, as well as woven chair seats. Lazore also creates dance costumes, quilts, and other types of clothing. The costumes are made for the Katerie Dance Group, to which she belongs.

MARY LEAF
Mohawk (1925 –   )
Basketmaker, splintworker, lacrosse stick weaving

EDUCATION: Learned her skills from her mother, Josephine Thompson.

AWARDS: Some of Leaf's work is held by the North American Indian Traveling College in Ontario.

ABOUT THE ARTIST: Leaf began making baskets at age eight to help her mother. Leaf creates sewing accessory baskets, as well as a variety of other types. Her work is well known and has been photographed for television and for the North American Indian Traveling College.

BESSIE LEE
Navajo (1921 –   ) Red Mesa/Teec Nos Pas, Arizona
Weaver

EDUCATION: Lee learned how to weave from other family members.

ABOUT THE ARTIST: Lee weaves Teec Nos Pas rugs but avoids bright colors that some other weavers choose to use. Her rugs usually have black backgrounds. She is one of the few weavers who sell to many dealers, negotiating until she gets the price she wants for her work.

CHARLIE LEE
(a.k.a. Huska Yelhayah, "Warrior Who Came Out")
Navajo (1926 –   ) Four Corners area/Navajo
Reservation, Arizona
Artist—watercolor

EDUCATION: Central Bible Institute, Springfield, Missouri.

ABOUT THE ARTIST: Lee lives with his people as a missionary, painting the Navajo people and their history.

CLARENCE LEE
Navajo (1952 –   ) Arizona
Jeweler, painter

AWARDS: In 1994, Lee was given the Grand Award at the Red Earth awards ceremony in Oklahoma. He has also won Best of Show at the 1982 and 1983 Eight Northern Indian Pueblos Artist and Craftsman Shows; Best of Classification in 1983 Indian Market; and many others.

REPRESENTATION: Eagle Plume Gallery, Allespark, Colorado; Mudhead Gallery, Denver and Beaver Creek, Colorado.

ABOUT THE ARTIST: Lee makes jewelry that tells a story about past and present Navajo life. He makes his own dyes and stamps and uses an appliqué technique where each piece of the work is cut from silver, gold, or copper, then soldered piece by piece to the base.

DAVID LEE
Navajo (N/A) Shiprock, Arizona
Sandpainter

ABOUT THE ARTIST: In the late 1970s, Lee created sandpaintings that had subsidiary themes such as the four sacred domesticated plants (corn, beans, tobacco, and squash) in them.

KATHY LEE
Navajo (N/A)
Weaver

AWARDS: Lee's work consistently wins awards.

ABOUT THE ARTIST: Lee uses vegetal-dyed wool. She began creating award-winning pieces while still in her twenties.

MIRIAM LEE

Seneca (N/A – 1993)
Basketmaker, beadworker, quilter

EDUCATION: Lee's mother-in-law taught her how to make baskets; she taught herself beadwork.

AWARDS: New York State Iroquois Conference Award, 7th annual Award to Iroquoian Individual (1976).

ABOUT THE ARTIST: Lee was one of the last Allegany basketmakers. Her specialties were corn washing, hominy, flower, and sewing baskets made in a twill or wicker weave from black-ash splints. She demonstrated her craft and taught others how to create baskets.

GRACE LEHI

San Juan/Paiute (N/A)
Basketmaker

ABOUT THE ARTIST: Lehi sometimes patterns her baskets after the traditional Navajo wedding basket.

MARY LEE (WEBSTER) LEMIEUX

Oneida (1946 –) Oneida, Wisconsin
Painter—oils, acrylics

EDUCATION: Took art classes in high school and at University of Wisconsin, Green Bay.

ABOUT THE ARTIST: Lemieux's painting entitled "Rib Cage" is now part of the University of Wisconsin's collection. She usually paints contemporary Indian people in modern-day reservation settings. She has a fairly realistic style.

JUANA LENO

Acoma (N/A) New Mexico
Potter

ABOUT THE ARTIST: When Leno and her family knead the clay for her pottery, they leave their sneakers on.

DOROTHEA LEROY

Seneca (1904 –)
Beadworker, leatherworker, quillworker

ABOUT THE ARTIST: Leroy's specialty is clan medallions. She creates designs that include the bear, heron, turtle, wolf, snipe, deer, beaver, and eel. She started doing beadwork through the Seneca Historical Society and has since designed some costumes and beadwork and has learned to make cornhusk dolls. In addition, Leroy can crochet, knit, and make quilts.

MARILYN LEROY

Mohawk (1943 –) Irving, New York
Beadworker, leatherworker

EDUCATION: Dot Leroy, Leroy's mother-in-law, taught her some of her skills.

AWARDS: Leroy's awards include second place for a necklace at the 1976 Indian Fall Festival and third place the following year.

ABOUT THE ARTIST: Leroy became involved with the Seneca Historical Society in the late 1960s where she took some beadwork and leather classes. Her first attempt at selling her work was from a stand set up outside her house. She creates beaded jewelry, papoose dolls, and leatherwork items such as vests, jackets and belts. She also teaches, passing on what she has learned to new students.

IVAN AND RITA LEWIS

Ivan—Acoma (1919 –) New Mexico
Rita—Cochiti (1920 –) New Mexico
Potters—Storyteller figures

EDUCATION: Both members of this husband -and-wife team are self-taught potters. Ivan observed his mother, Lucy Lewis, while Rita observed her mother, Ascencion Banada.

AWARDS: Rita started making Storyteller figures in 1973 with Ivan. They have been steadily winning awards at the Indian Market in Santa Fe ever since.

REPRESENTATION: Adobe Gallery, Albuquerque, New Mexico.

ABOUT THE ARTISTS: This pair comes from a long line of potters on both sides of the family. In the 1980s, Ivan became known for his reproductions of nineteenth century Cochiti caricatures. Rita assisted him in copying the designs. Their daughter, Patricia, and daughter-in-law, Mary, have also made Storyteller figures.

LUCY M. LEWIS

Acoma (approximately 1899 – 1992) Acoma
Pueblo, New Mexico
Potter

EDUCATION: Self-taught; influenced by polychrome pottery she saw in the kiva.

AWARDS: Lewis's awards are many and include honors from the governor of New Mexico (1983); the American Craft Council Gold Medal (1985); a citation from the College Art Association Women's Caucus (1992); an invitation to the Nixon White House; guest appearances on television programs; and having her work held by many museums.

REPRESENTATION: Adobe Gallery, Albuquerque, New Mexico.

ABOUT THE ARTIST: Lewis, the best known of the Acoma potters, exhibited her pottery in solo shows and at Indian markets, taught and demonstrated traditional pottery at the Idyllwild School of Music and the Arts in California, and made inroads for the many Acoma potters who have followed. Her children, Emma, Dolores, Ivan, and Andrew, are continuing her tradition by making pottery from the secret place where Lewis always gathered her clay.

NANCY LEWIS

Hopi (N/A) Arizona
Potter

ABOUT THE ARTIST: Lewis lives and works on her pottery in the village of Sichomovi atop the First Mesa.

GREG LIGHTBOWN

Haida (N/A) Masset, British Columbia, Canada
Carver

EDUCATION: Learned from watching other carvers and studying the ancient carvers' works.

ABOUT THE ARTIST: Lightbown often uses argilite in his work and has been known to carve pieces that tell of the Haida myths or legends.

JAMES LITTLE

Navajo (1947 –   ) Arizona
Jeweler

EDUCATION: Navajo Community College (1970–1972); studied jewelry under Kenneth Begay.

REPRESENTATION: Lovena Ohl Gallery, Scottsdale, Arizona; Galeria Capistrano, San Juan Capistrano, California; The Squash Blossom, Aspen, Vail, and Denver, Colorado; Galeria Capistrano, Santa Fe, New Mexico.

ABOUT THE ARTIST: Little is a minimalist, choosing to set off one stone rather than to surround it with a complex design. Though his designs are modern, they do reflect Navajo themes often suggested by his mother's rug patterns.

HAROLD LITTLEBIRD

Santo Domingo/Laguna (N/A)
Potter—stoneware; poet, ceramics

ABOUT THE ARTIST: Littlebird's work is reminiscent of pre-Colombian vessels, but he uses pastels rather than earth tones. The process he uses is called "terrasigilatta" or "sealed earth." He calls his work "skyscapes."

JAMES LITTLE CHIEF

(a.k.a. Tsen-T'ainte, "White Horse")
Comanche/Kiowa (1941 –   ) Lawton,
Oklahoma
Artist—acrylic

EDUCATION: Studied painting at Cameron Junior College, Lawton, and at Oklahoma University, Norman.

AWARDS: Little Chief's various awards include some won at the Indian Art Exhibit at the American Indian Exposition in Anadarko, Oklahoma (1966).

ABOUT THE ARTIST: Little Chief has had one- person shows in Oklahoma where his distinct style (he often uses odd-shaped canvases) garnered him a lot of attention.

CARM LITTLE TURTLE
Apache/Tarahumara/Mexican (1952 –) Santa Monica, California
Photographer

EDUCATION: Graduated from Navajo Community College as an R.N (1978); self-taught photographer.

AWARDS: Little Turtle has been exhibiting her work since 1981 and has won numerous honors.

ABOUT THE ARTIST: The photographs Little Turtle creates are deft depictions of her personal history. She is known for the way she manipulates light to her best advantage. Little Turtle also paints on the photographic image, making the photograph a mixture of the best of both the photographer's and artist's talents. Permanent collections of her work are held in many museums and universities such as the Southwest Museum in Los Angeles and the Southern Plains Indian Museum in Anadarko, Oklahoma.

JAKE LIVINGSTON
Zuni/Navajo (1947 –)
Jeweler

EDUCATION: Livingston credits Gibson Nez with teaching him the finer points of jewelry, but Livingston's father, Jacob Halso Su, taught him how to work with silver.

AWARDS: 1988 IACA "Artist of the Year"; top awards at Santa Fe Indian Market, the Heard Museum Show, and the Museum of Northern Arizona; and many others.

ABOUT THE ARTIST: Livingston won three Purple Hearts in the Marine Corps in Vietnam and did not begin selling his work until three years after he came home in 1972. His first award was for a reversible concho belt which won Best of Show at the 1974 Gallup Ceremonial. Livingston works with both silver and gold, as well as semiprecious stones.

CARNATION AND BILL LOCKWOOD
San Juan (N/A) New Mexico
Potters

EDUCATION: Carnation started making pottery with her sister after their mother died.

ABOUT THE ARTISTS: The Lockwoods create pottery that is banded and decorated with polychrome designs within the unpolished portion of the pot. Carnation states that once she starts polishing a pot, she does not want to be interrupted.

JAN LOCO
Warm Springs Apache (1949 –) Texas
Jeweler

REPRESENTATION: White River Trader, Indianapolis, Indiana; Dewey Galleries, Ltd., Santa Fe, New Mexico; Red Rock Trading Company, Alexandria, Virginia

ABOUT THE ARTIST: Loco did not know she was an Apache until her adoptive parents revealed that fact when Jan became an adult. Once she discovered her heritage, Loco moved to Santa Fe, met Allan Houser, and, with his help, reconstructed her past. She began making jewelry in 1988, working in copper and silver. She always makes her pins in multiples of four, a number sacred to the Apache.

101

BETTY ANNE LOGAN

Cayuga (1932 –   ) Gowanda, New York
Beadworker

EDUCATION: Logan took lessons from a neighbor; attended classes at Thomas Indian School and Gowanda High School.

ABOUT THE ARTIST: Logan specializes in beadwork lace collars and necklaces. She does freehand beadwork instead of loomwork. She also teaches her daughter and neighborhood children about the craft.

CHARLES LOLOMA

Hopi (1921 – 1991) Hotevilla, Arizona
Painter, potter, muralist, silversmith

EDUCATION: Studied under muralist Olaf Nordmark; received ceramics instruction at Alfred University, New York.

AWARDS: John A. Whiting Fellowship (1955); won awards in national and state competitions; the Arizona Governor's Art Award "for his courage and innovation in changing the look of Indian jewelry" (1990).

REPRESENTATION: Wheelwright Museum of the American Indian/Case Trading Post, Santa Fe, New Mexico.

ABOUT THE ARTIST: Loloma instructed special classes at the University of Arizona and Arizona State. He exhibited at the Arizona State Fair, the Museum of Modern Art in New York City, and the New Mexico State Fair, as well as internationally. He started out as a muralist who painted for the Federal Building on Treasure Island in San Francisco Bay. He then studied ceramics and the glazing properties of Hopi indigenous clays. He rented space at the Kiva Craft Center in Scottsdale where he and his wife, Otellie Pasivaya, sold their work. He began making jewelry in the 1950s.

A major force in Native American arts, Loloma spoke about his work all over the world, taught at the Institute of American Indian Art, was featured on television specials, and served as artist-in-residence in Japan and Korea for the National Endowment for the Arts. He also took on apprentices such as his niece, Verma Nequatewa, and her sister, Sherian Honhongva, and taught them how to create, innovate, and combine colors. After an accident in 1989, Loloma was forced to retire.

LINDA LOMAHAFTEWA

Hopi/Choctaw (1947 –   ) Phoenix, Arizona
Artist—various media

EDUCATION: Institute of American Indian Art, Santa Fe; Bachelor of Fine Art and Master of Fine Art, San Francisco Art Institute, California.

AWARDS: Lomahaftewa has exhibited in national and international shows, several one-woman shows, and has won many awards for her work.

REPRESENTATION: The Heard Museum, Phoenix, Arizona.

ABOUT THE ARTIST: In addition to holding teaching jobs at the San Francisco Art Institute, the University of California at Berkley, and the Institute of American Indian Arts in Santa Fe, Lomahaftewa has been an active artist. She unites the ancient Indian world with the contemporary in her modernistic paintings and has done a series of abstract landscapes which are considered the most powerful in her body of work. Her work is held in many private and public collections, such as the Millicent Rogers Museum in Taos and the Southern Plains Indian Museum in Anadarko, Oklahoma.

MILLARD DAWA LOMAKEMA

(a.k.a. Dawakema, "House of the Sun")
Hopi (1941 –   ) Arizona
Artist—acrylic

EDUCATION: Member of the Hopi artist group, the *Artists Hopid.*

ABOUT THE ARTIST: Lomakema paints Kachinas and Kachina maidens and surrounds them with traditional Hopi symbols. His work is an abstract interpretation of traditions within his tribe. He concerns himself with the spiritual and symbolic aspects of Hopi life.

JOSEPH LONEWOLF
Santa Clara (N/A) New Mexico
Potter

EDUCATION: Learned the trade from his famous father, Camilio Tafoya; has begun passing on his art to his own children.

ABOUT THE ARTIST: An innovative potter, Lonewolf uses an incised style of decoration on his pots, which are, for the most part, miniatures. His pottery is often decorated with wildlife and ancient symbolism. Though pottery is his first love, Lonewolf has also learned beadwork, drawing, painting, claywork and woodwork from his family members. His sister, Grace Medicine Flower, uses the same type of incised decoration on her pots.

ROSEMARY "APPLE BLOSSOM" LONEWOLF
Santa Clara (N/A) New Mexico
Potter

EDUCATION: Learned the pottery-making tradition from her father, Joseph Lonewolf.

AWARDS: Granted a Visual Arts Fellowship by the Arizona Commission on the Arts (1994).

ABOUT THE ARTIST: Like the other potters in her family, Lonewolf makes miniature pieces with incised decorations. She uses traditional designs in her pottery.

GEORGE LONGFISH
Seneca/Tuscarora (1942 –   ) Oshweken,
Ontario, Canada
Painter, sculptor, filmmaker

EDUCATION: Bachelor of Fine Art and Master of Fine Art, the Art Institute of Chicago.

AWARDS: Longfish has participated in and/or directed many one-person and group shows since 1967 and has been given many honors.

REPRESENTATION: California State University at Hayward, Hayward, California.

ABOUT THE ARTIST: Longfish has tried to incorporate European techniques with Indian traditions in his paintings. He uses mystical symbols on his large, unframed paintings; they often resemble the sides of tipis painted by his ancestors. In 1983, Longfish stated, "[I]t was this spirituality that made connections between making art and my cultural background . . ." In addition to his artwork, Longfish has directed the graduate program in American Indian Arts at the University of Montana, is a professor of Native American studies at the University of California at Davis, and is director of the C. N. Gorman Museum.

PHIL LORETTO
Jemez (1951 –   ) New Mexico
Jeweler, sculptor, painter, poet

EDUCATION: Bachelor of Art, painting major, Fort Lewis College (1976); Institute of American Indian Art (1968–1969); Arizona State University, studied under Paolo Soleri (1969). Learned how to create jewelry from his father-in-law, Chee Keams, a Navajo silversmith.

REPRESENTATION: Elaine Horwitch Gallery, Santa Fe, New Mexico; Packard's Indian Trading Co., Inc., Santa Fe, New Mexico; Wheelwright Museum of the American Indian/Case Trading Post, Santa Fe, New Mexico.

ABOUT THE ARTIST: Because Loretto is politically active, quite a bit of his work reflects his interests. One of his concha belts describes Columbus's arrival in the "new world." Each piece is individually stamped and hammered.

CHARLES F. LOVATO
Santo Domingo (1937 – 1987) Santo Domingo
Pueblo, New Mexico
Painter, ceramist, sculptor, poet, jeweler

EDUCATION: Learned art by helping his grand-mother, potter Monica Silva, decorate her pottery.

AWARDS: Honored posthumously with a show of his jewelry at Wheelwright Museum, Santa Fe.

REPRESENTATION: Eagle Plume Gallery, Allespark, Colorado.

ABOUT THE ARTIST: Lovato often used pottery designs in his work, a leftover influence of his early days of painting. He also incorporated traditional Pueblo images like the sun, mountains, and the plants of the Rio Grande Valley. He was known for shading the colors in his necklaces so that they shimmered and for using incredibly small beads. Lovato introduced other jewelers to the style of interchanging gold and turquoise with olive shell, white clamshell, sugilite, coral, and lapis lazuli.

JULIAN LOVATO
Santo Domingo (1925 –   ) Santo Domingo Pueblo, New Mexico
Jeweler

EDUCATION: Lovato comes from a family of jewelers and learned from his father and grandfather. He also picked up some techniques from his mentor, Frank Patania, an Italian silversmith and owner of the Thunderbird Shop in Santa Fe. Patania passed his thunderbird hallmark on to Lovato.

AWARDS: Entered his first Gallup Intertribal Ceremonial in 1977 and won three first prizes.

REPRESENTATION: Tanner Chaney Gallery, Albuquerque, New Mexico; Santa Fe East, Santa Fe, New Mexico; Brooks Indian Shop, Taos, New Mexico.

ABOUT THE ARTIST: Lovato's jewelry has a sculptural quality that is obviously an influence of Patania. His pieces have a spare, exact look that makes the stones appear to float.

RAY LOVATO
Santo Domingo (1946 –   ) Santo Domingo Pueblo, New Mexico
Jeweler

EDUCATION: Learned the art from his parents, Ike and Tonita Lovato.

REPRESENTATION: Notah-Dineh Trading Co., Cortez, Colorado; Mudhead Gallery, Denver and Beaver Creek, Colorado; The Squash Blossom, Aspen, Vail and Denver, Colorado; Dewey Galleries, Ltd., Santa Fe, New Mexico.

ABOUT THE ARTIST: Lovato uses only natural turquoise for his pieces and is recognized for his corn necklaces where the turquoise he uses is shaped like corn kernels.

TRUMAN LOWE
Winnebago (1944 –   ) Black River Falls, Wisconsin
Sculptor

EDUCATION: Bachelor of Science in Art Education, University of Wisconsin-LaCrosse (1969); Master of Fine Art, University of Wisconsin-Madison (1973).

AWARDS: Lowe's many awards include a Chancellor's Development Grant in 1991, many commissions, and honors.

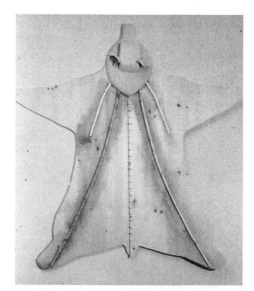

Lowe's "Hoonch," powdered pigment on wood with leather, 76 x 71½ inches, 1992, courtesy of the artist and Jan Cicero Gallery, Chicago, Illinois.

REPRESENTATION: Jan Cicero Gallery, Chicago, Illinois; Kathryn Sermas Gallery, New York City, NY; Lazzaro Signature Gallery of Fine Art.

ABOUT THE ARTIST: Lowe is interested in using natural forms in his sculptures and placing his materials in contemporary contexts. His Winnebago culture is strongly represented in his work. His work has been exhibited in solo and group shows around the world.

F. BRUCE LUBO, SR.

Laguna (1911 –) Old Laguna Pueblo, New Mexico
Artist—oil, watercolor, pastel

EDUCATION: Attended college for engineering and art; spent thirty years as an aircraft-design engineer.

AWARDS: Many honors, including Best of Show, Painting, Eight Northern Pueblo Art Exhibit, New Mexico (twice); forty-eight first, second, third, and honorable-mention awards; attended the Santa Fe Indian Market for twenty years and won best of class in pastel.

REPRESENTATION: In the past, Lubo's work has been represented by many Southwestern galleries, but since his eyesight loss, he has not been working.

ABOUT THE ARTIST: A very active artist, Lubo has sold thousands of paintings during his career. He attended many shows, sold works to collectors around the world, and was known for his roadrun-

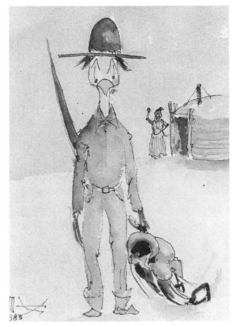

Lubo's watercolor painting, dated 1985, of birdlike cowboy dragging a saddle, courtesy of the artist.

ner pictures (he is a member of the Roadrunner Clan). In 1992, he was declared legally blind and now has to write using a magnifying glass.

DONALD D. LYNCH

Cayuga (1948 –) Ohsweken, Ontario, Canada
Painter—oils, watercolors

EDUCATION: Lynch took art courses at Cornell University (1966) and the State University of New York at Geneseo (1967–1969).

ABOUT THE ARTIST: Lynch likes to paint nostalgic views of the past. He often uses old photographs for ideas or plumbs his memory, imagining what the scene may have originally looked like. A talented artist, Lynch was a biology major at Cornell and an English and journalism major at Geneseo. He has spent most of his life at Six Nations.

OREN LYONS

(a.k.a. Jo-Ag-Quis-Ho)
Onondaga (1930 –)

Portrait of Lubo with first and second place awards in pastels, Indian Market, Santa Fe, New Mexico, courtesy of the artist.

105

Carver; painter—acrylics, oil, tempera, designer colors, pen and ink, pencil, charcoal, pastels

EDUCATION: Bachelor of Art, Syracuse University, College of Fine Art (1954–1958); Master of Art in Museum Technology and American History, Syracuse University

AWARDS: Lyons has exhibited and acted as director and co-director in many shows, has been commissioned to do silver medallion designs for the Franklin Mint, and won first prize from the Council of Interracial Books for Children for his illustrations in the children's book *Little Jimmy Yellow Hawk*.

ABOUT THE ARTIST: Lyons's work in the Iroquois nation has been significant since he became involved with the Council of Chiefs at Onondaga in the 1970s. He has taught at the State University of New York at Buffalo and been very involved with art exhibits. His work often depicts the Tree of Peace, the four winds, and clan animals.

DUANE MAKTIMA

Laguna/Hopi (1954 –   ) Holbrook, Arizona
Jeweler, carver

EDUCATION: Learned how to carve Kachinas from his grandfather; Northern Arizona University, art internship with Jacob Brookins; Bachelor of Fine Art, metalsmithing, 1982; Fellowship, Southwestern Association on Indian Affairs, 1982.

REPRESENTATION: Gallery 10, Inc., Scottsdale and Carefree, Arizona, and Santa Fe, New Mexico; Many Goats, Tucson, Arizona; Merrill B. Dumas American Indian Art, New Orleans, Lousiana; Wadle Galleries, Ltd., Santa Fe, New Mexico; Four Winds Gallery, Pittsburgh, Pennsylvania; Red Rock Trading Company, Alexandria, Virginia.

ABOUT THE ARTIST: Ancient artifacts on display at the Museum of Northern Arizona inspired Maktima and made him wonder what they meant. He learned more about his cultures and returned to

Northern Arizona University to study prehistoric and historical jewelry designs. He uses that knowledge to create unusual color combinations and abstract designs. Maktima signs his pieces with his initials and a stylized parrot, the insignia of the Laguna clan to which he belongs.

JOE MAKTIMA

Laguna/Hopi (N/A)
Artist—prisma color, pencil and pastel, other media

ABOUT THE ARTIST: Maktima likes to create abstract designs that reflect harmony and rhythm.

ALVIN JAMES MAKYA

Hopi (19) Old Oraibi, Arizona
Carver—Kachinas

EDUCATION: High school, Carson City, Nevada; studied under Peter Shelton.

ABOUT THE ARTIST: Makya considers his Kachinas something that "makes my living worthwhile." During the early 1970s, Makya Kachinas were not on the market, but those that had been sold earlier brought four-figure prices.

ANGIE MALONEY

Navajo (1951 –   ) Sand Springs, Arizona
Weaver

EDUCATION: Learned how to weave from her mother, Dorothy Walker; Bachelor of Science in Microbiology and Environmental Science, Northern Arizona University in Flagstaff.

AWARDS: Best of Show and Best of Its Kind at 1979 Gallup Indian Ceremonial.

ABOUT THE ARTIST: Maloney's first rug, a 2 x 2 feet weaving, was sold to the Oraibi Trading Post when Maloney was eight. Because she supports her family with her weavings, Maloney usually makes about four weavings a year. She is teaching one of her daughters to weave.

DAVID R. MARACLE
(a.k.a. Kanatawakhon)
Mohawk (1952 –   )
Beadworker, leatherworker, artist, basketmaker, potter,
    quillworker

EDUCATION: Mostly self-taught; has learned basketry from women on the reservation.

ABOUT THE ARTIST: A multitalented man, Maracle makes beadwork-decorated items such as belts, medallions, necklaces, cloth bandolier bags, tobacco bags, and moccasins. He also paints and sketches, has worked in clay to create pipes or pots with old Iroquois incised designs, has written articles about the Iroquoian people, and has encouraged others to use the traditional Iroquois designs in their crafts.

SALLY (ROSELLA) MARACLE
Mohawk (1933 –   )
Beadworker, quilter

EDUCATION: A friend taught Maracle how to bead; she learned the other crafts on her own.

ABOUT THE ARTIST: Maracle prefers to use shiny beads when she designs. She often works a turtle, horse, eagle, or rose into her composition and can work both freehand and on a loom. She also knits, crochets, and sews quilts. She exhibits her work at local events.

MARIA
Comanche (N/A)
Jeweler

EDUCATION: White Buffalo, Maria's father, taught her how to make jewelry.

ABOUT THE ARTIST: A fourth-generation silversmith, Maria often exhibits with her father.

GERRY MARKS
Haida (N/A) Masset, British Columbia, Canada
Carver; jeweler–silver, gold, wood

ABOUT THE ARTIST: Marks finds creating repoussé is one of the "more challenging techniques" (*Indian Artists at Work* by Ulli Steltzer). He makes his own tools and shapes them to his hands or to a particular job.

ROBIN MARR
Mohawk (1959 –   ) Hagersville, Ontario, Canada
Beadworker, leatherworker, wireworker

EDUCATION: Largely self-taught; has taken classes in beadwork, painting, leatherwork, cornhusk crafts, and copper enameling at the Six Nations Arts Council.

ABOUT THE ARTIST: Marr uses her talents to try to reach mentally retarded children by teaching them crafts. She makes a number of beadworked crafts, including jewelry, headbands, and strips. She also makes leather moccasins, pouches, necklaces, and plant hangers; bone chokers; and wirework chairs, tables, and rings.

ALVIN MARSHALL
Navajo (N/A)
Sculptor

EDUCATION: Marshall started drawing at age three or four after watching his father "draw on anything."

ABOUT THE ARTIST: Marshall uses alabaster, golden alabaster, and other materials to make his sculptures. His work makes a statement about Navajo ways of living in harmony with nature.

MARY MARTIN
Cochiti (1927 –   ) New Mexico
Potter–Storyteller figures

EDUCATION: Learned the art of pottery from her friend, Dorothy Trujillo.

ABOUT THE ARTIST: Martin's family has potted for generations. Some of the artists include Martin's grandmother, Seferina Suina; her cousins, Seferina Ortiz and Ada Suina; and her daughters, Gladys Martin and Adrienne Martin. Martin has also passed on her experience to Kathy Trujillo. Martin made her first Storyteller in 1974 and has since made a variety of Storytellers, nativities, and drummers.

MUNGO MARTIN

> *Kwakiutl (- 1962) Canada*
> *Carver*

EDUCATION: Learned his carving skills from his father.

ABOUT THE ARTIST: Martin taught many other Northwest Coast carvers the art of creating totem poles. He worked with his tools so well that he never cut himself. Considered a master among Northwest Coast carvers, Martin was responsible for passing on what he had learned to many others, including his stepgrandson-in-law, Henry Hunt.

TERESA MARTINE

> *Navajo (1920 –   ) Ramah, New Mexico*
> *Weaver*

EDUCATION: Was twelve when her mother taught her to weave; studied imported and local dyestuffs in workshops taught by weaver D. Y. Begay.

AWARDS: Martine brings her work to the Indian Market in Santa Fe and has won many awards for her weavings.

ABOUT THE ARTIST: Martine uses the wool of *churro* sheep, an old Navajo breed, to make her rugs, and raises the sheep herself. She creates twill and two-faced rugs, sash belts, and tapestry-weave rugs of old designs she finds in books and magazines.

JULIAN MARTINEZ

> *San Ildefonso (– 1943) San Ildefonso Pueblo,*
> *New Mexico*
> *Potter*

EDUCATION: Martinez worked alongside his famous wife, Maria Martinez.

ABOUT THE ARTIST: In 1919, Martinez perfected the technique of painting pots with a matte black design which became the couple's trademark. He also discovered the *puname* and *avanyu* designs which became distinctive of San Ildefonso pottery. When the couple worked, Maria polished the pottery while Julian painted the designs. After Julian died in 1943, other members of Maria's family took over the jobs which he had originally done.

MARIA MONTOYA MARTINEZ

> *San Ildefonso (1887 – 1980) San Ildefonso*
> *Pueblo, New Mexico*
> *Potter—black-on-black*

EDUCATION: Taught by her aunt, Nicolasa, how to make cookware and everyday ceremonial vessels.

AWARDS: Numerous honors, including honorary doctorates from New Mexico State University (1971) and Columbia College (1977).

REPRESENTATION: Adobe Gallery, Albuquerque, New Mexico; Freeport Art Museum and Cultural Center, Freeport, Illinois

ABOUT THE ARTIST: Martinez worked with her husband Julian, as well as her son, Popovi Da; her sister, Clara; her daughter-in-law (her son Adam's wife), Santana; her grandson, Tony Da; her sisters, Maximiliana and Desider; and her great-grand-daughter, Barbara Gonzales. Martinez also taught her son. With her husband, Martinez perfected the black-on-black process/design that became her signature. Most consider Maria the greatest Native American potter of all times. From 1904 to her death, she showed her pottery all over the world, met presidents, movie stars, and international celebrities. Her work is held by both national and international museums.

MARIO MARTINEZ

> *Yaqui (1953 –   ) near Scottsdale, Arizona*
> *Painter*

EDUCATION: Bachelor of Fine Art, Arizona State University (1979); Master of Fine Art, San Francisco Art Institute (1985).

Mario Martinez's "Ceremonial Landscape," acrylic and mixed media on canvas, 67 x 70 inches, 1993, courtesy of the artist and Jan Cicero Gallery, Chicago, Illinois.

REPRESENTATION: Jan Cicero Gallery, Chicago, Illinois.

ABOUT THE ARTIST: Martinez states that Monet, Kandinsky, and Picasso have influenced his vision of art, but he also delves into his own symbols from the Yaqui culture. His works are a combination of traditional and contemporary influences. They sometimes show his political leanings, and, most often, his feelings about the members of the Yaqui community.

RICHARD MARTINEZ

(a.k.a. Opa Mu Nu)
> *San Ildefonso (1904 –   ) San Ildefonso Pueblo, New Mexico*
> *Artist, muralist*

EDUCATION: One of the original students at the Santa Fe Indian School, Martinez helped paint a series of murals there in 1936.

ABOUT THE ARTIST: Most of Martinez's work was done between 1920 and 1950. His subjects were often mythological or ceremonial. His work was exhibited with the Exposition of Indian Tribal

Arts, Inc., in 1931 and collections are held by the Denver Art Museum, the Museum of New Mexico, the Chrysler Art Museum, and others.

SANTANA AND ADAM MARTINEZ

> *San Ildefonso (N/A) San Ildefonso Pueblo, New Mexico*
> *Potter*

EDUCATION: Santana learned how to decorate pottery by working with her famous mother-in-law, Maria Martinez.

ABOUT THE ARTISTS: Santana finds mixing the clay and temper the hardest step of making pottery. Santana decorated pots for Maria after Julian, Maria's husband, died in 1943. Adam and Santana worked together to produce pots after Maria died.

GEORGIA MASAYESVA

> *Hopi (N/A) Arizona*
> *Artist, photographer*

EDUCATION: Bachelor of Art and Master in Education, University of Arizona

ABOUT THE ARTIST: Masayesva was the first female to be selected the poster artist for the Festival of Native American Art in 1988. Her photographs are sepia-toned black-and-white images that are hand-tinted like they were 100 years ago.

JEAN McCARTY MAULDIN

> *Choctaw (N/A)*
> *Artist*

EDUCATION: Mauldin's work has been influenced by her sister, Val Jean Hessing, a well-known artist.

AWARDS: Mauldin's many awards come from exhibits such as the Philbrook Annual (1979), the Five Civilized Tribes Museum (1979), the Gilcrease Museum (1968), and many others.

ABOUT THE ARTIST: Included in *Who's Who in America* and *The Encyclopedia of American Indian Art*, Mauldin's work has been exhibited all over the United States. She also spent twenty-five years as a commercial artist and somehow found the time to raise four children.

MAXIMILIANA
San Ildefonso (N/A) San Ildefonso Pueblo, New Mexico
Potter

EDUCATION: Learned how to pot from members of her family, including Maria Martinez, her sister.

ABOUT THE ARTIST: A formidable potter in her own right, Maximiliana created valuable works that are held by museums and galleries throughout the United States.

LOUISE McCOMBER
Mohawk (1919 –   ) Caughnawaga, Quebec, Canada
Beadworker, quilter

EDUCATION: Learned basic beading techniques from her mother and loomwork beading from a kit she bought for her children.

ABOUT THE ARTIST: McComber began selling her jewelry when one of her children's teachers admired a necklace McComber had given her. McComber's rope necklaces are usually united by a beaded rosette which has a design on it. She sells directly to her customers.

SANDRA McCOMBER
Mohawk (1939 –   ) Caughnawaga, Quebec, Canada
Beadworker, leatherworker, dollmaker, ceramist

EDUCATION: Largely self-taught; has attended classes for sewing, pâpier-maché, macaroni art, beading, drawing, and ceramics.

ABOUT THE ARTIST: McComber opened a crafts store in 1976 and has continued to work with her own style. She makes beaded leatherwork, beaded jewelry, Indian dolls, and ceramic figures,and decorates tomahawks and toys made by her husband.

SOLOMON McCOMBS
(a.k.a. "Wolf Warrior")
Creek (1913 –   ) Eufala, Oklahoma
Artist—watercolor

EDUCATION: Studied at Bacone with Acee Blue Eagle.

ABOUT THE ARTIST: McCombs worked for the United States Department of State for seventeen years and traveled throughout Africa and Asia showing his paintings and lecturing about Indian culture. He focuses most of his interest on the Creek people and paints their customs and rituals.

CHEE McDONALD
Navajo (N/A) Sheep Springs, New Mexico
Sandpainter

EDUCATION: Taught by James Joe of Shiprock.

ABOUT THE ARTIST: McDonald either adds or subtracts details from his sandpaintings and also changes the color to placate the Holy People.

RITA McDONALD
Mohawk (1938 –   ) Hogansburg, New York
Basketmaking

EDUCATION: Her mother, Josephine Sunday, taught her.

REPRESENTATION: Mohawk Craft Fund.

ABOUT THE ARTIST: In the past, McDonald made some baskets with her sister, Agnes Phillips, but now she works alone. She uses black ash, sweet grass, and rope to create sewing and other types of baskets. She usually uses undyed splints.

CHRISTINE NOFCHISSEY McHORSE
Navajo (N/A)
Potter

EDUCATION: McHorse was influenced by her husband, Joel McHorse (Taos), who learned pottery from his grandmother.

REPRESENTATION: Jerome Evans Gallery, Lake Tahoe, Nevada.

ABOUT THE ARTIST: McHorse creates micaceous pottery that combines the influences of several tribes' cultures.

LUCY LEUPPE McKELVEY
Navajo (N/A)
Pottery

ABOUT THE ARTIST: This potter uses rug designs, wedding baskets, and supernatural spirits in her pottery. She has caused collectors to take a new look at traditional Navajo pottery.

BETTY McLESTER
Oneida (1940 –   ) Oneida, Wisconsin
Beadworker, quillworker, clothing designer, knitter, crocheter

EDUCATION: Learned from her friends; attended craft classes.

ABOUT THE ARTIST: McLester makes beaded jewelry, belts, wristbands, and headbands, and designs native clothing and porcupine-quill earrings. She is active in an Iroquois social dance group and often makes their costumes.

BERNIE McQUARY
Okanagan (N/A) Nautley Reserve, British Columbia, Canada
Beadwork jeweler

ABOUT THE ARTIST: McQuary often has ideas for new projects while she is sleeping and immediately tries them upon awakening.

ELIZABETH MEDINA
Zia (N/A) Arizona
Potter

EDUCATION: Learned some of her skill from working with her mother.

ABOUT THE ARTIST: Medina makes sure to fire her pots carefully to get the right color and leaves no smudges on her decorated pots. She decorates her pots the traditional family way, on a beige slip. Her husband, Marcellus, paints her traditional pots with highly detailed visions of Indian dancers.

RAFAEL MEDINA
(a.k.a. Teeyacheena)
Zia (1929 –   ) Zia Pueblo, Arizona
Artist—watercolor

EDUCATION: Studied with Velino Herrera and José Ray Toledo.

ABOUT THE ARTIST: Medina has tried many styles of painting but is most successful when he works in the traditional Rio Grande style. He paints the Zia ceremonials and is an active spokesman for the Zia people.

SOFIA MEDINA
Zia (N/A) Arizona
Potter

ABOUT THE ARTIST: Medina makes pottery in the traditional Zia way, though she is not as active as she once was.

MARY MICHELL
Okanagan (N/A) Burns Lake, British Columbia, Canada
Beadworker

ABOUT THE ARTIST: Michell uses different types of designs in her work and her children often watch her, probably learning the art at her feet.

DOROTHY MIKE
Navajo (1924 –   ) Toadlena, New Mexico
Weaver

EDUCATION: Learned how to weave from her mother.

ABOUT THE ARTIST: Mike wove her first rug at age thirteen. She stopped weaving in 1977 due to a back injury.

ROSE MIKE

Navajo (N/A) Toadlena, New Mexico
Weaver

ABOUT THE ARTIST: Rose, a well-known tapestry maker, is Dorothy Mike's sister-in-law.

FRANCIS MILLER

Navajo (N/A) Sheep Springs, New Mexico
Sandpainter

EDUCATION: Fred Stevens, Jr., encouraged Francis and his wife, Patsy, to become sandpainters and to experiment with their styles.

ABOUT THE ARTIST: Miller's work is often large and complex. His lines are thin and clear and every detail is intricate and fine.

PATSY MILLER

Navajo (N/A) Sheep Springs, New Mexico
Sandpainter

EDUCATION: Inspired by the master sandpainter Fred Stevens, Jr.; was a member of Stevens's same clan; Stevens, Jr., encouraged Miller and her husband, Francis, to experiment with their styles.

ABOUT THE ARTIST: Miller created a sandpainting of Big Blue Thunder, a figure which is not often made, but she changed the headdress and markings on the body so that the Holy Person would not be disturbed. Some women will not make this figure while pregnant because they believe it will damage the child they are carrying.

R. GARY MILLER

(a.k.a. Se-Honh-Yess)
Mohawk (1950 –   ) Toronto, Ontario, Canada
Painter, printmaker—oils, watercolors, pen and ink

EDUCATION: Art classes at Glenhurst Gardens in Toronto and the Mohawk Institute Residential School and Burlington High School; was an honor graduate of Ontario College of Arts (1974); took medical illustration and art history courses at the University of Toronto.

AWARDS: Miller has received much recognition for his work in the community and in exhibits. He even attended a dinner with the Queen of England and Prime Minister Trudeau for the Queen's Silver Jubilee in 1977.

EMMA MITCHELL

Acoma (N/A) New Mexico
Potter

EDUCATION: Learned from other family members.

ABOUT THE ARTIST: Mitchell, her mother, and her sister all use Argentine corned-beef tins as scrapers and trimmers. When Mitchell has a few pots ready, she lines them up and decides which design to use.

MARY MITCHELL

Mohawk (1906 –   ) St. Regis, Quebec, Canada
Basketmaker, quilter

EDUCATION: Learned by watching her mother.

REPRESENTATION: Mary Peachin's Art Company, Tucson, Arizona.

ABOUT THE ARTIST: Mitchell once created larger baskets, but as she grew older, she started making smaller baskets. She uses sweet grass, black-ash splints, and dyes.

THERESA MITTEN

(a.k.a. Guh Gwi Suh)
Seneca (1916 –   ) Caledonia, Ontario, Canada
Beadworker, cornhusk dollmaker, clothing designer

EDUCATION: Taught herself how to bead; learned to work with cornhusks from Isabell Skye.

ABOUT THE ARTIST: Mitten began beading during the late 1960s, remembering how her grandmother did beadwork on velvet. Mitten beads both free-hand and on a loom, creating jewelry, belts, key chains, wristbands, watchbands, headbands, arm-bands, and other items. She also makes native rib-bon clothing, action cornhusk dolls, and bone and bead chokers.

MADELINE MODESTE

Cowichan (N/A) Koksilah Reserve, British
Columbia, Canada
Knitter

EDUCATION: Learned from family members.

ABOUT THE ARTIST: Modeste, like other women in her business, dries, cleans, bleaches, cards, and spins her own wool.

SARAH MODESTE

Cowichan (N/A) Koksilah Reserve, British
Columbia, Canada
Knitter

EDUCATION: Learned from family members.

ABOUT THE ARTIST: Modeste dries and cleans her own wool. She counts on the sun and the night frost to bleach it. Modeste was the wholesale sup-plier for Central Marketing Service in Ottawa.

BRIAN MOHR

(a.k.a. Ga Hen Dí)
Seneca (1959 –) Salamanca, New York
Painter, beadworker—oils, pencil, watercolors, beads

EDUCATION: Learned beadwork skills from his grandmother, Deforest Abrams; Monroe Abrams; and others; studied painting and drawing in school; studied silverworking at the Seneca Nation Orga-nization for the Visual Arts.

AWARDS: Among Mohr's honors is a first prize for his work at the New York State Fair (1977).

ABOUT THE ARTIST: In addition to painting tradi-tional Iroquois life, Mohr beads his own dance cos-tumes and has learned to carve masks.

AL MOMADAY

(a.k.a. Haun Toa, "War Lance")
Kiowa (1913 –) Mountainview, Oklahoma
Artist—various media

EDUCATION: Bacone College (1931–1934); Uni-versity of New Mexico, Albuquerque (1936–1937); University of California, Los Angeles (1956); Famous Artists School correspondence course.

AWARDS: Momaday's numerous awards and honors include the Southwestern Indian Artists Award given by the Dallas Exchange Club (1956) and a Certificate of Appreciation awarded by the Indian Arts and Crafts Board, United States Department of the Interior (1967).

ABOUT THE ARTIST: The father of N. Scott Momaday, Momaday is the grandson of a Kiowa medicine man and thus knows the intricacies of tribal ceremonies, legends, and history. He brought some of this knowledge to his work and instructed others in art while at the Jemez Pueblo Day School in New Mexico. Momaday's work was commis-sioned by churches and other associations through-out the world and exhibited widely.

N. SCOTT MOMADAY

Kiowa (1934 –) Lawton, Oklahoma
Artist—illustrator, drawer, painter, printmaker

Portrait of Momaday, artist and writer. Photo by Cynthia Farah,
courtsy of LewAllen Gallery, Santa Fe, New Mexico.

Momaday's monotype entitled "Environmentalist," 30 x 22 inches. Photograph by Dan Morse, courtesy of LewAllen Gallery, Santa Fe, New Mexico.

EDUCATION: Bachelor of Art, University of New Mexico (1958); Master of Art, Stanford (1960); Ph.D., Stanford (1963); twelve honorary degrees.

AWARDS: Pulitzer Prize (literature), Guggenheim Fellowship, and numerous others.

REPRESENTATION: Horwitch LewAllen Gallery, Santa Fe, New Mexico.

ABOUT THE ARTIST: Momaday illustrates his own and other authors' books and lectures all over the world. He has held tenured positions at several United States universities, has won many writing awards, and his art has been exhibited widely, including at a one-person, twenty-year retrospective show at the Wheelwright Museum in Santa Fe (1992–1993).

BESSIE MONONGYE
Hopi (N/A)
Basketmaker

AWARDS: Won First Prize in the 1987 Museum of Northern Arizona Annual Hopi Artist's Exhibition.

JESSE LEE MONONGYE
Navajo/Hopi (1952 –   ) Arizona
Jeweler

EDUCATION: Apprenticed with his father, Preston Monongye.

AWARDS: Selected by the Heard Museum as artist-in-residence (1986–1987); has won many awards for his jewelry.

REPRESENTATION: Margaret Kilgore Gallery, Scottsdale, Arizona; Garland's, Sedona, Arizona; Galeria Capistrano, San Juan Capistrano, California; Galeria Capistrano, Santa Fe, New Mexico; Mosi Lakai-BI'Kisi, Santa Fe, New Mexico.

ABOUT THE ARTIST: Monongye did not take jewelry seriously until his mother came to him in a dream and told him he would be a famous artist. He did not know his father until they met in 1974. Once they made contact, Monongye began exploring the Hopi side of his heritage and added it to the designs he created for his jewelry. He combines Hopi and Navajo motifs in his work and is considered an exceptional lapidary artist.

PRESTON MONONGYE
Hopi/Mission (1929 – 1987) Arizona
Jeweler

EDUCATION: Self-taught.

REPRESENTATION: Christopher's Enterprises, Inc., Albuquerque, New Mexico; Tanner's Indian Arts, Gallup, New Mexico.

ABOUT THE ARTIST: A traditional jeweler, Monongye influenced the younger generation with his casting procedures. He often recreated Kachinas with explicit details and authenticity. One of the first to use gold in his jewelry, Monongye passed on his knowledge to his son, Jesse, as well as to other young jewelers.

DONALD MONTILEAUX
Ogala Sioux (1948 –   ) South Dakota
Artist—mixed media

EDUCATION: Studied under Oscar Howe and at the Institute of American Indian Arts.

ABOUT THE ARTIST: Montileaux combines the traditional Plains painting on hide (using watercolor and quills) to abstract symbols that appear to be futuristic. Though he frequently draws upon themes used by his Sioux forefathers, he often uses modern themes as well.

MARK D. MONTOUR
Mohawk (1952 –   ) Caughnawaga, Quebec, Canada
Painter—acrylics, mixed media

EDUCATION: Bachelor of Fine Art, Concordia University (1977); architecture courses at City College of New York (1973).

ABOUT THE ARTIST: Montour has worked with many media, has taught art, exhibited his work, and is a board member of the Native American Friendship Center in Montreal.

NANCY MONTOUR
(a.k.a. Skonwakwenni)
Mohawk (1934 –   )
Painter—oil pastels and oils

EDUCATION: Self-taught.

ABOUT THE ARTIST: Montour generally paints landscapes and sunsets. She has also passed on some of what she has learned to her mother, Margaret Etienne, and to her son.

ROSS MONTOUR
(a.k.a. Kakwiatkeron)
Mohawk (1954 –   ) Caughnawaga, Quebec, Canada
Illustrator, beadworker, leatherworker, wood and stone carver

EDUCATION: Self-taught; has attended various classes.

AWARDS: Scholarship to attend the School of Visual Arts.

ABOUT THE ARTIST: Montour's illustrations have been part of a number of books produced by Native people. He has also done beading on leather and on looms.

EUDORA MONTOYA
Santa Ana (N/A) New Mexico
Potter

EDUCATION: Learned how to pot with her sisters after their mother died.

ABOUT THE ARTIST: Montoya is responsible for keeping Santa Ana pottery alive. She makes bowls and water jars the old way using the ancient designs. She collects her red and grey clay, and her fine sand, from Santa Ana, but buys her white slip from the Zia pueblo. She has begun teaching some of the other women in the village so that they may continue the Santa Ana pottery tradition.

TOMMY EDWARD MONTOYA
(a.k.a. Than Ts'ay Ta)
San Juan (N/A)
Painter

REPRESENTATION: Adobe Gallery, Albuquerque, New Mexico.

ABOUT THE ARTIST: Montoya has a subtle, ethereal style.

TU MOONWALKER
Apache (1948 –   )
Basketmaker, beadworker, leatherworker, weaver —willow, grasses, beads, feathers, leather, wool

EDUCATION: Bachelor of Art in Anthropology, Bachelor of Science in Biochemistry, Master of Art in Museum Science, Master of Science in Geology.

AWARDS: First place, Miniature Baskets, 1986, 1987, and 1988, Gallup Inter-Tribal Ceremonial; First Place in Baskets, Denver Indian Market, 1986.

REPRESENTATION: Andrews Pueblo Pottery, Albuquerque, New Mexico; Evelyn Siegel Gallery, Fort Worth, Texas; Maison des Maison, Denver, Colorado; Serendipity Trading Company

ABOUT THE ARTIST: Moonwalker is considered the premier Apache basketweaver in the Southwest. She uses her skills to produce miniature baskets which have won almost all the awards given to basketweavers at shows throughout that area. In addition to weaving, Moonwalker teaches, lectures, and writes on the art. Her grandmother, Dorothy Naiche Moonwalker, is a descendant of the Apache chief Cochise.

STEPHEN MOPOPE
(a.k.a. Qued Koi, Wood-Coy, "Painted Robe")
*Kiowa (1900 – 1974) near Anadarko, (the
Kiowa Reservation) Oklahoma
Artist—watercolor, other media*

EDUCATION: Taught how to paint on hides a and about the techniques of Kiowa painting by his uncles; studied with Susie Peters of the Kiowa Agency in Anadarko, Oklahoma, and at the University of Oklahoma, Norman (1926–1929).

AWARDS: Mopope's many awards include a Certificate of Appreciation by the Indian Arts and Crafts Board, United States Department of the Interior (1966).

ABOUT THE ARTIST: Mopope broke out of the Kiowa tradition of painting by including more figures in his narrative paintings. He was one of the "Five Kiowas" at the University of Oklahoma. His work is represented in *Kiowa Art* and his paintings have been exhibited all over the world. His commissions include murals for the United States Department of the Interior, Washington, D.C. (1938), as well as works sponsored by the Works Progress Administration and the Public Works Administration.

CHARLOTTE MOREY
*Mohawk (1912 –) Potsdam, New York
Basketmaker*

EDUCATION: Learned by helping her mother, Margaret Brown Oaks.

REPRESENTATION: Mohawk Craft Fund.

ABOUT THE ARTIST: Morey uses black-ash splints, sweet grass, and rope to make a variety of baskets, as well as covered lamps and shades. She has taught basketry in New York and Massachusetts, exhibited throughout the United States, and has been recognized as a talented artist by some local newspapers.

MARY MOREZ
*Navajo (1938 –) Tuba City, Arizona
Artist—mixed media*

EDUCATION: Southwest Indian Art Project, University of Arizona, Tucson; constantly attending school and taking new classes.

ABOUT THE ARTIST: Morez paints Navajo deities symbolically and often translates her dreams into her paintings. Her style is a bit abstract, and combines traits from Cubism, Abstract Expressionism, and the style of Joe Herrera. She takes some of her ideas from life, especially the Indian dancers, and portrays them colorfully.

GEORGE MORRISON
*Ojibway/Chippewa (1919 –) Grand Marais,
Minnesota
Painter, sculptor*

EDUCATION: Studied art at the Minneapolis School of Art; honorary Master degree from the Minneapolis School of Art (now the Minneapolis College of Art and Design); studied at Art Students League in New York City.

AWARDS: Fulbright fellowship (1951) to study and work in France, Italy, and Spain.

REPRESENTATION: Bockley Gallery, Minneapolis, Minnesota; Minnesota Museum of American Art, St. Paul, Minnesota

ABOUT THE ARTIST: Morrison's style is a conglomeration of the styles he learned during his formal art training and the information he soaked up about his own quickly disappearing culture. His work has gone through many changes. As an artist, Morrison accepts those changes, works with them, and declares that he does not believe his art will make him immortal. Morrison believes that change is inevitable. He was the first Native artist on the faculty of Rhode Island School of Design and the first Indian artist on the New York art scene.

NORVAL MORRISSEAU
Ojibwa (1933 –   ) Canada
Artist–acrylic

EDUCATION: One of the founders of the "Ojibwa-Cree-Odawa School."

ABOUT THE ARTIST: Morrisseau is considered one of Canada's premier painters and has influenced the next generation of artists. When he first began painting, Morrisseau fought his tribe's tradition to prohibit painting certain subjects. His paintings and drawings are semi-abstract visions of how he sees his culture's mystic ways.

JAMES MOSES
(a.k.a. Kivetoruk)
Eskimo (1900 – 1982) near Cape Espenberg, Arkansas
Artist–pen and ink, colored pencils, watercolor, mixed media

EDUCATION: Self-taught.

ABOUT THE ARTIST: Moses painted people he knew and experiences and events he had seen. His drawings and paintings of the land in which he lived reflect the cold and the animals with which the Eskimo shares his land. Moses did not begin painting until after he was injured in a plane accident in 1953.

BRIAN MULDOE
Gitksan (N/A) British Columbia, Canada
Carver

EDUCATION: Often assisted Earl Muldoe and learned some of his carving skills.

ABOUT THE ARTIST: Muldoe worked with Earl Muldoe to carve a totem pole which now stands at the entrance to VanDusen Gardens in Vancouver.

EARL MULDOE
Gitksan (N/A) British Columbia, Canada
Carver

ABOUT THE ARTIST: Muldoe carves such items as the Raven Transformation mask. When closed, the mask is shaped like the Northwest Coast Raven. When strings are pulled, the mask opens to reveal a man's face. In Northwest Coast Indian folklore, the Raven came to Earth and was reborn as a man. Muldoe has also created totem poles such as the one carved for the entrance to the VanDusen Gardens in Vancouver in 1986.

JENNIFER MUSIAL
Navajo (1976 –   ) Flagstaff, Arizona
Weaver

EDUCATION: Musial's mother, Kalley Musial, and her grandmother, Carol Yazzie Keams, trained her.

AWARDS: This young artist has won many blue ribbons, including Best of the Juvenile Division and Best of Category at the 1991 Santa Fe Indian Market.

ABOUT THE ARTIST: Musial often uses yarns left over from her mother's rugs, a common practice among young weavers. Her rugs, like her mother's, reflect the feelings she has when weaving. She has collaborated on rugs with her maternal grandmother, Carol Yazzie Keams, and exhibited one of their projects in 1988 at the Coconino Center for the Arts in Flagstaff.

KALLEY MUSIAL
Navajo (1953 –   ) Flagstaff, Arizona
Weaver

117

EDUCATION: Learned how to weave from her mother, Carol Yazzie Keams.

ABOUT THE ARTIST: Musial has done workshops for museums and galleries all over the world, carrying a portable loom wherever she goes. She tries to keep her designs simple, preferring the all-over banded designs so that she can work with more colors. She regularly titles her rugs, which is something most weavers do not do. Kalley teaches beginning and advanced workshops for weavers throughout the United States and is teaching her two younger sisters, her daughter, and a niece. She exhibits at the Indian Market in Santa Fe, as well as at the Coconino Center for the Arts in Flagstaff.

SYLVIA NAHA
Hopi (N/A)
Potter

EDUCATION: Learned from her mother, Helen ("Feather Woman").

ABOUT THE ARTIST: Naha uses Mimbres designs in her work.

DAN NAMINGHA
Tewa/Hopi (1950 –   ) Polaca, Arizona
Artist—various media; printer

Portrait of Namingha at work. Photograph by Eric Swanson, courtesy of Nimán Fine Art, Santa Fe, New Mexico.

EDUCATION: University of Kansas; the Institute of American Indian Artists; the American Academy of Art in Chicago

AWARDS: NASA commissioned Namingha to interpret the three space programs in art (1991).

REPRESENTATION: Susan Duval Gallery, Aspen, Colorado; National Academy of Sciences, Washington, D.C.; Naravisa Press, Santa Fe, New Mexico; Níman Fine Art, Santa Fe, New Mexico

ABOUT THE ARTIST: Namingha is a member of a family with five artists. His style is almost abstract with some geometric qualities. He tends to paint on large canvases with bright colors.

Namingha"s "Kachina Symbolism," acrylic on canvas, 84 x 72 inches, courtesy of artist and Nimán Fine Art, Santa Fe, New Mexico.

BESSIE NAMOKI
Hopi (N/A) Arizona
Potter

EDUCATION: Learned some of her skills from her mother.

ABOUT THE ARTIST: Namoki uses a polishing stone that her mother used before her. She makes her pottery the old way, shaping the clay by hand and painting with a yucca brush.

CHRISTINA NARANJO

Santa Clara (N/A) New Mexico
Potter

EDUCATION: Learned the Tafoya potting tradition from her mother, Serafina Tafoya.

ABOUT THE ARTIST: Naranjo worked with her daughter, Mary Cain, in the 1970s and has taught other members of her family—her granddaughter, Linda; her daughter, Teresita; and her granddaughter, Stella Chavarria—the Tafoya potting tradition.

LOUIS AND VIRGINIA NARANJO

Louis—Cochiti (1932 –   ) New Mexico
Virginia—Cochiti (1932 –   ) New Mexico
Potters—Storyteller figures

EDUCATION: Louis taught himself the art of pottery making by watching his mother Frances Suina Virginia also watched Frances.

AWARDS: In 1973, Virginia won an award for one of her turtle Storytellers. Together, the Naranjos have won many awards for their pottery.

REPRESENTATION: Adobe Gallery, Albuquerque, New Mexico

ABOUT THE ARTISTS: This husband-and-wife team, who made their first Storyteller in 1974, are known for their nativities and Storyteller figures. Their Storytellers are unique because they feature animals. Louis was the first potter to make Bear Storytellers.

MICHAEL NARANJO

Santa Clara (N/A) Santa Clara, New Mexico
Sculptor

ABOUT THE ARTIST: Blinded in Vietnam, Naranjo works with his hands, using his memory and imagination to create his pieces. In 1983, he had an audience with the Pope and was allowed to touch the Vatican's collection of sculptures.

PAULA AND ANA NARANJO

Santa Clara (N/A)
Potters

ABOUT THE ARTISTS: This team create incised pottery, often using animals or serpents *(avanyu)* in their decorations.

ROSE NARANJO

Santa Clara (N/A) New Mexico
Potter

ABOUT THE ARTIST: Naranjo feels the day she fires her pots is "Judgement Day," the time when she can see whether her work will come out the way she wishes. She likes to make wedding vases.

TERESITA NARANJO

Santa Clara (N/A) New Mexico
Potter

EDUCATION: Learned the Tafoya pottery tradition from her mother, Christina Naranjo.

ABOUT THE ARTIST: Naranjo creates carved and polished black pottery and is in great demand at shows and galleries.

NORA NARANJO-MORSE

Santa Clara/Tewa (1953 –   ) Santa Clara Pueblo, New Mexico
Artist, sculptor, silversmith, poet

EDUCATION: Silversmithing program the Institute of American Indian Arts, Santa Fe (1991) Bachelor of University Studies degree, College of Santa Fe (1980); learned how to work clay from Jody Folwell.

AWARDS: Starting in 1979 with a third place award in clay sculpture at the SWAIA Indian Market in Santa Fe, Naranjo-Morse has won awards for her clay sculptures, forms, and scenes; her ceramic sculpture; and has had her poems published in many anthologies and books.

REPRESENTATION: American Indian Contemporary Arts, San Francisco, California

ABOUT THE ARTIST: Naranjo-Morse is a well-versed artist who has a wide range of abilities and interests. She has acted as artist-in-residence at the Santa Fe Indian School, taught pottery techniques, held workshops in basic silk screening and the culture of the Native Americans, toured Europe to teach pottery, given poetry readings throughout the United States, and held one-woman as well as group exhibits.

JOY NAVASIE

(a.k.a. Frog Woman)
Hopi (N/A) Arizona
Potter

ABOUT THE ARTIST: Navasie uses Sikyatki decorations on her pots, painting them on almost pure white slip.

PHIL NAVASYA

Hopi (N/A) Arizona
Jeweler

REPRESENTATION: American Indian Contemporary Arts, San Francisco, California

ABOUT THE ARTIST: Navasya's rings are made in the shape of spaceships. His abstract jewelry reflects his interpretation of Hopi life.

JENNY NAZIEL

Carrier (N/A) Moricetown, British Columbia,
Canada
Basketmaker

ABOUT THE ARTIST: Naziel strips the birch bark from the trees and scrapes it before cutting pieces to make her birch baskets. Her baskets are often hamper size and sewn at the seams. Smaller versions may resemble envelopes.

BOB NEEL

Kwakiutl (N/A) Canada
Carver

EDUCATION: The son of Ellen Neel, Neel learned some of his trade from his mother, as well as from other members of his family.

ABOUT THE ARTIST: Ellen Neel, one of the only women carvers in Northwest Coast art, passed on her knowledge to Neel. Using that education, he carved a pair of house posts for Foreshore Park's traditional plank house, as well as other works of art.

BARBARA NELSON

(a.k.a. Kawennahawi)
Mohawk (1944 –) Oka, Quebec, Canada
Beadworker, leatherworker

EDUCATION: Self-taught.

ABOUT THE ARTIST: Nelson creates beaded medallions, watchbands, and leather vests. She uses Mohawk clan symbols in her medallions, specifically decorating in different colored beads so that the animals will stand out; each animal also has a different expression. She sells her work on special order. Because she believes in passing her knowledge on, Nelson has taught her nephews how to do loom and freehand beadwork.

ELIZABETH NELSON

Mohawk (1959 –)
Beadworker, leatherworker

EDUCATION: Nelson learned some of her skills in a sixth-grade activity class.

ABOUT THE ARTIST: Nelson makes beaded necklaces and daisy chains and decorates leather vests and purses with beads. She likes to use flower designs.

EMILIENNE NELSON

(a.k.a. Kwaheniokwen)
Mohawk (1923 –) Oka, Quebec, Canada
Beadworker

EDUCATION: Nelson's sister, Mance, taught her.

ABOUT THE ARTIST: Though Nelson's whole family is artistic, she did not begin to bead as a child. She now likes to use both shiny and flat-colored beads (especially white and pink) to create beaded necklaces

FREDDIE NELSON
Navajo (N/A) Lupton, Arizona
Sandpainter

ABOUT THE ARTIST: Nelson has done innovative things with his sandpaintings. For instance, in 1977 he created a découpage board which was made into a clock for sale to the tourist trade.

BRYSON NEQUATEWA
Hopi (N/A) Arizona
Carver

ABOUT THE ARTIST: Nequatewa carves Kachinas that have a flowing look to them.

VERMA NEQUATEWA
Hopi (1949 –   ) Arizona
Jeweler

EDUCATION: Apprenticed with her uncle, Charles Loloma.

REPRESENTATION: Lovena Ohl Gallery, Scottsdale, Arizona; Dewey Galleries, Ltd., Santa Fe, New Mexico.

ABOUT THE ARTIST: With her sister, Sherian Honhongva, Nequatewa learned how to create unusual jewelry from the master jeweler, Loloma, and worked with him for twenty-three years. The sisters started exhibiting their own jewelry in 1989 under the name *Sonwai*, which means "beautiful" in Hopi. They use only top-quality stones and believe that quality is all that matters. Their studio is at the Third Mesa in Arizona.

JOYCE LEE TATE NEVAQUAYA
(a.k.a. Doc Tate Nevaquaya, Nevaquaya, "One Who Is Tired of Looking Nice")
Comanche/Apache (1932 –   ) Oklahoma
Painter, musician

EDUCATION: Self-taught; attended Haskell Institute, Lawrence, Kansas (1951-1952).

AWARDS: Nevaquaya's awards include the Grand Award at the All Indian Art Show in Chicago in 1969 and many others.

REPRESENTATION: Eagles Roost Gallery, Colorado Springs, Colorado.

ABOUT THE ARTIST: Nevaquaya began painting professionally in the late 1950s and has exhibited his work in one-person and group shows all over the United States. He is also a self-taught flutist and composer who has played all over the world.

ALICE NEW HOLY BLUE LEGS
Lakota (N/A) North Dakota
Quillworker

EDUCATION: New Holy Blue Legs is a descendant of a long line of quillworkers.

AWARDS: National Heritage Fellow, Folk Arts Program of the National Endowment for the Arts (1985).

ABOUT THE ARTIST: New Holy Blue Legs, a skilled quillworker, has taught other family members, as well as non-family members, to work with quills. Her work is held by private collections and in museums such as the Museum of New Mexico, Santa Fe.

NEW HOLY FAMILY
Lakota
Quillworkers, beadworkers, jewelers, miscellaneous
media

This family of artists includes many talented members such as Martha Good Voice Flute, Rosaline, Bernadine, Walter Ten Fingers, Mildred Catherine, Victor Young, Rosaline (Alice), Jackson, Dolores, Mary, Alton Eagle Louse, Joseph Al, Lucille Marie, Floydeen, Evelyn Sylvia, Eugene Christopher, Pearl May, Robin, and Monica.

Star Quilt of New Holy Family Nora Brings Him Back, courtesy of The Heritage Center, Inc., Pine Ridge, South Dakota.

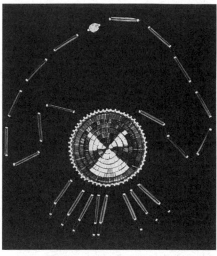

Blue Medallion, Tipi Design of New Holy Family/Martha New Holy, decorated with quillwork, 3 inches in diameter, courtesy of The Heritage Center, Inc., Pine Ridge, South Dakota.

Wapaglina/Roach Spreader of New Holy Family/Victor Young and Cathy (Patton) Young, decorated with quillwork, 14 x 3½ inches, courtesy of The Heritage Center, Inc., Pine Ridge, South Dakota.

ABOUT THE ARTISTS: This large Lakota family works together, both artistically and to support the extended family. The members share talents and offer each other the kind of familial contact that serves to bring each to his or her own level of talent. For further information about specific artist/members of this family, contact The Heritage Center, Inc., Pine Ridge, South Dakota (see the gallery contributors list in the front of this book).

AL NEZ

Navajo (1959 –) Tuba City, Arizona
Jeweler

REPRESENTATION: Lovena Ohl Gallery, Scottsdale, Arizona; Waddell Trading Company, Tempe, Arizona; Sherwoods, Beverly Hills, California; Eagle Plume Gallery, Allespark, Colorado; Mudhead Gallery, Beaver Creek and Denver, Colorado; The Indian Craft Shop, Washington, D.C.; Indian Post, Allentown, Pennsylvania

ABOUT THE ARTIST: Nez uses the style Kenneth Begay made popular in the 1940s, precisely chiseling lines around a stone. He uses silver, gold, and various semiprecious stones in his work.

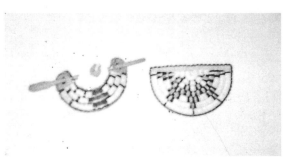

Two pony tail holders of New Holy Family/Bernadine Ten Fingers, courtesy of The Heritage Center, Inc., Pine Ridge, South Dakota.

BRUCE AND NADINE NEZ
Navajo (N/A)
   Weavers

ABOUT THE ARTISTS: Nadine designs the rug patterns and Bruce weaves the rugs. They make pictorials and rugs that are decorated with birds, flowers, and animals.

DESPAH NEZ
   Navajo (1908 –   ) Black Rock, New Mexico
   Weaver

EDUCATION: Nez learned how to weave from her stepmother.

REPRESENTATION: Edith and Troy Kennedy.

ABOUT THE ARTIST: Nez left school in the ninth grade to stay at home and care for her father. Shortly after, she sold her first weaving, a Yei rug. Today, she is considered an important weaver. Her two daughters also make rugs.

GIBSON NEZ
   Navajo/Apache (1944 –   ) Jicarilla Apache Res,
      New Mexico
   Jeweler, silversmith

EDUCATION: Self-taught.

AWARDS: Nez's many awards include Best of Show at the Heard Museum and at the 1994 Santa Fe Indian Market and 700 ribbons in the past decade.

REPRESENTATION: Hogan in the Hilton, Santa Fe, New Mexico; Moondancer Gallery, Redondo Beach, California; Gallery of the American West, Sacramento, California; Galeria Capistrano, San Juan Capistrano, California; Mudhead Gallery, Beaver Creek and Denver, Colorado; Tanner Chaney Gallery, Albuquerque, New Mexico; Indian Post, Allentown, Pennsylvania; SunWest Silver, Albuqerque, New Mexico

ABOUT THE ARTIST: Nez, a member of the Indian Cowboy Association Hall of Fame, is also credited with helping many of today's up-and-coming jewelers. Nez's jewelry is popular with many celebrities. His large, stunning works are produced in both silver and gold accented with turquoise, coral, and lapis lazuli. He exhibits at many Indian markets and travels to promote his jewelry. Nez recently started making silver pottery and won Best of Show at the 1994 Santa Fe Indian Market for that work.

Bracelet made by Gibson Nez and owned by the Berry family of California. Photograph courtesy of the Berry family and the artist.

Ring made by Gibson Nez and owned by the Berry family of California. Photograph courtesy of the Berry family and the artist.

GRACE HENDERSON NEZ
   Navajo (1913 –   ) Ganado, Arizona
   Weaver

EDUCATION: Taught how to weave by her mother.

ABOUT THE ARTIST: Nez still lives in the traditional Navajo hogan, speaks no English, raises sheep, and wears the gathered skirts and jewelry of her ancestors. She works on a heavy lumber loom her late husband built. It is easier for her to create bold designs because of her fading eyesight and limited dexterity.

IRENE JULIA NEZ

Navajo (1928 –) Kinlichee, Arizona
Weaver

EDUCATION: Learned how to weave from her mother, Edith James.

AWARDS: Has won awards for her two-faced and twill weaves.

ABOUT THE ARTIST: Nez creates twill-weave rugs, which are large and has become well known for combining the two-faced technique with her diamond-twill weaves.

LINDA NEZ

Navajo (N/A)
Weaver

EDUCATION: Learned how to weave by watching her mother and aunt.

ABOUT THE ARTIST: Nez fills her rugs with animals, butterflies, birds, and fish.

REDWING T. NEZ

Navajo (1961–)
Painter

AWARDS: First prize and Best of Show (1987), Annual Navajo Artist's Exhibition at the Museum of Northern Arizona

ABOUT THE ARTIST: Nez's painting, "Her Precious Time," reflects his feelings about his grandmother, a weaver, and her work.

TIM NICOLA

Penobscot (N/A)
Sculptor

ABOUT THE ARTIST: Nicola sometimes uses Utah alabaster for his simple, elegant figures.

GEORGINA NICHOLAS

(a.k.a. Ga Han De Yos)
Oneida (1928–) Southwold, Ontario, Canada
Artist–drawer and painter

EDUCATION: Took drawing and language classes at the Oneida Settlement Reserve.

AWARDS: Nicholas's many awards include first prize at the Oneida Fall Festival.

ABOUT THE ARTIST: Nicholas is multitalented. Not only does she draw and paint, but she has also knitted, crocheted, done leather tooling, and helped her grandmother make cornhusk mats, dolls, and baskets. Nicholas is also a dedicated teacher, offering her knowledge of the Oneida language to her students.

MURIEL NICHOLAS

(a.k.a. Kawenaehente)
Mohawk (1913–) Oka, Quebec, Canada
Beaded leatherworker

EDUCATION: Took beadwork classes.

ABOUT THE ARTIST: Nicholas started beading on leather when convalescing in the late 1970s. She creates beaded key chains, wallets, purses, hats, and moccasins. Her granddaughter is following in her footsteps.

PAT NICHOLAS

Oneida (1953–) Southwold, Ontario, Canada
Artist–pencil, oil pastels, chalk, acrylics, watercolors

EDUCATION: Self-taught.

ABOUT THE ARTIST: Nicholas does pencil portraits and watercolors of nature scenes. One of her designs graced the cover of *Three Generations*, a book about three generations of people on the reserve. She also does beadwork.

BEN NIGHTHORSE
(a.k.a. Ben Nighthorse Campbell)

Northern Cheyenne (1933–) Auburn, California
Jeweler–gold, sterling

EDUCATION: Learned the art of making jewelry from his father, Albert; Bachelor of Art, San Jose University; Meiji University, Tokyo.

AWARDS: More than 200 first place awards, including those received at the Santa Fe Indian Market, Gallup Inter-Tribal Ceremonial California State Fair Art Show, Indian Arts and Crafts Association, and G' Dam Tash. Nighthorse is now retired from juried competition.

REPRESENTATION: The Squash Blossom, Aspen, Vail, and Denver Colorado; TohAtin Gallery, Durango, Colorado; Fortunoff's, New York, NY; Interior Craft Shop, Washington, D.C.; Gallery of the West, Old Sacramento, California

ABOUT THE ARTIST: Nighthorse works with as many as five different metals. His work is so intricate that there is often as many as thirty-eight steps in creating a piece of jewelry. Sometimes he incorporates petroglyphs into his jewelry designs. Nighthorse has sold his work to many luminaries such as movie stars and Presidents Bush, Reagan,

Portrait of Nighthorse, courtesy of the artist.

Ford, Carter, and Nixon. His contemporary jewelry is admired by his peers; Nighthorse is considered one of the best in the business. In addition to being a talented artist, Nighthorse has also acted as a United States Congressman from Colorado's 3rd district. He currently is a United States Senator from Colorado.

SHELLEY NIRO
(a.k.a. Shelley Doxtater)

Mohawk (1954–) Niagara Falls, New York
Painter, sculptor, photographer, filmmaker

REPRESENTATION: Sacred Circle Gallery of American Indian Art, Seattle, Washington

ABOUT THE ARTIST: Niro's collection of photographs entitled *Mohawks in Beehives* showed at Ottawa's Ufundi Gallery in 1991 and surprised viewers. Since that time, Niro's sense of humor in her photographs has been recognized nationally. A film that Niro wrote in 1992, *It Starts with a Whisper*, starred her three sisters and won the Walking in Beauty Award at the Two Rivers Film and Video Festival in Minneapolis.

DENNIS NUMKENA
Hopi (N/A)
Painter, architect.

REPRESENTATION: Firehouse Gallery of Fine Arts, Bisbee, Arizona

ABOUT THE ARTIST: Numkena has designed sets and costumes for "The Magic Flute" by Mozart, an event held in Vienna.

J. NUMKENA-TALAYUMPTEWA
Navajo/Hopi (N/A) Tuba City, Arizona
Artist–watercolor and ink

ABOUT THE ARTIST: Numkena-Talayumptewa's Native teachings came mostly from her father's side of the family, the Hopi side. She often illustrates Hopi ceremonies and traditions in her work, using soft colors which blend traditional style with the contemporary.

THERESA OAKES
(a.k.a. Ta Ka Ne Ten Ha Wi)
Mohawk (1916–   ) St. Regis, Quebec, Canada
Basketmaker, quilter

EDUCATION: Learned by helping Mary Adams.

ABOUT THE ARTIST: Oakes uses black-ash splints and sweet grass to make small, fancy sewing baskets. An active basketmaker, she also teaches and creates quilts in her spare time.

DELORES OLDSHIELD
Seneca (1931–   ) Steamburg, New York
Beadworker, dollmaker, basketmaker

EDUCATION: Some of Oldshield's skills were learned from her mother, and sister, Ella; however, she also took cornhusk classes, learned how to make cloth costumes in classes taught by Dorothy Jimerson and Fie Jimerson, and took basketry classes from Nettie Watt, Kathryn Jamerson, and Miriam Lee.

ABOUT THE ARTIST: Oldshield, a prolific craftsperson, creates beaded medallions, necklaces, chokers, rings, earrings, and bracelets, as well as cornhusk dolls and black-ash splint baskets. She spends a lot of her time promoting Seneca arts and crafts, teaching beadwork classes, and helping the Allegany Arts & Crafts Coop.

BARBARA JEAN TELLER ORNELAS and ROSE ANN LEE
Navajo (1954–   ) Tucson, Arizona
Weavers

EDUCATION: Learned how to weave from their mother, Ruth Teller, and their grandmother, Susie Tom.

AWARDS: Best of Show, Santa Fe Indian Market (1987) for a rug made with sister Rosann Teller Lee—it was the first time a Navajo rug had taken Best of Show at the Market; Best of Show, Santa Fe (1991); Award for Excellence in Navajo Weaving, sponsored by Gloria Ross (1991).

ABOUT THE ARTISTS: These two sisters sell their rugs directly to clients at the Santa Fe Indian Market. They also demonstrate at museums and galleries. They create intricate patterns in shades of white, purple, yellow, gray, pale pink, and blue. Their outspoken thoughts on the subject of weaving are effective in bringing ethnic artists together and convincing others that weaving is an art, not just a craft. Rose weaves only in the Two Gray Hills style, while Barbara does Burnt Water and Ganado.

FELIPE ORTEGA
Jicarilla Apache (N/A) La Madera, New Mexico
Potter

EDUCATION: Jesucita Martinez of Petaca taught Ortega to make micaceous bean pots.

ABOUT THE ARTIST: Ortega continued Martinez's traditional pots. After Martinez's death, Ortega was the only Jicarilla making them. He has since taught others the art in order to keep the tradition alive.

SEFERINA ORTIZ
Cochiti (1931 –   ) Arizona
Potter—Storyteller figures

EDUCATION: Learned how to pot from mother, Laurencita Herrera.

ABOUT THE ARTIST: Ortiz's pottery-making family includes her grandmothers, Reyes Romero and Seferina Suina, and her great-aunt, Estephanita Herrera. Ortiz has also passed on her skills to her own children: Joyce Ortiz Lewis, Janice Ortiz, Juanita I. Ortiz, and Virgil Ortiz. Her style does not require special tools or techniques, she just creates as she "go(es) along and see(s) what comes out." Ortiz began making small dolls and animals in the early 1960s and created her first Storyteller in 1962. Her work, along with other Storyteller makers, was heralded in the 1973 Museum of International Folk Art in Santa Fe's show "What Is Folk Art?"

CLYDE LELAND OTIPOBY

Comanche (1940 –   ) Clinton, Oklahoma
Artist, illustrator, potter, sculptor

EDUCATION: Arkansas City Junior College, Kansas; Oklahoma State University (1966–1968).

ABOUT THE ARTIST: Otipoby worked as an illustrator in the Air Force for four years and taught art at the Lincoln Elementary School in Ponca City, Oklahoma. His work has been exhibited throughout the Southwest.

AMOS OWEN

Sioux/Dakotah (N/A) Sisseton, South Dakota
Carver–pipes

EDUCATION: Learned from the old Sioux men who carved.

ABOUT THE ARTIST: Owen carves pipes for the sacred pipe ceremony, as well as for collectors. Though he has studied the old ways, Owen uses modern tools such as an electric drill, sandpaper, and beeswax for polishing. He gets his stone from the Pipestone Quarries in Pipestone, Minnesota. The site has been the place where many tribes have mined their sacred stone, just as their ancestors did before them. Each pipe Owen makes is blessed before it is given to a person for ceremonial use.

ANGIE REANO OWEN

Santo Domingo (1946 –   ) Santo Domingo
Pueblo, New Mexico
Jeweler

EDUCATION: Owen worked with her parents, Joe I. Reano and Clara Lovato Reano, to make jewelry. As an adult, Owen researched ancient mosaic work and taught herself the tradition of creating mosaic "in the round" work originally done by the Hohokam.

AWARDS: Owen's mosaic bracelets have won numerous awards and have been included in exhibits at the American Craft Museum, the Millicent Rogers Museum, and the Albuquerque International Airport.

REPRESENTATION: Gallery 10, Inc., Scottsdale and Carefree, Arizona, and Santa Fe, New Mexico; American Indian Contemporary Arts, San Francisco, California; The Squash Blossom, Vail, Aspen, and Denver, Colorado; The Indian Craft Shop, Washington, D.C.; Dewey Galleries, Ltd., Santa Fe, New Mexico; Packard's Indian Trading Co., Inc., Santa Fe, New Mexico; Wheelwright Museum of the American Indian/Case Trading Post, Santa Fe, New Mexico; Quintana's Galleries, Portland, Oregon; Indian Post, Allentown, Pennsylvania; Texas Art Gallery, Dallas, Texas

ABOUT THE ARTIST: Owen slices the stones and shells she uses into smaller pieces, then glues them into a mosaic design. Once the design is completely dry, Owen grinds the piece and buffs and polishes it.

ROSE OWENS

Navajo (1929 –   ) Cross Canyon, Arizona
Weaver

EDUCATION: Self-taught.

ABOUT THE ARTIST: Owens had the idea to weave round rugs back in the 1950s. Today fewer than twenty-four weavers create round rugs. Owen mainly weaves in the Ganado Red design, but also uses twill and two-faced weaves. She is a versatile weaver who also makes full-scale chief blankets, rectangular Ganado Red rugs, experimental patterns, and twill saddle blankets. She also weaves special designs for customers all over the country. Owen credits weaving with keeping her healthy, sane, and strong. Owens is an herbalist and communicates that knowledge to others to keep the Navajo ways alive.

LOREN PAHSETOPAH

(a.k.a. "Four Hills")
Cherokee/Osage (1935 –   ) Pawhuska, Oklahoma
Artist

EDUCATION: Self-taught; began painting in 1941.

AWARDS: Pahsetopah's awards include three Second Awards at the American Indian Artists Exhibition at the Philbrook Art Center in Tulsa (1962, 1965, 1967).

ABOUT THE ARTIST: Pahsetopah's work has been exhibited nationally and internationally. His style is simple and natural, often focusing on the Native American family.

PAUL PAHSETOPAH

(a.k.a. "Four Hills")
> Cherokee/Osage (1932 –   ) Pawhuska, Oklahoma
> Artist

EDUCATION: Like his brother, Loren, Pahsetopah is self-taught.

AWARDS: Pahsetopah's awards include a First Award from the American Indian Artists Exhibition at the Philbrook Art Center (1967).

ABOUT THE ARTIST: Pahsetopah has exhibited his work throughout the United States in group shows. He also makes dance costumes and sings at various Native American events.

ALICE PAPINEAU

(a.k.a. De Wa Senta)
> Onondaga (1912–) Onondaga Nation, Nedrow, New York
> Beadworker, jeweler, basketmaker, leatherworker, dollmaker

EDUCATION: Papineau learned most of the Iroquois traditions by working with Mrs. Menros, a missionary Alice knew as a teenager.

ABOUT THE ARTIST: Papineau joined the American Indian Village group in 1964, traveling widely with the group, giving talks about herbs and caring for their traveling museum of Indian relics. After she returned to her home, she ran the Onondage Trading Post.

GLADYS PAQUIN

> Laguna (N/A) New Mexico
> Potter

ABOUT THE ARTIST: Paquin feels she puts a lot of herself in the pot and has to tell it how to be. Each of her pots is a little different.

CATHERINE PASCAL

> Mount Currie (N/A) Mount Currie, British Columbia, Canada
> Basketmaker

ABOUT THE ARTIST: Pascal gathers her own materials for her baskets—white straw made from red canary grass is picked along the highway, wild cherry bark is taken from an area far from her home. Pascal makes items such as baskets and cradleboards for babies.

ALICE PAUL

> Northwest Coast (N/A) Victoria, British Columbia, Canada
> Basketmaker

ABOUT THE ARTIST: Paul returns to her original home in Hesquiat every year to pick cedar and grass to make her baskets. She uses the Whale in her designs because her people always considered it a vital part of their lives. They used every bit of the whale in trading and making things for personal or household use.

DORA TSE PE PEÑA

> San Ildefonso (N/A) New Mexico
> Potter

REPRESENTATION: Gallery 10, Inc., Santa Fe, New Mexico

ROBERT PENN

> Artist—various media

REPRESENTATION: Toh Atin Gallery, Durango, Colorado

Peña's three pieces of pottery (vase, large bowl, small bowl with figure), courtesy of the artist and Gallery 10, Inc., Scottsdale, Arizona.

ABOUT THE ARTIST: Penn feels that today's Native American artist is a hybrid of two cultures—the ancient and the contemporary. Though he's proud to paint about his people, Penn, like many others, wishes to be known as a communicator through his art .

ELLA ROSE PERRY

Navajo (1929 –   ) near St. Michaels, Arizona
Weaver

EDUCATION: Perry's mother taught her how to weave.

REPRESENTATION: Toh Atin Gallery, Durango, Colorado

ABOUT THE ARTIST: The Crystal rugs Perry weaves are recognizable for their soft colors and mohair-like texture. Perry takes pains to give her side selvages near-perfect edges and is well-respected for her talent. For thirty years, Perry has worked at the Bureau of Indian Affairs boarding school in Crystal, New Mexico. That was where she learned the Crystal style of weaving. She is now teaching her daughter, Marlene, the art.

KEVIN PESHALAKAI

Cochiti (1963 –   ) Cochiti Pueblo, New Mexico
Potter—Storyteller figures

EDUCATION: Learned the trade from his grandmother, Helen Cordero, and other members of the Cordero family.

REPRESENTATION: Adobe Gallery, Albuquerque, New Mexico

ABOUT THE ARTIST: Peshalakai made his first Storyteller in 1981.

DAVID PESHLAKAI

Navajo (N/A) Sheep Springs, New Mexico
Sandpainter

ABOUT THE ARTIST: Peshlakai creates nontraditional sandpaintings, such as pictures of children in native costumes.

MARY LOU PESHLAKAI

Navajo (N/A) Sheep Springs, New Mexico
Sandpainter

ABOUT THE ARTIST: Peshlakai's first attempt at portraiture in 1977 was the "Indian Chief," a sandpainting of a chief holding a peace pipe. Because sandpainting mistakes are difficult to correct, Peshlakai started the painting at the top of the piece and worked downward, creating a man whose legs were too short simply because she had run out of room.

NORBERT PESHLAKAI

Navajo (N/A) Fort Defiance, Arizona
Jeweler, silversmith

EDUCATION: Studied painting and jewelry making at Haskell Junior College for Native Americans, Kansas.

ABOUT THE ARTIST: Peshlakai creates silver jewelry and miniature silver pots. He often stamps his designs on his pieces and is influenced by the

Crystal textiles woven by his mother. He is a fourth-generation silversmith; in fact, the word *peshlakai* means "silver" in Navajo.

JUNE PETERS
(a.k.a. Ga Yah Don Nes)
Seneca (1963 –   )
Beadworker

EDUCATION: Learned her beadworking skills from her grandmother, Ethel Hill.

ABOUT THE ARTIST: Peters makes beaded jewelry and has exhibited her work at the New York State Fair.

MARY PETERS
Salish (N/A) Seabird Island Reserve, British
Columbia, Canada
Weaver

EDUCATION: Peters learned the art of weaving from her family.

ABOUT THE ARTIST: Peters was the last of the Salish weavers until Oliver Wells started reviving the art. She has made blankets with the symbol of flying geese, which has become the trademark of Salish weaving.

NORA PETERS
Salish (N/A) Green Point, British Columbia,
Canada
Weaver

EDUCATION: Peters learned about working with wool from her family.

ABOUT THE ARTIST: Peters has acted as president of the Salish Weavers, spinning and dyeing wool for them. Her whole family, including her husband, daughters, sons, and other members helps with the weaving.

MYRTLE PETERSON
(a.k.a. Tidiwe: Nosah)
Seneca (1912 –   ) Allegany Reservation, New York
Beadworker, dollmaker, leatherworker

EDUCATION: Though Peterson learned most of her skills from her mother and grandmother, she also took some classes at the Allegany Indian Arts & Crafts Coop.

ABOUT THE ARTIST: Peterson is well respected for her large variety of beadwork pieces, as well as her cornhusk dolls, baskets, and corn and acorn necklaces. She travels to fairs to sell her work. Concerned with preserving Seneca history and its language, Peterson has instructed others in learning the language, and was working to compile a Seneca dictionary in the late 1970s. She is also well known for her storytelling, a skill she learned from her grandmother.

WAYNE PETERSON
Haida (N/A) Port Edward, Canada
Carver

ABOUT THE ARTIST: Peterson often carves from alder when he creates his masks.

DONNA PHILLIPS
Oneida (1941 –   ) London, Ontario, Canada
Beadworker, clothing designer, leatherworker, knitter,
crocheter

EDUCATION: Took some beadwork classes.

ABOUT THE ARTIST: Phillips learned about her culture from an Oneida woman in the States and began using old Iroquois design elements and symbols in her own beadwork. She uses beaded eels, wolves, thunderbirds, deer, turtles, and bears in her designs. She has created beaded dance costumes and has decorated leather goods with traditional Iroquois designs. Phillips teaches crafts as well as cultural topics.

ESTHER KANE PHILLIPS
(a.k.a. White Dove)
Mohawk (1920 –   )
Beadworker, weaver, dollmaker

EDUCATION: Learned how to bead from her grandmother and mother.

ABOUT THE ARTIST: Phillips makes beaded necklaces, headpieces, medallions, and rings. She weaves pillows, dresser scarves, and wall hangings, and also makes small leather dolls. She had a career in show business before returning to her craftwork and is an active member of a Mohawk dance and song group. Phillips also teaches the Mohawk language and encourages others to carry on Iroquois traditions.

LOREN PHILLIPS

Hopi (N/A) Arizona
Carver—Kachinas

REPRESENTATION: Adobe Gallery, Albuquerque, New Mexico

ABOUT THE ARTIST: Phillips gets anatomy books from the library and studies the muscles and ligaments so that his carved Kachinas are more lifelike.

MORGAN PHILLIPS

(a.k.a. Kahentonni)
Mohawk (1962 —   ) Caughnawaga, Quebec, Canada
Beadworker

EDUCATION: Learned how to bead from a friend.

ABOUT THE ARTIST: Phillips began loom beadwork at age ten and uses her own patterns or standard designs she sees in books. She prefers to let her customers choose their own colors.

RITA PHILLIPS

(a.k.a. Wita)
Mohawk (1929 —   ) Caughnawaga, Quebec, Canada
Illustrator, painter, beadworker, dollmaker

EDUCATION: Self-taught.

ABOUT THE ARTIST: Phillips's illustrations have been published in books on Quebec Native Americans. She is also an educator who feels that Iroquois arts should be recognized as legitimate art forms. She has worked closely with others to produce Mohawk language books.

VICTORIA PHILLIPS

Mohawk (1946 —   ) Hogansburg, New York
Basketmaker, splint worker

EDUCATION: Took basketmaking classes at the Akwesasne Library (1969).

REPRESENTATION: Mohawk Craft Fund.

ABOUT THE ARTIST: Phillips uses black-ash and sweet grass to make her sewing, fancy, strawberry, and button baskets. She also creates wastepaper baskets, doll bassinets, splintwork bells, and pincushions. She has attended many craft shows, powwows, and fairs.

OQWA PI

San Ildefonso (1900–1971) San Ildefonso, New Mexico
Painter

EDUCATION: Untrained.

AWARDS: Received awards from his constituents and at exhibits.

ABOUT THE ARTIST: Pi began painting around 1919 and was encouraged to continue. Because he turned out a large number of paintings during this life, he made a good living at his art. His first exhibit was at the 1931 Exposition of Indian Tribal Arts in New York City. After that time, his work was shown almost everywhere.

CONNIE PIERCE

Seneca (1932 —   )
Beadworker

EDUCATION: Learned how to do beadwork, leather tooling, fabric stenciling, and cross-stitch work at the Thomas Indian School.

ABOUT THE ARTIST: Pierce prefers to make bead jewelry, often using porcupine quills as accents in her designs. She does much of her work on a loom. Her medallion patterns include the wolf, turtle, bear, beaver, and snipe. The buyer decides what colors Pierce should use. Pierce has taught her daughter and her sister how to do beadwork.

DAVID PIERCE

Seneca (1961–) Gowanda, New York
Beadworker, quillworker, featherworker

EDUCATION: Self-taught.

ABOUT THE ARTIST: Pierce has exhibited his bead-work and God's eye pieces at the Indian Fall Festival. He creates his own native clothing and uses feathers, porcupine quills, claws, furs, and shells in his beadwork. Though he specializes in loomwork, Pierce takes orders for anything a customer may want. He has experimented with many craft forms and is always expanding his art background. He also dances and sings in the Longhouse and is now teaching his brothers and sisters both traditions so that they may keep the art forms alive.

RODNEY PIERCE

Seneca (1961 –)
Beadworker

EDUCATION: Self-taught.

ABOUT THE ARTIST: Pierce has made bone bead-work breastplates and chokers and loom beadwork belts and wristbands. He also works with feathers. A dancer who travels regularly to festivals and fairs, Pierce takes his items with him to show new customers. He has learned about his culture by being a guide at the Seneca Iroquois National Museum and passes on what he has learned to whomever wants the knowledge. Pierce's grandmother, Nettie Watt, a well-known basketmaker, taught him to make baskets.

LORENCITA PINO

Tesuque (N/A) Arizona
Potter

ABOUT THE ARTIST: Pino sculpts human faces into the sides of her pieces.

MARLIN PINTO

Zuni-Tewa (1957 –) Zuni, New Mexico
Carver– Kachinas

ABOUT THE ARTIST: Pinto specializes in miniature Zuni, Hopi, and Tewa dolls because those tribes interchange Kachinas. Every time Pinto carves a Kachina, he purposely makes a mistake to let the spirit out. He uses a pocketknife as his main tool and uses acrylic paint to make his dolls more realistic. His family is well known—his grandmother, Nampeyo, was a famous Tewa potter; his uncle, Ray Naha, was a Tewa painter; his grandmother, Daisy Nampeyo, was a Tewa potter; and his mother, Shirley Ben, is a Tewa jewelry maker.

PITSEOLAK

Eskimo (approximately 1900 –) Hudson Bay,
Canada
Graphic artist–stone cuts, engravings and drawings
with felt-tip pen

EDUCATION: Self-taught.

ABOUT THE ARTIST: Pitseolak creates images of myths and monsters she believes to be the past and about Eskimo life as she knows it. The wife of a migrant hunter, Pitseolak moved all over the Arctic, teaching herself how to be an artist, making a living with her work, then passing on her skills to some of her seventeen children (eleven are deceased).

LILLIAN PITT

Warm Springs Yakama/Wasco (1943 –) Warm
Springs, Oregon
Mask artist–ceramics, mixed media

EDUCATION: Associate of Art, Mt. Hood Community College, Gresham, Oregon.

AWARDS: Governor's Award for the Arts, Oregon (1990); City of Oguni, Niigata Prefecture, Japan, Gift to City; Purchase Award, Oregon Percent for Arts, Metropolitan Arts Commission; Purchase Award, Washington State Arts Commission.

REPRESENTATION: Adobe East, Summit, New Jersey; American Indian Contemporary Arts, San Francisco, California; Artique Gallery Ltd.,

Portrait of Pitt in her studio with her decorated clay masks, courtesy of the artist.

Pitt's Wasco totem pole, ceramic mixed, 6' feet x 18 x 5 inches, courtesy of the artist.

Anchorage, Alaska; Bailey Nelson Gallery, Seattle, Washington; Buffalo Gallery, Alexandria, Virginia; Images of the North, San Francisco, California; Quintana's Gallery, Portland, Oregon; Rattlesnake & Star, San Antonio, Texas; Scanlon Gallery, Ketchikan, Alaska; Sunbird Gallery, Bend, Oregon

ABOUT THE ARTIST: Pitt was first inspired by the Northwest Coast masks she owned and decided to try to imitate their style. Though she usually embellishes her work with Plateau and Wasco decorations and patterns, Pitt has also been influenced by those who use the Japanese ceramic firing method called Raku and the Anagama firing method, also Japanese. Her masks are both human and animal images derived from the long history of those masks carved by Northwest Coast tribes. Pitt shows all over the world. Her works are held by many museums and galleries and are featured in many publications.

McKEE PLATERO
Navajo (1957 —) New Mexico
Jeweler

REPRESENTATION: Teal McKibben, Santa Fe, New Mexico.

ABOUT THE ARTIST: Platero creates silverstamped, as gold, red brass, and iron work. He does his own lapidary work. Platero's inspiration comes from nature and worldly events. He often creates work related to the political strife of the day.

VERONICA POBLANO
Jeweler

AWARDS: Best of Division, Red Earth awards ceremony (1994).

TOM POLACCA
Tewa/Hopi (N/A) Arizona
Potter

EDUCATION: Learned how to pot from members of his famous family.

ABOUT THE ARTIST: Polacca, Fannie Nampeyo's son, could not show his pots at first because potters are traditionally female.

OTIS POLELONEMA

Hopi (1902–1981) Shungopovi, Second Mesa, Arizona
Painter—watercolor on paper

EDUCATION: Santa Fe Indian School, New Mexico.

REPRESENTATION: Amerind Foundation Museum, Dragoon, Arizona.

ABOUT THE ARTIST: Polelonema and Fred Kabotie are said to have started the "Hopi" style of painting. Polelonema's delicate touch with the brush captured details of Hopi life. His and Kabotie's skills were an apex that generations of other artists attempted to reach.

AMIE POODRY

Seneca (1954 –   ) Basom, New York
Beadworker

EDUCATION: Learned how to bead from her mother, Doris Sundown.

ABOUT THE ARTIST: Poodry does both loom and freehand beadwork to create neckties, headbands, wristbands and armbands, jewelry, and barrettes. She usually uses patterns from craft books or her mother's designs, but she sometimes relies on her own inspiration. She also makes native outfits for children and intends to become more involved with Iroquois crafts as time passes.

NANCY POODRY

Cayuga (1951 –   )
Beadworker, dollmaker

EDUCATION: Though largely self-taught, Poodry learned how to make cornhusk dolls from Edna Parker and Betsy Carpenter.

AWARDS: Include a first prize award at the New York State Fair for a cradleboard and coverings (1976).

ABOUT THE ARTIST: Poodry and her husband, Ken, began making traditional items in the early 1970s. Ken made cradleboards which Nancy decorated with beaded pieces. They both made cornhusk dolls, which Nancy dressed and beaded, using traditional materials, colors, and designs.

PHIL POSEYESVA

Hopi (1958 –   ) Arizona
Jeweler

EDUCATION: Was influenced by Charles Loloma and began combining traditional work with the contemporary.

REPRESENTATION: Lovena Ohl Gallery, Scottsdale, Arizona; Waddell Trading Company, Tempe, Arizona; Ansel Adams Gallery, Yosemite National Park, California; Mudhead Gallery, Beaver Creek and Denver, Colorado; Southwest Expressions, Chicago, Illinois; Adobe East Gallery, Millburn, New Jersey; Packard's Indian Trading Co., Inc., Santa Fe, New Mexico; The Turquoise Lady, Houston, Texas

ABOUT THE ARTIST: Poseyesva combines traditional Hopi overlay styles with asymmetry and lapidary touches. He uses both gold and silver in his work, draws his designs freehand, and often places his stones slightly off-center to accentuate his detailed overlay designs.

KAREN POWLESS

Seneca (N/A) Cattaraugus Indian Reservation, New York
Beadworker, moccasin designer, quillworker

EDUCATION: Taught herself a lot of techniques; also learned from her brother and friends; Associate of Art, Art major, Jamestown Community College.

ABOUT THE ARTIST: Powless is known for the variety of the types of beadwork she creates. The items she decorates include hair ties, necklaces, rings, medallions, key chains, lighter covers, belts, headbands, chokers, wristbands, watchbands, and barrettes. Her porcupine quill work is an added talent, as are her abilities to make bead chokers and earrings, bone chokers, and hair ties.

CHARLES PRATT

Cheyenne/Arapaho/French (N/A) Concho, Oklahoma
Sculptor, jeweler—various metals and semiprecious stones

EDUCATION: Self-taught; learned how to work with clay from his grandfather.

AWARDS: Listed in *Who's Who in American Art* and has won approximately 400 awards for his work.

REPRESENTATION: Silver Suns Traders, Albuquerque and Santa Fe, New Mexico.

ABOUT THE ARTIST: Pratt was influenced by Allan Houser's 1960s welded sculptures. Pratt creates large-scale and miniature creations in cast-bronze.

He also creates metal and stone sculpture and is an accomplished silversmith. Pratt weaves colors and textures from his heritage into his signature works which include "The Blue Corn People." Places that have commissioned his works include the Heard Museum, the Philbrook Art Center, the Oklahoma Science and Arts Foundation, and the A. Murrad Federal Building in Oklahoma City.

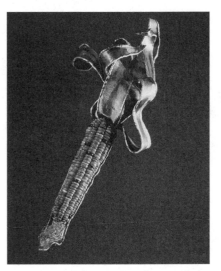

Pratt's signature piece, "Blue Corn," cast bronze and turquoise (with other semiprecious stones), 12 x 3 inches, courtesy of the artist.

KIM PRICE

Pawnee/Otoe/Kaw/Kiowa (1957 –   ) Pawnee, Oklahoma
Beadworker—leather, fabrics

EDUCATION: Two years of college.

REPRESENTATION: The Turquoise Lady, Wichita Falls, Texas

ABOUT THE ARTIST: Price's beaded work is a combination of contemporary and traditional styles. Though she often works with leather, as her ancestors did, she also creates beadwork-decorated denim jackets, pillows, earrings, vests, and bags. Her work has been sold to customers in the United States and Europe.

Portrait of Pratt with his "Standing Mudhead" (5 feet 6 inches tall), courtesy of the artist.

Portrait of Price, courtesy of the artist.

MAGGIE PRICE

Navajo (1934 —) Sanders, Arizona
Weaver

EDUCATION: All of the women in Price's family weave. They learn from each other.

ABOUT THE ARTIST: Price sold her first rug when she was nineteen and often turns out an average of three rugs a year. Price's daughter is also an excellent weaver.

WILSON PRICE

Navajo (N/A) Sheep Springs, New Mexico
Sandpainter

ABOUT THE ARTIST: When creating his sandpaintings, Price uses new color hues and new materials to counteract the power of the Holy People. He was one of the first sandpainters to create nontraditional sandpaintings, such as his 1977 work depicting the masked impersonator who dances in Big Godway and Nightway ceremonies.

ANNETTE PRINTUP

Cayuga/Tuscarora (1958 —) Lewiston, New York
Beadworker, wireworker, quillworker, graphic artist

EDUCATION: Learned by watching her mother, Marlene, and her grandmothers.

AWARDS: Printup has won awards for her beadwork and graphics. at the New York State Fair and New York State Iroquois Conference.

ABOUT THE ARTIST: Printup often uses her own designs, though she will make whatever her customers desire. She creatively blends the colors and designs in her beadwork so that her work is easily recognizable. Her beadwork adorns barrettes, bolo ties, necklaces, collars, picture frames, leather purses, and many other items. Her etchings, engravings, and woodcuts have also been award-winners.

DORIS PRINTUP

Cayuga (1930 —) Lewiston, New York
Beadworker, leatherworker, quillworker, wireworker,
clothes designer

EDUCATION: Learned most of her skills from her mother-in-law, Minnie Printup, and Inez Green. Printup also picked up other techniques on her own.

AWARDS: Among her prizes is a first prize from the New York State Fair for a pair of beaded moccasins (1977).

ABOUT THE ARTIST: Printup began making small decorated moccasin pins in her twenties and later began making rings. From there, she stepped into other crafts, usually incorporating a floral design into her work. She is a master craftswoman who also teaches others her arts.

MARLENE PRINTUP

Cayuga (1938 —)
Beadworker

EDUCATION: Learned from Harriet Pembleton, her husband's grandmother.

ABOUT THE ARTIST: Printup has made beaded medallions, belt buckles, jewelry, watchbands, picture frames, and cushions, working to decorate both cloth and leather items with her designs. She has exhibited at the New York State Fair, as well as other fairs, festivals, and crafts shows.

MARY LOU PRINTUP

Tuscarora (1939 –   ) Lewiston, New York
Beadworker, clothing designer

EDUCATION: Learned from her mother.

AWARDS: Among her awards are first and second prizes won at the New York State Fair for her beaded cushions.

ABOUT THE ARTIST: Printup is surrounded by family members who are proficient at beadwork and she follows in their tradition. She does shows, conventions, and takes orders for her belt buckles, medallions, jewelry, and beaded cushions. In addition, she makes ribbon shirts and beadwork designs on clothing. Printup encourages her children to follow in her footsteps.

TOM PRINTUP

Seneca (1940 –   )
Beadworker, leatherworker, dollmaker, basketmaker

EDUCATION: Tessie Snow taught Printup the art of beadwork, while his grandmother taught him how to make cornhusk dolls.

ABOUT THE ARTIST: Printup experiments in both technique and creative detail with his designs. Besides making beadwork jewelry, he does both flat and raised beadwork and creates decorative accents on costumes and leather purses. He likes using the traditional Iroquois or woodland floral designs. Prolific in his work, Printup also makes baskets, has carved masks, and teaches his skills to others.

CHARLES PUSHETONEQUA

(a.k.a. Wawabano Data, "Dawn Walker")
Sauk-Fox (1915 –   ) Tama City, Iowa
Painter

EDUCATION: Pipestone, Minnesota Indian School;Haskell Institute, Lawrence, Kansas; Santa Fe Indian School.

ABOUT THE ARTIST: Pushetonequa actively participated in the Sauk and Fox community's Indian Crafts organization at Tama. His paintings realistically depict the life and history of the Sauk-Fox people.

AL QÖYAWAYMA

(a.k.a. "Gray Fox Walking at Dawn")
Hopi (1938–) Los Angeles, California
Potter

EDUCATION: Studied with his aunt, Hopi potter Elizabeth White; worked with ceramics in high school; Bachelor of Science, Mechanical Engineering, California State Polytechnic University, San Luis Obispo (1961).

REPRESENTATION: Gallery 10, Inc., Santa Fe, New Mexico

ABOUT THE ARTIST: Though he had learned how to work with clay as a child, Qöyawayma has spent much of his life as a manager of environmental services and founded the American Indian Science and Engineering Society. As an artist, Qöyawayma

Three pieces of pottery by Qöyawayma (two decorated vases and one pot), courtesy of the artist and Gallery 10, Inc., Scottsdale, Arizona.

believes that ". . . most pottery today reflects the past . . ." His pottery is embellished with sculpted figures (sometimes Kachinas) and is often done in an elegant bone/white color. His pieces could be considered a blend of pottery and sculpture, a style which is unique and completely his own. Though he has been inspired by the ancient pottery, Qöyawayma brings his own talents to the art. He has also served as consultant to the Smithsonian Institute which is trying to identify the original clay sources used by ancient Hopi potters.

ANDRES QUANDELACY

Zuni (N/A) New Mexico
Jeweler, carver

EDUCATION: Learned some of his carving skills from his mother, as well as other members of his well-known family.

REPRESENTATION: The Indian Craft Shop, Washington, D.C.; Keshi-The Zuni Connection, Santa Fe, New Mexico; Wadle Galleries, Ltd., Santa Fe, New Mexico

ABOUT THE ARTIST: Quandelacy carves fetish necklaces and standing fetishes. His bears are standing bears.

ELLEN QUANDELACY

Zuni (1924 –   ) New Mexico
Jeweler, carver

EDUCATION: Learned from her father and her husband how to make fetish necklaces and tabletop fetishes.

REPRESENTATION: Wadle Galleries, Ltd., Santa Fe, New Mexico; The Indian Craft Shop, Washington, D.C.; Keshi-The Zuni Connection, Santa Fe, New Mexico; Quintana's Gallery, Portland, Oregon; Red Rock Trading Company, Alexandria, Virginia

ABOUT THE ARTIST: Quandelacy is the matriarch of a large Zuni family who have become noted for their fetish necklaces and tabletop fetishes. She

began making jewelry at age forty-six, creating channel inlay silver bracelets and necklaces (signed "E.Q. Zuni"). In the 1980s, Quandelacy had a stroke and began carving animals from stone, which are very collectible today.

FAYE QUANDELACY

Zuni (1958 –   ) New Mexico
Jeweler, carver, potter, sculptor

EDUCATION: Attended the Institute of American Indian Art, Santa Fe, New Mexico.

REPRESENTATION: The Indian Craft Shop, Washington, D.C.; Keshi-The Zuni Connection, Santa Fe, New Mexico; Wadle Galleries, Ltd., Santa Fe, New Mexico; Red Rock Trading Company, Alexandria, Virginia

ABOUT THE ARTIST: Quandelacy's Corn Maidens, decorated with crosses, dragonflies, and stars, are the most recognizable of her carvings. Her mother is Ellen Quandelacy.

GEORGIA QUANDELACY

Zuni (1957–) New Mexico
Jeweler, carver

EDUCATION: Learned some of her carving skill from her mother, Ellen.

REPRESENTATION: The Indian Craft Shop, Washington, D.C.; Keshi-The Zuni Connection, Santa Fe, New Mexico; Wadle Galleries, Ltd., Santa Fe, New Mexico

ABOUT THE ARTIST: Quandelacy bears are carved of jet and each has an inlaid sun design on the side.

STEWART QUANDELACY

Zuni (N/A) New Mexico
Jeweler, carver

EDUCATION: Learned some of his skills from his mother, Ellen.

REPRESENTATION: The Indian Craft Shop, Washington, D.C.; Keshi-The Zuni Connection, Santa Fe, New Mexico; Wadle Galleries, Ltd., Santa Fe, New Mexico

ABOUT THE ARTIST: Quandelacy carves fetish necklaces, as well as standing fetishes. His bears are medicine bears, with heart-lines and arched backs, and are the best known of the Quandelacy family carved bears.

MARGARET QUINTANA
Cheyenne/Arapaho (N/A) Watonga, Oklahoma
Potter—Storyteller figures

REPRESENTATION: Some Taos, New Mexico galleries carry her work.

ABOUT THE ARTIST: Quintana works with micaceous clay to create her Cochiti-style Storytellers. Her husband, Paul, is Cochiti. Quintana learned how to pot in the 1980s after moving to the Pueblo with him. Her work is held by museums such as the Millicent Rogers.

DEXTRA NAMPEO QUOTSKUYVA
Hopi-Tewa (1928 –   ) Arizona
Potter

EDUCATION: Learned how to pot from her mother, who learned from *her* grandmother, Nampeyo.

AWARDS: Her many awards include being designated one of Arizona's Indian Living Treasures (1994).

ABOUT THE ARTIST: Quotskuyva did not throw her first pot until 1967 when she was thirty-nine years old. When creating her work, Quotskuyva uses the same tools her great-grandmother, Nampeyo, did—organic and mineral paints, yucca leaf brushes, and polishing stones. Quotskuyva is recognized as one of the best potters in the Southwest.

WILLIAM RABBIT
Cherokee (19–) Oklahoma
Artist—oil

EDUCATION: Rabbit says he paints with the influence of Solomon McCombs, Fred Beaver, Blackbear Bosin, and Jerome Tiger.

AWARDS: Many honors, including first place at the Five Civilized Tribes Museum in Muskogee, Oklahoma (1981) and a number of prizes at the 61st Annual Gallup Ceremonial (1982); poster artist for the "Trail of Tears" art show (1985) and for an exhibit at the Smithsonian.

REPRESENTATION: Gomes Gallery Inc., St. Louis, Missouri

ABOUT THE ARTIST: Before producing the award-winning paintings for which he is well known, Rabbit worked as a silversmith in the early years of his career. Collections of his work are held all over the world.

GLEN RABENA
Yakima (N/A) Yakima Reservation, Washington
Carver

ABOUT THE ARTIST: Though Rabena is Yakima, he carves in the Gitksan style. He often uses birch for his masks.

HARVEY RATTEY
Pembina (1938–) near Harlem, Montana
Sculptor—bronze

Portrait of Rattey with his bronze "Down from the High Country," courtesy of the artist.

Rattey's bronze sculpture "Master of the Plains," 8½ x 9 x 5 inches, courtesy of the artist.

EDUCATION: Hines-Zemsky workshop with Robert Bateman; Zahourek, Anatomiken workshop; Edward Fraughton workshop.

AWARDS: Blue Chip Award, U.S. Chamber of Commerce, 1993; National Wild Turkey Federation Sculptor of the Year, 1992; and numerous others.

REPRESENTATION: Bridger Foundry & Gallery, Bozeman, Montana

ABOUT THE ARTIST: Rattey portrays his ancestors, cowboys, and animals in a "wild and wooly" fashion. His sculptures have been bought by dignitaries. His work has been exhibited in museums and shows all over the United States and Europe.

AUDREY RAY

Seneca (1949 –) Jimmersontown, New York
Beadworker, quillworker, dollmaker

EDUCATION: Self-taught.

ABOUT THE ARTIST: Ray works mostly with beading, though she has learned other crafts. She features clan animals and floral or geometric patterns in the wristbands and watchbands she makes. Her dolls are made with cornhusk, braided arms, and sometimes traditional clothing. She also has made baskets.

CHARLENE REANO

Santo Domingo (N/A) Santo Domingo Pueblo, New Mexico
Jeweler

EDUCATION: Reano learned her craft from her parents, Joe B. and Terry Reano.

CHARLOTTE AND PERCY REANO

Percy—Santo Domingo (1951 –)
Charlotte—Santo Domingo (1950 –) New Mexico
Jewelers—Mosaic, beadwork

EDUCATION: Percy learned how to make jewelry as a boy.

ABOUT THE ARTISTS: The couple work together; Percy cuts the material and does the final grinding of the beads while Charlotte drills and strings the beads. The Reanos use power-driven tools.

FRANK AND CHARLENE SANCHEZ REANO

Frank—Santo Domingo (1962 –)
Charlene San Felipe (1960 –)
Jewelers—mosaic

EDUCATION: Charlene studied art at New Mexico Highlands University. She and Frank worked with Angie Reano Owen (Frank's sister) to learn different techniques.

REPRESENTATION: Margaret Kilgore Gallery, Scottsdale, Arizona; American Indian Contemporary Arts, San Francisco, California

ABOUT THE ARTISTS: The Reanos have a unique earring style. They cut a shell in half, then cut a "kiva step" design inside each half. Charlene designs, cuts, and places the stones; Frank grinds the stones.

JOE B. AND TERRY REANO

Santo Domingo (N/A) New Mexico
Jewelers—turquoise

REPRESENTATION: Lovena Ohl Gallery, Scottsdale, Arizona

ABOUT THE ARTISTS: Joe and Terry (no relation to Charlotte and Percy Reano) make their necklaces by hand. They use only natural turquoise.

MARTIN E. RED BEAR

Ogala/Sicangu/Lakota Sioux (1951 –)
Painter

EDUCATION: Master of Art, Art Education, University of New Mexico (1982); Bachelor of Art, Visual Arts, College of Santa Fe (1980); Associate of Fine Art, Two-Dimension Design Painting , Institute of American Indian Arts (1978); Certificate in Fine Arts, Rocky Mountain School of Art (1976).

AWARDS: Red Bear has won many honors and awards for his teaching skills, including first place in Oil & Acrylic Painting Division, Northern Plains Tribal Arts Show, South Dakota (1992).

REPRESENTATION: The Heritage Center, Inc., Pine Ridge, South Dakota

ABOUT THE ARTIST: Red Bear has exhibited in the Northern Plains Tribal Arts show. A collection of his work is held by the Minneapolis Institute of Arts. His work has also been highlighted in a book published in concert with the Institute's exhibit in 1992.

Red Bear's painting entitled "Warrior of Bear Clan," courtesy of The Heritage Center, Inc., Pine Ridge, South Dakota.

ROBERT REDBIRD

Kiowa (1939 –) Lawton, Oklahoma
Artist—oil, watercolor

EDUCATION: Oklahoma State Tech., Okmulgee, Oklahoma (1960–1962)

AWARDS: Best of Class in Theme and First Place in Painting, Colorado Indian Market, Denver (1987); named to the top five of "Best Investments in Indian Art under $1,000 for 1987".

141

Red Bear's painting entitled "Dancers & Star Quilt," courtesy of The Heritage Center, Inc., Pine Ridge, South Dakota.

Redbird, Jr.'s acrylic on board of woman wrapped in red-and-black blanket against a background of moon and stars, 32 x 40 inches, courtesy of the artist and SunWest Silver, Albuquerque, New Mexico.

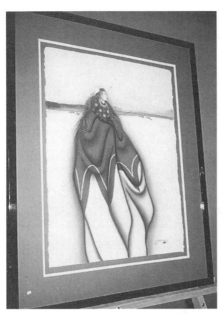

Redbird Jr.'s acrylic painting called Indian with landscape, 30 x 22 inches. courtesy of the artist and SunWest Silver, Albuquerque, New Mexico.

REPRESENTATION: Susan Peters Gallery, Anadarko, Oklahoma; Eagles Roost Gallery, Colorado Springs, Colorado

ABOUT THE ARTIST: Redbird is an associate pastor at the Tabernacle of Deliverance Church in Anadarko, Oklahoma. Collections of his work are held by Carnegie High School and private collectors. He has exhibited in one-person and group shows throughout the United States.

BILL REID
Haida (1920 –   ) Vancouver, British Columbia, Canada
Carver, jeweler—wood, silver, other materials

EDUCATION: One-year formal education at Victoria College(1937); largely self-taught; builds on traditional forms with his own innovative style.

ABOUT THE ARTIST: Reid is one of the best-known carvers in the Northwest, creating everything from abstract jewelry to house front poles to a four-and-one-half ton wooden sculpture. He has done jew-

elry and small and large carvings, using the crests known to the Haida people (i.e., the Raven, Eagle, Beaver, Bear, and Killer Whale). His larger carvings often adorn public buildings such as the Vancouver Public Aquarium and the University of British Columbia.

ELNORA REUBEN
(a.k.a. Joh Wehl Ah)
Seneca (1937 –   ) Basom, New York
Beadworker, dollmaker

EDUCATION: Learned by watching her stepfather.

ABOUT THE ARTIST: Reuben began actively working with beads in the mid 1960s. She designs her own medallion patterns; one of her specialties is a cameo medallion. Reuben often surrounds store-bought cameos with fancy beadwork. She also makes native clothing and costumes by order. Reuben has taught her children and others her crafts.

STEPHANIE C. RHOADES
(a.k.a. Snow Flake Flower)
Cochiti (1932 –   ) Cochiti Pueblo, New Mexico
Potter—Storyteller figures

EDUCATION: Learned some of her technique from Mary Martin, though mostly self-taught.

AWARDS: Some of the first awards Rhoades won for her Storytellers were at the New Mexico State Fair (1982) and the Indian Market (1983).

ABOUT THE ARTIST: Potters in Rhoade's family include her grandmother, Estephanita Herrera; her sister, Ada Suina; and her children, Jonathan Loretto and Morningstar Rhoades, to whom she has passed on her knowledge. Rhoades made her first Storyteller in 1979. She signs the name "Snow Flake Flower" to her works.

ROSE PECOS AND SUN RHODES
Rose—Jemez (1956 –   ) New Mexico
Sun—Jemez (N/A) New Mexico
Potters—Storyteller figures

ABOUT THE ARTISTS: This husband-and-wife team make Storytellers in the Navajo style. The children who gather round the Storyteller are often more realistically portrayed than the Storyteller. The figures are dressed in Navajo style and are often holding Navajo baskets or cradleboards.

MARGARET RICKARD

> *Tuscarora (1926 –)*
> *Beadworker, featherworker, wireworker, dollmaker,*
> *clothing designer*

EDUCATION: Learned from her mother, Hattie Williams.

ABOUT THE ARTIST: Rickard sells her beaded leather, felt and velvet items, feather earrings, wirework items, dolls in Iroquois dress, ribbon shirts, and cloth drawstring purses at Prospect Point, Niagara Falls; the New York State Fair; and many crafts shows in her area. She has taught her children her skills and also takes orders for special items such as quilts.

LEONARD RIDDLES

> (a.k.a. "Black Moon")
> *Comanche (1918 –) Walters, Oklahoma*
> *Artist*

EDUCATION: Studied mural techniques at the Indian Art Center in Fort Sill, Oklahoma (1938–1939).

AWARDS: His many awards include the First Award, Plains Division, from the Philbrook Art Center, Tulsa, Oklahoma (1969).

ABOUT THE ARTIST: Riddles has exhibited his work in many group and one-person shows throughout the United States. He paints scenes of Indian life in a clear and precise manner, using watercolors. He signs his work "Black Moon."

DOLONA ROBERT

> *Cherokee (N/A)*
> *Painter—acrylics*

ABOUT THE ARTIST: Robert paints in an abstract style.

WILMA LEE ROBERTS

> (a.k.a. Ga Sen Nee' Daeh')
> *Seneca (1919 –) Steamburg, New York*
> *Beadworker, dollmaker, basketmaker*

EDUCATION: Roberts' mother, Miriam Lee, taught her how to make baskets and beaded pieces; Roberts' sister, Doris Kenyon, taught her additional beadwork skills; Roberts took cornhusk craft classes at the Allegany Indian Arts & Crafts Coop.

ABOUT THE ARTIST: Roberts whole family has been involved in creating Iroquois products. Roberts' efforts in creating beaded jewelry, loom beadwork, cornhusk dolls, and baskets continue that tradition.

SADIE MARIE ROHLMAN

> (a.k.a. Gyn Da Nao)
> *Seneca (1898 –) Allegany Reservation*
> *Beadworker*

EDUCATION: Learned from her mother.

AWARDS: Won first prize for a Seneca beaded dress at the Seneca Indian Fall Festival in 1975; has also exhibited at the New York State Fair.

REPRESENTATION: Allegany Indian Arts & Crafts Coop

ABOUT THE ARTIST: Rohlman is known for the fineness of her beadwork. She created traditional raised beadwork as well as flat. She was always concerned about producing quality pieces and shared her concern for Iroquois traditions.

TONI ROLLER

> *Santa Clara (N/A) Santa Clara Pueblo,*
> *New Mexico*
> *Potter*

EDUCATION: Roller learned the pottery trade from her mother, Margaret Tafoya.

EDNA ROMERO

Taos (N/A) Taos Pueblo, New Mexico
Potter

EDUCATION: Learned from other potters in the area.

AWARDS: Romero has won awards for her pots at Indian markets.

ABOUT THE ARTIST: Romero began making pots during the late 1980s. Her micaceous style is graceful yet strong. She digs her clay from a mountain near Taos to make pots which can be used for cooking.

MARIA PRISCILLA ROMERO

Cochiti (1936 —) Cochiti Pueblo, New Mexico
Potter—Storyteller figures

EDUCATION: Learned the art of pottery from her mother, Maggie Chalan, and her mother-in-law, Teresita Romero.

ABOUT THE ARTIST: After making her first Storyteller in 1979, Romero has passed on what she has learned about pottery making to her daughter, Mary Eunice Ware. Romero is known for her small Storyteller Frogs.

VIRGINIA ROMERO

Taos (N/A) New Mexico
Potter

ABOUT THE ARTIST: Romero has not lost a pot since she began in 1919. According to Romero, that is because she uses wood instead of manure in her firing process. She does not add anything to her Taos clay; she just shapes her pots, smooths them (skipping the polishing process), and files them.

ROSIE ROSS

Salish (N/A) Lillooet, British Columbia, Canada
Basketmaker

ABOUT THE ARTIST: Ross makes lidded and unlidded baskets for sale to tourists and collectors.

LARRY ROSSO

Kwakiutl (N/A) Vancouver, British Columbia, Canada
Carver

ABOUT THE ARTIST: Rosso was adopted into the Mamalelekala through his wife, Alice. He makes bent wood boxes and storage chests. His designs are carved and painted and he often works with red cedar.

SKIP ROWELL

(N/A)
Painter

AWARDS: Won Best of Division (painting) at the Five Civilized Tribes Competitive Show (1994).

J. D. ROYBAL

(a.k.a. Oquwa, "Rain God")
San Ildefonso (1922 – 1978) San Ildefonso Pueblo, New Mexico
Artist—tempera

EDUCATION: Santa Fe Indian School, New Mexico.

REPRESENTATION: Adobe Gallery, Albuquerque, New Mexico.

ABOUT THE ARTIST: Roybal began painting in grade school, but he did not devote time to the art until the 1950s. He produced many paintings during the 1960s and 1970s. He was strongly influenced by San Ildefonso traditional painting styles, as well as by Santa Fe Studio designs.

THE RUNNELS FAMILY

Lakota
Sculptors, carvers—wood, clay, alabaster

The working artists in this family include Gerry, Ray, Gerry, Jr., and Carmel.

The Runnels Family creates dance sticks and clay and alabaster sculptures. They learn their crafts from each other and keep the work within the family. For more information about specific artists, contact The Heritage Center, Inc., Pine Ridge, South Dakota (see the gallery contributors list in the back of this book for the address).

MAMIE RYAN
Oneida (1903 –) Oneida, Wisconsin
Basketmaker, beadworker, jeweler, leatherworker

EDUCATION: Ryan's mother, Elizabeth Summers, taught her basketry. Ryan learned beadwork on her own.

ABOUT THE ARTIST: One of the last experienced basketmakers in Oneida, Ryan's baskets are made solely of black-ash splints (some are natural, some are dyed). She has passed on her skills to others in the hope that the art will not die. Ryan also creates cornhusk dolls, beadworked clothing and jewelry, and enthusiastically promotes all Native American arts.

RAMONA SAKIESTEWA
Hopi/Anglo (1948 –) Albuquerque, New Mexico
Weaver—various fibers

EDUCATION: Santa Fe Preparatory School (1966); Verde Valley School, Sedona, Arizona, (1966).

Black and white portrait of Sakiestewa. Photograph by Jack Parsons, courtesy of the artist and Horwitch LewAllen Gallery.

Sakiestewa has worked with Peruvian weavers to study their craft and native dyes.

AWARDS: Sakiestewa has won many honors from 1975 to the present, including a 1994 award for "Navajo Trail," a blanket design made for Pendleton; a 1988 Native American fellowship from the Smithsonian Institution; and a commission from the Frank Lloyd Wright Foundation in 1987–1989.

REPRESENTATION: Horwitch LewAllen Gallery, Santa Fe, New Mexico; Wheelright Museum of the American Indian, Santa Fe, New Mexico

ABOUT THE ARTIST: Sakiestewa uses a European horizontal (or floor) loom instead of a traditional vertical loom. She only uses plant dyes. Her stepfather (an Anglo) made certain Sakiestewa was surrounded by items that reflected her Native American heritage. Sakiestewa's weavings have been shown all over the world and at many important museums, such as the Smithsonian, the Heard, and the Wheelwright. In addition to her art, she is also a scholar. She was awarded several fellowships to study ancient textiles. In addition, she experiments with dyes, yarns, and looms, and interviews pueblo needleworkers. She was also the first woman, and the first Native American, to act as president of the Southwestern Association on Indian Affairs.

MARIA "LILLY" SALVADOR
Acoma (N/A) Acoma, New Mexico
Potter, jeweler, weaver

EDUCATION Grants High School; New Mexico State University, New Mexico; learned the basics of pottery from her mother, Frances Torivio.

AWARDS: First, second, third prizes, Santa Fe Indian Market (1994); Pasadena Craftsmen Show, Pasadena, California.

REPRESENTATION: Lilly's Pottery Gallery, Acoma Pueblo, New Mexico.

ABOUT THE ARTIST: Salvador's work is on permanent collection at several museums. She shows her work throughout the western United States and sells it from her own shop in the Acoma Pueblo. Pottery is Salvador's first love, though she is a multitalented artist. She makes Acoma pots in the traditional way, refusing to reveal the sources for her clay and her secrets of making pottery. Salvador has been known to paint the inside of a deep jar, something that is nearly impossible. She makes slip-decorated earthenware in the traditional Acoma style. Salvador is also a silversmith, acrylic artist, weaver, and native embroidery artist. Those items are available at her gallery as well.

WILL SAMPSON
Creek (– 1987) Oklahoma
Artist, actor

AWARDS: Won the Philbrook Art Center (Tulsa) art award (1951), as well as many other honors.

ABOUT THE ARTIST: As a member of the Screen Actors Guild, Sampson promoted the Indian in acting, directing, writing, and producing. He played the role of Chief Bromden in "One Flew Over the Cuckoo's Nest." As an artist, Sampson sold his first painting at age three. He did landscapes; western and Indian scenes in the style of Charles Russell, and exhibited at the Smithsonian, Library of Congress, Amon Carter Museum, and the Creek Council House Museum.

ABEL SANCHEZ
(a.k.a. Oqwa Pi, "Red Cloud")
San Ildefonso (1900 – 1972) San Ildefonso Pueblo,
New Mexico
Artist—watercolor

EDUCATION: Self-taught.

ABOUT THE ARTIST: One of the first Pueblo painters to win artistic recognition, Oqwa Pi's paintings were exhibited nationally and internationally. He helped establish the traditions of Rio Grande painting and is well known for his stylistic renderings of ceremonial dances.

RUSSELL SANCHEZ
Zia (N/A) New Mexico
Potter

EDUCATION: Learned how to pot from watching his great-aunt, Rose Gonzales, and her daughter-in-law, Dora.

REPRESENTATION: Gallery 10, Inc., Santa Fe, New Mexico.

ABOUT THE ARTIST: Sanchez's work includes two-tone sienna-and-black jars. He often adds bear-effigy lids, inlaid stones, and green slips to the jars.

PERCY SANDY
(a.k.a. Kai Sa, "Red Moon")
Zuni (1918 – 1974) Zuni Pueblo, New Mexico
Artist—watercolor

EDUCATION: Studied painting at Albuquerque Indian School and Santa Fe Indian School.

ABOUT THE ARTIST: Sandy created authentic and realistic depictions of his people, often painting the Kachinas in a detailed and meticulous manner.

ALLEN SAPP
Plains Cree (1929 –) Canada
Artist—acrylic

EDUCATION: Elected to the Royal Canadian Academy of Arts.

ABOUT THE ARTIST: Sapp paints in a realistic, narrative way. His works show how the Canadian Indians lived before World War II.

C. TERRY SAUL
(a.k.a. Tabaksi, "Ember of Fire")
Choctaw/Chickasaw (1921 – 1976) Sardis,
Oklahoma
Artist—acrylic, watercolor

EDUCATION: Studied at Bacone College with Woody Crumbo and Acee Blue Eagle; Bachelor of Art and Master of Fine Art, University of Oklahoma.

ABOUT THE ARTIST: As a painter, Saul turned to the legends and rituals of the Choctaw tribe for inspiration. His style made his figures light and floaty and created a spiritlike, otherworldly feel to his paintings. He felt a strong responsibility as spokesperson for his tribe and tried to relate that through his painting. When he died, he was chairperson of the art department at Bacone College.

EILEEN SAWATIS

(a.k.a. Looking for a Bluer Sky)

Mohawk (1943 –   ) Hogansburg, New York
Painter, sandpainter, silkscreener, woodcarver, clothing
designer, dollmaker, weaver

EDUCATION: Self-taught; learned some techniques from her mother and grandmother.

AWARDS: Sawatis has won many awards for her work at the Malone Fair in New York.

ABOUT THE ARTIST: Sawatis is a multitalented artist whose subjects include Iroquois legends, nature, scenery, wildlife and portraits. She also sews Iroquois clothing ornamented with beads or ribbons, makes apple-faced dolls, and writes poetry and short stories.

CHERYL SCHAPP

Seneca (1954 –   )
Beadworker; leatherworker; artist–drawer, painter

EDUCATION: Learned how to bead and make cornhusk dolls from Clara Redeye and Dorothy Jimerson. Leland John taught Schapp loom beadwork. She received a certificate in art from Salamanca Central High School in 1972.

ABOUT THE ARTIST: Schapp has always experimented with different styles and techniques, no matter what medium she is working with. She beads jewelry, does loom beaded work, creates beaded designs on leather, makes deer-tail roaches,

and draws and paints. Schapp has been very involved in the Allegany Arts & Crafts Coop and teaches her skills to her children so that they may carry on the Iroquois tradition.

MAISIE SCHENANDOAH AND FAMILY

(a.k.a. Wah-Lee)

Oneida (1932 –   ) Oneida, New York
Beadworkers, clothing designers, featherworkers,
cornhusk workers, potters, carvers, painters,
silversmiths, stonecarvers

EDUCATION: Maisie learned from her mother and, in turn, she has taught her five daughters and one son.

AWARDS: The Indian Arts and Crafts Board in Washington, D.C. holds some of this family's work.

ABOUT THE ARTISTS: The Schenandoah family, led by matriarch Maisie, combine their talents in both the visual and performing arts to present programs in schools, museums, and cultural centers throughout the United States. They also make a number of objects which have been exhibited at powwows and craft shows throughout the United States.

GARY SCHILDT

(a.k.a. "Lone Bull")

Blackfeet (1938 –   ) Helena, Montana
Sculptor

EDUCATION: Studied commercial art and photography at City College, San Francisco.

ABOUT THE ARTIST: Schildt is influenced by Western art, such as the work of Charles Russell. Schildt tries to give his sculptures the feeling of life you might see below the surface. His bronzes are realistic and are often of the very young or the very old.

FRITZ SCHOLDER

Mission/Luiseno (1937 –   ) Breckenridge,
Minnesota
Artist—oil on canvas; sculptor—bronze

EDUCATION: Studied under Francis Bacon, Bachelor of Fine Art, California State University, Sacramento; Master of Fine Art, University of Arizona, Tucson; Southwest Indian Art Project, Tucson.

REPRESENTATION: Riva Yares Gallery, Scottsdale, Arizona; Louis Newman Gallery, Beverly Hills, California; Bishop Gallery, Allenspark, Colorado; Susan Duval Gallery, Aspen, Colorado; John A. Boler, Indian and Western Art, Minneapolis, Minnesota; Nevada Institute of Contemporary Art, Las Vegas, Nevada; Albuquerque Museum of Art, Albuquerque, New Mexico; Charlotte Jackson Fine Art, Santa Fe, New Mexico; Wheelwright Museum of the American Indian/Case Trading Post, Santa Fe, New Mexico; Riva Yares Gallery, Santa Fe, New Mexico; Ed Hill Gallery, El Paso, Texas.

ABOUT THE ARTIST: Scholder challenges every stereotype of Native Americans as people and as artists. His feelings are that he is an artist, rather than an Indian artist. He purposely distorts his paintings of Native Americans so that he may relay the pain and confusion his people have felt. He believes that "[t]here is still real magic in the remnants of the American Indian" (*American Indian Painting & Sculpture* by Patricia Janis Broder). Scholder started instructing at the Institute of American Indian Art in 1962 and was one of the original four founding members to open the school.

HART MERRIAM SCHULTZ

(a.k.a. Nitoh Mahkwi, "Lone Wolf")
Blackfoot (1882 – 1970) Birch Creek, Minnesota
Painter, sculptor, illustrator

EDUCATION: Studied at the Art Students League, Los Angeles (1910) and the Chicago Art Institute (1914). Influenced by Thomas Moran and Harry Carr (art critic of *Los Angeles Times*).

ABOUT THE ARTIST: Schultz's work was often compared to Frederic Remington's because they both did active sculptures of men on horseback and "Wild West" scenes. Schultz painted scenes of Plains Indians in both oil and watercolor. In addition to painting and sculpting, Schultz also illustrated some of his father's (White writer James Willard Schultz) books. Schultz was at the height of his career in the 1920s.

LLAVALL SCROGG

(a.k.a. Gah Noh Sae Onh)
Seneca (1955 –   )
Beadworker

EDUCATION: Her mother, Doris Sundown, taught her.

ABOUT THE ARTIST: Scrogg designs loom beadworked pieces including wristbands, jewelry, chokers, and belts. She often attends powwows and fairs with other members of her family.

BERT D. SEABOURN

Cherokee (1931 –   ) Iraan, Texas
Artist—oil

EDUCATION: Certificate of Art from Oklahoma C.U. (1960); studied with the Famous Artists Correspondence Art School.

AWARDS: Include three awards from ITIC.

ABOUT THE ARTIST: Seabourn has exhibited throughout the Southwest and has had one-person shows at Henson Gallery, Oklahoma, and Chandler Galleries, Oklahoma. The Oklahoma Art Center holds a collection of his work.

RON SEBASTIAN

Carrier (N/A) Hagwilget, British Columbia,
Canada
Carver

ABOUT THE ARTIST: Though Sebastian is Carrier, he works in the Gitksan tradition. Some of his carved masks are decorated. For example, a birch

Porcupine mask Sebastian made for the 'Ksan Dancers was decorated with real quills.

DONALD HENRY SECONDINE, JR.
Cherokee/Delaware (1952 –   ) Nowata, Oklahoma
Artist—gouache on illustration board

EDUCATION: Haskell Indian Junior College, Lawrence, Kansas (early 1970s); studied art with Loren Pahsetopah; attended a workshop given by Jim Burden in Washington, D.C. (1970).

AWARDS: Secondine, Jr.'s, awards include an Honorable Mention from the Philbrook Art Center which was given to him when he was still in college.

ABOUT THE ARTIST: Secondine's work is his vision of what his ancestors may have looked like as they held court. He also depicts other scenes of Delaware or Cherokee life.

JOYCE SHARROW
(a.k.a. Te Kon Wa Ren Ken Nionh)
Mohawk (1949 –   ) St. Regis, Quebec, Canada
Basketmaking

EDUCATION: Learned from her mother, Margaret R. Lazore.

ABOUT THE ARTIST: Sharrow makes mail and wastepaper baskets, sometimes working alongside her mother. She has passed on her basketry skills to her own children as well.

HENRY SHELTON
Hopi (N/A) Arizona
Carver—Kachinas

ABOUT THE ARTIST: Shelton was first persuaded to carve a raw wood *Ho-ote* about forty years ago and proceeded to call it "very difficult." During the mid 1960s, however, Shelton went on to carve two Snake Dancers and an Eagle Dancer, both of which were eventually cast in bronze. His Kachina figures

caused other artists to change the way they carved the dolls.

EUSEBIA SHIJE
Zia (N/A) Arizona
Potter

EDUCATION: Learned some of her skills from her mother.

ABOUT THE ARTIST: Shije earns her living making pottery which is stone polished, then painted with a black pigment. Her trademark is the Zia bird, as it is for other Zia potters.

PERCY SHORTY
Navajo (N/A) Arizona
Jeweler

ABOUT THE ARTIST: Shorty works with unusual pieces of turquoise, such as Persian turquoises.

149

STELLA SHUTIVA
Acoma (N/A) New Mexico
Potter

ABOUT THE ARTIST: Shutiva's pottery is distinctive because she textures it with her corrugating tool.

HOWARD SICE
Hopi/Laguna (N/A) Arizona
Jeweler, engraver, sculptor

AWARDS: Sice has won numerous awards for his engraving and sculpting of precious and semi-precious metals.

REPRESENTATION: Long Ago & Far Away Gallery, Manchester Center, Vermont.

ABOUT THE ARTIST: Sice creates silver and gold jewelry, as well as engraved miniature Hopi pots. His bowls have won him national acclaim and are highly sought after collectibles.

LINDA SICKLES

Oneida (1948 –   )
Beadworker

EDUCATION: Took in-home classes to learn how to bead.

ABOUT THE ARTIST: Sickles sells her beaded barrettes, medallions, key chains, earrings, belts, and neckties at fairs and powwows. She decorates her medallions with bear or turtle designs. The neckties she weaves on a loom often feature eagle designs. Sickles also made baskets with her mother, Katie.

LANCE E. SILVERHORN

(a.k.a. Link Seger, Lance Haungooah)
Kiowa/Wichita (1948 –   ) Lawton, Oklahoma
Carver–flutes

EDUCATION: Bachelor of Science, Sociology (1975), University of Science and Arts of Oklahoma, Chickasha, Oklahoma; currently working on a Master degree in Counseling at the University of Oklahoma, Norman, Oklahoma.

ABOUT THE ARTIST: Silverhorn is enrolled with the Kiowa tribe of Oklahoma, is married to Sharlene Hansen Johnson (Silverhorn) and has five children. He makes handcarved cedar flutes which he sells personally to collectors.

KATHERINE SKYE

Cayuga (1957 –   ) Ohsweken, Ontario, Canada
Beadworker, featherworker, leatherworker

EDUCATION: Self-taught.

ABOUT THE ARTIST: Skye began doing beadwork in the late 1970s, but her specialties are dance costume items. She works with beads, feathers, and leather to decorate the costumes.

RUTH SKYE

Onondaga (1932 –   ) Hagersville, Ontario,
Canada
Beadworker, wireworker

EDUCATION: Learned from her mother.

AWARDS: Include a second prize for an Indian-head medallion she entered at the Caledonia Fair.

ABOUT THE ARTIST: Skye opened her own shop (Indian Crafts) in her home in 1974. She sold her own work, as well as that of her husband, Wilbur. Skye has taught others how to bead and is a member of the Independent Indian Handicrafters. She has also exhibited at fairs and powwows in the Northeast.

DUANE SLICK

Mesquakie (1961 –   ) Waterloo, Iowa
Painter, printmaker, lithographer

EDUCATION: Master of Fine Art, University of California–Davis (1990); Bachelor of Fine Art, University of Northern Iowa (1986).

AWARDS: Slick's many awards include a travel grant from the Rockefeller Foundation (1993) and a Robert Motherwell Fellowship (1991).

REPRESENTATION: Jan Cicero Gallery, Chicago, Illinois.

ABOUT THE ARTIST: Slick states that the focus of his work evolves around his identity as a Native American man and that his work has evolved into two separate categories: his abstract painting and his storytelling. Slick's work is held in collections

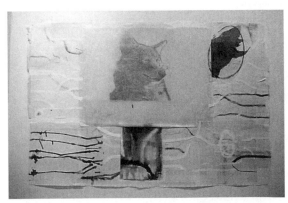

Slick's "Coyote's Mind," mixed media collage, 30 x 44 inches, 1992, courtesy of the artist and Jan Cicero Gallery, Chicago, Illinois.

such as the C. N. Gorman Museum and the Gallery of Art at the University of Northern Iowa.

WILBERT SLOAN
Navajo (N/A) Tohatchi, New Mexico
Sandpainter

ABOUT THE ARTIST: Sloan is one of the sand-painters who started painting rugs in 1977. His rug sandpaintings and still lifes have been made ever since.

ERNEST SMITH
Seneca (1907 – 1975) Tonawanda Reservation,
New York
Artist— oil, ink, watercolor

EDUCATION: Self-taught.

ABOUT THE ARTIST: Smith liked to paint stories of ancient legends; thus his work became narrative. Though he had no formal training, his style was delicate and finely executed.

JAUNE QUICK-TO-SEE SMITH
Flathead (1940 –   ) St. Ignatius, Montana
Artist—various media

EDUCATION: Bachelor of Art, Framingham State College, Massachusetts (1976); Master of Fine Art, University of New Mexico, Albuquerque (1980).

AWARDS: Among the many awards Smith has won are honorary degrees, awards, and commissions. She has also curated shows, organized cooperatives, and been very active in her field.

REPRESENTATION: Horwitch LewAllen Gallery, Santa Fe, New Mexico; Margaret Kilgore Gallery, Scottsdale, Arizona; Jan Cicero Gallery, Chicago, Illinois; Fort Wayne Museum of Art, Ft. Wayne, Indiana; Maine College of Art/The Baxter Gallery, Portland, Maine; Yellowstone Art Center, Billings, Montana; Tamarind Institute, Albu-

Jaune Quick-to-See Smith's "Talking Pictures: The Anthropologist," mixed media on paper, 44 x 30 inches, courtesy of the artist and Jan Cicero Gallery, Chicago, Illinois.

151

querque, New Mexico; DEL Fine Art Galleries, Santa Fe, New Mexico; Steinbaum Krauss Gallery, New York, NY; East Carolina University/ Wellington B. Gray Gallery, Greenville, North Carolina.

ABOUT THE ARTIST: Smith's work shows her knowledge of the European artists, as well as her ardor to show her Indian heritage. This effort often comes out in her narratives, which are quite abstract. She is an outspoken proponent of Native American issues and environmental concerns, and often brings those concerns to her work. Smith's works are owned by the American Medical Association, AT&T, The Denver Art Museum, the National Museum of American Art, and many others.

RICHARD ZANE SMITH
Wyandot (N/A)
Potter

REPRESENTATION: Gallery 10, Inc., Santa Fe, New Mexico.

ABOUT THE ARTIST: Smith makes pots in the ancient corrugated style, then decorates them with stunning painted designs. He has used Anasazi coiling methods when he creates his corrugated pots.

Richard Zane Smith's contemporary corrugated ceramic jar, 21 inches high x 19 inches diameter, courtesy of the artist and Gallery 10, Inc., Scottsdale, Arizona.

RUSSELL SMITH

Kwakiutl (N/A) Alert Bay, British Columbia, Canada
Carver—masks

ABOUT THE ARTIST: Smith likes to see his masks used in dances and believes it would take his whole lifetime to carve all the traditional masks.

VIRGIE SMITH

Oneida (1911 –)
Beadworker, quilter, crocheter

EDUCATION: Smith learned beadwork from her father and quilting from her mother-in-law.

ABOUT THE ARTIST: As a young girl, Smith learned how to make baskets from her uncle and how to do embroidery. Beadwork took over her interests as Smith grew older. She has made medallions, bolo ties, hair ties, jewelry, belts, and items like quilts.

SMOKEY

Zuni (1956 –) New Mexico
Jeweler, silversmith

EDUCATION: Smokey learned his needlepoint technique from his mother and his lapidary and silversmithing skills from the production shop in his father-in-law's trading post. He was inspired by Edith Tsabetsaye to experiment with his style.

AWARDS: First place in needlepoint, Indian Market, Santa Fe (1990).

ABOUT THE ARTIST: Smokey uses Sleeping Beauty turquoise as his primary stone. Because his experimental designs are modern, not traditional, he finds them hard to sell.

LOIS SMOKY

(a.k.a. Lois Smokey, Bougetah, Bou Ge Tah)
Kiowa (1907 – 1981) Anadarko, Oklahoma
Artist—mixed media

EDUCATION: Worked with Susan Peters at Anadarko Indian Agency; University of Oklahoma (1920s).

ABOUT THE ARTIST: During the 1920s, when they studied at the University of Oklahoma, Smoky was the only female of a group of five Kiowa Indians who became world renowned for their bold, broad style and knowledge of American Indian tribes and traditions. The group represented the United States in the International Folk Art Exhibition in Prague. The paintings and artists then toured museums throughout the United States. Smoky stopped painting because of prejudice against her and is often left out of history books as one of the original Five Kiowas, but her work is in Jacobson's *Kiowa Indian Art* and *American Indian Painters*. Her works are held by the Museum of the American Indian and McNay Art Institute in San Antonio.

CAROL SNOW

*Allegany/Seneca (N/A) Allegany Reservation,
New York*
Artist—pen and ink

EDUCATION: Two degrees in zoology.

REPRESENTATION: Long Ago and Far Away Gallery,
Manchester, Vermont.

ABOUT THE ARTIST: Snow draws wildlife because
of her strong background in zoology. All of her
art represents North American themes and her
series is called "Spirits of the Earth and Sky."
Her paintings have been reproduced as prints and
calendars.

VIRGINIA G. SNOW

Seneca (1909 –)
*Beadworker, moccasin maker, clothing designer,
silversmith, dollmaker*

EDUCATION: Snow learned beadwork from Lenora
George, dressmaking from Maud Hurd, and silverwork from Mrs. Barcus.

ABOUT THE ARTIST: Snow has lectured on Iroquois culture and crafts and taught classes in
beadwork, silverwork, cornhusk doll construc-
tion, and dress and moccasin making. She has also
judged costumes at the Indian Fall Festival. An
active woman, Snow has been particularly gener-
ous with her time and teaches anyone interested
in Iroquois art and crafts.

CAROL A. SOATIKEE

*Chiriahua Apache/Pima (1942 –) Phoenix,
Arizona*
Artist—oil on canvas

EDUCATION: Studied art at Cameron College,
Lawton, Oklahoma; studied art education at
Central State College, Edmond, Oklahoma; has
three art degrees.

Soatikee's many awards include a First
Place at the Heard Museum (1979) and a one-
woman exhibit at the Southern Plains Indian
Museum and Craft Center, Oklahoma (1973).

ABOUT THE ARTIST: Soatikee shared her knowledge
of art by teaching in the Anadarko, Oklahoma public school system and the United States Indian
School in Concho, Oklahoma. A fine poet as well as
an artist, Soatikee credits her mixed Native American background with giving her creativity, sensitiv-
ity to nature, and devotion to God and family.

ALICE SOULIGNY

Cherokee/Delaware (1931 –)
Artist

EDUCATION: Self-taught by watching the artists
who lived nearby.

AWARDS: Souligny's list of awards is long and
includes exhibits, television and radio appearances,
and publications.

ABOUT THE ARTIST: Souligny started painting after
raising her five children and now does portraits, as
well as fantasies and abstracts. She uses colors that
are vibrant and depict the heritage of her ancestors.
She uses spiritualistic symbolism in her work, combining traditional as well as contemporary values.

MARY SOUTHERLAND

*Okanagan/Necolslie Band (N/A) Sardis, British
Columbia, Canada*
Beadworker

EDUCATION: Learned the art from her mother and
still uses her designs.

ABOUT THE ARTIST: Having learned from her
mother, Southerland is glad she continued with
beadwork and today tries to improve on the designs
passed on to her.

LILY SPECK

*Kwakiutl (N/A) Alert Bay, British Columbia,
Canada*
Blanketmaker

153

ABOUT THE ARTIST: Speck sews using buttons and other materials. Sometimes her husband, Henry, creates a design.

MARJORIE SPENCER

Navajo (1936 –) Wide Ruins, Arizona
Weaver

EDUCATION: Spencer learned to weave when she was twenty-seven and was influenced by Bill Young, a Hubbell trader.

REPRESENTATION: Hubbell Trading Post, Ganado, Arizona.

ABOUT THE ARTIST: Spencer originally used the traditional colors of golds, yellows, browns, grays and whites for her Wide Ruins rugs, but she now uses pinks and blues to satisfy customers' desires. Spencer has taught three of her daughters (Vera Spencer, Irma Spencer Owens, and Geneva Scott Shabie) the Wide Ruins style. Another daughter, Brenda, weaves Burntwater patterns.

NANDELL SPITTAL

(a.k.a. Giyā Nu 'Ndyā, "Invisible Footprints")
Cayuga (1960 –) Ohsweken, Ontario, Canada
Beadworker

EDUCATION: Learned from her father, Buck Spittal.

ABOUT THE ARTIST: Spittal's whole family works in crafts. Spittal's beadwork includes jewelry made out of large beads, hairpipe bone beads, and leather. She also makes wolf headdresses and porcupine-quill earrings. In addition, she sketches animals and horses.

SHAWNEE SPITTAL

(a.k.a. Nyu Din 'Don, "Hanging Lake")
Cayuga (1958 –) Ohsweken, Ontario, Canada
Beadworker; carver–soapstone; painter

EDUCATION: Learned the basics of his crafts from his father, Buck Spittal.

ABOUT THE ARTIST: Spittal makes bone and beadwork necklaces and soapstone pendants and carvings, but his speciality is breastplates made from hairpipe bone beads, grass, glass beads, and leather.

ROGER STAATS

Mohawk (1964 –) Hagersville, Ontario, Canada
Beadworker

EDUCATION: Largely self-taught; has taken some summer classes at the Six Nations Art Council.

AWARDS: Honors include a first place for beadwork at the Six Nations Art Council (1976).

ABOUT THE ARTIST: Staats studies already-made pieces to see how they were created, then tries to make them on his own. His beadwork items include jewelry, bolo ties, medallions, watchbands, barrettes, Indian head rings, and hair ties usually worked in red, white, and black. He has passed his knowledge on to his brothers as well as to school children.

MILLIE STAFFORD

Seneca (1961 –) Versailles, New York
Beadworker, quillworker

EDUCATION: Taught by her grandmother, Juanita Lay.

ABOUT THE ARTIST: Stafford started doing beadwork at age twelve. She works on a variety of projects, sometimes beading hair ties or clothing, then creating God's eyes. Her talents are varied; she has been known to work as a television camera technician as well as a photographer for the school newspaper.

SEIDEL STANDING ELK

(a.k.a. Voaxaa'e – Vo'ko – Maestse, "White Eagle")
Northern Cheyenne (N/A) Crow Agency, Montana
Painter, actor

Portrait of Standing Elk with his work, courtesy of the artist and the Cheyenne Indian Museum.

EDUCATION: Mostly self-taught.

REPRESENTATION: Cheyenne Indian Museum, Ashland, Montana.

ABOUT THE ARTIST: Standing Elk describes his art as a "reflection of the values, visions, dreams, and stories told to me by my grandfather and other elders as shared the legends of the Northern Cheyenne." He teaches bilingual studies at the Northern Cheyenne Tribal School in Busby, Montana and has had starring roles in the "Return to Lonesome Dove" and "Last of the DogMen."

KEVIN RED STAR

Crow (1943 –   ) Montana
Artist–oil

EDUCATION: Graduated from the Institute of American Indian Arts, Santa Fe, New Mexico in 1965.

AWARDS: Special award, The Museum of New Mexico (1965).

REPRESENTATION: Custer County Art Center, Miles City, Missouri; 21st Century Fox Fine Art, Santa Fe, New Mexico.

ABOUT THE ARTIST: Red Star was exhibited at The Museum of New Mexico, the "First Annual Invitational Exhibition of American Indian Paintings"

Standing Elk's oil-on-canvas painting of a buffalo with a hunting spear in his side charging toward viewer, courtesy of the artist and the Cheyenne Indian Museum.

155

(1965) and at the Riverside Museum, New York City, "Young American Indian Artists" (1966). The Indian Arts and Crafts Board holds a collection of his work.

ELSIE M. STEFFANS

Mohawk (1917 –   ) Sanborn, New York
Beadworker

EDUCATION: Self-taught.

AWARDS: Include a first prize for a turtle medallion at the Optimist Club in Lockport, New York.

ABOUT THE ARTIST: Steffans has taken her beaded jewelry, clan medallions, bolo ties, headbands, chokers, jackets and wristbands to exhibits at pow-wows through the United States, She also makes ribbon shirts and rattles. Excited about what she makes, Steffans shares information about her art with anyone who is interested.

VERNON STEPHENS

Gitksan (N/A) British Columbia, Canada
Carver

ABOUT THE ARTIST: Stephens carves canoes the old way, using one whole and full-grown red cedar tree and the same type of tools his forefathers used.

ART STERRIT

Gitksan (N/A) British Columbia, Canada
Carver

ABOUT THE ARTIST: Sterrit carves decorated masks for the 'Ksan Dancers (i.e., a Sun mask made of alder) and other wooden items. The totem pole he made for the VanDusen Gardens in Vancouver was raised on June 11, 1976. It told the story of the Black Bear crest of the Killer Whale clan.

FRED STEVENS, JR.

Navajo (1922 –   ) Sheep Springs, New Mexico
Sandpainter

EDUCATION: Self-taught.

ABOUT THE ARTIST: Stevens fell into sandpainting by a fluke. An artist who had been creating sandpaintings for the tourists at a private museum along Route 66 fell ill and Stevens took over for him. Through the years, Stevens became well known as a sandpainting expert, demonstrating techniques first at the Arizona State Museum, then all over the United States, Europe, Mexico, Japan, South America, and Canada. Stevens was also a Navajo singer and an expert at Blessingway Ceremony chants and Nightway and Female Shootingway ceremonies. He decided to make permanent sandpaintings in 1946, but his early paintings were mediocre at best. He eventually mastered the art, leading the way for other Navajo sandpainters.

JACQUIE STEVENS

Winnebago (N/A)
Potter

EDUCATION: Stevens created her first piece at home when she was five—and ate it!

ABOUT THE ARTIST: Stevens makes unusual, large, hand-coiled pot pieces with micaceous clay which she smokes.

JUANITA STEVENS

Navajo (N/A) Chinle, Arizona
Sandpainter

ABOUT THE ARTIST: Stevens often creates some of the good subjects who help Earth people, such as Mother Earth and Father Sky. Like other sandpainters, she leaves out certain details or adds things to her paintings which are not made in the original sandpainting created by the medicine man.

ANABEL STEWART

Salish (by marriage), Skwaw Band (N/A) Canada
Weaver

EDUCATION: Oliver Wells taught some of the Salish weavers by taking Stewart's great-grandmother's rag rug apart and showing the weavers how it was done.

ABOUT THE ARTIST: Stewart is a prolific weaver.

SUSAN STEWART

Crow/Blackfeet (1953 –   ) Livermore,
*   California*
Painter, silkscreener, monoprintmaker

EDUCATION: Studied painting at the California College of Arts and Crafts, Oakland (1971–1975); Bachelor of Art, Fine Arts, Montana State University (1981).

AWARDS: Stewart's work has been shown in many exhibitions, has been honored many times, and is held in permanent collections at the Museum of the Plains Indian in Browning, Montana, and the North Dakota Museum of Art in Grand Forks.

ABOUT THE ARTIST: Stewart has used watercolors and pastels and oils and monoprints throughout her career. She likes to be spontaneous in her work and believes her paintings to be a "reflection of my inner visions." Her work has been influenced by Frank LaPena, George Longfish, Jean LaMarr, Kandinsky, and Klee.

WILLARD STONE
Cherokee (1916 – 1985) near Oktaha, Oklahoma
Sculptor—wood

EDUCATION: Bacone Junior College, Bacone, Oklahoma.

ABOUT THE ARTIST: Stone was considered by many to be the finest wood sculptor in America. His works were commissioned for the Cherokee Cultural Center in Tahlequah, Oklahoma, as well as many others. In his work, Stone strived to reflect the suffering and survival of his people. His style is original.

DOROTHY STRAIT
Cherokee (N/A) Arizona
Painter

EDUCATION: Self-taught.

AWARDS: Strait has won many purchase awards, honorable mentions, prizes, and ribbons for her work.

ABOUT THE ARTIST: Strait works mostly in oils, but she does also use acrylics, watercolors, and occasionally does portraits in pastels. She is a careful artist who researches her subjects completely so that she can incorporate their historic values into her work. Her paintings are held by many private collections and are exhibited widely, including at the Annual Invitational at the Heard Museum in Phoenix.

VIRGINIA STROUD
Cherokee (1949 –   ) Tennessee
Artist—various media

REPRESENTATION: Eagles Roost Gallery, Colorado Springs, Colorado; Earthstar Gallery, Klamash Falls, Oregon.

ABOUT THE ARTIST: Stroud draws on her studies of all different styles of Native American art, as well as on the themes that originate within each tribe. She paints the traditions, as well as the contemporary, with her art.

BERNICE SUAZO-NARANJO
Taos (N/A) Taos, New Mexico
Potter

EDUCATION: Suazo-Naranjo's grandmother gave her the information she needed to start making pottery in 1981.

ABOUT THE ARTIST: Suazo-Naranjo respects the clay she works with, believing in the cycle of nature. Her husband, Tito, often works with her. She keeps her micaceous clay in plastic bags for three or four months to age so that it will be plastic-like. Some of Suazo-Naranjo's pots are left undecorated while others are carved with her design before she fires them.

ADA SUINA
Cochiti (1930 –   ) Cochiti Pueblo, New Mexico
Potter—Storyteller figures

EDUCATION: Learned the art of pottery from her cousin, Virginia Naranjo, and her mother-in-law, Aurelia Suina.

AWARDS: Suina has won awards for her work since she began potting in 1976.

ABOUT THE ARTIST: Suina creates nativities, Storytellers, and drummers with large, distinctive faces. She has begun to teach her four daughters (Caroline Grace Suina, Marie Charlotte Suina, Maria Suina, and Patty Suina) the art of pottery, and they are already winning prizes for their work.

157

ANTONITA (TONY CORDERO) SUINA

Cochiti (1948 –) Cochiti Pueblo, New Mexico
Potter–Storyteller figures

EDUCATION: Learned the trade from her mother, master Storyteller creator, Helen Cordero.

REPRESENTATION: Adobe Gallery, Albuquerque, New Mexico.

ABOUT THE ARTIST: Suina created her first Storyteller in 1983. Other members of her family, such as her brother, George Cordero, her niece, Buffy Cordero, and her nephews, Tim Cordero and Kevin Peshlakai, are also Storyteller makers.

AURELIA SUINA

Cochiti (1911 –) Cochiti Pueblo, New Mexico
Potter–Storyteller figures

EDUCATION: Learned her potting skills from her mother, Victoria Montoya, and her aunt, Reycita Romero.

AWARDS: Suina began winning prizes for her Storytellers at the 1980 Indian Market.

ABOUT THE ARTIST: Suina's family is filled with pottery artists, such as her mother and aunt; her daughter-in-law, Ada Suina; and her granddaughters, Caroline Grace Suina, Marie Charlotte Suina, Maria Suina, and Patty Suina. Aurelia, who learned how to make figures and traditional vessels in the 1920s, started making Storytellers in 1968. The identifying features of her figures are widely spaced eyes set high on the forehead and a tiny line of a mouth. In 1973, Suina was one of three Cochiti potters featured in the Folk Art exhibit in Santa Fe.

CAROLINE GRACE SUINA

Cochiti (1955 –) Cochiti Pueblo, New Mexico
Potter–Storyteller figures

EDUCATION: Learned her art from her mother, Ada Suina.

ABOUT THE ARTIST: Suina created her first Storyteller around 1980. Other members of her family who are potters include her grandmother, Aurelia Suina, and her sisters, Marie Charlotte, Maria, and Patty Suina.

FRANCES SUINA

Cochiti (1902 –) Cochiti Pueblo, New Mexico
Potter–Storyteller figures

EDUCATION: Self-taught.

ABOUT THE ARTIST: Suina's son, Louis Naranjo, her daughter-in-law, Virginia Naranjo, and her daughter, Sarah Suina, are all involved with pottery. Suina's work was included in the 1973 "What Is Folk Art?" exhibit held at the Museum of International Folk Art in Santa Fe. One of the distinguishing features of her work is the traditional Cochiti vessel designs she paints on the back of her Storytellers' shirts. Suina began creating traditional pottery vessels in the 1920s, made "Singing Mothers" in the 1940s and 1950s, then began making larger, seated Storyteller figures in the 1960s and early 1970s.

JUDITH SUINA

Cochiti (1960 –) Cochiti Pueblo, New Mexico
Potter–Storyteller figures

EDUCATION: Taught by mother, Dorothy Trujillo.

ABOUT THE ARTIST: Suina's family is filled with pottery makers like Suina's sisters Frances Pino and Cecilia Valencia, brother Onofre Trujilio II, mother-in-law Louise Q. Suina, sister-in-law Vangie Suina, and aunts and great-aunts. Suina created her first Storyteller in 1978.

LOUISE Q. SUINA

Cochiti (1939 –) Cochiti Pueblo, New Mexico
Potter–Storyteller figures

EDUCATION: Self-taught; learned some techniques from cousin Dorothy Trujillo.

ABOUT THE ARTIST: Suina's daughter Vangie, cousins Helen Cordero and Seferina Ortiz, and daughter-in-law Judith Suina, are also potters.

LUCY R. SUINA

Cochiti (1921 –   ) Cochiti Pueblo, New Mexico
Potter–Storyteller figures

EDUCATION: Suina learned the art of pottery from her mother and father, Reyes T. and Vicente Romero; shares grandfather, Santiago Quintana, with Helen Cordero, her first cousin.

ABOUT THE ARTIST: Suina created her first Storyteller in 1974 and comes from a large family of potters that includes her sister, Laurencita Herrera; her niece, Seferina Ortiz; her cousin, Helen Cordero; and her daughter, Evangeline Suina. Suina has even helped her son-in-law, Tony Dallas, with the art of creating Storytellers.

MARIE CHARLOTTE SUINA

Cochiti (1954 –   ) Cochiti Pueblo, New Mexico
Potter–Storyteller figures

EDUCATION: Suina's mother, Ada, taught her how to pot.

AWARDS: Suina began winning prizes for her Storytellers in 1983 at the Indian Market.

ABOUT THE ARTIST: Suina created her first Storyteller in 1980. She comes from a large family of potters that includes her grandmother, Aurelia Suina; her cousins, Josephine and Martha Arquero; and her sisters, Caroline, Maria, and Patty.

THEODORE SUINA

(a.k.a. Kuperu, "Snow")
Cochiti (1918 –   ) Cochiti Pueblo, New Mexico
Artist–tempera

EDUCATION: Studied with Geronima Montoya (Po-Tsuni) at Santa Fe Indian School.

ABOUT THE ARTIST: Permanently crippled by a fall from a horse, Suina began painting when a friend provided him with paints and paper. He then went on to learn more about art. He has followed the basic designs of the Santa Fe Indian School and with abstract elements found on prehistoric pottery and petroglyphs.

VANGIE SUINA

Cochiti (1959 –   ) Cochiti Pueblo, New Mexico
Potter–Storyteller figures

EDUCATION: Taught by her mother, Louise Q. Suina.

AWARDS: Since her first Storyteller in the early 1980s, Suina has won many awards for her work.

ABOUT THE ARTIST: Suina's grandmother, Anita, and great-aunt, Marianita Venado, were both potters. Suina began making Storytellers in the early 1980s. Most of the children on her figures hold something. She uses acrylic paints and kiln-firing in her work—the process produces a brighter, glossier, whiter polychrome finish.

AGNES SUNDAY

(a.k.a. Ka Ra Kwine)
Mohawk (1909 –   ) St. Regis, Quebec, Canada
Basketmaker, quilter

EDUCATION: Sunday learned from her mother, as well as from her mother-in-law, Annie Sunday.

AWARDS: One of Sunday's baskets was on display at the United Nations exhibit held in 1977.

REPRESENTATION: Mohawk Craft Fund.

ABOUT THE ARTIST: Sunday was a founding member of Akwesasne Homemakers and Cultural Committee. She uses black-ash splints, sweet grass, dyes, and hickory when making her sewing, shopping, and pack baskets, among others.

CECILIA SUNDAY

Mohawk (1919 –   ) St. Regis, Quebec
Basketmaker

159

EDUCATION: Learned by watching her father and mother-in-law.

REPRESENTATION: Mohawk Craft Fund.

ABOUT THE ARTIST: Sunday has been making baskets since she was thirteen. She uses black-ash splints, sweet grass, and white ash handles for shopping, picnic, pie, hampers, clothes, pack, bushel, and corn-washing baskets. She has taught basketry to others and often works with her husband, Joe. The couple have taught their eldest daughter and granddaughter how to create baskets.

DORIS SUNDOWN

(a.k.a. Gie Onh Won Noeh)

Seneca (1925 –) Basom, New York
Beadworker, clothing designer

EDUCATION: Learned from Malinda Parker.

AWARDS: Sundown's talent was recognized when the New York State Iroquois Conference commissioned her to make the bolo ties given to honor famous Iroquois in 1976.

ABOUT THE ARTIST: Sundown makes beaded medallions, bolo ties, hair ties, barrettes, jewelry, belt buckles, and lighter covers. Her designs are original and though she may start with a pattern in mind, it often changes as the work progresses. Sundown has taught others how to bead.

MOLLIE SUNDOWN

Seneca (1950 –) Basom, New York
Beadworker

EDUCATION: Taught by her mother, Doris Sundown.

ABOUT THE ARTIST: Sundown has exhibited her work and taught others how to bead. She does both loom and freehand beading to create jewelry, key chains, cigarette cases, and other items. She uses beads and porcupine quills in her designs. Sundown usually joins her family to bead and show her work.

PEARL SUNRISE

(a.k.a. Gleh-Dez-Bah, Pearl Pintohorse)

Navajo (1944 –) Whitewater, New Mexico
Weaver, basketmaker

EDUCATION: Learned how to weave and make baskets, clothing, and jewelry from her parents and aunts. Studied fine arts on a scholarship to the University of New Mexico.

ABOUT THE ARTIST: A traditional weaver, Sunrise uses raw wool and natural dyes as her ancestors did hundreds of years ago. She also follows the Native American's unwritten law—to never take more than she needs from the earth. All of her designs are her own variations. Sunrise's baskets are used in the Navajo healing ceremonies. She only uses one pattern, the one that depicts the clouds, rainbow, and four Sacred Mountains. Sunrise also makes clothing and jewelry, though she prefers weaving.

CHARLES SUPPLEE

Hopi/French (1959 –) Arizona
Jeweler

EDUCATION: Worked with Pierre Touraine from 1982–1984.

REPRESENTATION: Lovena Ohl Gallery, Scottsdale, Arizona; Eagle Plume Gallery, Allenspark, Colorado; Mudhead Gallery, Beaver Creek and Denver, Colorado; Santa Fe East, Santa Fe, New Mexico.

ABOUT THE ARTIST: Supplee has been commended for his superior inlay work and elegance. He incorporates some of his early memories of Navajo jewelry (he grew up in Ganado, Arizona, where his father worked as a schoolteacher on the Navajo reservation) with what he learned with Touraine, then bends the idea so that his creation becomes distinctly his own. Supplee has also collaborated with Al Qöyawayma, a Hopi artist/potter, on ceramic and metal sculptures.

ROXANNE SWENTZELL

Santa Clara/Anglo (1962 –   ) Taos, New Mexico
Sculptor—clay

EDUCATION: Institute of American Indian Art, Santa Fe; Portland Museum Art School, Portland, Oregon.

AWARDS: Swentzell's many awards include annual awards at the Santa Fe Indian Market, as well as the Joy Levine Art Scholarship (1980).

REPRESENTATION: Four Winds Gallery, Pittsburgh, Pennsylvania; Studio 53, New York, NY; Heard Museum, Phoenix, Arizona; Denver Art Museum, Denver, Colorado.

ABOUT THE ARTIST: Swentzell comes from a family of potters, sculptors, educators, and architects.

Portrait of Swentzell sitting with "Poh-Povi Clown," courtesy of the artist.

Swentzell's clay sculpture entitled "Despairing Clown," courtesy of the artist.

She is a fifth-generation artist (her aunt is potter Jody Falwell and her grandparents are Michael and Rose Naranjo). Swentzell's sculptures are figures that are studies of the human body and the emotions. She builds her sculptures in the coiling style some potters use. All of her figures have gestures and humanistic expressions that appear to change as you study them.

CAMILIO TAFOYA

Santa Clara (N/A) Santa Clara Pueblo, New Mexico
Potter

EDUCATION: Learned the trade from his famous mother, Serafina, as well as other members of the Tafoya family.

ABOUT THE ARTIST: Tafoya carries on the tradition of pottery making within his family, creating pots that are both contemporary and traditional. His children, Joseph Lonewolf and Grace Medicine Flower, have also become noted for their pots and are teaching their own families the art.

MARGARET TAFOYA

Santa Clara (N/A) Santa Clara Pueblo, New Mexico
Potter

EDUCATION: Learned the trade from her family; some of her pieces are inspired by tales she heard from her parents and grandparents.

AWARDS: National Heritage Fellow, National Endowment for the Arts Folk Arts Program (1984).

REPRESENTATION: Adobe Gallery, Albuquerque, New Mexico.

ABOUT THE ARTIST: Tafoya's trademark is polished blackware. Her work is often decorated with bear-paw designs, which she considers good luck. Tafoya is considered a master of the art. She makes deeply carved blackware and redware vessels which are highly valued by collectors. She believes the secret to her technique are her polishing stones, which have been passed down through the generations.

Tafoya is teaching her children, Virginia Ebelacker, Mela Youngblood, Toni Roller, and Esther Archuleta, her pottery-making skills.

MAISA P. TAHAMONT

(a.k.a. Ko Noh So Tyooh)
Seneca (1895 –   )
Beadworker, rugmaker, basketmaker

EDUCATION: Learned from some of her friends.

ABOUT THE ARTIST: Tahamont, a versatile craftsperson, created beadwork jewelry, hooked rugs, pillows, wall hangings, baskets, and cornhusk wreaths. She also ran a crafts shop from 1920–1940 and helped her husband when he headed the Works Progress Administration (WPA) Indian Arts and Crafts Project. Tahamont continued to support the Iroquois Nation's activities by actively participating in organizations such as the National Conference on Aging, where, in 1971, she represented the New York State Native Americans.

MARK TAHBO

Hopi-Tewa (N/A) Arizona
Potter

ABOUT THE ARTIST: Tahbo uses anything that works to shape and create his pottery, often even using discarded bowls and dinnerware that might serve as a *puki* (a base to support the coils of clay).

JOSIAH TAIT

Nishga (N/A) British Columbia, Canada
Carver

ABOUT THE ARTIST: Tait helped his son, Norman, create a totem pole for the Port Edward community. The elder Tait has passed on his skills to his son.

NORMAN TAIT

Nishga (N/A) Kincolith, Nass River, Canada
Carver

EDUCATION: Tait learned some of his carving skills from his father, Josiah Tait.

AWARDS: Tait's work was exhibited by the Museum of Anthropology in British Columbia in 1977.

ABOUT THE ARTIST: Tait has made totem poles with tools of the same type as those used by his ancestors. One of his poles, made for the Port Edward community, included all of the community's family crests.

ROY TALAHAFTEWA

Hopi (1955 –   ) Shungopavi, Arizona
Jeweler

EDUCATION: Took art classes in elementary school; attended the Institute of American Indian Art, Santa Fe, while in high school; was influenced by sculptor Allan Houser.

AWARDS: Talahaftewa won his first prize at age eight for a painting he entered in a Museum of Northern Arizona contest; Best of Show, the Indian Market (1986); Best of Jewelry and Best of Division, the Indian Market (1990).

REPRESENTATION: Many Hands, Sedona, Arizona; Ansel Adams Gallery, Yosemite National Park, California; The Indian Craft Shop, Washington, D.C.; Southwest Trading Company, Saint Charles, Illinois.

ABOUT THE ARTIST: Talahaftewa started making jewelry full-time in 1977. He creates concha belts with realistic silver-stamped Kachinas on them. At first, Talahaftewa worked only with silver, but he now incorporates some stones and gold into his designs as well.

LOWELL TALASHOMA

Hopi (N/A) Arizona
Carver—Kachinas; bronze caster

EDUCATION: Learned how to carve from other members of his family.

ABOUT THE ARTIST: A well-known carver, Talashoma creates small traditional dolls in a contemporary style. His carved wooden Kachinas are now being cast in bronze. Talashoma's agent markets and sells copies to galleries and collectors.

TERRANCE TALASWAIMA
(a.k.a. Honvantewa, "Bear Making Tracks")
Hopi (1939 –   ) Arizona
Artist–acrylic

ABOUT THE ARTIST: Talaswaima often paints about the spirit world, something which connects him strongly with his ancestors.

ANNA MAE TANNER
Navajo/Hopi (1929 –   ) Phoenix, Arizona
Weaver

EDUCATION: Learned how to weave from her mother, Despah Nez.

REPRESENTATION: Edith and Troy Kennedy.

ABOUT THE ARTIST: Tanner wove her first rug at age six, but believed the task so impossible that she cried. Since then, Tanner has begun weaving sandpainting rugs at the suggestion of Edith and Troy Kennedy. Weaving is her only source of income.

BELEN AND ERNEST TAPIA
Santa Clara (N/A) New Mexico
Potters

ABOUT THE ARTISTS: Belen makes the pottery and Ernest does the designing. The Tapia couple regularly show their work at the Indian Market in Santa Fe. They make traditional polished redware that is painted with white, buff, blue-grey, and matte red. Belen makes evenly patterned melon jars with sculptured squash ribs around the entire jar. Ernest uses his hands when shaping the clay because he believes working with a wheel is "not art."

DAISY TAUGLECHEE
Navajo (1909 – 1990) Two Grey Hills,
New Mexico
Weaver

EDUCATION: Learned how to weave from family members.

ABOUT THE ARTIST: By the 1940s, Tauglechee had the reputation of being a top weaver and was often called the "greatest living Navajo weaver." Her rugs were tightly woven, sometimes with 115 weft threads to the inch. She wove in the Two Grey Hills style, but brought that style to even greater heights with her own impeccable weaving skills. When her eyesight began to fail, Tauglechee worked with her daughter-in-law, Priscilla.

PRISCILLA TAUGELCHEE
Navajo (1947 –   ) Near Tonalea, Arizona
Weaver

EDUCATION: Taugelchee learned how to weave from her mother and her mother-in-law, Daisy Taugelchee.

ABOUT THE ARTIST: Priscilla and her mother-in-law are considered two of the finest Two Grey Hills weavers.

DANIEL J. TAULBEE
Comanche (1924 –   ) Flathead Reservation,
Montana
Artist

EDUCATION: Self-taught.

AWARDS: Taulbee has been the recipient of many awards and honors.

ABOUT THE ARTIST: Taulbee owned the Heritage American Gallery in Butte, Montana. His own work has been exhibited widely throughout the United States.

HERBERT TAYLOR
Navajo (1951 –   ) Indian Wells, Arizona
Jeweler–gold, silver

EDUCATION: Self-taught.

AWARDS: Several first-place ribbons from the Santa Fe Indian Market, including three in 1994;

163

"Best of Show," Heard Museum, Phoenix, Arizona (1992); "Best of Show," Southwest Museum, Los Angeles, California (1992).

REPRESENTATION: Cristof's of Santa Fe, Santa Fe, New Mexico; Blue-eyed Bear, Sedona, Arizona; Desert Son, Tucson, Arizona.

ABOUT THE ARTIST: Taylor's whole family is in the jewelry business. He learned some of his early skills from watching his father make jewelry, then continued to learn on his own. He creates silver concho belts, jewelry, makes his own tools, and sketches out his designs before stamping the silver. though he considers himself a traditional jeweler, Taylor is versatile, always looking for different ways to approach the art. Taylor's work has been shown all over the United States at museum shows and markets.

Taylor's double Kachina figure bolo tie, courtesy of the artist.

MABEL TAYLOR
Northwest Coast (N/A) Port Alberni, British Columbia, Canada
Basketmaker

ABOUT THE ARTIST: Taylor weaves different types of baskets and sometimes uses a wooden basket form to shape the piece.

MARY TEBO
(a.k.a. Wen Ni Si Ri Io Sta)
Mohawk (1906 –   ) Rooseveltown, New York
Basketmaker, splintworker

EDUCATION: Learned from Minnie Thompson, her mother.

ABOUT THE ARTIST: Tebo has been creating baskets all her life and has passed her skills on to her five children. She often works with her daughter, Annabell, traveling to exhibits and demonstrations. Tebo has also taught classes on basketry in her home. She uses black-ash splints and sweet grass to make a variety of baskets that include sewing baskets, jardinieres, and hampers. She also makes splint bookmarkers.

STELLA TELLER
Isleta (N/A) New Mexico
Potter

REPRESENTATION: Adobe Gallery, Albuquerque, New Mexico.

ABOUT THE ARTIST: Teller likes to work alone.

ROBERT TENORIO
Santo Domingo (N/A) New Mexico
Potter

ABOUT THE ARTIST: Tenorio made contemporary stoneware before turning back to the old Santo Domingo way of creating pots. When Tenorio starts painting a pot, the design just comes to him. He does not plan ahead. Tenorio's pots are still being used to carry food, like similar pots did centuries before. Tenorio uses a special white slip to achieve his unique color.

BOBBIE TEWA
San Juan/Hopi (1948 –   ) San Juan Pueblo, New Mexico
Jeweler

EDUCATION: Took an eight-week silversmithing course sponsored by the federal Manpower Program.

AWARDS: Two Best of Division awards, Indian Market (1982).

REPRESENTATION: The Squash Blossom, Aspen, Vail, and Denver, Colorado; Mosi Lakai-Bi'Kisi, Santa Fe, New Mexico; Santa Fe East, Santa Fe, New Mexico; Four Winds Gallery, Pittsburgh, Pennsylvania; Pot Carrier American Indian Arts, Vashon Island, Washington.

ABOUT THE ARTIST: Tewa was encouraged to enter his first Indian Market by his friend and mentor, the late Harvey Chavarria. Tewa's pieces sold immediately. The artist combines traditional Hopi motifs with Pueblo pottery designs to create goblets as well as jewelry.

DENNIS TEWA
Hopi (N/A) Arizona
Carver

Tewa's contemporary Hopi Kachina Maiden, 16 inches high, carved cottonwood, 1990. Photograph by Bill McLemore Photography, transparency courtesy of the artist and Gallery 10, Inc., Scottsdale, Arizona.

REPRESENTATION: Gallery 10, Inc., Santa Fe, New Mexico.

ABOUT THE ARTIST: According to Hopi prophecy, Tewa believes that the Kachinas he carves may someday no longer exist. By carving them, he hopes that people will remember them and what they stood for.

WILFRED TEWAWINA
Hopi (N/A) Arizona
Carver—Kachinas

ABOUT THE ARTIST: Tewawina carved several plain wood Hopi figures during the period 1965–1970.

ALBERTA THOMAS
Navajo (1927 –   ) Oak Springs, Arizona
Weaver

EDUCATION: Learned how to weave from her mother, Despah Nez, and her sister, Anna Mae Tanner.

REPRESENTATION: Troy Kennedy.

ABOUT THE ARTIST: Thomas sold her first rug at age ten. She now weaves to help support the family.

CECELIA THOMAS
Mohawk (1899–) St. Regis, Quebec, Canada
Basketmaker

EDUCATION: Learned from her parents, John and Marion Adams.

AWARDS: Thomas has presented one of her baskets to the Queen of England (1973) and has one first prize at the New York State Fair.

ABOUT THE ARTIST: Thomas learned how to weave baskets at a young age and started selling them when she was in her early twenties. Her husband often helped her with the bindings on her laundry baskets. Thomas creates quite colorful, memorable baskets, often naming her original designs.

JENNIE THOMAS

Navajo (1957 –   ) St. Michaels, Arizona
Weaver

EDUCATION: Thomas and her three sisters learned how to weave from their mother, Betty B. Roan.

REPRESENTATION: Garland's, Sedona, Arizona; Cristof's of Santa Fe, Santa Fe, New Mexico.

ABOUT THE ARTIST: Thomas comes from a large family of weavers, most of whom have used the Wide Ruins style. Jennie creates Burntwater bordered patterns that highlight small-scale details and a subtle change of pastel colors. Though she is inspired by the Two Grey Hills and Ganado styles, Thomas reworks the design to fit her own creative sense. She has passed on her knowledge to other women and to her daughter, Desiree.

JOHN BIGTREE THOMAS

Mohawk (1958 –   ) Hogansburg, New York
Woodcarver, painter—acrylics, pen and ink, pencil,
tempera, charcoal

EDUCATION: Self-taught.

AWARDS: Thomas has been commissioned to do posters for the North American Indian Traveling College.

ABOUT THE ARTIST: Thomas started painting when his father, Frank, encouraged him. Now he paints the history of his people and their legends. Sometimes he does borders of his scenes, including geometric designs derived from Peyote symbols used by the Native American Church. Thomas's family is active in the Akwesasne Library and Culture Center.

MARY THOMAS

(a.k.a. Wa Rie Wa Thon Tha)
Mohawk (1901 –   ) St. Regis, Quebec
Basketmaker

EDUCATION: Learned her skills from her parents.

ABOUT THE ARTIST: Thomas began making baskets at a very young age and can weave a wide variety of baskets, often creating new styles. Thomas has taught others the Mohawk names for her baskets. She works with black ash and sweet grass to create sewing, Easter, shopping, and clothes baskets, among others.

SOPHIE THOMAS

Okanagan (N/A) Stony Creek Reserve, Canada
Leatherworker

ABOUT THE ARTIST: Thomas herself stretches, dries, scrapes, washes, restretches and softens the hides she uses. It is a long project and has to be perfectly timed so that the hide will turn the right color.

DANIEL THOMPSON

(a.k.a. Rokwaho)
Mohawk (1953 –   ) Rooseveltown, New York
Illustrator; carver—wood, stone; photographer

EDUCATION: Self-taught.

AWARDS: Thompson has won awards for his stonecarvings and has illustrated many books for presses throughout the country.

ABOUT THE ARTIST: Thompson not only does illustrating, he also writes poetry. A multitalented artist, Thompson carves with soapstone and wood to make pipes, sculptures, and canes. He demonstrates and teaches his craft at culture centers.

ELIZABETH THOMPSON

(a.k.a. Katsitsainnie)
Mohawk (1916 –   ) Cornwall Island, Ontario,
Canada
Basketmaker, splintworker, lacrosse stick lacer, textiles

EDUCATION: Thompson learned her basketry skills from her mother, Christie Phillips, and her stick-lacing skills from her husband and mother-in-law.

ABOUT THE ARTIST: Thompson has passed on her skills to her daughter and others. She makes a variety of baskets, including an egg-shaped knitting basket which has a hole in one end through which yarn can be pulled. She is always trying new styles.

ELLA THOMPSON

Northwest Coast (N/A) Ucluelet, British Columbia, Canada
Basketmaker

ABOUT THE ARTIST: Thompson states that all of the women she knew created baskets long ago, but that the number who weave today has dwindled. Thompson makes smaller baskets with interwoven designs.

HAZEL THOMPSON

(a.k.a. Deh Gah Nego Wes)
Seneca (1933 –   )
Beadworker

EDUCATION: Taught by Rose John and her husband, Philip.

ABOUT THE ARTIST: Thompson started making necklaces and loomwork in the late 1960s but did not begin going to shows with her work until almost twenty years later. Her medallion designs include clan animals and geometric and flora patterns. She is active in Longhouse activities, teaches the Seneca language, and works with her husband who creates traditional Iroquois items. She also has passed on some of her beading techniques to her son.

JOSEPHINE THOMPSON

Northwest Coast (N/A) Ahousat, British Columbia, Canada
Basketmaker

ABOUT THE ARTIST: Lidded baskets created by Thompson often have narrative stories—stories Thompson heard when growing up—woven into their design.

MARITA THOMPSON

(a.k.a. Kawenninon)
Mohawk (1956 –   ) Cornwall Island, Ontario, Canada

Painter, basketmaker, beadworker, leatherworker, quilter

EDUCATION: Mostly self-taught; has taken some classes.

ABOUT THE ARTIST: Marita can make baskets (she used to help her mother, Elizabeth, make them); does beadwork (floral designs on leather or felt); has made wooden rocking horses and other items; and sews, crochets, and makes quilts. Thompson demonstrates at fairs and craft shows in both Canada and Florida. Her whole family is involved in arts and crafts and all work to help the Native Arts Cultural Organization spread information about their work and their people.

JOHNNY TIGER, JR.

Creek/Seminole (N/A) Tahlequah, Oklahoma
Painter, sculptor

AWARDS: Tiger, Jr., has won many awards since he began working as an artist in 1967, including first place awards from many shows/fairs throughout the Southwest; the Governor's Award at the Five Civilized Tribes Museum (1977); Grand Prize,

Johnny Tiger, Jr.'s limited edition print "Warrior for Peace," courtesy of the artist.

First Place, and the Heritage Award (as well as two others) at the Five Civilized Tribes Museum Annual Indian Exhibition (1978); and many others for both his paintings and his sculptures.

REPRESENTATION: Tiger Art Gallery, Muskogee, Oklahoma.

ABOUT THE ARTIST: Tiger, Jr.'s, brother, Jerome, was also a renowned artist. The two men learned about the Creek people and their native language from their grandfather. Tiger's work has been shown throughout the United States, in England and in Russia.

NOWETAH TIMMERMAN
(a.k.a. Nowetah, Karen Timmerman)

> *Abenaki/Susquehanna-Cherokee (1947 –   ) New Haven, Connecticut*
> *Weaver, porcupine quillworker, glass beadworker, glass blower, leatherworker, teacher, writer*

EDUCATION: Some college and glass blowing apprenticeship.

Portrait of Nowetah (Karen) Timmerman, courtesy of Nowetah's Indian Museum & Gift Store, New Portland, Maine.

Nowetah (Karen) Timmerman's handwoven, 100 percent wool, "Storm Pattern" rug, 31 x 62 inches, courtesy of Nowetah's Indian Museum & Store, New Portland, Maine.

AWARDS: Received awards for educational programs on Indian History/Dancing/Crafts and blue ribbons at county, state, and local fairs for her arts.

REPRESENTATION: Nowetah's American Indian Museum and Gift Store, New Portland, Maine.

ABOUT THE ARTIST: The mother of seven daughters, Timmerman has brought at least one of her daughters into the Indian crafts business. Timmerman owns a museum/store in Maine where she showcases her work and her daughter's work. A believer in keeping the earth free of garbage, Timmerman's catalogs for items sold in her shop are simply "lent" to customers rather than sent out in mass mailings. Timmerman has received local recognition for her store as well as for the items she produces. She works hard to keep the public informed about New England Indian life and history.

WAHLEYAH ANNE TIMMERMAN-BLACK

> *Abenaki/Susquehanna-Cherokee/Paugusset (1976 –   ) Strong, Maine*

Potter, basketmaker, beadworker, dollmaker, jeweler, birchbark creator, painter

EDUCATION: Learned her crafts from her mother, Nowetah; attends University of Maine, Farmington.

AWARDS Community, state, and school awards for Outstanding Pottery, Advanced Art, and others.

REPRESENTATION: Nowetah's Indian Museum and Gift Store, New Portland, Maine.

ABOUT THE ARTIST: Timmerman designed the "Don't Drink and Drive" Maine State Christmas card (1992). Some of her art is on display at the Maine State House in Augusta. She makes coiled clay pottery, baskets, quill and bead jewelry, dream-catchers, cornhusk dolls, and birch-bark, cone-shaped wigwams.

Wahleyah Anne Timmerman at work in her yard by birch-bark wigwam, courtesy of Nowetah's Indian Museum & Store, New Portland, Maine.

BEA TIOUX

Tesuque (N/A) Tesuque Pueblo, New Mexico
Potter, weaver, drummaker

EDUCATION: Tioux learned how to pot from her mother and great aunt.

ABOUT THE ARTIST: Tioux produces micaceous pots with Tesuque symbols such as those for day, night, corn, rivers, and mountains. She also pro-duces woven items, does embroidery, makes drums, and keeps a herd of cattle.

JIMMY TODDY

(a.k.a. Beatien Yazz, "Little No Shirt")
Navajo (1928 –) Navajo Reservation, near Wide Ruins, Arizona
Artist—various media

EDUCATION: Studied with Yasuo Kuniyoshi at Mills College for two years; Santa Fe Indian School, New York; The Art Institute of Chicago, Illinois.

REPRESENTATION: Tohono Chul Park, Tucson, Arizona.

ABOUT THE ARTIST: Toddy uses watercolors and natural colors to paint Navajo life on the reservations—the traditions and ceremonies. One of his paintings, done in 1946, depicted the "Gallup Ceremonial Parade."

JOSÉ REY TOLEDO

(a.k.a. Sho-Bah-Woh-Hon, "Morning Star")
Jemez (1915 –) Jemez Pueblo, New Mexico
Artist—watercolor

EDUCATION: Started learning about art from his brother-in-law, John Sahmon; his uncle, Juanito Moquino; and his cousin, Velino; received Bachelor of Art and Master of Art degrees in art from the University of New Mexico.

AWARDS: Toledo has received awards at the Gallup Inter-Tribal and the Philbrook Art Center, Oklahoma, among others.

ABOUT THE ARTIST: Toledo regularly creates paintings of the Native American ceremonials and dance rituals. He tries to convey a deeper meaning of those traditions in his paintings. He shows the "far-away" look some Native American dancers have when they perform, and he tries to perfect his style.

MIKE TOM AND JOSEPHINE TOM

Mike—Northwest Coast (N/A) Canada
Josephine—Northwest Coast (N/A) Canada
Basketweavers, carvers

ABOUT THE ARTISTS: This couple make totem-pole-style baskets, masks, canoes, and other smaller wooden carved items. Josephine's basketmaking also extends to mats which she might design with whales and halibut, both part of Northwest Coast legends.

KERRY TOME

Seneca (1960 —) Steamburg, New York
Painter—pastels, pen and ink, some oils

EDUCATION: Salamanca Central High School art classes.

ABOUT THE ARTIST: Tome has worked on the art staff of a newsletter produced by the Indian Health, Education and Welfare (HEW) Program. His mother, Lorraine, and sister, Cheryl Schapp, are also involved in arts and crafts.

LORRAINE TOME

Seneca (1933 —) Salamanca, New York
Beadworker

EDUCATION: Self-taught; has taken some classes at the Allegany Indian Arts & Crafts Coop.

AWARDS: One of Tome's belts and necklaces was presented to Mrs. Krupsack, Lieutenant Governor of the State of New York (1977); one was presented to Miss Cattaraugus County as well (1977).

ABOUT THE ARTIST: Tome creates her own patterns for her medallions. They are usually geometric and in red, white, blue, or turquoise. Tome also uses floral designs for loom beadwork. Her mother taught her to make dolls when she was a child (which she sold at a stand in front of her house). Tome has passed her own skills on to two of her children.

TOOKOOME

Inuit (N/A) Baker Lake, Canada
Stone printmaker

ABOUT THE ARTIST: Tookoome creates prints about the stories of his clan. His narratives are always recognizable, though often abstract in style.

HERMAN TOPPAH

(a.k.a. All-Guat-Kou, "Yellow Hair")
Kiowa (1923 —) Carnegie, Oklahoma
Artist

EDUCATION: Studied with muralist Olaf Nordmark at Indian Art Center, Fort Sill, Oklahoma; informal training from James Auchiah, Spencer Asah, Leonard Riddles, Archie Blackowl, and Cecil Murdock.

AWARDS: Among Toppah's awards are a Second Award in Special Category, American Indian Artists Exhibition, from the Philbrook Art Center in Tulsa.

ABOUT THE ARTIST: Toppah has exhibited his work throughout the Southwest and is a member of the American Indian Artists Association.

DOROTHY TORIVIO

Acoma (N/A)
Potter

EDUCATION: Taught by her mother and her mother-in-law.

REPRESENTATION: Adobe Gallery, Albuquerque, New Mexico.

ABOUT THE ARTIST: Torivio often repeats the same design in different sizes and shapes on her pots, which makes the designs appear to be optical illusions.

MARY E. TOYA

Jemez (1934 —) Jemez Pueblo, New Mexico
Potter—Storyteller figures

AWARDS: Toya has won prizes for almost every kind of pottery, though her specialty is Storytellers.

ABOUT THE ARTIST: Toya's claim to fame is that she made an extremely large Storyteller that holds 115 children. Her seven daughters are following in the pottery-making tradition.

MAXINE TOYA

Jemez (N/A) Jemez Pueblo, New Mexico
Potter

EDUCATION: Toya learned from her mother, Marie Romero, the first Jemez to make a Storyteller in 1968.

ABOUT THE ARTIST: Toya works with her sister, Laura, and their mother. She creates figures that are experimental in form, though simple in design. Toya shares her clays and skills with her fifth-grade class.

RAY TRACEY

Navajo (1953 –   ) Navajo Reservation near
Ganado, Arizona
Jeweler—14 carat gold and sterling silver, inlaid
precious and semiprecious stones

EDUCATION: University of Utah; Brigham Young University; Trenton School of Jewelry.

Tracey's signature white heishi rope necklaces with inlaid mosaic "danglers" and eagle feathers, courtesy of Tracey Galleries, Santa Fe, New Mexico.

AWARDS: Niche Magazine Awards (1993); First Place, Santa Fe Indian Market (1993); First Place, Santa Fe Indian Market (1992); Best in Division, Santa Fe Indian Market (1991), and others

REPRESENTATION: Ray Tracey Galleries, Santa Fe, New Mexico; Southwest Studio Connection, Southampton, New York; The Squash Blossom, Aspen, Denver, and Vail, Colorado; Margaret Kilgore Gallery, Scottsdale, Arizona.

ABOUT THE ARTIST: Tracey's jewelry is known for its unusual use of color and shapes. He rarely uses more than two or three colors in the same piece. Many pieces feature eagle feathers because "the eagle is sacred to most Indian tribes . . . (and is) considered to be the messenger for the Great Spirit," Tracey says.

WANDA TRACEY

Navajo
Weaver

AWARDS: Best of Division, Scottsdale Native American Indian Cultural Foundation Arts and Crafts Competition (1987).

Portrait of Tracey at work, courtesy of Tracey Galleries, Santa Fe, New Mexico.

DEL TRANCOSA
San Felipe/Cochiti (1951 –) New Mexico
Potter–Storyteller figures

EDUCATION: Learned his art from mother-in-law, Helen Cordero.

REPRESENTATION: Adobe Gallery, Albuquerque, New Mexico.

ABOUT THE ARTIST: Trancosa made his first Story-teller in 1980. His figures are often reminiscent of Helen Cordero's.

DOROTHY TRUJILLO
Cochiti (1932 –) New Mexico
Potter–Storyteller figures

EDUCATION: Taught the art of pottery by her mother, Carrie Reid Loretto, and her grandmother, Lupe Madalena Loretto.

AWARDS: Began winning awards in the 1970s throughout the Southwest and later the United States for her Storytellers and Nativities.

ABOUT THE ARTIST: Trujillo's family is full of potters such as her aunts, Loretta Cajero and Damacia Cordero; her sisters, Marie Edna Coriz, Alma Concha Loretto, Fannie Wall Loretto, Leonora (Lupe) Lucero, and Mary E. Toya; her daughters, Frances Pino, Judith Suina, and Cecilia Valencia; and her son, Onofre Trujillo II. Dorothy made her first Storyteller in 1966 and has passed on her experience to others, including her friend, Mary Martin.

EVON TRUJILLO
Cochiti (1959 –) New Mexico
Potter–Storyteller figures

EDUCATION: Learned from her mother, Kathy Trujillo.

ABOUT THE ARTIST: Trujillo comes from a long line of potters that includes her grandmothers, Rosalie Aguilar and Helen Cordero; her grandfather, Jose A. Aquilar; her aunts, Florence A.

Naranjo and Annie A. Martinez; her uncles, Alfred Aguilar and Jose V. Aguilar, Sr.; and her cousin, Becky Martinez. Trujillo began making Storytellers in the late 1970s.

FELIPA TRUJILLO
Cochiti (1908 –) New Mexico
Potter–Storyteller figures

EDUCATION: Trujillo's mother, Estephanita Herrera, taught her how to make large bowls, figurines, and effigy pitchers. Trujillo learned how to make Storytellers on her own.

REPRESENTATION: Adobe Gallery, Albuquerque, New Mexico.

ABOUT THE ARTIST: Trujillo's daughter, Angel Quintana, and niece, Helen Cordero, are also potters. Trujillo's first "Storytellers" were actually "singing ladies" which resembled those made during the early twentieth century. She began producing Storytellers in earnest in the 1960s. Most of these pieces have her trademark baby in the cradle-board. Trujillo was one of the six potters exhibited at the "What Is Folk Art?" show at the Museum of International Folk Art in Santa Fe in 1979.

KATHY TRUJILLO
San Ildefonso/Cochiti (1931 –) San Ildefonso
Pueblo, New Mexico
Potter–Storyteller figures

EDUCATION: Learned how to pot from her parents, Rosalie and José A. Aguilar; learned how to make Storytellers from Dorothy Trujillo and Mary Martin.

ABOUT THE ARTIST: Trujillo's family is heavily involved in pottery. Active pottery-making members include Trujillo's daughter, Evon Trujillo; her sisters, Florence A. Naranjo and Annie A. Martinez; her brothers, Alfred Aguilar and Jose V. Aguilar, Sr.; her niece, Becky Martinez; and her mother-in-law, Helen Cordero.

Trujillo originally made the black-on-black pottery produced in San Ildefonso, but she began making figures in the 1970s after she married into the Cordero family and moved to Cochiti.

MARY TRUJILLO

> *San Juan / Cochiti (1937 –   ) San Juan Pueblo, New Mexico*
> *Potter–Storyteller figures*

EDUCATION: Learned to pot from her mother, Leondias C. Tapia; Taught the art of Storytellers by Trujillo's mother-in-law, Helen Cordero, and her neighbor, Ada Suina.

AWARDS: Trujillo won her first award in 1982 at the Indian Market for her piece "Corn Husking Party."

ABOUT THE ARTIST: Trujillo's family members are also potters: Trujillo's aunts, Belen Tapia, Santianita Suazo, and Martina Aquino; her great-aunt, Rose Gonzales; and her cousins, Anita Suazo and Tse-Pe. Trujillo started making Storytellers in the late 1970s to early 1980s. She uses the traditional Cochiti materials—white clay for figures, white slip, and bee plant for black paint. Like other potters, Trujillo thinks of her ancestors. especially her grandfather, when creating her Storytellers.

ONOFRE TRUJILLO II

> *Cochiti (1969 –   ) New Mexico*
> *Potter–Storyteller figures*

EDUCATION: Dorothy Trujillo, Trujillo's mother, taught him how to pot.

ABOUT THE ARTIST: Pottery-making members of Trujillo's family include his sisters, Frances Pino, Judith Suina and Cecilia Valencia and his aunts and great-aunts. Trujillo created his first Storyteller in 1982.

EDITH TSABETSAYE

> *Zuni (1940 –   ) New Mexico*
> *Jeweler, silversmith*

AWARDS: Best of Show, Indian Market, Santa Fe (1980), among many others.

REPRESENTATION: Many Goats, Tucson, Arizona; Tanner Chaney Gallery, Albuquerque, New Mexico; The Turquoise Village, Zuni Pueblo, New Mexico.

ABOUT THE ARTIST: Tsabetsaye is a master of needlepoint designs in jewelry and has inspired younger jewelers to continue in her footsteps. She sometimes uses over 1,000 stones for concha belts, but is not producing as much work as she used to because she has arthritis in her hands.

LEE MONETT TSATOKE

(a.k.a. Tsa-Toke, "Hunting Horse")
> *Kiowa (1929 –   ) Lawton, Oklahoma*
> *Artist*

EDUCATION: Self-taught.

AWARDS: Among Tsatoke's awards are a First Prize, Indian Art Exhibit, American Indian Exposition, Anadarko, Oklahoma (1960).

ABOUT THE ARTIST: Tsatoke began painting in 1943 and has exhibited his works throughout the United States. He is also well known as a fancy war dancer in the Kiowa Dance troupe.

ANDY TSINAHJINNIE

(a.k.a. Yazzie Bahe, Andrew Tsinnajinne, "Little Gray")
> *Navajo (1918 –   ) Rough Rock, Arizona*
> *Artist–mixed media*

EDUCATION: Studied with Dorothy Dunn at the Santa Fe Indian School in the 1930s.

AWARDS: Among this artist's many awards is a first prize in the 1962 Scottsdale National Indian Art Show for his painting "Slayer of Enemy Gods-Nayeinezani."

ABOUT THE ARTIST: One of the most influential Native American painters, Tsinahjinnie and his style have been studied by artists of all generations. His style and choice of medium have changed during his career, but his choice of subject matter has always been the same: the Navajo lifestyle.

HULLEAH TSINHNAHJINNIE
Seminole/Creek/Navajo (1954 –   ) Phoenix, Arizona
Artist—multimedia

EDUCATION: Institute of American Indian Art, Santa Fe; California College of Arts and Crafts, Oakland.

REPRESENTATION: San Francisco Art Institute, Walter/McBean Gallery, San Francisco, California; Temple University, Tyler School of Art/Temple Gallery, Philadelphia, Pennsylvania; Sacred Circle Gallery of American Indian Art, Seattle, Washington.

ABOUT THE ARTIST: Tsinhnahjinnie uses his photography in conjunction with other media to produce pieces that often have significance (i.e. an anniversary or Columbus's arrival in America).

DANNY RONDEAU TSOSIE
Hopi (N/A)
Painter—prisma on paper, other media

ABOUT THE ARTIST: Tsosie paints while playing songs or *yeibichai* chants as inspiration. One of his paintings, "October Song," reflects the impact music has on his work.

RICHARD TSOSIE
Navajo (1953 –   ) Arizona
Jeweler

REPRESENTATION: Lovena Ohl Gallery, Scottsdale, Arizona; October Art Ltd., New York, NY; Garland's, Sedona, Arizona; Many Hands, Sedona, Arizona.

ABOUT THE ARTIST: Tsosie uses the technique of reticulation to decorate his contemporary jewelry.

KEVIN SKYPAINTER TURNER
Choctaw (1958 –   ) St. Louis, Missouri
Custom handpainter—acrylics, oils, varnishes

EDUCATION: Self-trained signpainter and designer.

REPRESENTATION: Turner Artworks Trading Post and Art Gallery, DeSoto, Missouri; Red Cloud, St. Petersburg, Florida; Indian Sun, Sarasota, Florida; Dockside Gifts, Panama City Beach, Florida.

ABOUT THE ARTIST: Turner's unusual work includes creating a family coat of arms; creating Indian design fingernails (Turner is also a licensed manicurist); and decorating crayfish pincher necklaces, earrings, pins, and shell-amulet necklaces. He also makes arrowhead necklaces and chokers and turtle-shell wall hangings, paintings, and decorated skulls. Turner's work is sold through his catalog and the galleries that represent him.

Sepia portrait of Turner in full headdress, courtesy of the artist.

Turner's handpainted Villarreal family coat of arms, courtesy of the artist.

JAMES TURPEN, JR.
Cherokee/Navajo (1930 –) Winslow, Arizona
Painter, sculptor, jeweler

EDUCATION: University of Arizona.

ABOUT THE ARTIST: Turpen, Jr., who came from a family of traders, lived in the Southwest during his childhood, then moved after he married. While he traveled, he picked up a knowledge of art and continued to draw and to study western and Indian history. His bronzes have been shown throughout the Southwest and his jewelry is sometimes shown at Tobe Turpen's Indian Trading Company in Gallup, New Mexico, where he manages the shop.

FRANK TUTTLE
Yuki/Wailaki/Koncow Maidu (1957 –)
Oroville, California
Painter—various media

EDUCATION: Bachelor of Art, Fine Arts, emphasis in Native American Studies, Humboldt State University (1981).

REPRESENTATION: Meridian Gallery Society for Art Publications of the Americas, San Francisco, California.

ABOUT THE ARTIST: Tuttle lectures in Native American art, studies at Medocino College, and exhibits his work at Humboldt State University, among other places. He experiments with different imagery and materials in his work, often combining the traditional with the contemporary. He has exhibited in solo and group exhibitions for many years at places that include the Heard Museum.

THE TWO BULLS FAMILY
Lakota
Painters—acrylic, oil, acrylic on leather, ink on leather

Among the working artists in this family are Zachary; Linda; John; Loren; Lori; Marty (M. Grant); Matthew; Marvin Helper; Robert, Jr.; Sam, Jr.; Ed, Jr.; and Andrea.

The work of this family of painters is extensive and diverse. Though most of the members

Two Bulls, Jr.'s "Beadwork Design #7," courtesy of The Heritage Center, Inc., Pine Ridge, South Dakota.

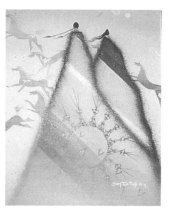

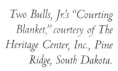

Two Bulls, Jr.'s "Courting Blanket," courtesy of The Heritage Center, Inc., Pine Ridge, South Dakota.

work in acrylic, some have chosen oils or ink as their media. Most paintings are done on canvas, though velvet and leather may be used. The Two Bulls Family shares skills and techniques; each helps the other advance in his or her art.

SHIRLEY VANATTA
Seneca (1922 – 1975)
Painter—oils, watercolors, pastels, pen and ink

EDUCATION: Self-taught.

AWARDS: In 1972, Governor Nelson Rockefeller of New York State presented Vanatta the award of "Indian of the Year"; she has also won many other honors.

ABOUT THE ARTIST: Vanatta's paintings and work in the Allegany community were appreciated by her community as well as the newspapers and magazines for which she illustrated during the 1950s–1960s. She was also the publicist for the Seneca Nation and editor-in-chief of *O-He-Yah-Noh*. During her career, Vanatta painted wildflowers, nature scenes, or portraits of famous Indians.

DONALD VANN
Cherokee (1952 –) South Carolina
Artist—watercolor

REPRESENTATION: Eagles Roost Gallery, Colorado Springs, Colorado.

ABOUT THE ARTIST: Vann's paintings show the despair the Indians feel about how they have been deceived. Vann believes that his people have turned from their strong beliefs and are on the road leading to war, illness, violence, and despair. His paintings reflect a barren, stark landscape where it is always winter and always dreary.

GORDON VAN WERT
Red Lake Chippewa (N/A)
Sculptor

ABOUT THE ARTIST: Van Wert often uses translucent alabaster when sculpting.

BETTY VAN WINKLE
Navajo (N/A)
Weaver

ABOUT THE ARTIST: Van Winkle creates traditional designs such as Burnt Water-style weavings.

PABLITA VELARDE
(a.k.a. Tse Tsan)
Santa Clara (1918 –) Santa Clara Pueblo, New Mexico
Artist; muralist; portraitist—various media

EDUCATION: Velarde was the first full-time female student in Dorothy Dunn's art class at the Santa Fe Indian School (The Studio); she also studied with Tonita Pena.

REPRESENTATION: Amerind Foundation Museum, Dragoon, Arizona; Wheelwright Museum of the American Indian/Case Trading Post, Santa Fe, New Mexico.

ABOUT THE ARTIST: Velarde painted in the "traditional" style of Santa Fe and did accurate portraits of Indian life and culture. At first she worked in watercolor, but later learned how to prepare paints from natural pigments (a process called *fresco secco*). Velarde painted murals for the Bandelier National Monument in New Mexico (1939–1948). She was also known to create art derived from the Navajo sandpainting tradition. Clara Tanner called her the "greatest woman artist in the Southwest." Velarde's daughter, Helen Hardin, was also quite well known.

ROY VICKERS
Tsimshian (N/A) Canada
Carver, painter

REPRESENTATION: Orca Aart Gallery, Chicago, Illinois.

ABOUT THE ARTIST: Vickers creates crests for family use, often incorporating Northwest Coast animals such as the killer whale into his designs.

EVELYN VIGIL

Jemez (N/A) New Mexico
Potter

ABOUT THE ARTIST: Vigil discovered the ancient way that the Pecos people painted their pottery, and in a sense recreated an old tradition. She now passes that skill on to the next generation of potters or to anyone else who wants to learn.

LONNIE VIGIL

Nambé (N/A) New Mexico
Potter

EDUCATION: Learned from members of his family.

AWARDS: Vigil has won major awards with his pottery.

ABOUT THE ARTIST: Vigil first began making pots in 1983 and micaceous pots in 1990. Some pieces are extremely large (22 inches in height).

MANUEL AND VICENTA VIGIL

Tesuque (N/A) New Mexico
Potters

ABOUT THE ARTISTS: This couple create Storytellers and nativities. The figures are fully clothed and have hair made of rabbit's fur.

PAUL VIGIL

Tesuque (1940? –   ) Tesuque Pueblo, New Mexico
Artist—oil

EDUCATION: Learned some of his skills from his father.

AWARDS: First-place ribbon, Indian Market, Santa Fe (1991).

ABOUT THE ARTIST: Vigil paints traditional Tewa dancers in the style of the early Pueblo artists using delicate brushwork and geometric designs and traditional motifs like corn, water, and Pueblo architecture. One of Paul's nine children, a son, is now learning to carry on the family's artistic tradition.

ROMANDO VIGIL

(a.k.a. Tse Ye Mu)
San Ildefonso (1902–1978) San Ildefonso Pueblo, New Mexico
Artist—watercolor on paper

EDUCATION: Self-taught.

ABOUT THE ARTIST: A leader within the San Ildefonso Watercolor Movement, Vigil used a stylized design to represent ceremonial dances. He was a master at creating stylized images with a simple line.

LILLIE WALKER

Navajo (1929 –   ) Coal Mine Mesa, Arizona
Weaver

EDUCATION: Learned how to weave from family members.

ABOUT THE ARTIST: Walker weaves side-by-side with her daughter, Cecilia Nez, at her daughter's house in Tuba City. Walker's rugs are simple geometric designs with a limited color range and rough texture. They resemble the rugs made in the 1930s. Walker uses processed yarn because she no longer keeps sheep.

KAY WALKINGSTICK

Cherokee (1935 –   ) Syracuse, New York
Artist—mixed media

EDUCATION: Bachelor of Fine Art, Beaver College, Glenside, Pennsylvania; Master of Fine Art, Pratt Institute, Brooklyn, New York.

AWARDS: WalkingStick has exhibited both solo and in museums. Her work is held in a number of public and private collections and has been honored by many awards.

REPRESENTATION: Wenger Gallery II at Hotel Nikko, Los Angeles, California; Wenger Gallery, Santa Monica, California; University at Albany/Rathbone Gallery, Albany, New York; Long Island University/Hillwood Art Museum, Brookville, New York; June Kelly Gallery, New York, NY;

177

State University College at Potsdam/Roland Gibson Gallery, Potsdam, New York; Cleveland State University Art Gallery, Cleveland, Ohio

ABOUT THE ARTIST: WalkingStick uses a diptych format where each painting needs the other to complete the picture. In 1987, WalkingStick stated that she is "interested in the interrelationship between ideas and empirical reality." She is considered one of the leading contemporary Native American artists and is currently an assistant professor of art at Cornell University.

ALAN WALLACE

Taos (N/A) Taos Pueblo, New Mexico
Jeweler, artist

EDUCATION: Largely self-taught.

AWARDS: Wallace has won many awards for his mosaic work.

ABOUT THE ARTIST: Wallace creates necklaces, rings, and bracelets with finely worked mosaic designs and scenes. Some of his pieces reflect pueblo life. An image of a Kachina, for example, may find its way into Wallace's larger bracelets. He works with many semiprecious stones, as well as with silver and gold.

ROBERTA WALLACE

(N/A)
Potter

AWARDS: Best of Division, Red Earth awards ceremony (1994).

MARY EUNICE WARE

Cochiti (1958 –   ) New Mexico
Potter–Storyteller figures

EDUCATION: Ware's mother, Maria Priscilla Romero, taught her how to pot.

ABOUT THE ARTIST: Other members of Ware's family who are potters include Ware's grandmother,

Teresita Romero, and her great-grandmother, Cresencia Quintana. Ware created her first Storyteller in 1980 and continues to make inroads in the art.

ANDREW WARREN

Dineh (1963 –   ) Albuquerque, New Mexico
Painter–acrylic paints on hide

EDUCATION: High-school graduate and trade-school electrician.

REPRESENTATION: Native Reflections, Salt Lake City, Utah.

ABOUT THE ARTIST: Born to the Folding Arm People and for the Red House People, Warren does paintings on hide and is also a recording artist with the Indian Creek Singers. His work has been purchased by celebrities and collectors throughout the United States.

Warren's painting on hide depicting Pueblo man with pottery, courtesy of the artist and Native Reflections, Salt Lake City, Utah.

Warren's painting on hide depicting chief with buffalo headdress on head and various shots of buffalos throughout the montage, courtesy of the artist and Native Reflections, Salt Lake City, Utah.

FRANK WARREN

Dineh (1962 –   ) Shiprock, New Mexico
Potter, painter, etcher

EDUCATION: Warren learned a lot of his skills from family members, all of whom are well known for their art work.

REPRESENTATION: Native Reflections, Salt Lake City, Utah.

Portrait of Warren holding one of his vases, courtesy of the artist and Native Reflections, Salt Lake City, Utah.

Warren's seed pot with geometric designs and buffalo decorations, done in shades of blue and peach, courtesy of the artist and Native Reflections, Salt Lake City, Utah.

ABOUT THE ARTIST: A versatile artist, Warren sells his pottery, paintings, and etchings to collectors from all over the world. He is also a singer/drummer with the Indian Creek Singers who recently recorded some of their powwow music.

ALFREDO WATCHMAN

Navajo (N/A) Sheep Springs, New Mexico
Sandpainter

ABOUT THE ARTIST: Watchman worked with extensive color changes when creating sandpaintings in the late 1970s. In so doing, he counteracted any negative reactions that would have been caused by recreating a holy symbol.

ELSIE Y. WATCHMAN

Navajo (N/A) Sheep Springs, New Mexico
Sandpainter

ABOUT THE ARTIST: As with many other sandpainters, Watchman intentionally makes errors on her paintings, such as neglecting to put hands on her figures, so that the religious intent of the work is negated. She usually creates simple, single-figure

Holy People because of economic and religious considerations.

PEARL WATCHMAN

Navajo (N/A) Sheep Springs, New Mexico
Sandpainter

ABOUT THE ARTIST: Watchman's commercial sandpaintings that sold on the market during the mid 1960s often had figures that were reversed.

SUSIE WATCHMAN

Navajo (N/A) Sheep Springs, New Mexico
Sandpainter

ABOUT THE ARTIST: Watchman created Pueblo dancers in the late 1970s, a diversion from her usual sandpainting subjects.

WALTER Z. WATCHMAN

Navajo (N/A) Sheep Springs, New Mexico
Sandpainter

ABOUT THE ARTIST: Like other members of his family, Watchman creates sandpaintings which deliberately include elements that are not religious or lack religious connotation.

CARSON R. WATERMAN

Seneca (1944 –   ) Salamanca, New York
Painter, graphic artist, printmaker, carver, sculptor

EDUCATION: Fine Arts certified instructor degree (1965–1967), Cooper School of Art; Smithsonian Institution internship program.

AWARDS: Waterman's honors include commissions from the Seneca Nation, the Department of Transportation, Housing and Urban Development (HUD), and others. One of his paintings (included in the exhibit "Famous Presidential Quotations") now hangs in the Lyndon B. Johnson Library.

ABOUT THE ARTIST: Waterman's mural paintings are well known in the Cattaraugus and Allegany

Nation's buildings. His work centers around Iroquois themes and has been political.

He has extensive teaching experience, has acted as exhibit curator, has exhibited his own work, and, with Pete Jemison, was cofounder of Seneca Nation Organization for the Visual Arts.

MARIE WATSON

Navajo (N/A)
Weaver

ABOUT THE ARTIST: Watson is known for her rug-within-a-rug or double-rug designs.

NETTIE WATT

(a.k.a. Ah Wen Non Gon)
Seneca (1901 –   ) Steamburg, New York
Basketmaker, dollmaker, beadworker

EDUCATION: Walt learned her skills by experimenting and watching her in-laws.

ABOUT THE ARTIST: One of the last basketmakers at Allegany, Watt passed her skills on to her daughter, Ruth. Nettie has made baskets since the Depression days, making most of them during the winter months. The majority of her baskets are made of black-ash splints; however, she does make some sweet-grass and sea-grass rope. She also creates cornhusk dolls and has tried to pass those skills on to others so that the craft will not die.

RUTH WATT

Seneca (1921 –   ) Steamburg, New York
Basketmaker

EDUCATION: Watt's mother, Nettie Watt, taught her how to make basket bottoms. Later, Watt learned how to make the rest of the basket on her own.

ABOUT THE ARTIST: Watt makes market, cake, shopper, and mail baskets out of black-ash splints which have rope or hickory handles. She often uses colored splints to accent the baskets, but most pieces are made from natural fibers. Ruth also makes colored corn necklaces.

KATIE WAUNEKA

Navajo (1941 –   ) near Fort Defiance, Arizona
Weaver

EDUCATION: Learned how to weave from mother, Nellie Williams.

ABOUT THE ARTIST: Wauneka, the sister of Daisy Redhorse and Betty Jumbo, wove her first rug at seven and has been weaving ever since. She and her sisters gather the materials for their dyes themselves.

WA-WA-CHAW

(a.k.a. Wawa Calac Chaw, "Keep From the Water," Benita Nunez)

Luiseno (1888 – 1972) Valley Center, California
Artist, writer

EDUCATION: Self-taught.

ABOUT THE ARTIST: Wa-Wa-Chaw was raised by Dr. Cornelius Duggan and his sister Mary because Wa-Wa-Chaw was ill at birth. A child prodigy, Wa-Wa-Chaw sketched Pierre and Marie Curie's experiments and started talking about her work and Indian matters to the public while still a teenager. Her oil paintings were done on large canvases and were usually portraits of people who were important at that time. A very active speaker on the equality of Indian women, Wa-Wa-Chaw met many of the intellectuals and leaders of her day, including Sir Arthur Conan Doyle, General Richard H. Pratt, and Arthur C. Parker. After she married Manuel Carmonia-Nunez, she changed her name to Benita Nunez.

JESSIE WEBSTER

Northwest Coast (N/A) Ahousat, British
Columbia, Canada
Basketweaver

EDUCATION: Webster watched her grandmothers weave hats. One grandmother would start a project for her, then Webster would work on it later.

ABOUT THE ARTIST: Webster creates woven basketry hats—fancy ones for the chief and plain varieties for the people.

PETER WEBSTER

Northwest Coast (N/A) Ahousat, British Columbia,
Canada
Carver

ABOUT THE ARTIST: Webster teaches his children and grandchildren the old dances. Their grandmother, Jessie, makes the costumes; Peter carves rattles and masks for the ceremonials.

LEE AND MARY WEEBOTHIE

Lee—Zuni (1927 –   ) New Mexico
Mary—Zuni (1933 –   ) New Mexico
Jewelers, silversmiths

REPRESENTATION: Tanner Chaney Gallery, Albuquerque, New Mexico.

ABOUT THE ARTISTS: Mary does the stonework and Lee the silversmithing when creating their jewelry.

CLARENCE WELLS

Tsimshian (N/A) Canada
Artist

ABOUT THE ARTIST: Wells often paints the legends of the Northwest Coast.

W. RICHARD (DICK) WEST

(a.k.a. Wapah Nahyah, Wah-Pah-Nah-Yah, "Lightfooted Runner"or "Lightfoot")

Cheyenne (1912 –   ) near Darlington, Oklahoma
Artist—watercolor; sculptor—wood

EDUCATION: West studied with Acee Blue Eagle at Bacone College. He was the first full-blooded Indian to graduate from the University of Oklahoma (Bachelor of Fine Art, 1941; Master of Fine Art, 1950) and also studied with the muralist Olaf Nordmark.

AWARDS: West has won many awards, including the Grand Award at the Philbrook Art Center (1955).

ABOUT THE ARTIST: For almost thirty years (1947–1970), West taught and was director of Bacone College's art department. He has received honors for both his artistic and teaching abilities, as well as his painstaking research as tribal historian. West's paintings show his knack for detail and historical accuracy. His career has often been said to reflect that of the entire Native American arts community—West has explored and experimented with a number of styles, techniques, and arts.

JOHN WHEELER

(a.k.a. Se Wa Tis)
Mohawk (1956 –   ) Rooseveltown, New York
Painter, woodcarver, beadworker

EDUCATION: Self-taught.

AWARDS: Wheeler won his first award in eighth grade when a Christmas card he had designed for the Muscular Dystrophy competition received worldwide distribution.

ABOUT THE ARTIST: Wheeler sketches portraits of contemporary and historical Native Americans and draws animals and cars.

ANDREW WHITE

(a.k.a. Tekaronhaneka)
Mohawk (1947 –   ) Hogansburg, New York
Painter—oils, charcoal, pencil

EDUCATION: Self-taught.

AWARDS: White has exhibited at the Iroquois Confederacy Arts and Crafts Exhibition.

ABOUT THE ARTIST: White has become well known for the paintings he does of Iroquoise history, culture, and traditions. He sometimes also paints about other Indian cultures as well.

ELIZABETH WHITE

(a.k.a. Polingaysi)
Hopi (N/A)
Potter, educator, writer

ABOUT THE ARTIST: White is Al Qöyawayma's aunt.

GLADYS WHITE

Mohawk (1942 –   )
Basketmaker, quilter

EDUCATION: White learned her basketmaking skills at the Akwesasne Homemakers and Cultural Committee.

ABOUT THE ARTIST: White makes planters and 4-inch baskets in natural splints and a simple pattern. She also sews quilts.

LARRY WHITE

(a.k.a. Kanatakeniate)
Mohawk (1945 –   ) Hogansburg, New York
Painter—oils, acrylics, charcoal

EDUCATION: Mostly self-taught; has taken some community college classes in Texas and Nevada.

ABOUT THE ARTIST: White's brother, Andy, encouraged White to start painting. He does mostly portraits or Native American scenes.

MADELINE WHITE

Mohawk (1917 –   ) Caughnawaga, Quebec, Canada
Beadworker, carver

EDUCATION: Self-taught; continues to expand her knowledge by studying books and traditional Iroquois designs.

ABOUT THE ARTIST: White likes to use dark-colored beads when making her medallions, Indian head ties, and clan animal patches. She has also carved cradleboards. White teaches her art at home and promotes Iroquois crafts.

RANDY LEE WHITE

Sioux (1941 –   ) North Dakota
Painter—mixed media

REPRESENTATION: MacLaren/Markowitz Gallery, Boulder, Colorado.

ABOUT THE ARTIST: White roots his work in truth,

though he often combines the past with the present in an abstract, mixed media way. His paintings are often political in nature.

White's style often reflects the stick figures Plains Indians used when drawing on ledger paper, but his figures might represent modern rather than ancient imagery. For example, in White's *Custer's Last Stand Revised*, the narrative is of the battle, but the horses are replaced by cars and tanks.

EMMI WHITEHORSE
Navajo (1957 –   ) Crownpoint, New Mexico
Artist—oil and chalk on paper, mounted in canvas

EDUCATION: Bachelor of Art, University of New Mexico (1980); Master of Art, University of New Mexico (1982).

REPRESENTATION: Horwitch LewAllen, Santa Fe, New Mexico.

ABOUT THE ARTIST: Whitehorse brings abstract and Navajo metaphysical views into her paintings. Her conceptualization sometimes appears in recognizable symbols—snakes, spirals, leaves, and branches. Collections of Whitehorse's work are held by many institutions including The Heard Museum (Phoenix), The Wheelwright Museum of the American Indian (Santa Fe), and the United States Department of State.

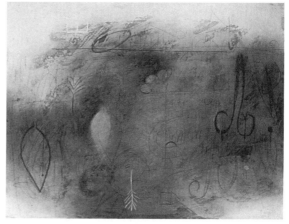

Whitehorse's "Microcosm I," Oil/paper/canvas, 39½ x 51 inches, 1992, courtesy of the artist and Jan Cicero Gallery, Chicago, Illinois.

ROLAND N. WHITEHORSE
(a.k.a. "Whitehorse")
Kiowa (1920 –   ) Carnegie, Oklahoma
Artist, sculptor

EDUCATION: Bacone College, Muskogee, Oklahoma (1947–1948); Dallas Art Institute, Texas (1951–1952).

AWARDS: Among Whitehorse's honors are awards for his bronze sculptures and First and Second Awards given at the Oklahoma Indian Trade Fair (1970).

ABOUT THE ARTIST: Whitehorse has exhibited his work throughout the United States. He was an illustrator for the Fort Sill School Training Aids, worked at the Fort Sill Museum, and acted as director of arts and crafts at the American Indian Exposition in Anadarko, Oklahoma.

Portrait of Whitehorse by Dirk DeBruycker, courtesy of LewAllen/Butler Fine Art, Santa Fe, New Mexico.

ALFRED WHITEMAN, JR.
(a.k.a. "Sitting Bear")
Cheyenne/Arapaho (1928 –   ) Colony, Oklahoma
Artist

EDUCATION: Certificate in commercial art, Oklahoma State Tech, Okmulgee, Oklahoma (1960–1962).

AWARDS: Whiteman, Jr., has been awarded prizes in exhibits throughout the West and Southwest.

ABOUT THE ARTIST: Whiteman worked as an artist and designer for Oklahoma State University. He has exhibited his work throughout the United States.

JUNIOR WHITEROCK

Dineh (1964 –   ) Ponca City, Oklahoma
Sandpainter

EDUCATION: WhiteRock attended Utah Community College (1985–1987), but was influenced strongly by his parents (John and Cecilia) and grandparents (Archie and Mary), all of whom were artistic.

AWARDS: WhiteRock's work has won first and second place awards at the Northern Arizona Museum, Navajo Nation Fair, Phoenix Indian Market, and Native American Art Show in Phoenix.

REPRESENTATION: Native Reflections, Salt Lake City, Utah.

ABOUT THE ARTIST: WhiteRock does the Denver Indian Pow Wow, as well as other shows. Born to the Salt People and born for the Edgewater People, he has the distinction of being one of the best-known sandpainters in the business. His work is held in private collections throughout the world.

BAJE WHITETHORNE

Navajo (N/A) near Shonto and Black Mesa, Arizona
Artist

EDUCATION: Learned his early painting skills from his family.

REPRESENTATION: Sage Brush Limited Editions, Flagstaff, Arizona.

ABOUT THE ARTIST: Whitethorne's trademark is a small folding chair which he tries to include in all his paintings. The chair is part of what he remembers as a child living in a hogan. He has had work exhibited in the Museum of Northern Arizona, The Heard Museum, and at the Santa Fe Indian Market. He likes to paint near his home and the Shonto and Tsegi Canyons.

Photograph of Whiterock (right) with artist Frank Salcido (left) after Salcido had purchased one of Whiterock's works, courtesy of the artist and Native Reflections, Salt Lake City, Utah.

A selection of Whiterock's sandpainted pottery, courtesy of the artist and Native Reflections, Salt Lake City, Utah.

ELIZABETH WHITETHORNE-BENALLY

Navajo (N/A) near Shonoto and Black Mesa, Arizona
Artist

EDUCATION: Learned from her family, especially Baje, her brother.

REPRESENTATION: Sage Brush Limited Editions, Flagstaff, Arizona.

ABOUT THE ARTIST: Whitethorne-Benally's work often reflects the memories she has of watching her mother and grandmother weave rugs and take them to market. Other traditions are also incorporated into her work.

ANNE WILLIAMS

Okanagan (N/A) Burns Lake, British Columbia, Canada
Beadworker

ABOUT THE ARTIST: Williams has made beaded gloves, moccasins, and other items.

DAVID EMMETT WILLIAMS

(a.k.a. Tosque, Tos-Que, "Apache Man")

Kiowa/Tonkawa/Apache (1933 –   ) Anadarko, Oklahoma
Artist—oil on canvas, tempera on illustration board

EDUCATION: Studied art at Bacone College, Muskogee, Oklahoma (1960–1962).

AWARDS: Williams has won awards for his work throughout the United States.

ABOUT THE ARTIST: Williams, who is descended from the famous Kiowa chief Sitting Bear, has made his career with exhibits at such places as the Sporting Gallery in Williamsburg, Virginia, and Stouffer's Manor Gate House in Pittsburg, Pennsylvania. He is a member of the Oklahoma Indian Arts and Crafts Cooperative.

FRANCIS WILLIAMS

Haida (N/A) Masset, British Columbia, Canada
Carver, jeweler—wood, silver

ABOUT THE ARTIST: Williams is well known for his silver jewelry, but also carves with wood occasionally to create spoons and other objects.

FRED WILLIAMS, SR.

(a.k.a. Ha Ehen Nos, "Watching Traps," Chief Red Cloud)

Cayuga (1889 –   )
Beadworker, carver, leatherworker

EDUCATION: Self-taught.

ABOUT THE ARTIST: Williams was not only a craftsperson/artist, but, as Chief Red Cloud, performed as a trick rider, roper, and bullwhip expert, first with Buffalo Bill's Wild West Show and later with a company that toured Europe. He had created beadwork items; birch-bark canoes; wood-carved items such as bowls, spoons, arrow tomahawks, and snowsnakes; and leather items such as clothing and moccasins.

HATTIE WILLIAMS

Tuscarora (1908 –   )
Beadworker, dollmaker

EDUCATION: Learned from her mother.

AWARDS: Among the awards Williams has received are New York State Fair honors for her beadwork.

ABOUT THE ARTIST: Williams helped her mother sell her crafts in Niagara Falls before she started beading herself. She mostly creates raised beadwork style items on velvet.

JULIANNA WILLIAMS

Mount Currie (N/A) Mount Currie, British Columbia, Canada
Basketmaker

EDUCATION: Learned the skills of basketmaking from her mother, Matilda Jim.

ABOUT THE ARTIST: Williams makes lidded and unlidded baskets, as her mother did before her.

ROSE WILLIAMS

(N/A)
Potter

AWARDS: Williams was designated one of Arizona's Indian Living Treasures in 1994.

SUSANNE WILLIAMS

Seneca (1962 –   ) Versailles, New York
Artist, beadworker, quillworker

EDUCATION: Mostly self-taught; has taken art classes in school and a costume class from Edith John (1975).

ABOUT THE ARTIST: Williams draws landscapes, animals, and cartoon characters. She also does beadwork and is learning woodcarving and pottery.

TOM WILLIAMS AND FAMILY

Cayuga (N/A)
Beadworker, carver

EDUCATION: Tom is largely self-taught, though his children have attended craft classes.

ABOUT THE ARTISTS: The Williams family is talented and diverse. Janice, mother to the six children, makes beaded items, both freehand and on a loom. She often creates her own designs or helps friends fill orders. Her daughters, Arlene, Darlene, and Sharon, create woodwork while the boys, Duane and Richard, carve soapstone pendants. Tom, the eldest son, is a leathercrafter.

JOHN JULIUS WILNOTY

Cherokee (1940 –   ) Bigwitch, North Carolina
Sculptor—pipestone, catlinite, other stone

EDUCATION: Self-taught.

ABOUT THE ARTIST: Wilnoty concentrates on bringing the history of his people to life. His carv-

ings are meticulous and often influenced by his study of pre-Colombian pipe bowls of the Southeastern United States.

AUDREY SPENCER WILSON

Navajo (1920 –   ) Indian Wells, Arizona
Weaver

EDUCATION: Learned how to weave from her mother.

REPRESENTATION: J. B. Tanner Trading Company, Ya-Ta-Hey, New Mexico.

ABOUT THE ARTIST: Wilson often makes large, ambitious projects. She uses the same kind of loom she learned on and often weaves sash belts and other items while working on a large rug. Her designs reflect the Two Grey Hills rugs though her weavings are often a little more innovative. Wilson usually weaves complex two-faced and fancy weaves, as well as designs that incorporate *yei* figures. Wilson cannot card and dye her own wool any longer because of painful arthritis.

DOUG WILSON

Haida (N/A) Skidegate, British Columbia, Canada
Carver—wood, stone

ABOUT THE ARTIST: Wilson likes working with Queen Charlotte argillite when doing his small totem poles or bowls. He believes it to be easily carveable.

DUFFY WILSON

Tuscarora/Iroquois (1925 –   ) Lewiston, New York
Sculptor—stone

EDUCATION: Self-taught.

ABOUT THE ARTIST: Wilson is often credited with bringing the Iroquois art of sculpting back to his people. His modern works reflect his heritage and traditions.

ELSIE JIM WILSON

Navajo (1924 –   ) Kinlichee, Arizona
Weaver

EDUCATION: Learned how to weave at a young age.

AWARDS: One of four Native American artists to be awarded the 1990 Arizona Indian Living Treasure Award.

REPRESENTATION: Hubbell Trading Post, Arizona.

ABOUT THE ARTIST: Wilson makes a version of the Ganado Red regional style (a style recognized by its central diamond, fancy borders, and predominately red color). She repeats finely stepped motifs in the center and border areas of her rugs and frequently uses hooked frets and small stepped triangles. Wilson works on an unusual welded steel loom. Her sisters, Sadie Curtis and Mae Jim, are also weavers and Wilson has taught her daughters to weave. As Wilson grew older, her youngest daughter, Ruby, began assisting her with the large rugs.

ERROL WILSON

Oneida (1957 –   ) Oneida, Wisconsin
Painter, beadworker, dollmaker, potter

EDUCATION: Painting major at the Institute of American Indian Arts (1975–1978); art major at the University of Wisconsin, Milwaukee (1978); has taken beadwork classes and learned how to do cornhusk work from his grandmother, Amelia Metoxin.

AWARDS: Among Wilson's awards is a Congressional Certificate of Merit in the Painting category from the Institute of American Indian Arts.

ABOUT THE ARTIST: Wilson likes to work with oils for paintings and with pen and ink for illustrations. His scenes are frequently portraits of nature which he sometimes borders with traditional Iroquois patterns.

GRACE WILSON

Haida (N/A) Masset, British Columbia, Canada
Basketmaker

ABOUT THE ARTIST: Wilson weaves spruce root hats, baskets, and other items.

LYLE WILSON

Haisla/Kwakiutl (1955 –   ) Canada
Carver, artist

EDUCATION: Wilson learned about carving from his uncle, Sam Robinson, as well as by his own research in the study of graphic design.

ABOUT THE ARTIST: Wilson often uses a multi-shade pencil in his work, which is a new medium for Northwest Coast artists. His work represents the Beaver, Fish, Blackfish, Raven, and Eagle (his crest) clans.

CRYING WIND

Navajo (N/A) Arizona
Artist, freelance writer, lecturer

AWARDS: Received the "Distinguished Christian Service in the Highest Tradition of the American Indian" award from the CHIEF organization.

ABOUT THE ARTIST: Crying Wind achieved success with her first book, *Crying Wind* and her second, *My Searching Heart*, a novelized biography about her and her family. Her paintings have been shown in museums and at art shows.

GLENN WOOD

Gitksan (N/A) Kitwancool, Canada
Carver

ABOUT THE ARTIST: Wood carves panels, masks, and other items. He often shares ideas and obtains new knowledge from other carvers in the Prince Rupert area.

CARL WOODRING

(a.k.a. Wasaba Shinga, "Little Bear")
Osage (1920 –   ) Arkansas City, Kansas
Artist—watercolor

EDUCATION: Studied under Acee Blue Eagle.

AWARDS: Woodring won more awards in one year than any other competitor during the history of the Philbrook Museum's annual competitions.

ABOUT THE ARTIST: Woodring's narrative paintings have been exhibited both nationally and internationally, often reflecting the Osage ceremonies and rituals.

KEN WOODWARD
(N/A)

AWARDS: Woodward won the Cecil Dick Award at the 1994 Five Civilized Tribes show in Muskogee, Oklahoma.

TEX WOUNDED FACE
Mandan/Hidatsa (N/A)
Sculptor

ABOUT THE ARTIST: Wounded Face works in stone, porcelain, and other materials.

BEATIEN YAZZ
(a.k.a. Jimmy Toddy, Bea Etin Yazz, Beatian Yazz, Beatian Yazzia, Beatin, Yazz, B. Yazz, "Little Shirt")
Navajo (1930 –) Arizona
Artist

EDUCATION: Mostly self-taught; he spent time with the artist James Swann and the Japanese artist Kuniyoshi at Mills College.

AWARDS: Yazz has won many awards.

ABOUT THE ARTIST: Yazz's first exhibit at the tender age of ten began to reap him rewards—both monetary and emotional—which would continue throughout his artistic career. Yazz paints simple watercolors of animals and his people. His style is clear and clean, yet one can feel the effect of his learning process which linked his pan-Indian illustrative style with the changes in his life. As he approached his upper middle-age years, Yazz began painting less because his eyes were bothering him.

BETTY JOE YAZZIE
Navajo (1932 –) Red Rock, Arizona
Weaver

EDUCATION: Grace Joe, Yazzie's mother, taught Yazzie how to weave.

ABOUT THE ARTIST: Yazzie has woven all her life, but did not become a regular weaver until the 1970s. She passes on her knowledge to the younger weavers and asks for input from the people who buy her rugs.

CORNELIA AKEE YAZZIE
Navajo (N/A) Tuba City, Arizona
Sandpainter

ABOUT THE ARTIST: Yazzie has created sandpaintings that are completely enclosed in a border so that the power of the symbols will not escape. The figures are also placed differently than they would be in a medicine man's sandpainting.

ELLEN YAZZIE
Navajo (N/A)
Weaver

ABOUT THE ARTIST: Yazzie does pictoral rugs, some with hundreds of figures which depict daily Navajo life.

JAMES WAYNE YAZZIE
Navajo (N/A) Sheep Springs, New Mexico
Sandpainter

ABOUT THE ARTIST: One of the sandpainters who started creating works for tourists in the 1970s, Yazzie was encouraged to improve his craftsmanship so that retailers could better sell his work.

JOHNNY YAZZIE
Navajo (N/A)
Artist

REPRESENTATION: SunWest Silver, Arizona.

Yazzie's acrylic on canvas of horse with spirits, 36 x 24 inches, courtesy of the artist and SunWest Silver, Albuquerque, New Mexico.

ABOUT THE ARTIST: Yazzie has been producing award-winning art for a few years.

LARRY YAZZIE

> *Navajo (1955 –   ) Coal Mine Mesa, Arizona*
> *Weaver*

EDUCATION: Yazzie learned how to weave from his mother and grandmother when he was very young. He had four years of art in school.

AWARDS: Yazzie has won blue ribbons for his work.

REPRESENTATION: Garland's, Sedona, Arizona.

ABOUT THE ARTIST: Yazzie's whole family is involved with the art of weaving; both males and females excel at the task. Yazzie is teaching the younger children how to weave. He elaborates on the old-style, raised outline designs and uses some of the figures from the Teec Nos Pas and Two Grey Hills styles in his work. He likes experimenting with color and size, often making hall runners.

LEE YAZZIE

> *Navajo (1946 –   ) south of Gallup, New Mexico*
> *Jeweler*

EDUCATION: Learned about his craft by watching his parents, both silversmiths, and, later, by taking a course at Fort Wingate Boarding School, Fort Wingate, New Mexico.

AWARDS: Three Best of Show Awards at the Gallup Inter-Tribal Ceremonial (between 1969–1990).

REPRESENTATION: Lovena Ohl Gallery, Scottsdale, Arizona; Waddell Trading Company, Tempe, Arizona; Eagle Plume Gallery, Allenspark, Colorado; The Indian Craft Shop, Washington, D.C.; Tanner's Indian Arts, Gallup, New Mexico.

ABOUT THE ARTIST: Yazzie worked with Tanner's Indian Arts and Crafts Center, Gallup, New Mexico, and learned how to cut good stones. The design for which Yazzie is best known is his corn bracelets. He shapes and polishes each "kernel" before placing it in the bracelet itself.

LEO YAZZIE

> *Navajo (1940 –   ) New Mexico*
> *Jeweler*

REPRESENTATION: Gallery 10, Inc., Scottsdale and Carefree, Arizona, and Santa Fe, New Mexico; Beckwith Gallery, Wellesley, Massachusetts; Quintana's Gallery, Portland, Oregon.

ABOUT THE ARTIST: Yazzie juxtaposes traditional Navajo textile patterns with lapis stones.

MARGARET YAZZIE

> *Navajo (1929 –   ) near Newcomb Trading Post, New Mexico*
> *Weaver*

EDUCATION: Learned how to weave by watching her foster grandmother, Adzani Baah.

ABOUT THE ARTIST: Yazzie weaves rugs to support her family. She is regarded as one of the better weavers on the Navajo reservation.

PHILOMENA YAZZIE

> *Navajo (1935 –   ) Sanders, Arizona*
> *Weaver*

189

EDUCATION: Learned how to weave by watching her mother.

AWARDS: Yazzie frequently wins prizes for her weavings at exhibits and fairs.

ABOUT THE ARTIST: Yazzie's sister and one of her daughters, Delores Grisley, are also weavers. Philomena has her own herd of sheep, shears them, dyes their wool, and does her own spinning. She works her rugs in the traditional way and usually produces two smaller (4 x 6 feet) rugs every year.

PHILOMENA YAZZIE
Navajo (1927 –   ) Querino, Arizona
Weaver

AWARDS: First prize in New Mexico and Arizona state fairs (1971 and 1972).

ABOUT THE ARTIST: One of the creators of the style called "Burntwater," Yazzie and her aunt, Mary Goldtooth Smith, and cousin, Maggie Price, are considered the premier weavers of the style which was introduced in 1968. Yazzie uses as many as twelve colors in a single rug and her designs have been copied by both Native Americans and Europeans. Because her eyesight is failing and she has arthritis, Yazzie tries to keep her designs simple and her colors bold.

FRANCIS YELLOW
(N/A)
Artist

AWARDS: Received the Presidents Award from the Red Earth Awards Ceremony, Oklahoma (1994).

YELLOWBIRD
San Ildefonso (N/A) San Ildefonso Pueblo,
New Mexico
Potter

ABOUT THE ARTIST: Yellowbird creates figural animals with his hands, using clay and shaping the pieces until they are recognizable. After the piece

is dry, he paints it with slip, polishes it with stone, and fires it.

ASON YELLOWHAIR
(a.k.a. "Mrs. Yellowhair," "Old Lady Yellowhair")
Navajo (1930 –   ) Smoke Signal, Arizona
Weaver

EDUCATION: Learned how to weave from family members.

REPRESENTATION: J. B. Tanner's Yah-Ta-Hey, New Mexico.

ABOUT THE ARTIST: Yellowhair has passed on her skills to her nine daughters and to two of her daughters-in-law. Most of the women learned how to weave before they were ten. Yellowhair has begun to teach her grandchildren as well. She specializes in large rugs, often uses birds in her weavings, and gets her inspiration from her love of the outdoors.

THE YELLOW HORSE FAMILY
Lakota
Beadworkers, jewelers, dollmakers, medallion makers,
belt buckle makers, watchband makers, barrette
makers, knife makers, bolo tie makers.

Working artisans of this family include Dorothy, Geraldine, Josephine, Raymond Pipe on Head, Yolanda Gertrude (Wanda), Sara Hope, Alvin, Dianne, Beverly, Stephanie Red Paint, Donny Stephan, Marvin Aloysius, Patricia Ann, Katherine (Kathy), John Wayne, Carol Jean, Darlene May, Stephan Kills Enemy, Felicia Caroline (Phyllis), Narcissus Stephen, Dennis Peter, and Priscilla Lynn.

ABOUT THE ARTISTS: This large Lakota family mainly creates bead decorated items. They share their skills and support each other artistically and familiarly. For more information on each artist, contact The Heritage Center, Inc., Pine Ridge, South Dakota for the address (see the gallery contributors list in the back of this book).

Hair strings of Yellow Horse Family/Alvin Pipe on Head, decorated with beadwork, 12 x 3 inches, courtesy of The Heritage Center, Inc., Pine Ridge, South Dakota.

Pony tail holder of Yellow Horse Family/Narcisse Kills Enemy, decorated with beadwork, 3 x 6 inches, courtesy of The Heritage Center, Inc., Pine Ridge, South Dakota.

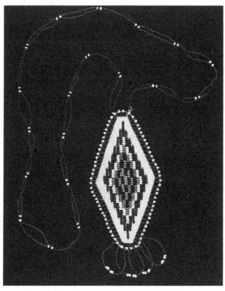

Diamond Medallion of Yellow Horse Family/Josephine Yellow Horse, decorated with beadwork, 5½ x 2¼ inches. Courtesy of The Heritage Center, Inc., Pine Ridge, South Dakota.

Marine Corps knife of Yellow Horse Family/Dianne Pipe on Head, decorated with beadwork, courtesy of The Heritage Center, Inc., Pine Ridge, South Dakota.

GEORGE YELTATZIE
Haida (N/A) Masset, British Columbia, Canada
Carver, jeweler—wood, stone

ABOUT THE ARTIST: Using the traditional Northwest Coast animal symbols, Yeltatzie often creates pieces that are narrative in nature. He believes that his art reaches people and helps them to understand who he is.

DON YEOMANS
Haida (1957 –) Prince Rupert, British Columbia, Canada
Carver, artist, jeweler

EDUCATION: Studied Fine Arts at Langara College, Vancouver, Canada.

ABOUT THE ARTIST: Yeomans carves masks, small totems, and other wooden items from his home in Prince Rupert. The head of the Fine Arts Department where Yeomans studied asked him to carve a totem pole for the college's entrance. It was only Yeoman's second pole, but he had already established himself as an artist.

MELA YOUNGBLOOD

Santa Clara (N/A) New Mexico
Potter

EDUCATION: Learned the pottery-making tradition from her mother, Margaret Tafoya.

NATHAN YOUNGBLOOD

Santa Clara (N/A) New Mexico
Potter

EDUCATION: Learned his trade from members of his family.

ABOUT THE ARTIST: Like his sister Nancy, Youngblood creates miniature pottery. He mixes his own clay and estimates that it takes over a day of work to mix one cubic foot.

NANCY YOUNGBLOOD-CUTLER

Santa Clara (N/A) Santa Clara, New Mexico
Potter

EDUCATION: Learned from her family, a branch of the Tafoya pottery-making clan.

Three contemporary Santa Clara black pots of Youngblood's (left to right): black carved jar, 12 inches high x 8½ inches diameter, black swirl melon jar, 4 inches high x 4¼ inches diameter, black swirl melon jar, 4½ inches high x 6½ inches diameter, courtesy of the artist and Gallery 10, Inc., Scottsdale, Arizona.

ABOUT THE ARTIST: Youngblood-Cutler is the niece of Mary Archuleta and the sister of Nathan Youngblood. Youngblood-Cutler creates old-style black miniatures. All of her tools are miniature as well. She is always experimenting with different designs.

ALBENITA YUNIE

Zuni (1944 –   ) New Mexico
Jeweler, carver

EDUCATION: Learned some of her technique from her famous mother, Ellen Quandelacy.

REPRESENTATION: Wadle Galleries, Ltd., Santa Fe, New Mexico.

ABOUT THE ARTIST: Yunie comes from the Quandelacy family, a group of carvers who have their own distinctive styles. Yunie creates fetish bears in all colors.

CHRISTINE C. ZUNI

(a.k.a. Povi, "Flower")
San Juan (N/A) San Juan Pueblo, New Mexico
Potter

EDUCATION: Learned the pottery techniques by watching her mother, Flora A. Cata.

AWARDS: Zuni's work has won numerous blue ribbons at Native American shows in Nevada and is on display at the Heard Museum and the Indian Pueblo Cultural Center in Albuquerque.

ABOUT THE ARTIST: Zuni signs her work with her Indian name, Povi, which means "flower" in the Tewa language. She has taught at the Smithsonian Institute as well as in the Maryland public schools. Her pottery reflects both contemporary and traditional influences. The majority of her work is hand-coiled, painted, and carved with traditional designs.

art appendix

A–B

Basketmaking

Eliza Abraham
Mary Adams
Sally Anne Adams
Agnes Alfred
Josephine Angus
Norma Antone
Christie Arquette
Jake Arquette
Margaret Arquette
Virginia (Hill) Beaver
Amy Begay
Agnes Black
Lorraine Black
Mary Black
Christine Bobb
Elsie Charlie
Florence Cook
Julius Cook
Cecilia Cree
Felicity Dan
Florence David
Florence Davidson
Nora Deering
Charlotte Delormier
Minnie Delormier
Charlotte Diabo
Mavis Doering
Frances Edgar
Margaret Etienne
Delfina Francisco
Mary Mitchell Gabriel
Sylvia Gabriel
Dorina Garcia
Ruby Garcia
Mildred Garlow
Agnes Garrow

Agnes George
Pat Courtney Gold
Gertrude Gray
Tom Gray
Liz Happynook
Mary Herne
Maggie Jacks
Vernon Jacks
Mary Jackson
Theresa Jemison
Matilda Jim
Fidelia Jimerson
Christina Jock
Joyce Johnson
Charlene Juan
Elaine Jumbo
Lena Jumbo
Beatrice Kenton
Madeline Lamson
Agnes Lazore
Margaret R. Lazore
Sarah Lazore
Mary Leaf
Miriam Lee
Grace Lehi
David R. Maracle
Rita McDonald
Mary Mitchell
Bessie Monongye
Tu Moonwalker
Charlotte Morey
Jenny Naziel
Theresa Oakes
Delores Oldshield
Alice Papineau
Catherine Pascal
Alice Paul
Victoria Phillips

Tom Printup
Wilma Lee Roberts
Rosie Ross
Mamie Ryan
Joyce Sharrow
Agnes Sunday
Cecilia Sunday
Pearl Sunrise
Maisa P. Tahamont
Mabel Taylor
Mary Tebo
Cecelia Thomas
Jennie Thomas
Mary Thomas
Elizabeth Thompson
Ella Thompson
Josephine Thompson
Marita Thompson
Wahleyah Anne
    Timmerman-Black
Josephine Tom
Mike Tom
Nettie Watt
Ruth Watt
Jessie Webster
Gladys White
Julianna Williams
Grace Wilson

Beadwork

Jeannine Aaron
D. Monroe Abrams
Eula Antone
Charla Bach
Ruth Baird
Virginia (Hill) Beaver
Mary (Thompson) Beckman
Dorothy M. Biscup

Winona Esther Blueye
Grace Bonspille
Perry Bonspille
Arkene Bova
Darlene Bova
Mamie Brown
Helen Burning
Gertrude Chew
Dorial Clark
Karen Clark
Darelyn Clause
Ann Coho
Ruth Conklin
Carl Cook
Toni Cooke
Bernice Crouse
Kathleen D'Arcy
Florence David
Agnes Decaire
Kristen Deer
Nora Deering
Diane Demarco
Elizabeth (Betty) Dennison
Luella Derrick
Alice Diabo
Marjorie Diabo
Victor K. Diabo
Betty Doxtator
Laura Doxtator
Deborah Drouin
Nancy Diabo Drouin
Sarah Dubuc
Black Eagle
Shannon Elijah
Gail Ellis
Jane Elm
Adeline Etienne
Karen Etienne
Margaret Etienne
Ida Gabriel
Mildred Garlow
Ruth Garlow
Sarah Garrow
Fidelia George
Mildred George
Leona Gray
Irene Greene
Mary Halftown
Ariel Harris

Hazel Harrison
Louise Henry
Margie Henry
Ethel Hill
Rita Hill
Penny Hudson
Jerry Ingram
Gōwá Djōwá Alsea Isaacs
Connie Jacobs
Emily Jacobs
Mary Scott Jacobs
Jacqueline "Midge" Jamison
Theresa Jamison
Fidelia Jimerson
Christina Jock
Velma Jocko
Elaine John
Estella John
Rose John
Darla Johnson
Tracy Johnson
Evelyn Jonathan
Louise Joseph
Maude Kegg
Celeste (Rooney) Kettle
Ivy Kibbe
Dorothy K. Lahache
Brenda Laughing
Juanita Lay
Robbie Lazore
Miriam Lee
Dorothea Leroy
Marilyn Leroy
Betty Anne Logan
David R. Maracle
Sally (Rosella) Maracle
Robin Marr
Louise McComber
Sandra McComber
Betty McLester
Bernie McQuary
Mary Michell
Theresa Mitten
Brian Mohr
Ross Montour
Tu Moonwalker
Barbara Nelson
Elizabeth Nelson
Emilienne Nelson

New Holy Family
Muriel Nicholas
Delores Oldshield
Alice Papineau
June Peters
Myrtle Peterson
Donna Phillips
Esther Kane Phillips
Morgan Phillips
Rita Phillips
Connie Pierce
David Pierce
Rodney Pierce
Amie Poodry
Nancy Poodry
Karen Powless
Kim Price
Annette Printup
Doris Printup
Marlene Printup
Mary Lou Printup
Tom Printup
Audrey Ray
Elnora Reuben
Margaret Rickard
Wilma Lee Roberts
Sadie Marie Rohlman
Mamie Ryan
Cheryl Schapp
Maisie Schenandoah and
    Family
Llavall Scrogg
Linda Sickles
Katherine Skye
Ruth Skye
Virgie Smith
Virginia G. Snow
Mary Southerland
Nandell Spittal
Shawnee Spittal
Roger Staats
Millie Stafford
Elsie M. Steffans
Doris Sundown
Mollie Sundown
Maisa P. Tahamont
Hazel Thompson
Marita Thompson
Nowetah Timmerman

Wahleyah Anne Timmerman-
Black
Lorraine Tome
Nettie Watt
John Wheeler
Madeline White
Anne Williams
Fred Williams, Sr.
Hattie Williams
Susanne Williams
Tom Williams and Family
Errol Wilson
The Yellow Horse Family

Blanketmaking
Emma Beans
Sadie Harris
Lily Speck

C

Carving
D. Monroe Abrams
Abraham Apakark Anghik
Johnson Antonio
Dempsey Bob
Cecil Calnimptewa
Dale Campbell
Jeffrey Chapman
Simon Charlie
Ray P. Cornelius
Doug Cranmer
Gordon Cross
Nelson Cross
Bill Crouse
Joe David
Neil David, Sr.
Claude Davidson
Reg Davidson
Robert Davidson
Fred Davis
John Deer
Diane Demarco
Victor K. Diabo
Jimmy Dick
Freda Diesing
Pat Dixon
John Fadden
Mitch Farmer
James (Jim) Fred

John Fredericks
Ros George
Harley Gordon
Leona Gray
Herbert Green
Stan Greene
Ron Hamilton
Monica Hansen
Roy Hanuse
Richard Harris
Walter Harris
James Hart
Bill Henderson
Ernie Henderson
Mark Henderson
Sam Henderson
Donald Hill
Delbridge Honanie
Brian Honyouti
Ronald Honyouti
Walter Howato
Calvin Hunt
Henry Hunt
Richard Hunt
Tony Hunt
Robert Jackson
Alvin James, Sr.
Doreen Jensen
Jimmy John
Norman John
Tracy Johnson
Harrison Juan
Presley La Fountain
Dorothy K. Lahache
Greg Lightbown
Oren Lyons
Duane Maktima
Alvin James Makya
Gerry Marks
Mungo Martin
Ross Montour
Brian Muldoe
Earl Muldoe
Bob Neel
Bryson Nequatewa
Amos Owen
Wayne Peterson
Loren Phillips
Marlin Pinto

Andres Quandelacy
Ellen Quandelacy
Faye Quandelacy
Georgia Quandelacy
Stewart Quandelacy
Glen Rabena
Bill Reid
Larry Rosso
The Runnels Family
Eileen Sawatis
Maisie Schenandoah and
Family
Ron Sebastian
Henry Shelton
Lance E. Silverhorn
Richard Zane Smith
Russell Smith
Shawnee Spittal
Vernon Stephens
Art Sterrit
Josiah Tait
Norman Tait
Lowell Talashoma
Dennis Tewa
Wilfred Tewawina
John Bigtree Thomas
Daniel Thompson
Josephine Tom
Mike Tom
Roy Vickers
Carson R. Waterman
Peter Webster
John Wheeler
Madeline White
Francis Williams
Fred Williams, Sr.
Tom Williams and Family
Doug Wilson
Lyle Wilson
Glen Wood
George Yeltatzie
Don Yeomans
Albenita Yunie

Ceramics
Pegie Ahvakana
Marjorie Barnes
Karita Coffey
David A. Gordon

Marguerite Lee Haring
Donald Hill
Peter B. Jones
Harold Littlebird
Charles F. Lovato
Sandra McComber

Claywork
Elizabeth Abeyta
Peter B. Jones

Clothing decorating/designing
Mary (Thompson) Beckman
Helen Burning
Toni Cooke
Nora Deering
Betty Doxtator
Anita Fields
Gertrude Gray
Irene Greene
Ariel Harris
Louise Henry
Ethel Hill
Rita Hill
Mary Scott Jacobs
Fidelia Jimerson
Darla Johnson
Celeste (Rooney) Kettle
Sarah Lazore
Betty McLester
Theresa Mitten
Donna Phillips
Doris Printup
Mary Lou Printup
Doris Printup
Mary Lou Printup
Margaret Rickard
Eileen Sawatis
Maisie Schenandoah and
    Family
Virginia G. Snow
Doris Sundown

Cornhusk Work
Virginia (Hill) Beaver
Margie Henry
Theresa Mitten
Maisie Schenandoah and
    Family

Crochet
Laura Doxtator
Ariel Harris
Betty McLester
Donna Phillips
Virgie Smith

D
Dollmaking
D. Monroe Abrams
Charla Bach
Mamie Brown
Ruth Conklin
Nora Deering
Diane Demarco
Alice Diabo
Marjorie Diabo
Deborah Drouin
Nancy Diabo Drouin
Sarah Dubuc
Mildred Garlow
Ruth Garlow
Margie Henry
Jacqueline "Midge" Jamison
Fidelia Jimerson
Estella John
Darla Johnson
Juanita Lay
Sandra McComber
Theresa Mitten
Delores Oldshield
Alice Papineau
Myrtle Peterson
Esther Kane Phillips
Rita Phillips
Nancy Poodry
Tom Printup
Audrey Ray
Elnora Reuben
Margaret Rickard
Wilma Lee Roberts
Eileen Sawatis
Virginia G. Snow
Wahleyah Anne Timmerman-
    Black
Nettie Watt
Hattie Williams
Errol Wilson
The Yellow Horse Family

E-F
Featherwork
D. Monroe Abrams
Mamie Brown
Darla Johnson
David Pierce
Margaret Rickard
Maisie Schenandoah and
    Family
Katherine Skye

G
Glassmaking
Tony Jojola

Graphic art
Joe Fedderson
Gaston Gaspé
Marguerite Lee Haring
Jerry Ingram
Pitseolak
Annette Printup
Carson R. Waterman

H
Headdress Work
Dorial Clark
Alice Diabo

I
Illustrations
Harrison Begay
Archie Blackowl
Les Bucktooth
Velina Shije Herrera
G. Peter Jemison
Fred Kabotie
N. Scott Momaday
Ross Montour
Clyde Leland Otipoby
Rita Phillips
Hart Merriam Schultz
Daniel Thompson

J
Jewelry
Andy Abeita
Roberta Abeita

Florence Aguilar
Marie Aguilar
Tony Aguilar
Alvarez
Mary Avery
Victor Beck
Mary (Thompson) Beckman
Abraham Begay
Alvin Begay
Harvey Begay
Kenneth Begay
Kyle Begay
Charlie Bird
Gail Bird
Mike Bird
Carolyn Bobelu
White Buffalo
"Ca Win" Jimmy Calabaza
Joe Caté
Rosey Caté
Ric Charlie
Ted Charveze
Elizabeth Charveze-Caplinger
Richard Chavez
John Christiansen
Carl Clark
Irene Clark
Victor Coochwytewa
Rita Joe Cordalis
Cippy Crazy Horse
Gordon Cross
Nelson Cross
John Deer
Pat Dixon
Tom "Two Arrows" Dorsey
Black Eagle
Dennis Edaakie
Nancy Edaakie
Elk Woman
Christina Eustace
Barbara Garcia
Raymond Garcia
Larry Golsh
Shal Goshorn
Watson Honanie
Sherian Honhongva
Sidney Hooee
Thomas Jim
Yazzie Johnson

Joe Jojola
Fred Kabotie
Bennett Kagenveama
Roderick Kaskalla
Clarence Lee
James Little
Jake Livingston
Jan Loco
Phil Loretto
Charles F. Lovato
Julian Lovato
Ray Lovato
Duane Maktima
Maria
Gerry Marks
Bernie McQuary
Jesse Lee Monongye
Preston Monongye
Phil Navasya
Verma Nequatewa
New Holy Family
Al Nez
Gibson Nez
Ben Nighthorse
Angie Reano Owen
Alice Papineau
Norbert Peshlakai
McKee Platero
Veronica Pablano
Phil Poseyesva
Charles Pratt
Andres Quandelacy
Ellen Quandelacy
Faye Quandelacy
Georgia Quandelacy
Stewart Quandelacy
Charlene Reano
Charlotte Reano
Frank Reano
Joe B. Reano
Percy Reano
Terry Reano
Charlene Sanchez Reano
Bill Reid
Lela Romero
Mamie Ryan
Maria "Lilly" Salvador
Percy Shorty
Howard Sice

Smokey
Charles Supplee
Roy Talahaftewa
Herbert Taylor
Bobbie Tewa
Wahleyah Anne Timmerman-
   Black
Ray Tracey
Edith Tsabetsaye
Richard Tsosie
James Turpen, Jr.
Alan Wallace
Lee Weebothie
Mary Weebothie
Francis Williams
Lee Yazzie
Leo Yazzie
The Yellow Horse Family
George Yeltatzie
Don Yeomans
Albenita Yunie

K

Knitting
Dennis Charlie
Marge Charlie
Nora Deering
Laura Doxtator
Hilda Henry
Evelyn Joe
Monica Joe
Betty McLester
Madeline Modeste
Sarah Modeste
Donna Phillips

L

Leatherwork
Mary Abel
D. Monroe Abrams
Arthur D. Amiotte
Eula Antone
Virginia (Hill) Beaver
Winona Esther Blueye
Grace Bonspille
Perry Bonspille
Helen Burning

Florence David
John Deer
Elizabeth (Betty) Dennison
Alice Diabo
Victor K. Diabo
Laura Doxtator
Deborah Drouin
Nancy Diabo Drouin
Black Eagle
Adeline Etienne
Karen Etienne
Margaret Etienne
Ida Gabriel
Ruth Garlow
Irene Greene
Rita Hill
Mary Scott Jacobs
Christina Jock
Velma Jocko
Estella John
Tracy Johnson
Ivy Kibbe
Dorothy K. Lahache
Brenda Laughing
Dorothea Leroy
Marilyn Leroy
David R. Maracle
Robin Marr
Sandra McComber
Ross Montour
Tu Moonwalker
Barbara Nelson
Elizabeth Nelson
Muriel Nicholas
Alice Papineau
Myrtle Peterson
Donna Phillips
Doris Printup
Tom Printup
Mamie Ryan
Cheryl Schapp
Katherine Skye
Sophie Thomas
Marita Thompson
Nowetah Timmerman
Fred Williams, Sr.

Lithographs
Jerry Ingram
Duane Slick

M-N
Mask Making
Lillian Pitt
Miscellaneous Media
Arthur D. Amiotte
Farrell Cockrum
New Holy Family
Muralist
Harrison Begay
Archie Blackowl
Woodrow Wilson Crumbo
John George-Mathews
Tom Hill
Charles Loloma
Richard Martinez
Pablita Velarde

O-P
Painting
Jimmy Abeita
Narcisso Platero Abeyta
Tony Abeyta
José Vicente Aguilar
Pegie Ahvakana
Norman Akers
Gail Albany
Alvin Eli Amason
Nadema Agard
Clara Archilta
Pitseolak Ashoona
Alice Asmar
Gilbert Atencio
James Auchiah
Marjorie Barnes
Rick E. Bartow
Joseph Beauvais
Fred Beaver
Clifford Beck
Larry Beck
Mary (Thompson) Beckman
Harrison Begay
Dennis Belindo
Mike Bero
Woody Big Bow
Archie Blackowl
Alex Bomberry
F. Blackbear Bosin
Parker Boyiddle, Jr.

Lynda (Hayfield) Brant
Clifford Brycelea
Les Bucktooth
Benjamin Franklin Buffalo
Diane M. Burns
Jerome Gilbert Bushyhead
Tom Wayne Cannon
Pop Chalee
Jeffrey Chapman
Robert Chee
Leslie Claus
Farrell Cockrum
Grey Cohoe
Don Conklin
Toni Cooke
Ray P. Cornelius
Larry D. B. (Butch) Cottrell
Bill Crouse
Woodrow Wilson Crumbo
Tony Da
Richard Glazer Danay
David Dawangyumptewa
Joe David
Neil David, Sr.
Robert Davidson
Frank Day
Andy Deer
John Deer
Diane Demarco
Patrick DesJarlait
Victor K. Diabo
Cecil Dick
Freda Diesing
Bill Dixon
Tom "Two Arrows" Dorsey
Tomas Dougi, Jr.
Alta Doxtador
Black Eagle
Tennyson Eckiwaudah
Ken Edwards
Elk Woman
Marshall Ellis
Sam English
Margaret Etienne
John Fadden
Mitch Farmer
Joe Fedderson
Phyllis Fife
Harry Fonseca
W. B. Franklin

Gaston Gaspé
George Geionety
Jack TóBaahe Gene
John George-Mathews
John Gibson
Rick Glazer-Danay
Henry Gobin
Larry Golsh
Stephen Gonyea
David A. Gordon
Harley Gordon
R. C. Gorman
Shal Goshorn
Enoch Kelly Haney
Roy Hanuse
Helen Hardin
Marguerite Lee Haring
Marcelle Sharron Ahtone
   Harjo
James Hart
James Havard
Hachivi Edgar Heap of Birds
Mark Henderson
Sue Ellen Herne
Joe H. Herrera
Velino Shije Herrera
Valjean McCarty Hessing
Alva Martin Hill
Bobby Hill
Donald Hill
Joan Hill
Rick Hill
Ron Hill
Tom Hill
Jack Hokeah
Delbridge Honanie
Rance Hood
Allan C. Houser
Oscar Howe
James Humetewa, Jr.
Jerry Ingram
Arnold Jacobs
G. Peter Jemison
Willie Jock
Velma Jock
David Johns
Darla Johnson
Harrison Juan
Joseph Kabance
Fred Kabotie

Michael Kabotie
Ernie Keahbone
George Keahbone
Michael Lacapa
Greg La Forme
Dorothy K. Lahache
Elgin W. Lamarr
Jean Lamarr
Frank Lapena
James Lavadour
Charlie Lee
Clarence Lee
Mary Lee (Webster) Lemieux
James Little Chief
Charles Loloma
Linda Lomahaftewa
Millard Dawa Lomakema
George Longfish
Phil Loretto
Charles F. Lovato
F. Bruce Lubo, Sr.
Donald D. Lynch
Oren Lyons
Joe Maktima
David R. Maracle
Mario Martinez
Richard Martinez
Georgia Masayesva
Jean McCarty Mauldin
Solomon McCombs
Rafael Medina
R. Gary Miller
Brian Mohr
Al Momaday
N. Scott Momaday
Donald Montileaux
Mark D. Montour
Nancy Montour
Tommy Edward Montoya
Stephen Mopope
Mary Morez
Norval Morrisseau
George Morrison
James Moses
Dan Namingha
Nora Naranjo-Morse
Joyce Lee Tata Nevaquaya
Redwing T. Nez
Georgina Nicholas
Pat Nicholas

Shelley Niro
Dennis Numkena
J. Numkena-Talayumptewa
Clyde Leland Otipoby
Loren Pahsetopah
Paul Pahsetopah
Robert Penn
Rita Phillips
Oqwa Pi
Otis Polelonema
Charles Pushetonequa
William Rabbit
Martin E. Red Bear
Robert Redbird
Leonard Riddles
Dolona Robert
Skip Rowell
J. D. Roybal
Will Sampson
Abel Sanchez
Percy Sandy
Allen Sapp
C. Terry Saul
Eileen Sawatis
Cheryl Schapp
Maisie Schenandoah and
   Family
Fritz Scholder
Hart Merriam Schultz
Bert D. Seabourn
Donald Henry Secondine, Jr.
Duane Slick
Ernest Smith
Jaune Quick-to-See Smith
Lois Smoky
Carol A. Soatikee
Alice Souligny
Shawnee Spittal
Seidel Standing Elk
Kevin Red Star
Susan Stewart
Virginia Stroud
Dorothy Strait
Theodore Suina
Terrance Talaswaima
Daniel J. Taulbee
John Bigtree Thomas
Marita Thompson
Johnny Tiger, Jr.

Wahleyah Anne Timmerman-
  Black
Jimmy Toddy
José Rey Toledo
Kerry Tome
Herman Toppah
Lee Monett Tsatoke
Andy Tsinahjinnie
Hulleah Tsinhnahjinnie
Danny Rondeau Tsosie
Kevin Skypainter Turner
James Turpen, Jr.
Frank Tuttle
The Two Bulls Family
Shirley Vanatta
Donald Vann
Pablita Velarde
Roy Vickers
Romando Vigil
Kay WalkingStick
Alan Wallace
Andrew Warren
Carson R. Waterman
Wa-Wa-Chaw
Clarence Wells
W. Richard (Dick) West
John Wheeler
Andrew White
Larry White
Randy Lee White
Emmi Whitehorse
Roland N. Whitehorse
Alfred Whiteman, Jr.
Baje Whitethorne
Elizabeth Whitethorne-Benally
David Emmett Williams
Susanne Williams
Errol Wilson
Lyle Wilson
Crying Wind
Carl Woodring
Beatien Yazz
Francis Yellow
Don Yeomans

Pen and Ink
George A. Ahgupuk
Alex Bomberry
Lynda (Hayfield) Brant

Les Bucktooth
Florence Nupok Chauncey
Don Conklin
Bill Crouse
Ken Edwards
Stephen Gonyea
Tom Hill
Willie Jock
Greg La Forme
Oren Lyons
R. Gary Miller
James Moses
Carol Snow
John Bigtree Thomas
Kerry Tome

Petroglyphs
Arthur D. Amiotte

Photography
Marjorie Barnes
Leslie Claus
Joe Fedderson
Gaston Gaspé
Shal Goshorn
Rick Hill
Jean Lamarr
Carm Little Turtle
Georgia Masayesva
Shelley Niro
Daniel Thompson

Pottery
Karen Abeita
Tamra L. Abeita
Elizabeth Abeyta
Pauline Abeyta
Blanche Antonio
Hilda Antonio
Clarice Aragon
Delores Aragon
John Aragon
Wanda Aragon
Esther Archuleta
Mary E. Archuleta
Josephine Arquero
Martha Arquero
Nathan Begay
Mabel Brown
Mary Cain

Barbara Cerno
Connie Cerno
Joe Cerno
Karen Kahe Charley
Carrie Chino Charlie
Stella Chavarria
Evelyn Cheromiah
Lee Ann Cheromiah
Gilbert Chino
Grace Chino
Keith Chino
Karita Coffey
Carolyn Concho
Sheila Concho
Toni Cooke
Buffy Cordero
Damacia Cordero
George Cordero
Helen Cordero
Tim Cordero
Blue Corn
Dawn'a D
Popovi Da
Tony Da
Tony Dallas
Raymond Lee Deschene
Desider
Tom "Two Arrows" Dorsey
Virginia Duran
Juanita DuBray
Virginia Duran
Anthony Durand
Cora Durand
Virginia Ebelacker
Marshall Ellis
Grace Medicine Flower
Jody Folwell
Juanita Fragua
Candelaria Gachupin
Delores Lewis Garcia
Dolores Garcia
Goldenrod Garcia
Joanne Chino Garcia
Wilfred Garcia
Sandra Garcia
Cordi Gomez
Glen Gomez
Barbara Gonzales
Rose Gonzales

David A. Gordon
Lois Gutierrez-da la cruz
Luther Gutierrez
Margaret Gutierrez
Petra Gutierrez
Stephanie Gutierrez
Pula Gutierrez
Val Gutierrez
Virginia Gutierrez
Daisy Hooee
Rondina Huma
Peter B. Jones
Harrison Juan
Marie Juanico
Marcella Kahe
Rena Kavena
Tracy Kavena
Juana Leno
Ivan Lewis
Lucy M. Lewis
Nancy Lewis
Rita Lewis
Harold Littlebird
Bill Lockwood
Carnation Lockwood
Charles Loloma
Joseph Lonewolf
Rosemary "Apple Blossom"
    Lonewolf
David R. Maracle
Mary Martin
Adam Martinez
Julian Martinez
Maria Montoya Martinez
Santana Martinez
Maximiliana
Christine Nofchissey McHorse
Lucy Leuppe McKelvey
Elizabeth Medina
Sofia Medina
Emma Mitchell
Eudora Montoya
Sylvia Naha
Bessie Namoki
Ana Naranjo
Christina Naranjo
Louis Naranjo
Paula Naranjo
Rose Naranjo

Teresita Naranjo
Virginia Naranjo
Joy Navasie
Felipe Ortega
Seferina Ortiz
Clyde Leland Otipoby
Gladys Paquin
Dora Tse Pe Pena
Kevin Peshalakai
Lorencita Pino
Tom Polacca
Al Qöyawayma
Faye Quandelacy
Margaret Quintana
Dextra Nampeo Quotskuyva
Stephanie C. Rhoades
Rose Pecos
Sun Rhodes
Toni Roller
Edna Romero
Maria Priscilla Romero
Virginia Romero
Maria "Lilly" Salvador
Russell Sanchez
Maisie Schenandoah and
    Family
Eusebia Shije
Stella Shutiva
Richard Zane Smith
Jacquie Stevens
Bernice Suazo-Naranjo
Ada Suina
Antonita (Tony Cordero) Suina
Aurelia Suina
Caroline Grace Suina
Frances Suina
Judith Suina
Louise Q. Suina
Lucy R. Suina
Marie Charlotte Suina
Vangie Suina
Camillo Tafoya
Margaret Tafoya
Mark Tahbo
Belen Tapia
Ernest Tapia
Stella Teller
Robert Tenorio

Wahleyah Anne Timmerman-
    Black
Bea Tioux
Dorothy Torivio
Mary E. Toya
Maxine Toya
Del Trancosa
Dorothy Trujillo
Evon Trujillo
Felipa Trujillo
Kathy Trujillo
Mary Trujillo
Onofre Trujillo II
Evelyn Vigil
Lonnie Vigil
Manuel Vigil
Paul Vigil
Vincenta Vigil
Roberta Wallace
Mary Eunice Ware
Elizabeth White
Rose Williams
Errol Wilson
YellowBird
Mela Youngblood
Nathan Youngblood
Nancy Youngblood-Cutler
Christine C. Zuni

Printmaking
Tony Abeyta
Abraham Apakark Anghik
Harrison Begay
Don Conklin
Robert Davidson
Black Eagle
Joe Fedderson
Enoch Kelly Haney
R. Gary Miller
N. Scott Momaday
Dan Namingha
Duane Slick
Susan Stewart
Tookoome
Carson R. Waterman

Q
Quillwork
D. Monroe Abrams
Virginia (Hill) Beaver

Darlene Bova
Mamie Brown
Toni Cooke
Kathleen D'Arcy
Agnes Decaire
Elizabeth (Betty) Dennison
Marjorie Diabo
Gail Ellis
Sarah Garrow
Leona Gray
Rita Hill
Christina Jock
Evelyn Jonathan
Celeste (Rooney) Kettle
Dorothea Leroy
David R. Maracle
Betty McLester
Alice New Holy Blue Legs
New Holy Family
David Pierce
Karen Powless
Annette Printup
Doris Printup
Audrey Ray
Millie Stafford
Nowetah Timmerman
Susanne Williams

Quilting

Mary Adams
Sally Anne Adams
Josephine Angus
Eula Antone
Margaret Arquette
Ruth Baird
Florence Cook
Cecilia Cree
Florence David
Charlotte Delormier
Elizabeth (Betty) Dennison
Laura Doxtator
Gertrude Gray
Mary Herne
Mary Scott Jacobs
Sarah Lazore
Miriam Lee
Sally (Rosella) Maracle
Louise McComber
Mary Mitchell

Theresa Oakes
Virgie Smith
Agnes Sunday
Marita Thompson
Gladys White

R

Rattles
Karen Clark

Rugweaving
Eula Antone
Bessie Barber
Maisa P. Tahamont

S–T

Sandpainting
Danny Akee
Harry A. Begay
Joe Begay
Keith Begay
Gladys Ben
Joe Ben, Jr.
Wilson Benally
Notah H. Chee
Gracie Dick
Timothy Harvey
Marian Herrera
Edward Jim
Eugene Joe
James Joe
George Johns
Margaret Johns
David Lee
Chee McDonald
Francis Miller
Patsy Miller
Freddie Nelson
David Peshlakai
Mary Lou Peshlakai
Wilson Price
Eileen Sawatis
Wilbert Sloan
Fred Stevens, Jr.
Juanita Stevens
Wilbert Sloan
Alfredo Watchman

Elsie Y. Watchman
Pearl Watchman
Susie Watchman
Walter Z. Watchman
Junior Whiterock
Cornelia Akee Yazzie
James Wayne Yazzie

Sculpture

Andy Abeita
Roberta Abeita
Elizabeth Abeyta
Abraham Apakark Anghik
Arnold D. Aragon
Rick E. Bartow
Larry Beck
Mike Bero
Parker Boyiddle, Jr.
Jeffrey Chapman
Randall Chitto
Dennis R. Christy
Leslie Claus
Farrell Cockrum
Jon DeCelles
Victor K. Dibo
Gracie Dick
Tomas Dougi, Jr.
Elk Woman
Anita Fields
Cliff Fragua
Retha Walden Gambaro
Ted Garner
Jack Glover
Larry Golsh
David A. Gordon
R. C. Gorman
Craig Goseyun
Rollie A. Granbois
Judith Greene
Monica Hansen
Robert Haozous
James Pepper Henry
Ron Hill
Delbridge Honanie
John J. Hoover
Allan C. Houser
Doug Hyde
Jim Jackson
Oreland Joe

Harrison Juan
Presley La Fountain
George Longfish
Phil Loretto
Charles F. Lovato
Truman Lowe
Alvin Marshall
George Morrison
Michael Naranjo
Nora Naranjo-Morse
Tim Nicola
Shelley Niro
Clyde Leland Otipoby
Charles Pratt
Faye Quandelacy
Harvey Rattey
The Runnels Family
Gary Schildt
Fritz Scholder
Hart Merriam Schultz
Howard Sice
Willard Stone
Roxanne Swentzell
Johnny Tiger, Jr.
James Turpen, Jr.
Gordon Van Wert
Carson R. Waterman
W. Richard (Dick) West
Roland N. Whitehorse
John Julius Wilnoty
Duffy Wilson
Tex Wounded Face

Silkscreen
Mitch Farmer
Eileen Sawatis
Susan Stewart

Silversmithing
Abraham Apakark Anghik
Victor Coochwytewa
Cippy Crazy Horse
Popovi Da
Victor K. Diabo
Dennis Edaakie
Nancy Edaakie
Marshall Ellis
Margie Henry
Ron Hill

Joe Jojola
Fred Kabotie
Dorothy K. Lahache
Charles Loloma
Nora Naranjo-Morse
Gibson Nez
Norbert Peshlakai
Maisie Schenandoah and
   Family
Smokey
Virginia G. Snow
Edith Tsabetsaye
Lee Weebothie
Mary Weebothie

Splintwork
Mary Adams
Josephine Angus
Christie Arquette
Florence David
Charlotte Delormier
Minnie Delormier
Agnes Garrow
Agnes Lazore
Margaret R. Lazore
Sarah Lazore
Mary Leaf
Victoria Phillips
Mary Tebo
Elizabeth Thompson

Storyteller Figures
Hilda Antonio
Josephine Arquero
Martha Arquero
Buffy Cordero
Damacia Cordero
George Cordero
Helen Cordero
Tim Cordero
Tony Dallas
Ivan Lewis
Rita Lewis
Mary Martin
Louis Naranjo
Virginia Naranjo
Serefina Ortiz
Kevin Peshalakai
Margaret Quintana

Stephanie C. Rhoades
Maria Priscilla Romero
Ada Suina
Antonita (Tony Cordero) Suina
Aurelia Suina
Caroline Grace Suina
Frances Suina
Judith Suina
Louise Q. Suina
Lucy R. Suina
Marie Charlotte Suina
Vangie Suina
Dorothy Trujillo
Evon Trujillo
Felipa Trujillo
Kathy Trujillo
Mary Trujillo
Onofre Trujillo II
Mary Eunice Ware

T
Textiles
Norman Bushyhead

U–W
Weaving
Bessie Barber
Virginia (Hill) Beaver
Alice N. Begay
Amy Begay
Gloria Begay
Mamie P. Begay
Mary Lee Begay
Vera Begay
Alice Belone
Helen Bia
Mary Brown
Helen Burbank
Norman Bushyhead
Irene Clark
Toni Cooke
Sadie Curtis
Susie Shirley Dale
Virginia Deal
Luella Derrick
Tom "Two Arrows" Dorsey
Gail Ellis

Margaret Emery
Adeline Etienne
Bessie George
Margie Henry
Penny Hudson
Martha James
Margaret Jimmie
Theresa Jimmie
Grace Joe
Isabell John
Julia Jumbo
Josephine Kelly
Marie Lapahie
Bessie Lee
Kathy Lee
Rose Ann Lee
Angie Maloney
Teresa Martine
Dorothy Mike
Rose Mike
Tu Moonwalker
Jennifer Musial
Kalley Musial
Bruce Nez
Despah Nez

Grace Henderson Nez
Irene Julia Nez
Linda Nez
Nadine Nez
Barbara Jean Teller Ornelas
Rose Owens
Ella Rose Perry
Mary Peters
Nora Peters
Esther Kane Phillips
Maggie Price
Ramona Sakiestewa
Maria "Lilly" Salvador
Eileen Sawatis
Marjorie Spencer
Anabel Stewart
Pearl Sunrise
Anna Mae Tanner
Daisy Tauglechee
Priscilla Tauglechee
Alberta Thomas
Jennie Thomas
Elizabeth Thompson
Nowetah Timmerman
Bea Tioux

Wanda Tracey
Betty Van Winkle
Lillie Walker
Marie Watson
Katie Wauneka
Audrey Spencer Wilson
Elsie Jim Wilson
Betty Joe Yazzie
Ellen Yazzie
Larry Yazzie
Margaret Yazzie
Philomena Yazzie
Ason Yellowhair

Wirework

Dorial Clark
Sarah Dubuc
Ariel Harris
Robin Marr
Annette Printup
Doris Printup
Margaret Rickard
Ruth Skye

gallery/representation appendix

21st Century Fox Fine Art, Santa Fe, NM
   Tom Wayne Cannon
   R. C. Gorman
   Kevin Red Star

A

Ansel Adams Gallery, Yosemite National Park, CA
   Phil Poseyesva
   Roy Talahaftewa
Adobe East, Summit, NJ
   Lillian Pitt
Adobe East Gallery, Millburn, NJ
   Harvey Begay
   Phil Poseyesva
Adobe Gallery, Albuquerque, NM
   Tony Abeyta
   Cecil Calnimptewa
   Buffy Cordero
   Damacia Cordero
   George Cordero
   Helen Cordero
   Tim Cordero
   Tony Dallas
   James (Jim) Fred
   Ronald Honyouti
   Ivan Lewis
   Lucy M. Lewis
   Rita Lewis
   Maria Montoya Martinez
   Tommy Edward Montoya
   Louis Naranjo
   Virginia Naranjo
   Kevin Peshalakai
   Loren Phillips
   J. D. Roybal
   Antonita (Tony Cordero) Suina
   Margaret Tafoya
   Stella Teller

   Dorothy Torivio
   Del Trancosa
   Felipa Trujillo
Akwesasne Notes, Roosvelt Town, NY
   Florence Cook
   Charlotte Diabo
Alaska State Museum Show, Juneau, AK
   George A. Ahgupuk
Albuquerque Museum of Art, Albuquerque, NM
   Fritz Scholder
Allard's Gallery, Fresno, CA
   R. C. Gorman
Allegany Indian Arts & Crafts Coop, Salamanca, NY
   Charla Bach
   Sadie Marie Rohlman
American Indian Contemporary Arts, San Francisco, CA
   Christina Eustace
   Nora Naranjo-Morse
   Phil Navasya
   Angie Reano Owen
   Lillian Pitt
   Charlene Sanchez Reano
   Frank Reano
Amerind Foundation Museum Shop, Dragoon, AZ
   Harrison Begay
   Allan C. Houser
   Otis Polelonema
   Pablita Velarde
Amerind Gallery, Daleville, VA
   Retha Walden Gambaro
Ancestral Spirits Gallery, Port Townshend, WA
   Pat Courtney Gold
Andrews Pueblo Pottery, Albuquerque, NM
   Tu Moonwalker
Argus Fine Arts, Eugene, OR
   R. C. Gorman
Artables Gallery, Houston, TX
   Anita Fields

Artique Gallery Ltd., Anchorage, AK
  Lillian Pitt
Attic-Hogan Gallery, Prescott, AZ
  Elk Woman

B
Bailey Nelson Gallery, Seattle, WA
  Lillian Pitt
Bear Skin Trading Co., NY
  Rose John
Beckwith Gallery, Wellesley, MA
  Harvey Begay
  Richard Chavez
  Leo Yazzie
Bishop Gallery, Allenspark, CO
  Fritz Scholder
Black Wolf Art Gallery, Lake Worth, FL
  Ken Edwards
Blue-eyed Bear, Sedona, AZ
  Herbert Taylor
Bockley Gallery, Minneapolis, MN
  George Morrison
John A. Boler, Indian and Western Art, Minneapolis, MN
  R. C. Gorman
  Fritz Scholder
Bridger Foundry & Gallery, Bozeman, MT
  Harvey Rattey
Brooks Indian Shop, Taos, NM
  Julian Lovato
Broschofsky Galleries, Ketchum, ID
  Tom Wayne Cannon
Suzanne Brown Galleries, Scottsdale, AZ
  Harry Fonseca
Buffalo Gallery, Alexandria, VA
  Retha Walden Gambaro
  Lillian Pitt
Buffalo Gallery, McLean, VA
  Retha Walden Gambaro
Amy Burnett Gallery, Bremerton, WA
  John J. Hoover

206

C
C & L Fine Arts, Inc., Bohemia, NY
  R. C. Gorman
John Cacciola Galleries, NY
  Tony Abeyta
California State University at Hayward, Hayward, CA
  George Longfish
Joan Cawley, Scottsdale, AZ
  R. C. Gorman

Tanner Chaney Gallery, Albuquerque, NM
  Dennis Edaakie
  Nancy Edaakie
  Watson Honanie
  Julian Lovato
  Edith Tsabetsaye
Channing, Santa Fe, NM
  James Havard
Cheyenne Indian Museum, Ashland, MT
  Seidel Standing Elk
Christopher's Enterprises, Inc., Albuquerque, NM
  Preston Monongye
Jan Cicero Gallery, Chicago, IL
  Norman Akers
  Jeffrey Chapman
  Hachivi Edgar Heap of Birds
  Joe Fedderson
  Ted Garner
  Tony Jojola
  Truman Lowe
  Mario Martinez
  Duane Slick
  Jaune Quick-to-See Smith
Civic Fine Arts Center, Sioux Falls, SD
  Oscar Howe
Cleveland Institute of Art/Reinberger Galleries, Clevelend, OH
  Hachivi Edgar Heap of Birds
Cleveland State University Art Gallery, Cleveland, OH
  Kay WalkingStick
Crazy Horse, Frandor, IL
  Elk Woman
Cristof's of Santa Fe, Santa Fe, NM
  Herbert Taylor
  Jennie Thomas
Custer County Art Center, Miles City, MO
  Kevin Red Star

D
Davis Museum, Claremare, OK
  Joyce Johnson
Denver Art Museum, Denver, CO
  Roxanne Swentzell
Desert Son, Tucson, AZ
  Herbert Taylor
Dewey Galleries, Ltd., Santa Fe, NM
  Charlie Bird
  Gail Bird
  Mike Bird
  Joe Caté

Rosey Caté
Rita Joe Cordalis
Cippy Crazy Horse
Christina Eustace
Yazzie Johnson
Jan Loco
Ray Lovato
Verma Nequatewa
Angie Reano Owen
Dockside Gifts, Panama City Beach, FL
  Kevin Skypainter Turner
Merrill B. Dumas American Indian Art,
    New Orleans, LA
  Victor Beck
  Mike Bird
  Richard Chavez
  Duane Maktima
Susan Duval Gallery, Aspen, CO
  Dan Namingha
  Fritz Scholder

E

Eagle Plume Gallery, Allenspark, CO
  Clarence Lee
  Charles F. Lovato
  Al Nez
  Charles Supplee
  Lee Yazzie
Eagles Roost Gallery, Colorado Springs, CO
  Woodrow Wilson Crumbo
  Joyce Lee Tate Nevaquaya
  Robert Redbird
  Virginia Stroud
  Donald Vann
EarthStar Gallery, Klamath Falls, OR
  Ken Edwards
  Joyce Lee Tata Nevaquaya
  Robert Redbird
  Virginia Stroud
  Donald Vann
East Carolina University/Wellington B. Gray Gallery,
    Greenville, NC
  Jaune Quick-to-See Smith
Jerome Evans Gallery, Lake Tahoe, NV
  Harry Fonseca
  Jean Lamarr
  Frank Lapena
  Christine Nofchissey McHorse

F

Federico on Montana, Santa Monica, CA
  Mike Bird

Fields and Rosen Fine Arts, Inc., Jupiter, FL
  R. C. Gorman
Fields and Rosen Fine Arts, Inc., Southampton, NY
  R. C. Gorman
Fine Art Galleries, Santa Fe, NM
  Jaune Quick-to-See Smith
Firehouse Gallery of Fine Arts, Bisbee, AZ
  Dennis Numkena
Fort Wayne Museum of Art, Ft. Wayne, IN
  Jaune Quick-to-See Smith
Fortunoff's, New York, NY
  Ben Nighthorse
Four Winds Gallery, Naples, FL
  Retha Walden Gambaro
Four Winds Gallery, Pittsburgh, PA
  Victor Beck
  Mike Bird
  Richard Chavez
  Duane Maktima
  Roxanne Swentzell
  Bobbie Tewa
Freeport Art Museum and Cultural Center, Freeport, IL
  R. C. Gorman
  Maria Montoya Martinez

207

G

Galeria Capistrano, San Juan Capistrano, CA, and
Santa Fe, NM
  Harvey Begay
  Larry Golsh
  James Little (Santa Fe)
  Jesse Lee Monongye (both locations)
  Gibson Nez
Galeria Primitivo, Santa Monica, CA
  Mike Bird
  Christina Eustace
Gallery 10, Inc., Scottsdale; NY and Carefree, AZ; Santa
Fe, NM
  Victor Beck
  Mike Bird
  Carl and Irene Clark
  Christina Eustace
  Jody Fowell
  Duane Maktima
  Angie Reano Owen
  Dora Tse Pe Pena
  Al Qöyawayma ("Gray Fox Walking at Dawn")
  Russell Sanchez
  Richard Zane Smith

Dennis Tewa
Leo Yazzie
Gallery Mack NW , Seattle, WA
  R. C. Gorman
Gallery of the American West, Sacramento, CA
  Harvey Begay
  Dennis Edaakie
  Nancy Edaakie
  Gibson Nez
  Ben Nighthorse
Gallery of the West, Old Sacramento, CA
  Ben Nighthorse
Garland's, Sedona, AZ
  Jesse Lee Monongye
  Jennie Thomas
  Richard Tsosie
  Larry Yazzie
Georgetown Gallery of Art, Washington, D.C.
  R. C. Gorman
Gilcrease Museum Gift Shop, Tulsa, OK
  Thomas Jim
  Joyce Johnson
Glover's Old West Museum and Trading Post, Bowie, TX
  Jack Glover
Gomes Gallery Inc., St. Louis, MO
  R. C. Gorman
  William Rabbit
Glenn Green Galleries, Santa Fe, NM
  Tony Abeyta
  Larry Golsh
  John J. Hoover
  Allan C. Houser
Grycner Studio/Gallery Taos, Taos, NM
  R. C. Gorman

H

Hahn Gallery, Philadelphia, PA
  Doug Hyde
Kelly Haney Art Gallery, Shawnee, OK
  Enoch Kelly Haney
Fred Harvey Enterprises, Grand Canyon, AZ
  Elk Woman
Rena Haveson Gallery, Pittsburgh, PA
  Harry Fonseca
Heard Museum, Phoenix, AZ
  Elk Woman
  James Joe
  Linda Lomahaftewa
  Roxanne Swentzell

The Heritage Center, Inc., Pine Ridge, SD
  Arthur D. Amiotte
  Martin E. Red Bear
Ed Hill Gallery, El Paso, TX
  Fritz Scholder
Hogan in the Hilton, Santa Fe
  Gibson Nez
Horwitch LewAllen Gallery, Santa Fe, NM
  N. Scott Momaday
  Ramona Sakiestewa
  Jaune Quick-to-See Smith
  Emmi Whitehorse
Elaine Horwitch Gallery, Santa Fe, NM
  Tony Aguilar
  Phil Loretto
Perry House Galleries, Alexandria, VA
  Pat Courtney Gold
Hubbell Trading Post, Ganado, AZ
  Mary Lee Begay
  Susie Shirley Dale
  Marjorie Spencer
  Elsie Jim Wilson

I

Images of the North, San Francisco, CA
  Lillian Pitt
The Indian Craft Shop, Washington, DC
  Harvey Begay
  Cippy Crazy Horse
  Dennis Edaakie
  Nancy Edaakie
  Bennett Kagenveama
  Al Nez
  Angie Reano Owen
  Andres Quandelacy
  Ellen Quandelacy
  Faye Quandelacy
  Georgia Quandelacy
  Stewart Quandelacy
  Roy Talahaftewa
  Lee Yazzie
Indian Post, Allentown, PA
  Cippy Crazy Horse
  Al Nez
  Gibson Nez
  Angie Reano Owen
Indian Sun, Sarasota, FL
  Kevin Skypainter Turner

Indian Way Gallery, Olympia, WA
    Pat Courtney Gold
Interior Craft Shop, Washington, DC
    Ben Nighthorse

J

JRS Fine Art, Providence, RI
    R. C. Gorman
Charlotte Jackson Fine Art, Santa Fe, NM
    Fritz Scholder

K

Kanawake Handicrafts Workshop, Quebec, Canada
    Connie Jacobs
Kanesatake Indian Arts & Crafts, Quebec, Canada
    Adeline Etienne
    Velma Jocko
June Kelly Gallery, New York, NY
    Kay WalkingStick
Keshi-The Zuni Connection, Santa Fe, NM
    Andres Quandelacy
    Ellen Quandelacy
    Faye Quandelacy
    Georgia Quandelacy
    Stewart Quandelacy
Robert Kidd Gallery, Birmingham, MI
    James Havard
Margaret Kilgore Gallery, Scottsdale, AZ
    Jesse Lee Monongye
    Charlene Sanchez Reano
    Frank Reano
    Jaune Quick-to-See Smith
    Ray Tracey
Kline's Gallery, Boonesboro, MD
    Retha Walden Gambaro
Kopavi International, Sedona, AZ
    Michael Kabotie

L

La Fonda Indian Shop and Gallery, Santa Fe, NM
    Harvey Begay
    Richard Chavez
Landing Gallery of Woodbury, Inc., Woodbury, NY
    R. C. Gorman
Allene La Pides Gallery, Santa Fe, NM
    James Havard
Lazzaro Signature Gallery of Fine Art
    Truman Lowe
Lelooska Gallery, Ariel, WA
    Pat Courtney Gold

Lilly's Pottery Gallery, Acoma Pueblo, NM
    Maria "Lilly" Salvador
Littman Gallery, Portland, OR
    James Pepper Henry
Long Ago and Far Away, Manchester Center, VT
    Abraham Begay
    Randall Chitto
    Sam English
    Howard Sice
    Carol Snow
Long Island University/Hillwood Art Museum,
    Brookville, NY
    Kay WalkingStick
Joanne Lyon Treasures, Aspen, CO
    Gail Bird
    Yazzie Johnson

M

MacLaren/Markowitz Gallery, Boulder, CO
    Randy Lee White
Maine College of Art/The Baxter Gallery, Portland, ME
    Jaune Quick-to-See Smith
Maison des Maison, Denver, CO
    Tu Moonwalker
Many Goats, Tucson, AZ
    Duane Maktima
    Edith Tsabetsaye
Many Hands, Sedona, AZ
    Carl Clark
    Irene Clark
    Watson Honanie
    Roy Talahaftewa
    Richard Tsosie
McGee's Indian Art, Keams Canyon, AZ
    Dennis Edaakie
    Nancy Edaakie
    Watson Honanie
Meridian Gallery Society for Art Publications of the
    Americas, San Francisco, CA
    Frank Tuttle
Micah Gallery, Calgary, Alberta, Canada
    Ken Edwards
R. Michelson Galleries, Amherst, MA
    R. C. Gorman
The Mill Gallery, Seneca, SC
    Ken Edwards
Joe Milo's Trading Company, Vanderwagen, NM
    Dennis Edaakie
    Nancy Edaakie

Minnesota Museum of American Art, St. Paul, MN
George Morrison
Mohawk Craft Fund
Josephine Angus
Christie Arquette
Jake Arquette
Margaret Arquette
Florence Cook
Julius Cook
Cecilia Cree
Florence David
Agnes Garrow
Mary Herne
Agnes Lazore
Sarah Lazore
Rita McDonald
Charlotte Morey
Victoria Phillips
Agnes Sunday
Cecilia Sunday
Monongye's Gallery, Old Oraibi, AZ
Watson Honanie
Moondancer Gallery, Redondo Beach, CA
Elk Woman
Gibson Nez
Morefields Gallery, Ruidoso, NM
Elk Woman
Mosi Lakai-Bl'Kisi, Santa Fe, NM
Jesse Lee Monongye
Bobbie Tewa
Mudhead Gallery, Beaver Creek and Denver, CO
Clarence Lee
Ray Lovato
Al Nez
Gibson Nez
Phil Poseyesva
Charles Supplee

N

Naravisa Press, Santa Fe, NM
James Havard
Dan Namingha
Natchez Indian Museum, Natchez, MI
Joyce Johnson
National Academy of Sciences, Washington, DC
Dan Namingha
Native Reflections, Salt Lake City, Utah
Raymond Lee Deschene
Harrison Juan
Andrew Warren

Frank Warren
Junior Whiterock
Navajo Gallery, Taos, NM
R. C. Gorman
Nevada Institute of Contemporary Art, Las Vegas, NV
Fritz Scholder
Louis Newman Gallery, Beverly Hills, CA
Fritz Scholder
The New Riverside Gallery, Red Bank, NJ
R. C. Gorman
Robert F. Nichols Gallery, Canyon Road, Santa Fe, NM
Karen Abeita
Delores Aragon
Marie Juanico
Nímán Fine Art, Santa Fe, NM
Dan Namingha
Notah-Dineh Trading Co., Cortez, CO
Ray Lovato
Nowetah's American Indian Museum and Gift Store,
New Portland, ME
Nowetah Timmerman
Wahleyah Anne Timmerman-Black

O

O B Enterprises, Denver, CO
Elk Woman
October Art Ltd., New York, NY
Richard Chavez
Rita Joe Cordalis
Christina Eustace
Watson Honanie
Richard Tsosie
Lovena Ohl Gallery, Scottsdale, AZ
Harvey Begay
Elk Woman
Larry Golsh
Delbridge Honanie
Sherian Honhongva
Thomas Jim
David Johns
Michael Kabotie
James Little
Verma Nequatewa
Al Nez
Phil Poseyesva
Joe B. Reano
Terry Reano
Charles Supplee
Richard Tsosie
Lee Yazzie

Okmulgee Creek Museum, Okmulgee, OK
  Joyce Johnson
Orca Art Gallery, Chicago, IL
  Tony Hunt
  Roy Vickers
Out West, Walker, CA
  Arnold D. Aragon

P
Packard's Indian Trading Co., Inc., Santa Fe, NM
  Charlie Bird
  Joe Caté
  Rosey Caté
  Cippy Crazy Horse
  Thomas Jim
  Phil Loretto
  Angie Reano Owen
  Phil Poseyesva
Mary Peachin's Art Company, Tucson, AZ
  Mary Mitchell
Susan Peters Gallery, Anadarko, OK
  Robert Redbird
Philbrook Art Institute, AZ
  Woodrow Wilson Crumbo
  Robert Haozous
Philbrook Museum, Tulsa, OK
  Woodrow Wilson Crumbo
  Robert Haozous
  Joyce Johnson
Philharmonic Galleries/Philharmonic Center for the
    Arts, Naples, FL
  Allan C. Houser
Phoenix Gallery, Coeur d'Alene, ID
  Elk Woman
Pierce Fine Art, Santa Fe, NM
  Oreland Joe
Pot Carrier American Indian Arts, Vashon Island, WA
  Bobbie Tewa

Q
Quintana's Gallery, Portland, OR
  John J. Hoover
  Angie Reano Owen
  Lillian Pitt
  Ellen Quandelacy
  Leo Yazzie

R
Rattlesnake & Star, San Antonio, TX
  Lillian Pitt

Red Cloud, St. Petersburg, FL
  Kevin Skypainter Turner
Red River Indian Museum, Bartleville, OK
  Joyce Johnson
Red Rock Trading Company, Alexandria, VA
  Harvey Begay
  Watson Honanie
  Jan Loco
  Duane Maktima
  Ellen Quandelacy
  Faye Quandelacy
David Rettig Fine Arts, Inc., Santa Fe, NM
  Robert Haozous
Riata Gallery, Virginia City, NV
  Arnold D. Aragon
Donna Rose Galleries/Art Brokerage, Inc., Ketchum, ID
  R. C. Gorman
Roswell Museum and Art Center, Roswell, NM
  R. C. Gorman

S
Sage Brush Limited Editions, Flagstaff, AZ
  Michael Lacapa
  Baje Whitethorne
  Elizabeth Whitethorne-Benally
San Francisco Art Institute Walter/McBean Gallery,
    San Francisco, CA
  Hulleah Tsinhnahjinnie
Sacred Circle Gallery of American Indian Art, Seattle, WA
  Shelley Niro
  Hulleah Tsinhnahjinnie
Santa Fe Connection, San Antonio, TX
  Elk Woman
Santa Fe East, Santa Fe, NM
  Julian Lovato
  Charles Supplee
  Bobbie Tewa
Santa Fe Gallery, Madison, WI
  R. C. Gorman
Santa Fe Trails Gallery of Southwestern Art, Sarasota, FL
  R. C. Gorman
Saper Galleries, East Lansing, MI
  R. C. Gorman
Scanlon Gallery, Ketchikan, AK
  Lillian Pitt
Seminole Museum, Wewoka, OK
  Joyce Johnson
Serendipity Trading Company
  Tu Moonwalker

Kathryn Sermas Gallery, New York, NY
    Truman Lowe
Sherwoods, Beverly Hills, CA
    Ric Charlie
    Al Nez
Evelyn Siegel Gallery, Fort Worth, TX
    Tu Moonwalker
Silver and Sand Trading Company, Taos, NM
    Watson Honanie
Silver Sun/Hardin Estate, Santa Fe, NM
    Elk Woman
    Helen Hardin
Silver Sun Traders, Canyon Road, Albuquerque and
        Santa Fe, NM
    Andy and Roberta Abeita
    Charles Pratt
Inee Yang Slaughter Gallery, Santa Fe, NM
    Helen Hardin
Snow Goose Associates, Inc., Seattle, WA
    Pat Courtney Gold
Southwest Expressions, Chicago, IL
    Phil Poseyesva
Southwest Studio Connection, Southampton, NY
    Ray Tracey
Southwest Trading Company, Saint Charles, IL
    Carl Clark
    Irene Clark
    Roy Talahaftewa
The Squash Blossom, Aspen, Vail, and Denver, CO
    Victor Beck
    Richard Chavez
    Larry Golsh
    James Little
    Ray Lovato
    Ben Nighthorse
    Angie Reano Owen
    Bobbie Tewa
    Ray Tracey
State University College at Potsdam/Roland Gibson
        Gallery, Potsdam, NY
    Kay WalkingStick
Steinbaum Krauss Gallery, New York, NY
    Jaune Quick-to-See Smith
Stonington Gallery, Anchorage, AK, and Seattle, WA
    John J. Hoover
Studio 53, New York, NY
    R. C. Gorman
    Roxanne Swentzell
Sunbird Gallery, Bend, OR
    Lillian Pitt
Sun/Silver West Gallery, Sedona, AZ
    Elk Woman

SunWest Silver, Albuquerque, NM
    Jerry Abeita
    Dennis R. Christy
    Farrell Cockrum
    Jon DeCelles
    Bill Dixon
    Rollie A. Granbois
    Jerry Ingram
    Presley La Fountain
    Gibson Nez
SunWest Silver, Inc., Santa Fe, NM
    Parker Boyiddle, Jr.

T
El Taller Gallery, Austin, TX
    R. C. Gorman
Tamarind Institute, Albuquerque, NM
    Jaune Quick-to-See Smith
Tanner Chaney Gallery, Albuquerque, NM
    Elk Woman
    Watson Honanie
    Julian Lovato
    Gibson Nez
    Edith Tsabetsaye
    Lee Weebothie
    Mary Weebothie
Tanner's Indian Arts, Gallup, NM
    Preston Monongye
    Lee Yazzie
J. B. Tanner's, Ya-Ta-Hey, AZ
    Susie Shirley Dale
    Preston Monongye
    Audrey Spencer Wilson
    Ason Yellowhair
Teal McKibben, Santa Fe, NM
    McKee Platero
Temple University/Temple Gallery, Philadelphia, PA
    Hulleah Tsinhnahjinnie
Texas Art Gallery, Dallas, TX
    Richard Chavez
    Cippy Crazy Horse
    Angie Reano Owen
Jamison Thomas Gallery, Portland, OR
    Rick E. Bartow
Three Flags, Walker, CA
    Arnold D. Aragon
Tiger Art Gallery, Muskogee, OK
    Johnny Tiger, Jr.
TóBaahe Fine Art, Winslow, AZ
    Jack TóBaahe Gene
J. Todd Galleries, Wellesley, MA
    R. C. Gorman

Toh Atin Gallery, Durango, CO
    Bessie Barber
    Ben Nighthorse
    Robert Penn
    Ella Rose Perry
Tohono Chul Park, Tucson, AZ
    Jimmy Toddy
Ray Tracey Galleries, Santa Fe, NM
    Ray Tracey
Tribal Expressions Gallery, Arlington Heights, IL
    Elk Woman
Turner Artworks Trading Post and Art Gallery,
      DeSoto, MO
    Kevin Skypainter Turner
The Turquoise Lady, Houston, TX
    Phil Poseyesva
The Turquoise Lady, Wichita Falls, TX
    Kim Price
Turquoise Tortoise, Sedona, AZ
    Tony Abeyta
The Turquoise Village, Zuni Pueblo, NM
    Edith Tsabetsaye
Turquoise Tortoise, Tubac, AZ
    Elk Woman

U

University at Albany/Rathbone Gallery, Albany, NY
    Kay WalkingStick
University of Alaska Museum Shop, Fairbanks, AK
    George A. Ahgupuk
University of North Texas Art Gallery/Cora Stafford
      Gallery, Denton, TX
    Hachivi Edgar Heap of Birds
University of South Dakota/University Art
      Galleries, Vermillion, SD
    Oscar Howe

V

Via Gambaro Gallery, Washington, DC
    Pegie Ahvakana
Vigil's Native American Gallery, Nevada City, CA
    Arnold D. Aragon
Vision Quest, Dallas, TX
    Elk Woman

W–X

Waddell Trading Company, Tempe, AZ
    Thomas Jim

    Bennett Kagenveama
    Al Nez
    Phil Poseyesva
    Lee Yazzie
Wadle Galleries, Ltd., Santa Fe, NM
    Christina Eustace
    Duane Maktima
    Andres Quandelacy
    Ellen Quandelacy
    Faye Quandelacy
    Georgia Quandelacy
    Stewart Quandelacy
    Albenita Yunie
Wenger Gallery II at Hotel Nikko, Los Angeles, CA
    Kay WalkingStick
Wenger Gallery, Santa Monica, CA
    Kay WalkingStick
Western Heritage Art Gallery, Taos, NM
    Retha Walden Gambaro
Wheelwright Museum of the American Indian/Case
      Trading Post, Santa Fe, NM
    Tom Wayne Cannon
    Joe Caté
    Rosey Caté
    R. C. Gorman
    Robert Haozous
    Allan C. Houser
    Frank Lapena
    Charles Loloma
    Phil Loretto
    Angie Reano Owen
    Ramona Sakiestewa
    Fritz Scholder
    Pablita Velarde
White Pelican, Dana Point, CA
    Elk Woman
White River Trader, Indianapolis, IN
    Jan Loco
Wrights Gallery, Albuquerque, NM
    Elk Woman

Y–Z

Yah-Ta-Hey Gallery, New London, CT
    Elk Woman
    Retha Walden Gambaro
Riva Yares Gallery, Scottsdale, AZ, and Santa Fe, NM
    Fritz Scholder
Yellowstone Art Center, Billings, MT
    Jaune Quick-to-See Smith

213

tribe appendix

A

Abenaki
Nowetah Timmerman
Wahleyah Anne Timmerman-
Black

Acoma
Tamra L. Abeita
Pauline Abeyta
Blanche Antonio
Hilda Antonio
Clarice Aragon
Delores Aragon
John Aragon
Wanda Aragon
Mabel Brown
Barbara Cerno
Connie Cerno
Joe Cerno
Carrie Chino Charlie
Gilbert Chino
Grace Chino
Keith Chino
Carolyn Concho
Sheila Concho
Delores Lewis Garcia
Dolores Garcia
Joanne Chino Garcia
Wilfred Garcia
Sandra Garcia
Marie Juanico
Juana Leno
Ivan Lewis
Rita Lewis
Lucy M. Lewis
Emma Mitchell
Maria "Lilly" Salvador
Stella Shutiva
Dorothy Torivio

Aleut
Alvin Eli Amason

John J. Hoover

Algonquin
Darelyn Clause

Alleghany
Carol Snow

Anishinabe
Diane M. Burns

Apache
Clara Archilta
Beatrice Kenton
Michael Lacapa
Carm Little Turtle
Tu Moonwalker
Gibson Nez
David Emmett Williams

Arapaho
Hachivi Edgar Heap of Birds
Charles Pratt
Margaret Quintana
Alfred Whiteman, Jr.

Arikara
Elk Woman

Assiniboin
Doug Hyde

Assiniboin Sioux
Jon DeCelles

B

Blackfeet
Gary Schildt
Hart Merriam Schultz
Susan Stewart

Blackfoot
Farrell Cockrum

C

Caddo
Tom Wayne Cannon

Carrier
Agnes George

Jenny Naziel
Ron Sebastian

Cattaraugus Seneca
G. Peter Jemison

Cayuga
Dorial Clark
Alta Doxtador
Margie Henry
Donald Hill
Gōwá Djōwa Alsea Isaacs
Arnold Jacobs
Betty Anne Logan
Donald D. Lynch
Nancy Poodry
Annette Printup
Doris Printup
Katherine Skye
Nandell Spittal
Shawnee Spittal
Fred Williams, Sr.
Tom Williams and Family

Chemehuevi
Diane M. Burns

Cherokee
Nadema Agard
Cecil Dick
Mavis Doering
Jack Glover
Larry Golsh
Shal Goshorn
Joan Hill
Joyce Johnson
Lela Romero
Loren Pahsetopah
Paul Pahsetopha
William Rabbit
Dolona Robert
Bert D. Seabourn
Donald Henry Secondine, Jr.
Alice Souligny

Willard Stone
Virginia Stroud
Dorothy Strait
Nowetah Timmerman
Wahleyah Anne Timmerman-
  Black
James Turpen, Jr.
Donald Vann
Kay WalkingStick
John Julius Wilnoty

Cheyenne
Archie Blackowl
Benjamin Franklin Buffalo
Jerome Gilbert Bushyhead
Norman Bushyhead
Hachivi Edgar Heap of Birds
Charles Pratt
Margaret Quintana
W. Richard (Dick) West
Alfred Whiteman, Jr.

Chickasaw
Parker Boyiddle, Jr.
C. Terry Saul

Chippewa
Jeffrey Chapman
Patrick DesJarlait
Sam English
John George-Mathews
Rollie A. Granbois
James Havard
Doug Hyde
Presley La Fountain
George Morrison

Chiricauha Apache
Robert Haozous
Allan C. Houser
Carol A. Soatikee

Choctaw
Randall Chitto
James Havard
Valjean McCarty Hessing
Jerry Ingram
Linda Lomahaftewa
Jean McCarty Mauldin
C. Terry Saul
Kevin Skypainter Turner

Coast Salish
Simon Charlie
Stan Greene

Cochiti
Josephine Arquero
Martha Arquero

Buffy Cordero
Damacia Cordero
George Cordero
Helen Cordero
Tim Cordero
Cippy Crazy Horse
Christina Eustace
Joe H. Herrera
Rita Lewis
Mary Martin
Louis Naranjo
Virginia Naranjo
Seferina Ortiz
Kevin Peshalakai
Stephanie C. Rhoades
Maria Priscilla Romero
Ada Suina
Antonita (Tony Cordero) Suina
Aurelia Suina
Caroline Grace Suina
Frances Suina
Judith Suina
Louise Q. Suina
Lucy R. Suina
Marie Charlotte Suina
Theodore Suina
Vangie Suina
Del Trancosa
Dorothy Trujillo
Evon Trujillo
Felipa Trujillo
Kathy Trujillo
Mary Trujillo
Onofre Trujillo II
Mary Eunice Ware

Colville Confederated Tribes
Ken Edwards
Joe Fedderson

Comanche
Alvarez
F. Blackbear Bosin
White Buffalo
Karita Coffey
Tennyson Eckiwaudah
Rance Hood
James Little Chief
Maria
Joyce Lee Tata Nevaquaya
Clyde Leland Otipoby
Leonard Riddles
Daniel J. Taulbee

Cowichan
Dennis Charlie
Marge Charlie
Hilda Henry
Evelyn Joe
Monica Joe
Madeline Modeste
Sarah Modeste

Cree
Rollie A. Granbois

Creek
Fred Beaver
Woodrow Wilson Crumbo
Anita Fields
Phyllis Fife
Retha Walden Gambaro
Enoch Kelly Haney
James Pepper Henry
Joan Hill
Solomon McCombs
Will Sampson
Johnny Tiger, Jr.
Hulleah Tsinhnahjinnie

Crow
Arnold D. Aragon
Kevin Red Star
Susan Stewart

D

Dakotah
Amos Owen

Delaware
Parker Boyiddle, Jr.
Donald Henry Secondine, Jr.
Alice Souligny

Dineh
Raymond Lee Deschene
Harrison Juan
Andrew Warren
Frank Warren
Junior Whiterock

E

East Indian
Pop Chalee

Eskimo
George A. Ahgupuk
Abraham Apakark Anghik
Florence Nupok Chauncey
James Moses
Pitseolak

F

Flathead
Jaune Quick-to-See Smith

G

Gitksan
Herbert Green
Richard Harris
Walter Harris
Robert Jackson
Doreen Jensen
Brian Muldoe
Earl Muldoe
Vernon Stephens
Art Sterrit
Glen Wood
Gros Ventre
Jon DeCelles

H

Hagwilget
Louise Joseph
Haida
Eliza Abraham
Doug Cranmer
Gordon Cross
Nelson Cross
Joe David
Claude Davidson
Florence Davidson
Reg Davidson
Robert Davidson
Fred Davis
Freda Diesing
Pat Dixon
James Hart
Greg Lightbown
Gerry Marks
Wayne Peterson
Bill Reid
Francis Williams
Doug Wilson
Grace Wilson
Lyle Wilson
George Yeltatzie
Don Yeomans
Hopi
Karen Abeita
Nathan Begay
Cecil Calnimptewa

Karen Kahe Charley
Victor Coochwytewa
Tony Dallas
Neil David, Sr.
David Dawangyumptewa
James (Jim) Fred
John Fredericks
Ros George
Delbridge Honanie
Watson Honanie
Sherian Honhongva
Brian Honyouti
Ronald Honyouti
Daisy Hooee
Walter Howato
Rondina Huma
James Humetewa, Jr.
Alvin James, Sr.
Fred Kabotie
Michael Kabotie
Bennett Kagenveama
Marcella Kahe
Rena Kavena
Tracy Kavena
Michael Lacapa
Madeline Lamson
Nancy Lewis
Charles Loloma
Linda Lomahaftewa
Millard Dawa Lomakema
Duane Maktima
Joe Maktima
Alvin James Makya
Georgia Masayesva
Bessie Monongye
Jesse Lee Monongye
Preston Monongye
Sylvia Naha
Dan Namingha
Bessie Namoki
Joy Navasie
Phil Navasya
Bryson Nequatewa
Verma Nequatewa
Dennis Numkena
J. Numkena-Talayumptewa
Loren Phillips
Tom Polacca
Otis Polelonema
Phil Poseyesva

Al Qöyawayma
Dextra Nampeo Quotskuyva
Ramona Sakiestewa
Henry Shelton
Howard Sice
Charles Supplee
Mark Tahbo
Roy Talahaftewa
Lowell Talashoma
Terrance Talaswaima
Anna Mae Tanner
Bobbie Tewa
Dennis Tewa
Wilfred Tewawina
Danny Rondeau Tsosie
Elizabeth White

I

Inuit
Piseolak Ashoona
Tookoome
Iroquois
Jeannine Aaron
Peter B. Jones
Duffy Wilson
Isleta
Andy Abeita
Ted Charveze
Elizabeth Charveze-Caplinger
Joe Jojola
Tony Jojola
Stella Teller

J

Jemez
Cliff Fragua
Juanita Fragua
Phil Loretto
Rose Pecos
Sun Rhodes
José Rey Toledo
Mary E. Toya
Maxine Toya
Evelyn Vigil
Jicarilla Apache
Felipe Ortega

K

Kaw
James Pepper Henry
Kim Price

Kiowa
Clara Archilta
James Auchiah
Dennis Belindo
Woody Big Bow
F. Blackbear Bosin
Parker Boyiddle, Jr.
Tom Wayne Cannon
George Geionety
Marcelle Sharron Ahtone
    Harjo
Bobby Hill
Jack Hokeah
Ernie Keahbone
George Keahbone
James Little Chief
Al Momaday
N. Scott Momaday
Stephen Mopope
Kim Price
Robert Redbird
Lance E. Silverhorn
Lois Smoky
Herman Toppah
Lee Monett Tsatoke
Roland N. Whitehorse
David Emmett Williams

Kispiox
Sadie Harris

Klamath Modoc
Jim Jackson

Kwakiutl
Agnes Alfred
Emma Beans
Jimmy Dick
Roy Hanuse
Bill Henderson
Ernie Henderson
Mark Henderson
Sam Henderson
Calvin Hunt
Henry Hunt
Richard Hunt
Tony Hunt
Mungo Martin
Bob Neel
Larry Rosso
Richard Zane Smith
Russell Smith
Lily Speck
Lyle Wilson

L

Laguna
Arnold D. Aragon
Charlie Bird
Gail Bird
Evelyn Cheromiah
Lee Ann Cheromiah
Harold Littlebird
F. Bruce Lubo, Sr.
Duane Maktima
Joe Maktima
Gladys Paquin
Howard Sice

Lakota
Charging Thunder Family
Alice New Holy Blue Legs
New Holy Family
The Runnels Family
The Two Bulls Family
The Yellow Horse Family

Lakota Sioux
Martin E. Red Bear

Lower Cayuga
Alex Bomberry

Luiseno
Wa-Wa-Chaw

M

Maidu
Frank Day
Harry Fonseca

Malahat
Simon Charlie

Mandan/Hidatsa
Elk Woman
Tex Wounded Face

Mesquakie
Duane Slick

Mission
Preston Monongye

Mission/Luiseno
Fritz Scholder

Mississippi Choctaw
Joyce Johnson

Mohawk
Mary Adams
Sally Anne Adams
Gail Albany
Josephine Angus

Christie Arquette
Jake Arquette
Margaret Arquette
Marjorie Barnes
Joseph Beauvais
Virginia (Hill) Beaver
Mike Bero
Grace Bonspille
Perry Bonspille
Lynda (Hayfield) Brant
Leslie Claus
Darelyn Clause
Carl Cook
Florence Cook
Julius Cook
Cecilia Cree
Richard Glazer Danay
Florence David
Agnes Decaire
Kristen Deer
Nora Deering
Charlotte Delormier
Minnie Delormier
Alice Diabo
Charlotte Diabo
Marjorie Diabo
Victor K. Diabo
Betty Doxtator
Deborah Drouin
Nancy Diabo Drouin
Adeline Etienne
Karen Etienne
Margaret Etienne
John Fadden
Ida Gabriel
Agnes Garrow
Sarah Garrow
Gaston Gaspé
John Gibson
Rick Glazer-Danay
Gertrude Gray
Leona Gray
Tom Gray
Mary Herne
Sue Ellen Herne
Alva Martin Hill
Donad Hill
Connie Jacobs
Mary Scott Jacobs
Jacqueline "Midge" Jamison

217

Theresa Jemison
Christina Jock
Willie Jock
Velma Jocko
Ivy Kibbe
Dorothy K. Lahache
Brenda Laughing
Agnes Lazore
Margaret R. Lazore
Robbie Lazore
Sarah Lazore
Mary Leaf
Marilyn Leroy
David R. Maracle
Sally (Rosella) Maracle
Robin Marr
Louise McComber
Sandra McComber
Rita McDonald
R. Gary Miller
Mary Mitchell
Mark D. Montour
Nancy Montour
Ross Montour
Charlotte Morey
Barbara Nelson
Elizabeth Nelson
Emilienne Nelson
Muriel Nicholas
Shelley Niro
Theresa Oakes
Esther Kane Phillips
Morgan Phillips
Rita Phillips
Victoria Phillips
Eileen Sawatis
Joyce Sharrow
Roger Staats
Elsie M. Steffans
Agnes Sunday
Cecilia Sunday
Mary Tebo
Cecelia Thomas
John Bigtree Thomas
Mary Thomas
Daniel Thompson
Elizabeth Thompson
Marita Thompson
John Wheeler
Andrew White
Gladys White

Larry White
Madeline White
Mount Currie
Felicity Dan
Matilda Jim
Catherine Pascal
Julianna Williams

N
Nambé
Virginia Gutierrez
Lela Romero
Lonnie Vigil
Navajo
Jimmy Abeita
Roberta Abeita
Elizabeth Abeyta
Narcisso Platero Abeyta
Tony Abeyta
Danny Akee
Johnson Antonio
Gilbert Atencio
Mary Avery
Bessie Barber
Clifford Beck
Victor Beck
Abraham Begay
Alice N. Begay
Alvin Begay
Amy Begay
Gloria Begay
Harrison Begay
Harry A. Begay
Harvey Begay
Joe Begay
Keith Begay
Kenneth Begay
Kyle Begay
Mamie P. Begay
Mary Lee Begay
Nathan Begay
Vera Begay
Dennis Belindo
Alice Belone
Gladys Ben
Joe Ben, Jr.
Wilson Benally
Helen Bia
Agnes Black
Lorraine Black
Mary Black

Mary Brown
Clifford Brycelea
Helen Burbank
Ric Charlie
Notah H. Chee
Robert Chee
Carl Clark
Irene Clark
Irene Clark
Grey Cohoe
Rita Joe Cordalis
Sadie Curtis
Dawn'a D
Susie Shirley Dale
Virginia Deal
Gracie Dick
Bill Dixon
Tomas Dougi, Jr.
W. B. Franklin
Jack TóBaahe Gene
Bessie George
R. C. Gorman
Robert Haozous
Timothy Harvey
Marian Herrera
Edward Jim
Thomas Jim
Eugene Joe
Grace Joe
James Joe
Oreland Joe
Isabell John
David Johns
George Johns
Margaret Johns
Yazzie Johnson
Julia Jumbo
Marie Lapahie
Bessie Lee
Charlie Lee
Clarence Lee
David Lee
Kathy Lee
Rose Ann Lee
James Little
Jake Livingston
Angie Maloney
Alvin Marshall
Teresa Martine
Chee McDonald
Christine Nofchissey McHorse

Lucy Leuppe McKelvey
Dorothy Mike
Rose Mike
Francis Miller
Patsy Miller
Jesse Lee Monongye
Mary Morez
Jennifer Musial
Kalley Musial
Freddie Nelson
Al Nez
Bruce Nez
Despah Nez
Gibson Nez
Grace Henderson Nez
Irene Julia Nez
Linda Nez
Nadine Nez
Redwing T. Nez
J. Numkena-Talayumptewa
Barbara Jean Teller Ornelas
Rose Owens
Ella Rose Perry
David Peshlakai
Mary Lou Peshlakai
Norbert Peshlakai
McKee Platero
Maggie Price
Wilson Price
Percy Shorty
Wilbert Sloan
Marjorie Spencer
Fred Stevens, Jr.
Juanita Stevens
Pearl Sunrise
Anna Mae Tanner
Daisy Tauglechee
Priscilla Tauglechee
Herbert Taylor
Alberta Thomas
Jennie Thomas
Jimmy Toddy
Ray Tracey
Wanda Tracey
Andy Tsinahjinnie
Hulleah Tsinhnahjinnie
Richard Tsosie
James Turpen, Jr.
Betty Van Winkle
Lillie Walker
Alfredo Watchman

Elsie Y. Watchman
Pearl Watchman
Susie Watchman
Walter Z. Watchman
Marie Watson
Katie Wauneka
Emmi Whitehorse
Baje Whitethorne
Elizabeth Whitethorne-Benally
Audrey Spencer Wilson
Elsie Jim Wilson
Crying Wind
Beatien Yazz
Betty Joe Yazzie
Cornelia Akee Yazzie
Ellen Yazzie
James Wayne Yazzie
Larry Yazzie
Lee Yazzie
Leo Yazzie
Margaret Yazzie
Philomena Yazzie
Philomena Yazzie
Ason Yellowhair
Necolslie Band
Mary Southerland
Nez Percé
Doug Hyde
Nishga
Josiah Tait
Norman Tait
Nomtimpom Wintu
Frank Lapena
Nootka
Jimmy John
Norman John
Northern Cheyenne
Ben Nighthorse
Seidel Standing Elk
Northwest Coast
Christine Bobb
Elsie Charlie
Frances Edgar
Ron Hamilton
Liz Happynook
Ellen Jumbo
Lena Jumbo
Alice Paul
Mabel Taylor
Ella Thompson
Josephine Thompson

Josephine Tom
Mike Tom
Jessie Webster
Peter Webster
Norwegian
Elk Woman

O

Ogala
Martin E. Red Bear
Ogala Sioux
Arthur D. Amiotte
Donald Montileaux
Ojibwa (Ojibway)
John George-Mathews
Maude Kegg
George Morrison
Norval Morrisseau
Okanagan
Mary Abel
Louise Joseph
Bernie McQuary
Mary Michell
Mary Southerland
Sophie Thomas
Anne Williams
Oneida
Eula Antone
Ruth Baird
Mamie Brown
Toni Cooke
Ray P. Cornelius
Larry D. B. (Butch) Cottrell
Elizabeth (Betty) Dennison
Laura Doxtator
Shannon Elijah
Gail Ellis
Marshall Ellis
Jane Elm
Irene Greene
Ron Hill
Emily Jacobs
Mary Lee (Webster) Lemieux
Betty McLester
Georgina Nicholas
Pat Nicholas
Donna Phillips
Mamie Ryan
Maisie Schenandoah and
    Family
Linda Sickles

Virgie Smith
Errol Wilson

Onondaga
Mary (Thompson) Beckman
Les Bucktooth
Helen Burning
Gertrude Chew
Andy Deer
John Deer
Luella Derrick
Tom "Two Arrows" Dorsey
Mitch Farmer
Stephen Gonyea
Ariel Harris
Peter B. Jones
Greg La Forme
Oren Lyons
Alice Papineau
Ruth Skye

Osage
Norman Akers
Anita Fields
Loren Pahsetopah
Paul Pahsetopha
Carl Woodring

Otoe
Kim Price

Owikeeno
Roy Hanuse

P

Paiute
Jean Lamarr
Grace Lehi

Pala Mission
Larry Golsh

Passamaquoddy
Mary Mitchell Gabriel
Sylvia Gabriel

Paugusset
Wahleyah Anne Timmerman-
Black

Pawnee
Norman Akers
Kim Price

Pembina
Harvey Rattey

Penelakut
Marge Charlie
Maggie Jacks
Vernon Jacks

Penobscot
Tim Nicola

Picuris
Virginia Duran
Anthony Durand
Cora Durand

Pima
Carol A. Soatikee

Pitt River
Jean Lamarr

Plains Cree
Allen Sapp

Pojoaque
Cordi Gomez
Glen Gomez
Virginia Gutierrez

Portugese
Harry Fonseca

Potawatomi
Woodrow Wilson Crumbo
Joseph Kabance

Powatan
Nadema Agard

Q-R

Ramah Navajo
Ann Coho

Red Lake Chippewa
Gordon Van Wert

S

Sac and Fox
John Christiansen

Saginaw Chippewa
Dennis R. Christy

Salish
Margaret Emery
Martha James
Margaret Jimmie
Theresa Jimmie
Josephine Kelly
Mary Peters
Nora Peters
Rosie Ross
Anabel Stewart

San Felipe
Richard Chavez
Charlene Sanchez Reano
Del Trancosa

San Ildefonso
José Vicente Aguilar

Gilbert Atencio
Blue Corn
Popovi Da
Tony Da
Desider
Barbara Gonzales
Rose Gonzales
Adam Martinez
Julian Martinez
Maria Montoya Martinez
Richard Martinez
Sandra Martinez
Maximiliana
Dora Tse Pe Pena
Oqwa Pi
J. D. Roybal
Abel Sanchez
Kathy Trujillo
Romando Vigil
YellowBird

San Juan
Mary E. Archuleta
Mike Bird
Grace Lehi
Bill Lockwood
Carnation Lockwood
Tommy Edward Montoya
Bobbie Tewa
Mary Trujillo
Christine C. Zuni

Santa Ana
Eudora Montoya

Santa Clara
Esther Archuleta
Mary E. Archuleta
Mary Cain
Stella Chavarria
Virginia Ebelacker
Goldenrod Garcia
Grace Medicine Flower
Jody Folwell
Goldenrod Garcia
Lois Gutierrez-de la Cruz
Luther Gutierrez
Margaret Gutierrez
Petra Gutierrez
Pula Gutierrez
Stephanie Gutierrez
Val Gutierrez
Helen Hardin
Joseph Lonewolf

Rosemary "Apple Blossom"
  Lonewolf
Ana Naranjo
Christina Naranjo
Michael Naranjo
Paula Naranjo
Rose Naranjo
Teresita Naranjo
Nora Naranjo-Morse
Toni Roller
Roxanne Swentzell
Camilio Tafoya
Margaret Tafoya
Belen Tapia
Ernest Tapia
Pablita Velarde
Mela Youngblood
Nathan Youngblood
Nancy Youngblood-Cutler
Santo Domingo
Florence Aguilar
Marie Aguilar
Tony Aguilar
Charlie Bird
Gail Bird
"Ca Win" Jimmy Calabaza
Joe Caté
Rosey Caté
Barbara Garcia
Raymond Garcia
Harold Littlebird
Charles F. Lovato
Julian Lovato
Ray Lovato
Angie Reano Owen
Charlene Reano
Charlotte Reano
Frank Reano
Joe B. Reano
Percy Reano
Terry Reano
Charlene Sanchez Reano
Robert Tenorio
Sauk-Fox
John Christiansen
Charles Pushetonequa
Sechelt
Mary Jackson
Seminole
Fred Beaver
Enoch Kelly Haney

Johnny Tiger, Jr.
Hulleah Tsinhnahjinnie
Seneca
D. Monroe Abrams
Charla Bach
Dorothy M. Biscup
Winona Esther Blueye
Arkene Bova
Darlene Bova
Karen Clark
Don Conklin
Ruth Conklin
Bernice Crouse
Bill Crouse
Kathleen D'Arcy
Mildred Garlow
Ruth Garlow
Fidelia George
Mildred George
David A. Gordon
Harley Gordon
Judith Greene
Mary Halftown
Marguerite Lee Haring
Hazel Harrison
Ethel Hill
Rita Hill
Tom Hill
Fidelia Jimerson
Elaine John
Estella John
Rose John
Darla Johnson
Evelyn Jonathan
Peter B. Jones
Celeste (Rooney) Kettle
Juanita Lay
Miriam Lee
Dorothea Leroy
George Longfish
Theresa Mitten
Brian Mohr
Delores Oldshield
June Peters
Myrtle Peterson
Connie Pierce
David Pierce
Rodney Pierce
Amie Poodry
Karen Powless
Tom Printup

Audrey Ray
Elnora Reuben
Wilma Lee Roberts
Sadie Marie Rohlman
Cheryl Schapp
Llavall Scrogg
Ernest Smith
Carol Snow
Virginia G. Snow
Millie Stafford
Doris Sundown
Mollie Sundown
Maisa P. Tahamont
Hazel Thompson
Kerry Tome
Lorraine Tome
Shirley Vanatta
Carson R. Waterman
Nettie Watt
Ruth Watt
Susanne Williams
Shoshone
Black Eagle
Sicangu
Martin E. Red Bear
Sioux
Nadema Agard
Ted Garner
Amos Owen
Randy Lee White
Skohomish
Henry Gobin
Suquamish
Pegie Ahvakana
Susquehanna
Nowetah Timmerman
Wahleyah Anne Timmerman-
  Black

T
Tahltan
Dempsey Bob
Dale Campbell
Taos
Pop Chalee
Juanita DuBray
Edna Romero
Virginia Romero
Bernice Suazo-Naranjo
Alan Wallace

221

Tarahumara
  Carm Little Turtle
Tesuque
  Lorencita Pino
  Bea Tioux
  Paul Vigil
  Manuel Vigil
  Vincenta Vigil
Tewa
  Daisy Hooee
  Michael Iacapa
  Dan Namingha
  Nora Naranjo-Morse
  Marlin Pinto
  Tom Polacca
  Dextra Nampeo Quotskuyva
  Mark Tahbo
Tlingit
  Dempsey Bob
  Pat Courtney Gold
Tohono O'odham
  Norma Antone
  Dorina Garcia
  Ruby Garcia
  Charlene Juan
Tonkawa
  Clara Archilta
  David Emmett Williams
Tsimshian
  Roy Vickers
  Clarence Wells
Tuscarora
  Dorial Clark
  Diane Demarco
  Sarah Dubuc
  Louise Henry
  Donald Hill
  Rick Hill
  Penny Hudson
  Tracy Johnson

George Longfish
Annette Printup
Mary Lou Printup
Margaret Rickard
Hattie Williams
Duffy Wilson

U-V
Ute
  Mary Black
  Oreland Joe

W
Walla Walla
  James Lavadour
Warm Springs Apache
  Jan Loco
Warm Springs Yakama/Wasco
  Lillian Pitt
Wasco
  Pat Courtney Gold
White
  Rick Glazer-Danay
Wichita
  Parker Boyiddle, Jr.
  Elgin W. Lamarr
  Lance E. Silverhorn
Winnebago
  Truman Lowe
  Jacquie Stevens
Wyandote
  Richard Zane Smith

X-Y
Yakima
  Glen Rabena
Yanktonai Sioux
  Oscar Howe

Yaqui
  Mario Martinez
Yokut
  Black Eagle
Yuki/Wailaki/Koncow Maidu
  Frank Tuttle
Yup'ik
  Larry Beck
Yurok
  Rick E. Bartow

Z
Zia
  Candelaria Gachupin
  Velino Shije Herrera
  Elizabeth Medina
  Rafael Medina
  Sofia Medina
  Russell Sanchez
  Eusebia Shije
Zuni
  Carolyn Bobelu
  Dennis Edaakie
  Nancy Edaakie
  Christina Eustace
  Sidney Hooee
  Roderick Kaskalla
  Jake Livingston
  Marlin Pinto
  Andres Quandelacy
  Ellen Quandelacy
  Faye Quandelacy
  Stewart Quandelacy
  Percy Sandy
  Smokey
  Edith Tsabetsaye
  Lee Weebothie
  Mary Weebothie
  Albenita Yunie

bibliography

Abbott, L. (Ed.) (1994). *I stand in the center of the good.* University of Lincoln and London: Nebraska Press.

Lost and found traditions—Renwick Gallery Show in view through March 6. (1988, February 5). *Antiques and Arts Weekly.*

Ethnographic art to be sold at Hesse Galleries February 20. (1988, February 12). *Antiques and Arts Weekly,* 100–101.

Navajo rug exhibition opening in Lexington. (1988, February 12). *Antiques and Arts Weekly,* 35.

It's westward ho at the Springfield Art Museum. (1987, September 25). *Antiques and Arts Weekly,* 20.

Appleton, L. H. (1971). *American Indian design and decoration.* New York: Dover.

Archuleta, M. & Stickland, R. (1991). *Shared visions: Native American painters and sculptors in the twentieth century.* New York: The New Press.

Hopi Kachina Artist Alwin James Makya. (1973, June). *Arizona Highways.*

Basket Making in Arizona by Don Dedera. (1973, June). *Arizona Highways.*

Arnold, D. L. (1982, November). Pueblo artistry in clay. *National Geographic.*

Atwater, H. F. (1992, June). Pottery's stepchild. *Americana,* 41–45.

Barash, L. (1992, August/September). On the cutting edge. *National Wildlife,* 29.

Bennett, K. W. (1981, Winter). The Navajo chief blanket—A trade item among non-Navajo groups. *American Indian Art Magazine,* 62–68.

Bland, E. (1993, August 23). Desert dazzlers. *Time,* 65.

Bowman, J. (1991, August/September). A few reservations. *Reason,* 49–50.

Broder, P. J. (1979). *Hopi painting: The world of the Hopis.* New York: Brandywine Press.

Broder, P. J. (1981). *American Indian painting & sculpture.* New York: Abbeville Press.

Bunzel, R. L. (1972). *The pueblo potter: A study in primitive art.* New York: Dover Publications.

Cembales, R. (1994, October 10). Native American pride and prejudice. *ARTnews,* 86–91.

Cirillo, D. (1988, Spring). Back to the past: Tradition and change in contemporary pueblo jewelry. *American Indian Art,* 46–63.

We are part of the earth and it is part of us. (1991, October 9). *The Chronicle of Higher Education,* B60.

Cirillo, D. (1992). *Southwestern Indian jewelry.* New York/London/Paris: Abbeville Press.

Clark, J. (1987, November). The 1988 IACA Artist of the Year. *The Indian Trader,* 4–5.

Colp, J. (1991, October 28). An artist first, a politician second. *Insight,* 42–43.

Currier, W. T. (1987). *Currier's price guide to American artists 1645–1945 at auction.* Brockton, MA: Currier Publications.

Dallas, S. (1988, June). Triumph on a loom. *Americana,* 54–57.

Denton, C. (1991, Summer). The American Indian Share-Art Gallery. *Whole Earth Review,* 36–37.

Dillingham, R. with Elliott, M. (1992). *Acoma & Laguna pottery.* School of American Research Press: Santa Fe, NM.

Dockstader, F. J. (1987). *The song of the loom: New traditions in Navajo weaving.* New York: Hudson Hills Press.

Dockstader, J. (1977). *Great North American Indians: Profiles in life and leadership.* New York: Van Nostrand Reinhold Co.

Elliott, M. (1987, October). Basic techniques in beading. *The Indian Trader,* 14–15.

Elliott, M. (1987, October). Material and techniques of beadwork. *The Indian Trader,* 14–15.

Ewers, J. C. (1986). *Plains Indian sculpture—A traditional art from America's heartland.* Washington, DC: Smithsonian Institution Press.

Fielding, M. (1974). *Dictionary of American painters, sculptors and engravers.* Connecticut: Modern Books & Crafts, Inc.

Frank, L. (1978). *Indian silver jewelry of the Southwest, 1868–1930.* Boston: New York Graphic Society.

Gillman, C. (1988, Spring). The way to independence: An exhibition at the Minnesota Historical Society. *American Indian Art*.

Hale, J. C. (1994, October). Native voices. *Travel & Leisure*, 40.

Harsant, W. J. (1988, Spring). The Otago Museum, Dunedin, New Zealand: The North American Indian Collection. *American Indian Art*.

Harmsen, D. *American western art*. New York: R. R. Donnelly & Sons Company.

Hedlund, A. L. (1992). *Reflections of the weaver's world: the Gloria F. Ross Collection of contemporary Navajo weaving*. Denver, CO: Denver Art Museum.

The folk art carvings of Johnson Antonio—The Making of a Bisti Carver. (1987, August). *The Indian Trader*, 4.

Indian art enjoying a second renaissance, (1988, January). *The Indian Trader*, 3–4.

The meanings behind decorative symbols used in Indian art, (1988, January). *The Indian Trader*, 6.

The beauty of California mission basketry, (1988, January). *The Indian Trader*, 7–9.

The diamond rattlesnake basket, (1988, January). *The Indian Trader*, 9–11.

Southern Plains Museum features works by Tony Jojola, (1988, March). *The Indian Trader*, 21.

Masayesva selected poster artist for Festival of Native American Arts, (1988, March). *The Indian Trader*, 11.

Newlands outline: A new regional style rug (1988, March). *The Indian Trader*, 3–4.

Jacka, J. & Essary, L. (1988). *Beyond tradition: Contemporary Indian art and its evolution*. Flagstaff, AZ: Northland Publishing Co.

Jacka, J. (1984, Spring). Innovations in Southwestern Indian jewelry: Fine art in the 1980s. *American Indian Art Magazine*, 28–37.

Jacobsen, A. (1983). *Jacobsen's sixth painting and bronze price guide* (Vol. 6). Author.

James, G. W. (1974). *Indian blankets and their makers*. New York: Dover Publications.

James, G. W. (1972). *Indian basketry*. New York: Dover Publications.

Johannsen, C. B., & Ferguson, J. P. (Eds.). (1993). *Iroquois arts: A directory of a people and their work*. Warnerville, NY: The Association for Advancement of Native North American Arts and Crafts.

Sacred land: Indian and Hispanic cultures of the Southwest. (1994, June). *The Journal of American History*, 185–193.

Kabotie, F. & Belknap, B. (1977). *Fred Kabotie: Hopi Indian artist*. Flagstaff, AZ: Museum of Northern Arizona with Northland Press.

Karasik, C. (1993). *The turquoise trail: Native American jewelry and culture of the Southwest*. New York: Harry N. Abrams, Inc., Publishers.

Katz, J. (Ed.). (1980). *This song remembers: Self portraits of Native Americans in the arts*. Boston: Houghton Mifflin Company.

Kent, K. P. (1981, Winter). Pueblo weaving. *American Indian Art Magazine*, 32–45.

LeFree, B. (1975). *Santa Clara pottery today*. Albuquerque, NM: University of New Mexico Press.

Libhart, M. (Ed.). (1972). *Contemporary Southern Plains Indian painting*. Anadarko, OK: Oklahoma Indian Arts and Crafts Cooperative.

Milton, J. R. (Ed.). (1969). *The American Indian speaks*. Vermillion, SD: Dakota Press, University of South Dakota.

Navajo School of Indian Basketry. (1975). *Indian basket weaving*. New York: Dover Publications.

New, L. K. (1991, October/November). Remembering Charles Loloma. *American Craft*, 18–19.

Parezo, N. J. (1983). *Navajo sandpainting: From religious act to commercial act*. Albuquerque, NM: University of New Mexico Press.

Peterson, S. (1992, June/July). Lucy M. Lewis, 95, legendary acoma potter. *American Craft*, 16.

Ray, D. J. (1967). *Graphic arts of the Alaskan Eskimo*. Washington DC: United States Department of the Interior.

Ripp, B. (1988, March). Eleven Indian painters created a treasure at Maisel's. *Indian Trader*.

Sagel, J. (1988, February). Frank Waters. *New Mexico Magazine*, 52–57.

Schiffer, N. N. (1991). *Miniature arts of the Southwest*. West Chester, PA: Schiffer Publishing Ltd.

Schiffer, N. N. (1991). *Navajo arts and crafts*. West Chester, PA: Schiffer Publishing Ltd.

Schiffer, N. N. (1991). *Pictorial weavings of the Navajo*. West Chester, PA: Schiffer Publishing Ltd.

Scott, J. (1989). *Changing woman: The life and art of Helen Hardin*. Flagstaff, AZ: Northland Publishing.

Shadbolt, D. (1986). *Bill Reid*. Seattle/London: University of Washington Press.

Shaw, R. (1993). *America's traditional crafts*. New York: Hugh Lauter Levin Associates, Inc., Macmillan Publishing Company.

Sides, D. S. (1961). *Decorative art of the Southwestern Indians*. New York: Dover Publications.

Snodgrass, J. O. (1968). *American Indian painters—A biographical directory.* New York: Museum of American Indian, Heye Foundation.

Sommer, R. L. (1994). *Native American art.* New York: Smithmark Publishers, Inc.

Stanger, K. (1993, February). Golden artist colors opens its doors to the community. *American Artist,* 56–57+.

Starline, M. (1988, March). Karen Charley, traditional Hopi potter. *The Indian Trader,* 19.

Steltzer, U. (1976). *Indian artists at work.* Seattle and London: University of Washington Press.

Stewart, H. (1979). *Looking at Indian art of the Northwest Coast.* Seattle and London: University of Washington Press.

Stifter, A. (1994, October 15). Dream weaver. *Kennebec Journal.*

Tanner, C. L. (1983). *Indian baskets of the Southwest.* Tucson, AZ: University of Arizona Press.

Thom, I. M. (Ed.). (1993). *Robert Davidson: Eagle of the dawn.* Seattle: University of Washington Press.

Trimble, S. (1987). *Talking with the clay: The art of pueblo pottery.* Santa Fe, NM: School of American Research Press.

Turano, J. V. N. (1988, February). Sotheby's Winter Sale of American Indian Art. *Maine Antique Digest.*

Turnbaugh, W. A., & Peabody, S. (1988). *Indian jewelry of the American Southwest.* West Chester, PA: Schiffer Publishing Ltd.

Wade, E. L. (Ed.). (1986). *The arts of the North American Indian: Native traditions in evolution.* New York: Hudson Hills Press.

Wade, E. L. & Strickland, R. (1981). *Magic images: Contemporary Native American art.* Norman, OK: Philbrook Art Center and University of Oklahoma Press.

Wagner, S. R., Brody, J. J., & Yazz, B. (1983). *Yazz: Navajo painter.* Flagstaff, AZ: Northland Press.

Whiteford, A. H. (1973). *North American Indian arts.* New York: Golden Press.

Whitt, J. (1983, June). The art of the Plains Indians. *The Indian Trader,* 5–10.

Wright, R. K. (1988, Spring). The Burke Museum: Northwest Coast Collection. *American Indian Art,* 32–37.

Wright, B. (1973). *Kachinas: A Hopi artist's documentary.* Flagstaff, AZ: Northland Press, with the Heard Museum, Phoenix, Arizona.

Wright, B. (1984, Spring). Kachina carvings. *American Indian Art Magazine,* 38–45, 81.

Zuend, P. (1987, November). Michael Paul, Colville Indian Storypole Carver. *The Indian Trader,* 9, 11, 13.

225

contributors

artist contributors

Tony Abeyta
Arnold D. Aragon
Black Eagle
Anita Fields
Retha Walden Gambaro
Pat Courtney Gold
Judith Greene
Enoch Kelly Haney
James Pepper Henry
John J. Hoover
Jim Jackson
Joyce Johnson
Joe Jojola
F. Bruce Lubo, Sr.
N. Scott Momaday
Tu Moonwalker
Nora Naranjo-Morse
Gibson Nez
Ben Nighthorse

Lillian Pitt
Charles Pratt
Kim Price
Harvey Rattey
Martin E. Red Bear
Ramona Sakiestewa
Maria "Lilly" Salvador
Lance E. Silverhorn
Jaune Quick-to-See Smith
Seidel Standing Elk
Roxanne Swentzell
Herbert Taylor
Johnny Tiger, Jr.
Nowetah Timmerman
Wahleyah Anne Timmerman-Black
Ray Tracey
Kevin Skypainter Turner
Emmi Whitehorse

gallery contributors

Adobe Gallery, 413 Romero, NW , Albuquerque, NM 87104

Col. L. Doug Allard, Auctioneer, PO Box 460, #1 Museum Ln., St. Ignatius, MT 59865

American Indian Contemporary Arts, San Francisco, CA

Amerind Gallery, 885 Roanoke Rd., Daleville, VA 24083   703/992-1066

The Association for the Advancement of North American Arts and Crafts, Star Route 1, Box 144, Warnerville, NY 12187

Blue-eyed Bear, 299 N. Hwy. 89A, Sedona, AZ 86336   602-282-1158.

Bridger Foundry & Gallery/Harvey Rattey, 1460 Bear Canyon Rd., Bozeman, MT 59715 406/587-1028.

Buffalo Gallery, Tysons Corner Center, 1961 Chainbridge Rd., McLean, VA 22102   703/556-3343

Anna Gambaro Butler, Via Gambaro, Box 1117, Stafford, VA 22554   703/659-0130

Cheyenne Indian Museum, St. Labre Indian School, PO Box 216, Ashland, MT 59003

Jan Cicero Gallery, 221 W. Erie St., Chicago, IL 60610   312/440-1904

Denver Art Museum, 100 W. 14 Avenue Pkwy., Denver, CO 80204   303/640-7572

Desert Son, 4759 E. Sunrise, Tucson, AZ 85718   602/299-0818

Black Eagle, 54 Aseoleado Dr., Carmel Valley, CA 93924

Four Winds Gallery, 5512 Walnut St., Pittsburgh, PA 15232   412/682-5092

Gallery 10, Inc., 7045 Third Ave., Scottsdale, AZ 85251

Glenn Green Galleries, 50 E. San Francisco, Santa Fe, NM 87501   505/988-4168

Kelly Haney Art Gallery, 723 E. Independence, Shawnee, OK 74868   405/275-2270

Heard Museum, 22 E. Monte Vista, Phoenix, AZ 85004   602/252-8840

The Heritage Center, Inc., Red Cloud Indian School, Box 100, Pine Ridge, SD 57770

Horwitch LewAllen Gallery, 129 W. Palace Ave., Santa Fe, NM 87501   505/988-8997

The New Iroquois Indian Museum, Box 7, Howes Cave, NY 12092

Jamison Thomas Gallery, 1313 NW Guisan, Portland, OR 97209   503/222-0063

Kline's Gallery, Alt. Rt. 40, Boonesboro, MD 21713   301/432-6650

Long Ago and Far Away Gallery, PO Box 809, Manchester Ctr., VT 05255

Museum of Indian Culture, RD #2, Fish Hatchery Rd., Allentown, PA 18103-9801

Native Reflections, 526 E. Broadway, Salt Lake City, UT 84102   800/414-9111 or 801-322-0730

New York State Archaeological Association, The Incorporated Long Island Center, PO Box 268, Southold, NY 11971

Niman Fine Art, 125 Lincoln Ave., Suite 116, Santa Fe, NM 87501

Nowetah's Indian Museum and Gift Store, Rt. 27, Box 40, New Portland, ME 04954-9602 207/628-4991

Lovena Ohl Gallery, 7373 Scottsdale Mall, Scottsdale, AZ 85251 and Lovena Ohl Gallery, 4251 N. Marshall Way, Scottsdale, AZ 85251   602-945-8212

Quintana Gallery, 139 NW Second Ave., Portland, OR 97209   503/223-1729

Evelyn Siegel Gallery, 3700 W. Seventh St., Fort Worth, TX 76107   817/731-6412

Sioux Indian Museum, PO Box 1504, Rapid City, SD 57709   605/348-0557

Southwest Studio Connection, 65 Main St., Southampton, NY 11968   516/283-9649

The Squash Blossom, (Vail, Aspen, and Denver, CO.), 306 Tenth St., Alamogordo, NM 88310

Studio 53, 424 Park Ave., New York, NY 10022   212/755-6650

SunWest Silver, 324 Lomas Blvd. NW , Albuquerque, NM 87102   505/243-3781

Jamison Thomas Gallery, 1313 NW Glisan, Portland, OR 97209

TóBaahe Fine Art, PO Box 328, Winslow, AZ 86047

Ray Tracey Galleries, 135 W. Palace Ave., Santa Fe, NM 87501   505/989-3430

The Turquoise Lady, 2310 Brook St., Wichita Falls, TX 76301   817/766-2626

United States Department of the Interior, Indian Arts and Crafts Board, Washington, DC 20240

Vigil's Native American Gallery, Nevada City, CA

Western Heritage Art Gallery, S. Side Plaza, Taos, NM 78571   505/758-4376

Yah-Ta-Hey Gallery, 279 State St., New London, CT 06320   203/443-3204

Photo by: Bob Reno

Lecturer, award-winning author, teacher, and antiques expert, Dawn Reno (a.k.a. Diana Lord) has published non-fiction, fiction, children's books, and articles.

Reno's December 1994 collectible book, *Native American Collectibles*, has received national attention, as has her first novel, *All That Glitters*, (nominated for *Romantic Times'* 1993 "Best Contemporary Glitz" award). *Collecting Romance Novels*/Alliance Publishing (written with Jacque Tiegs), caught the attention of romance readers everywhere and when introduced to the reading public at a convention in April, quickly sold out (300 copies within three hours).

The *Silver Dolphin*, written under the pseudonym Diana Lord, is a new novel which will debut in August. *The Encyclopedia of Black Collectibles* (Chilton) will be released in October.

Next year will be another busy one with a book on Marilyn Monroe and a new children's book, a story about Beryl Markham, called *The Good Lion* (Lothrop, Lee and Shepard), and will be illustrated by Caldecott-award winner Ted Lewin.

Reno, teaches writing at the college level and lives in Central Florida with her husband, a professional photographer.